Wheeler & Woolsey

McFarland Classics

1997–1998

Archer. *Willis O'Brien* • Cline. *In the Nick of Time* • Frasier. *Russ Meyer—The Life and Films* • Hayes. *3-D Movies* • Hayes. *Trick Cinematography* • Hogan. *Dark Romance* • Holland. *B Western Actors Encyclopedia* • Jarlett. *Robert Ryan* • McGee. *Roger Corman* • Okuda & Watz. *The Columbia Comedy Shorts* • Pitts. *Western Movies* • Selby. *Dark City* • Warren. *Keep Watching the Skies!* • West. *Television Westerns*

1999–2000

Benson. *Vintage Science Fiction Films, 1896–1949* • Cline. *Serials-ly Speaking* • Darby & Du Bois. *American Film Music* • Hayes. *The Republic Chapterplays* • Hill. *Raymond Burr* • Horner. *Bad at the Bijou* • Kinnard. *Horror in Silent Films* • McGhee. *John Wayne* • Nowlan. *Cinema Sequels and Remakes, 1903–1987* • Okuda. *The Monogram Checklist* • Parish. *Prison Pictures from Hollywood* • Sigoloff. *The Films of the Seventies* • Slide. *Nitrate Won't Wait* • Tropp. *Images of Fear* • Tuska. *The Vanishing Legion* • Watson. *Television Horror Movie Hosts* • Weaver. *Poverty Row HORRORS!* • Weaver. *Return of the B Science Fiction and Horror Heroes*

2001

Byrge & Miller. *The Screwball Comedy Films* • Chesher. *"The End"* • Erickson. *Religious Radio and Television in the United States, 1921–1991* • Fury. *Kings of the Jungle* • Galbraith. *Motor City Marquees* • Langman & Gold. *Comedy Quotes from the Movies* • Levine. *The 247 Best Movie Scenes in Film History* • McGee. *Beyond Ballyhoo* • Mank. *Hollywood Cauldron* • Martin. *The Allied Artists Checklist* • Nollen. *The Boys* • Quarles. *Down and Dirty* • Smith. *Famous Hollywood Locations* • Watz. *Wheeler & Woolsey*

Wheeler & Woolsey
The Vaudeville Comic Duo and Their Films, 1929–1937

by EDWARD WATZ

with forewords by
DOROTHY LEE
TOM DILLON

McFarland & Company, Inc., Publishers
Jefferson, North Carolina, and London

*To one of my life's greatest heroes,
writer-director Edward Bernds,
who always encourages me to follow my dreams.*

*And to Lucy—
"In any case, you're the top"*

The present work is a reprint of the library bound edition of Wheeler & Woolsey: The Vaudeville Comic Duo and Their Films, 1929–1937, *first published in 1994.* **McFarland Classics** *is an imprint of McFarland & Company, Inc., Publishers, Jefferson, North Carolina, who also published the original edition.*

Frontispiece: Wheeler & Woolsey in an RKO publicity photo.

Title page caricature: courtesy J.P. Graphics

Library of Congress Cataloguing-in-Publication Data

Watz, Edward, 1958–
    Wheeler & Woolsey : the vaudeville comic duo and their films, 1929–1937 / by Edward Watz.
       p.   cm.
    Includes bibliographical references and index.
    ISBN 0-7864-1141-4 (softcover : 50# alkaline paper) ∞
    1. Wheeler, Bert, 1895–1968   2. Woolsey, Robert, 1889–1938.
3. Motion picture actors and actresses—United States—Biography.
4. Comedians—United States—Biography. I. Title. II. Title: Wheeler and Woolsey.
PN2287.W4569W38   2001
                          791.43'028'092273—dc20 [B]   94-26995

British Library cataloguing data are available

©1994 Edward Watz. All rights reserved

No part of this book may be reproduced or transmitted in any form or by any means, electronic or mechanical, including photocopying or recording, or by any information storage and retrieval system, without permission in writing from the publisher.

Manufactured in the United States of America

*McFarland & Company, Inc., Publishers
  Box 611, Jefferson, North Carolina 28640
    www.mcfarlandpub.com*

Acknowledgments

No book is the product of a single individual. I would like to express my sincere thanks to all those who had a hand in the shaping of this modest volume. Words of appreciation cannot express my thanks—even toward the few who repeatedly asked, "Why are you writing about Wheeler and Woolsey?" Now they can see, and read, for themselves.

First, let me thank those who knew and worked with Bert Wheeler and Robert Woolsey for sharing their memories with me: Marjorie Lord, Esther Muir, Gil Perkins, Mary Carlisle, George "Spanky" McFarland, H. N. Swanson, Edward Bernds, Buster Libott, Eddie Quillan, Betty Furness, Henny Youngman, Marilyn Cantor Baker, Mike Baker, Janet Cantor Gari, E. G. Marshall, Yvette Vickers, Jules White, Frank Melfo, Florence Henderson, Pat Harrington, Jr., Paul Landres, Nat Perrin, Rudy Vallee, June Havoc, John Lahr, Joey Adams, Elwood Ullman, Missy McMahon, Eli Wallach, George Burns, Buddy Howe, Joe Hardy, Buddy Rogers, Jeff Morrow, Madge Kennedy, Raymond Rohauer. I give a warm nod of thanks to the late, great original Sunshine Boy, Joe Smith of Smith and Dale, who suggested the idea of a W & W book to me back in 1979.

Special thanks are in store for Dorothy Lee, Bert's on-screen costar and lifelong friend; and Tom and Alice Dillon, who befriended Bert in later years and became his real family. Tom's warm recollections are the cornerstone of this book, and I will be forever grateful for his enormous help.

Leonard Maltin was the real catalyst behind this project; his pioneering work, *Movie Comedy Teams* (1970), sparked my initial curiosity about Wheeler and Woolsey. Maltin was the first film historian concerned enough to reappraise the forgotten generation of comedians who graced the Depression and World War II eras. Comedically, we are all in his debt.

Ted Turner graciously allowed me to examine the original RKO production files from which I quote freely throughout the text. Turner's dedication to cinema past has prevented Hollywood's early history from becoming a lost memory. Without the considerable assistance from Roger Mayer and the staff of Turner Entertainment, this book would have been an abruptly short one.

Acknowledgments

For unfailing moral support and grandstand cheerleading, I must thank my parents, Alexander and Caroline Watz, and my brothers and sister—Steve, Andy, Chris, Tom, and Connie—who grew up knowing that vintage comedy is the best kind. Thanks, guys.

Research associates (and good pals) Tom Weaver, Maurice Terenzio, and Cody Morgan dug into their vast resources of Wheeler and Woolsey memorabilia to provide many valuable facts and much invaluable nonsense. John Cocchi is a walking compendium of film facts and a darned nice person to boot; the generous Fred D. Leich, Joe Proscia, and Eddie Brandt's Saturday Matinee crew provided most of the fascinating photos contained herein.

The numerous Bert Wheeler quotes found throughout this text were tracked down through rare, one-of-a-kind recordings. Richard Lamparski conducted an interview with Bert for his talk show *Whatever Became Of*, originally aired over WBAI (New York) in 1966. Dr. Ronald Grele, director of Columbia University's Rare Book and Manuscript Library, located a Wheeler dialogue conducted by Joan and Bob Franklin in 1958. John Lahr allowed me access to his 1964 conversation with Wheeler, preserved at Lincoln Center's Rodgers and Hammerstein Archive of Recorded Sound. Maurice Terenzio transferred from reel-to-reel onto cassette tape Dorothy Lee's 1958 Wheeler monologue, while Cody Morgan unearthed the original aluminum discs of various Bert Wheeler radio shows, not to mention Bert and Bob's only commercial recording, made in 1933 for Victor Records. Besides my own interviews with Dorothy Lee, both Joe Savage and Maurice Terenzio lent me their taped conversations with Dorothy from 1976 to 1978.

Additional support came from Brigitte J. Kueppers of the Film Archives at UCLA, Sister Margaret Mary Lawler of the Paterson Diocesan Center, Howard Prouty of the Academy of Motion Picture Arts and Sciences Research Library, Michael Feinstein, Bob Socci, John Hall of RKO General, Joe Rodriguez, Alex Gordon, Tom Royall, Mary Phillips, Peter J. Hicks, Miles Kreuger of the Institute of the American Musical, Rich Ares, the Cook County (Chicago) Office of Court Records, Bill Fuchs, Rachel Sweet, Alan Seeger of Saint John's University, Sue Zuba, Marc Baca, Jon Weaver, everybody's avuncular editor Sam Rubin (Classic Images), Edward I. Koch and the City of New York Marriage License Bureau (Manhattan), Cal Romney, Jim and Gerry Ruth, Mary Saia, Joe Riley, William M. Drew, Andrea Battifarano, Marvin Grossman, Stuart Ira Soloway of the Museum of the City of New York, Jim Cullinan, Kristian Chester, Richard Conaty of WFUV-FM (Fordham University), Herb Graff, Steve Fishkin, Richard Anderson, the Los Angeles Hall of Records, Steve Thorpey, Kim Stypulkowski, Sam Gill, the wonderful clan at the Lambs Club, Jim Przybylski, Steve Tencza, Erwin Dumbrille,

Acknowledgments

Sister Maureen Gibbons of Saint Malachy's Church (New York), Bob Gilroy, Sanjeev Nath, Ann V. McKee of Tinseltown Titles, Eugene Sorenson, Paul Myers of the Billy Rose Theater Collection/Library at Lincoln Center, Laurence Lande, Al O'Hagan, Sherd-Bear, Charlie Kiersted, Marcy Levine of Ed Sullivan Productions, Inc., Marty Kearns, Lenore Puleo, Alex Lugones, Bill Brent, Mike Hawks, Linda Brown of the Paterson Free Public Library, Dolores Boettjer, Harry Sutherland, Alan Hoffman, Lia Sweet, Justin Orlando, Mark Jungheim, Ralph Locascio, Jack LaMantia, John O'Connell of Films, Inc., Mary McLaughlin, Larry Urbanski, Mike LaSalle, Greg Mank, Artie Goldberg, Brian Anthony, Clare Augustine, Christine Berardi, Peggy Beretta, Scott Cohen, Kevin Engel, Steve Epstein, Al Gerber, Ron Hutchinson, Tai Huynh, Karen Levin, Arden Melick, Bob Moore, Denis Szabaga, Mike Taunton, Lee Weal, and Elaine Wilkinson.

Finally, a special word of thanks to my good friend, Lucy Stypulkowski, whose valuable advice and sound criticism grace these pages. Whatever virtues this book possesses, Lucy contributed in no small way toward all of them. Here's looking at you, kid.

Contents

ACKNOWLEDGMENTS		v
FOREWORD (by Dorothy Lee)		1
FOREWORD (by Tom Dillon)		3
PREFACE		11
1	Bert Wheeler	15
2	Robert Woolsey	41
3	*Rio Rita* (1929)	55
4	*The Cuckoos* (1930)	73
5	*Dixiana* (1930)	85
6	*Half Shot at Sunrise* (1930)	93
7	*Hook Line and Sinker* (1930)	103
8	*Cracked Nuts* (1931)	113
9	Wheeler and Woolsey Split Asunder	123
10	*The Stolen Jools* (1931)	129
11	*Caught Plastered* (1931)	133
12	*Oh! Oh! Cleopatra* (1931)	139
13	*Peach O'Reno* (1931)	143
14	*Girl Crazy* (1932)	155
15	*Hold 'Em Jail* (1932)	165
16	*So This Is Africa* (1933)	173
17	*Diplomaniacs* (1933)	187
18	*Signing 'Em Up* (1933)	197
19	*Hips, Hips, Hooray!* (1934)	201

20	*Cockeyed Cavaliers* (1934)	209
21	*Kentucky Kernels* (1934)	219
22	*The Nitwits* (1935)	229
23	*The Rainmakers* (1935)	241
24	*Silly Billies* (1936)	251
25	*Mummy's Boys* (1936)	261
26	*On Again—Off Again* (1937)	269
27	*High Flyers* (1937)	279

EPILOGUE	291
APPENDIX	
Miscellaneous Film Appearances	303
SOURCES AND NOTES ON THE CHAPTERS	305
INDEX	317

Foreword
Dorothy Lee

Editor's note: Lovable Dorothy Lee was more than just the perfect ingenue in Wheeler and Woolsey's comedy world; in real life she was Bert Wheeler's cherished friend for forty years. A former singer and dancer with Fred Waring's Pennsylvanians, Lee established herself as a comedian while appearing in the musical comedy *Hello Yourself* (1928). During one performance her stockings would not stay up, causing Dottie to fuss with them all through her big number. She stole the show (bare legs were forbidden onstage) and made a hit with the audience. During the 1930s, she knew or worked with many of the great comedians—Joe E. Brown, Bob Hope, Buster Keaton, Thelma Todd, Milton Berle, the Ritz Brothers, "even John Barrymore." Her work with Wheeler and Woolsey spanned thirteen feature films, one short subject, vaudeville tours between pictures, and a solo feature with Bert. Retired from show business since the early 1940s, Dorothy divides her whirlwind social life between San Diego, Palm Springs, and Chicago, enjoying her grandchildren and "once in a great while" reminiscing about her days with Bert and Bob.

There's a saying that goes "Youth is wasted on the young," but when I was very young, I had the good fortune of working with Bert Wheeler and Bob Woolsey. I had never seen them perform before, but in 1929 they were famous Broadway stars and I was a teenager appearing in New York with Fred Waring's show. Wheeler and Woolsey had just signed with RKO to make their first picture, *Rio Rita*, one of the big films that year. I owe a lot to Bert, that darling man. He was allowed to choose his leading lady for the movie. Out of all the actresses in New York, Bert chose me. The studio brought me back out to Los Angeles, my hometown, and we made *Rio Rita*. I thought, "What an experience—too bad it's over."

A few months later I was back with Fred Waring's band in vaudeville, playing the Palace Theater in New York. There were probably eight acts appearing on the program. Bert Wheeler was also appearing there that week, but Bert was the headliner on the bill. All the other performers, skits, and everything else were window dressing—it was Bert's show. I watched his act from the wings that week. He would come out on a bare stage and talk to the audience while he was eating an apple. I don't remember what he said, but the audience took to Bert and loved him. That's when it hit me that Bert was already a major celebrity in his own right. He didn't need the movies to make him a Somebody. His friend Georgie Jessel once called Bert "the King of Vaudeville." Now I could see why.

After the first performance, it dawned on Bert to put me in his act, too. We traded some quips and sang a number, probably "Sweetheart, We Need Each Other." I found out that some of the gags we used were things he had done with his ex-wife, Betty. Betty left him for another man, which seemed like such an awful thing. There wasn't anyone in show business who was kinder or more generous than Bert Wheeler, but he had no luck in marriage and gave all his money away, often to people who didn't deserve it.

Bob Woolsey, on the other hand, held on to every buck he could. He was a real character. Once when I was getting remarried after a divorce, Bob gave me a wedding present and grumbled, "Lee, these wedding gifts are too damned expensive. Don't do this again, girl." Bob more or less kept to himself while Bert and I had fun learning our dance numbers and duets together. But Woolsey was more concerned about what showed up on the screen. He would always ask, "Do you think it was funny enough?" The only times I ever saw the boys argue was over how a gag should be played. They wanted the films to be the best they could be.

Ed Watz has spent seven years putting together this book about Bert, Bob, and their films. Everything is here—oh dear, even about the bombs we made—as well as my personal favorites, *Hips, Hips, Hooray!* and *Cockeyed Cavaliers*. I used to wonder, "Gee, these films are so silly, is there an audience for this stuff anymore?" But today, because of cable television, I can't get away from Wheeler and Woolsey. It's amazing—we've been rediscovered by a generation born fifty years after the pictures were made. Fifteen-year-old kids write me fan letters, telling me how much they love us. It's all very sweet—I'm only sorry that Bert and Bob aren't around to take the bows they deserve.

Foreword
TOM DILLON

Editor's note: Singer, actor, and gentleman—Tom Dillon was Bert Wheeler's longest-running partner (thirteen lucky years) at the twilight of Wheeler's performing days and at the start of Tom's own wide-ranging career. Besides numerous Broadway, television, and nightclub credits, he has known and worked with many of the legends of show business—Milton Berle, Victor Borge, Martha Raye, Bert Lahr, Frank Fay, Phil Silvers, Smith and Dale, Perry Como, Imogene Coca, Kate Smith—but he is most fondly associated with his beloved late partner and friend, Bert Wheeler. Today he is the very active president of the Actor's Fund of America ("Night of 100 Stars"), although he still finds time for occasional screen appearances (including the recent Sean Connery–Dustin Hoffman film *Family Business*).

The following address was delivered on "Bert Wheeler Night" at the Lambs Club, New York City, in 1988.

I can vividly recall the first time I ever stepped onstage with Bert Wheeler. A fellow named Nat Goldstein was the circulation director for the *New York Times*. He was an old friend of mine, and he was always calling me to do shows for the Newspaper Guild. The Guild was directly across the street from the Lambs Theater on West Forty-fourth Street. So one Sunday night I drove over, parked in front, and went inside the Lambs to check my mail. Who do I see sitting there but little Bert, all alone. There is nothing worse than being by yourself in the club on a Sunday night; no one is there. Bert was sitting with a work light reading the Sunday *Times* at the table. He looked so dejected. I said, "Gee, Bert, I'm going to a corned-beef-and-cabbage party across the street—would you like to come? You wouldn't have to do anything." His face beamed with that beautiful smile I got to know so well. "Oh, I'd love to," he said. So we go across the street—I'm thrilled to be walking over there with this great performer. Incidentally, my father worked for the *Times*, and the people at this party were mainly old-timers who worked with my dad.

Bert marches down the aisle dressed as an old biddy in the act he performed with Tom Dillon.

Anyway, we arrived at the party, ate, and then I got up and gave Bert a lavish introduction. There was a fellow present named Dennis Harris who worked with my father. Denny was then in his eighties and had two hearing aids, neither of which he ever turned on. So when Denny whispered, you could hear him two miles away. I gave Bert this elaborate introduction, and he's walking out into the audience, up onto the stage. Deaf Denny Harris "whispered" in his booming voice, "Jesus Christ, he must be ninety!" I absolutely froze. There was a hush over the audience. Everybody was embarrassed—except Bert! Bert was bent over, dying of laughter, and the reason being, he was so used to people saying that.

When I started to work with Bert, I realized that people don't use much tact. I can't tell you how many times people came up to him in restaurants and said, "Bert Wheeler, I thought you were dead!" This happened over and over again, so Bert wasn't shocked at all.

How did I team up with Bert Wheeler? It basically started a few years later, in 1955. I was a very small boy. Frank Fay came up to me when I was doing an act with Smith and Dale. We were disbanding the act because Charlie Dale wasn't really well. Frank Fay approached me and said, "Listen, Wheeler is afraid to ask you—will you consider doing this mother act with him?" In the routine, Bert would play the "mother" of his straight man, and they would heckle each other back and forth. I had already seen the act when Fay asked me about it—as a matter of fact, Bert had tried the routine with two people: Jack Pepper, who was famous as Ginger Rogers's first husband, and Pat Harrington, Sr. Frank said, "It's a great premise except those fellows are basically in the same age range as Bert. It doesn't come off as a mother-and-son routine. He needs a much younger partner." Anyway, Bert and I got together, and I thought it was fun. We got Jack Whiting, a great song-and-dance artist, to help us polish the act. And all of a sudden we started to work closely.

Bert had bought a black dress at the Salvation Army out in Hollywood. It was in tatters when he bought it, and the dress just kept getting worse. My poor wife, Alice, was always repairing this terrible outfit. And he wore a horrible wig. Bert just looked awful! For the purpose of the act, I would sing, "*M* is for the million things she gave me..." We had it timed so that after two choruses Bert would come out into the audience. He had a little pocketbook, and he kept groping inside until he reached my side of the stage, where I'd still be singing. He would say, "Son, I just got off the bus," and I'd say, "Ma, get back on it!" That was the start of the act. Twenty minutes into the segment Bert's last line was, "He's just like his father. Thank God I never married him!" For the second part of the act we'd do a song and dance.

One memorable night in Washington, D.C., we played in one of the city's biggest ballrooms. Two thousand people were at a testimonial honoring Arlene Francis. Two thousand people—and I get up and sing, "*M* is for the million things..." Two-and-a-half choruses pass—but Bert doesn't make his entrance; *five* choruses pass—still no Wheeler! I'm up there and, boy, you talk about sweating! I think I did about twelve choruses on that lonely stage. Finally, Bert came up, huffing and puffing. He said, "They wouldn't let me in!" The security men thought he was an old hag and wouldn't let him into the ballroom. Arlene loved the act and the next day she called Ed Sullivan. Ed immediately contacted Bert. Bert called me, saying, "Hey, Ed Sullivan wants us on his show." "Great," I answered. He said, "I don't think so. We're doing well, and we're having fun. Give this act to television and we're dead." Well, the whole routine was his idea, so I replied, "That's up to you." Mark Leddy, who knew Bert from vaudeville days, was Sullivan's chief agent. Mark called Bert and convinced him that the exposure couldn't hurt our bookings. We went on the show after all and scored a big hit.

Things I tell you might not sound particularly funny unless if you knew and understood Bert. For instance, we had a play date in Washington, and I said I'd drive by the Lambs Club at 9:00 A.M. to pick him up. On the way over, I turned the car radio on and heard a news

6　　　　　　　　Foreword (Tom Dillon)

Tom Dillon and Bert Wheeler on *The Ed Sullivan Show*, **November 20, 1960.**

bulletin: "Famous comedian, Bert Wheeler, almost drowned last night on Long Island Sound." He had been on a yacht and went into a dinghy with two other men when suddenly the little boat overturned. Bert grabbed a buoy and held tight for forty-five minutes before he was rescued. Fortunately no one died, but here I was, a nervous wreck, thinking, "Oh, my God, poor Bert, I'll have to contact the theater and call the show off." I get to the Lambs, and Bert is standing in front of the place! I asked him, "How do you feel?" He answered, "Fine, let's go." Not one word from him about the accident. I said, "I just heard a radio bulletin about what happened last night." He replied, "Isn't it awful—I lost my elevator shoes." I said, "You *what*?" He said, "I lost my elevator shoes. I spent a hundred bucks for them. They're gone." Bert had enough good sense when he grabbed the buoy to take off his elevator shoes; they weighed a ton. He might have drowned, and anybody else would still be in a state of shock, but losing those shoes was what bothered Bert.

　　Bert was an incredibly generous guy, and it's easy for me to understand why he couldn't save anything from his Wheeler and Woolsey days, when he made the big money. This story epitomizes Bert: when we were playing the Latin Quarter here in New York, I told him I wouldn't let him go out of the dressing room at night before I checked both exits — the stage door and the main entrance. Outside there would always be little old ladies waiting for him. They'd say, "Remember Sam, my husband? You were in vaudeville with him." Bert had no idea of who they were but he'd be reaching into his pocket to give them money. I can best sum up this characteristic with a story involving Bert and Harry Delmar. Harry told me this story himself. He had been a hoofer and Broadway showman since the 1920s, producing *Harry Delmar's Revels*, which starred people like Bert Lahr, Blossom Seeley, and Frank Fay. Years later, Harry was strapped for cash while trying to stage a new show. Things weren't going well for him when he walked into the Lambs and saw Bert standing there. Wheeler asked, "What's the matter with you?" Harry sighed, "I need five hundred dollars." Bert said, "Oh, sure!" He reached into his pocket and gave Delmar the money. Crisis averted. Harry's money problem was solved within a few days, so he went over to the Lambs and called on Bert. Harry told him, "Gosh, Bert, I'm so grateful for the loan. Here's your money back." Bert started to cry. Harry asked, "What are you crying about?" Wheeler said, "You're the first guy that ever paid me back!" Well, I think that kind of sums up Bert Wheeler.

I'll never forget the worst experience I had onstage with Bert. We were playing the Riverside Hotel, a beautiful resort in Reno, Nevada. We went there for a two-week engagement and we stayed there for fourteen weeks in all. It was a wonderful occasion; we were quite a smash. On a Saturday night, packed house, we overhear the chorus girls while we're sitting in the dressing room: "That guy's a nitwit, he's trying to trip us!" What are they talking about? I don't know. So we go out onstage and start the act. Then we see it: there's a guy with a crutch in the front row. The stage is right up against him, and he's swinging the crutch, trying to knock us over. Poor Bert. He just stood there, and I didn't know what to do. I finally went up to the footlights and said to this character, "You do that once more, and I'm going to come down there and shove the crutch down your throat!" As I look at the guy, I see that he's a cowboy: boots, broken leg, with a crutch — and about eight feet tall. I thought, "What am I doing?" Fortunately, security men came and got him out of there.

Now the funny thing is, when Bert blew his lines (which didn't happen often), I could tell from the expression on his face that he had gone blank. That's what happened on this particular night with the crazy giant cowboy. Bert just stood there for a minute and he sang:

> McCarthy is dead, O'Brien don't know it.
> O'Brien is dead, McCarthy don't know it.
> They're both of 'em dead, and neither one knows it.
> They're in the same bed, and both of 'em's dead!

On that particular night it took us twenty minutes to get back into the act.

Bert became sick in the mid-1960s. He had emphysema; for years he had smoked three packs of cigarettes a day. Although he hadn't smoked for a number of years when I knew him, the emphysema finally caught up with him. So we used to send him up to the Will Rogers Institute at Saranac Lake, New York. He had a doctor who was considered one of the top practitioners in his field. He helped Bert tremendously, giving him the best medication and treatment possible. Anytime Bert took sick, he'd go up there and stay a weekend. The pure, clean air itself was so invigorating that Bert would start feeling better the minute he arrived.

In any case, the doctor would use Bert as a role model for people with emphysema because he could still sing and dance despite the illness. When Bert was staying at Saranac, my wife, Alice, and I would drive upstate, pick Bert up at the hospital, do a club date at Lake Placid, and then take Bert back to the hospital. One day Bert's doctor called me: could I come up and do a show with Wheeler for a medical convention? I replied that I'd be happy to oblige. We set a date and I drove up with the fellow who had always done the arranging for our act, Joe Berman. Joe was one of the great characters of all time. I don't think he had ever been outside of New York City before. His idea of a great vacation was to sit in the Stage Delicatessan with a big black cigar, a pastrami sandwich, and a two-cent plain.

Before Joe and I left for Saranac, I told Conrad Nagel where I was headed and that Bert was there. You remember Conrad — distinguished actor, outstanding gentleman, that magnificent voice. He had a bronchial condition and loved to go up to the Will Rogers Institute. Connie and Bert were good pals, and in the past they had been at Saranac at the same time. Connie always called Bert "Blue Eyes." He told me, "When you're up there, tell Blue Eyes to take care of our ducks." I said, "Your ducks?" Connie replied, "Bert will know. Go there in the morning, walk across the bridge. There's a little bakery on the right side, opposite this little stream. Go in and tell them that Conrad Nagel said you need a bag of rolls."

Joe and I drove up to Saranac for this early morning show. We picked Bert up at the hospital around seven o'clock in the morning and had breakfast. Then I told him, "Bert — Blue Eyes — Connie Nagel wants me to see your ducks." He said, "Sure." So we walk across town. Sure enough, there is this beautiful little bridge and this bakery. I go in and say that Conrad Nagel sent me to feed the ducks. The baker gives me a bag of two or three dozen rolls, right out of the oven. I thanked him and returned to Bert and Joe Berman. There isn't a duck in sight, and here I am holding this huge bag of rolls. I asked Bert, "What kind of a place is this? There aren't any ducks here." "Just a minute," Bert replied. He cupped his hands to his face and called, "Quack, quack, quack!" Well, I never saw so many ducks in my life! They came from around the bend. I thought we were going to be invaded by ducks. Joe Berman went bananas and nearly swallowed his cigar—he had never seen a duck before. The three of us are standing there throwing rolls to these silly ducks. The ducks knew they could trust their friend Bert, with his New York–accented birdcall. You had to be there to appreciate it.

Onstage and in his films, Bert was always eating. Usually he'd be munching on an apple or a sandwich; that was part of his routine. I have to tell you about Bert's appetite. He had certain likings and strange eating habits because he had eaten in so many vaudeville boardinghouses. When you ate with Bert, you had to have a very strong stomach—especially at breakfast. He'd have eggs every morning. Before he'd taste them he'd say. "Boy, they look good!" Then he'd cover the eggs with ketchup, Lea and Perrins, salt and pepper. You wouldn't know what the mess was that he was eating, but he'd say, "Ohhh, this is good!" That was when you'd really start to get sick. When he'd come over to the house, he loved Alice's cooking. Alice knew his tastes—he loved fish chowder. Alice used to make that and he'd say, "Boy, I can't wait to eat it!" But then he'd pour on his ketchup, salt, et cetera, all over this chowder and ruin it. She wanted to kill him!

When we'd drive all over the country going to our club dates, it reminded Bert of his beloved vaudeville days. He'd tell me how happy he was to be performing before live audiences again, and he'd reminisce, singing these silly patter songs from his youth. One song that he sang was reminiscent of the vaudeville boardinghouses, and I'll finish with this:

> On Monday we had bread and gravy
>   On Tuesday, gravy and bread
> On Wednesday and Thursday was gravy and toast
>   Which was nothing but gravy and bread
> On Friday I said to the landlord
>   "Won't you please give me something instead?"
> So on Saturday morning by way of a change
>   We had gravy without any bread!

I can only hope that Bert is smiling down on us and eating a huge steak smothered in gravy. It's been a very nostalgic evening for me, and I loved it. He was a remarkable man and a wonderful human being. Thank you, ladies and gentlemen.

Preface

It's long overdue—but at last, Wheeler and Woolsey make their comeback!

Bert Wheeler and Robert Woolsey were Broadway musical comedy stars who invaded Hollywood with the Ziegfeld extravaganza *Rio Rita* (1929). Their unpretentious and risqué dialogue routines were not always welcomed by the critics, but they were an instant hit with audiences. Dapper, good-looking, and pint-sized Bert Wheeler exuded good cheer with his singing and dancing, all the while fracturing the English language with his "Noo Yawk" accent. Horsey, bespectacled, and spindly Robert Woolsey defended himself with his mouth, trading outrageous barbs and cooking up crazy schemes that formed the basis of their many films. Throughout the 1930s, Wheeler and Woolsey starred in over twenty breezy comedies, saving their studio, RKO, from financial disaster during those dark Depression days. The boys were second only to Laurel and Hardy as comedy duo favorites (on at least one occasion they beat Stan and Ollie in a British popularity poll).

Yet until recently, Bert and Bob were unjustly overlooked by the pop culture generation. Why were they ignored for so many years, and how did their renaissance finally come about?

In comedy films—as in real life—I've always rooted for the underdog. The great comedy teams of the thirties and forties were everyone's television favorites—mine included—in the sixties. It was always the neglected partner who held my attention, however. My favorite Marx Brother is Chico; Shemp Howard strikes me as the most talented Stooge; and Bud Abbott (in the half-hour television series) seems ten times funnier than Lou Costello ever hoped to be. In horror movie parlance, I'd be the guy who prefers a mangy Bela Lugosi Monogram potboiler over a slick Boris Karloff Columbia production. Say what you will, but the underdog has been, and always will be, numero uno with me.

Bert Wheeler and Robert Woolsey's situation presented a real problem in my comedy-tutored childhood. I had heard of the team (in 1968 they were still listed as "famous celebrities" in the *Information Please Almanac*) and I had seen gag photos of them in film-reference books. My parents fondly remembered the W & W movies from *their* childhood (Dad

Wheeler and Woolsey

would describe *So This Is Africa*, his personal favorite, in hilarious detail), and my grandfather had seen them on stage—live—in *Rio Rita*. But the Wheeler and Woolsey films were not shown on New York City television when I grew up. As far as I was concerned, Wheeler and Woolsey were the original Unknown Comics.

Thanks to Leonard Maltin's groundbreaking book *Movie Comedy Teams* (1970), the 1970s saw the rediscovery of several forgotten comedy duos—Clark and McCullough, Olsen and Johnson, Moran and Mack—along with occasional revivals of their comedies. But these films were not appealing; the "humor" seemed too remote and bizarre to have ever been regarded as funny. Although an excellent chapter of Maltin's book was devoted to Bert and Bob, their movies did not resurface as a result of this exposure. I began to wonder whether Wheeler and Woolsey would live up to my expectations—if I ever got the chance to see their films.

In 1978 the Museum of Modern Art in Manhattan ran a fiftieth-anniversary tribute to RKO, including a representative sampling of the studio's output. *Rio Rita* (1929), RKO's first blockbuster musical, was being shown in a pristine 35 mm print. All I knew about the film was that Wheeler and Woolsey were in it—not as the stars, but as comic relief. That was enough for me. I knew that I *had* to be there, no matter how brief their participation. Quite a few other curious comedy buffs made the pilgrimage to New York City during that blustery Christmas season. One fan, Maurice Terenzio, came from as far away as Chicago, his sole traveling provisions consisting of some cash and a toothbrush.

The museum's six-hundred-seat theater was SRO that night, an unusual event in itself. Bert and Bob's first appearance on-screen generated scattered laughs, without a flicker of recognition from the audience. But as the film unspooled, a curious thing happened. People in the theater warmed up to Wheeler and Woolsey's appealing characterizations. When the boys undertook their next scene, getting drunk on Aztec wine, the entire audience was with them; by the end of the episode, Bert and Bob had the crowd in hysterics. The main plot would interrupt now and then, we would endure five or ten minutes of schmaltzy operetta, but you could sense the anticipation in the air: what would Wheeler and Woolsey do next? Then a double whammy hit: Bert's exhilarating song-and-dance number, "Out on the Loose." As he finished this show stopper, blissfully pleased with himself and dancing down a dirt road, the audience applauded Bert into the next scene. Sustained applause followed each subsequent Wheeler and Woolsey sequence. If ghosts do exist and are aware of mere mortals' behavior, I hope that a certain pair were listening that night. By the end of *Rio Rita*, Wheeler and Woolsey had endeared themselves to the jaded crowd just as they had done the first time around, in 1929.

As we left the theater, sharing the afterglow from Bert and Bob's great performances, I realized that I had to see the rest of the story. It took me eight years, but I managed eventually to view all of Wheeler and Woolsey's full-length comedies. Like the work of any comedy team, some of the films were mediocre, a couple were outright bad, but from 1931 through 1935 they had a winning streak of first-rate gems. A book devoted solely to Wheeler and Woolsey seemed the logical follow-up, since there was not one in existence and I wanted to learn more about them. But to read such a book I had to write such a book. You now hold it in your hands, the product of seven years' research.

During those years of comedic archaeology, Wheeler and Woolsey began to make a real comeback on their own. With the widespread popularity of cable television, VCRs, and laser disc players, Bert and Bob have become popular fixtures on the home screen. While fans may not be quite so rabid as Curly Howard fanatics, Wheeler and Woolsey supporters are very real nonetheless, thank you, and their numbers continue to grow. It has been a long intermission in the wings, but for Wheeler and Woolsey, the curtain has gone back up.

1
Bert Wheeler

While Wheeler and Woolsey movies run the gamut from extremely good to excruciatingly bad, the surprise to be found in all of them is Bert Wheeler's own remarkable comic talent. A little fellow—he was five feet, four inches in his elevator shoes—with the homespun mien of a Norman Rockwell schoolboy, china-blue eyes, and a mop of wavy brown hair that rippled atop his head, Bert was an intuitive actor who fashioned a winsome characterization as well rounded as Chaplin's tramp or Fields's huckster. Yet he never saw himself on a par with his more-celebrated contemporaries. "I'm just a shanty Irishman," he would say, "with a Brooklyn accent."

Bert could be equally disparaging about his movie career. Late in life he conceded to a reporter that the films he had made with Robert Woolsey were "bloody awful." Such evaluations would ordinarily discourage the most dedicated comedy enthusiasts, but the best of the Wheeler and Woolsey comedies have recently resurfaced to refute Bert's claim. Bert Wheeler was his own worst spokesman, too busy creating laughter for the masses to erect a monument to his own memory.

For Bert, the laughter he created was its own reward. At the age of seventy-one he was still on the road, performing in nightclubs and the straw-hat theater circuit. "I keep working all the time. I never stop," he admitted. "I'm a worse ham today than when I started, and I've been in show business fifty-five years." Though Wheeler had earned and lost several million dollars in his lifetime, he never pitied himself: "I always feel sorry for people if they're not in show business. I say, 'Oh, you poor soul! If you had the fun that I've had—and still have....'"

The trials that Bert encountered during his lifetime might have evoked a curse from St. Patrick himself, yet Wheeler's high spirits seemingly overcame all obstacles. During a particularly low point in his career he applied for a television commercial audition where the interviewer never looked up. Name? "John Barrymore," Bert replied. What work had he done recently? "Nothing," Wheeler answered, "because I've been dead eighteen years." Saddled with a small role in his last Broadway play, *The Gang's All Here* (1959), Bert looked on the bright side: "I get killed early enough in the play to have time to go out on club dates."

Onstage, his puckish demeanor could not be suppressed. Tom Dillon, a close friend of Wheeler's, recalled an incident that occurred in the late 1950s:

> Bert was appearing in a summer stock production of *Finian's Rainbow*, but he didn't have enough time to rehearse for his part. So for the first several performances Wheeler had the script wedged in his back pocket. Whenever he'd forget his lines, he'd pull out the script, scratch his head, and ask aloud, "Now, let me see—where was I?" When Bert would find his place he'd gleefully exclaim, "Ah-ha!" and the show would continue.
>
> Now, ordinarily such behavior wouldn't be tolerated in the theater—but Bert had such great appeal that the audience loved this nonsense. He made the people feel like they were in on his little joke.

Along with the laughter, Bert created friendships. Joe Smith, of the comedy team Smith and Dale, knew Bert for over half a century, and called Wheeler "a real extrovert, always laughing and joking, just a big kid." Florence Henderson was a starlet during Wheeler's tenure as president of the Catholic Actors Guild. Her election as treasurer afforded Bert the opportunity to befriend her. She reminisced, "I do remember his great kindness, his encouragement and his warm, impish smile. His attitude about himself and about show business only strengthened my respect and love for him and that same business." In 1955 Bert and a young singer named Tom Dillon devised a popular nightclub act, teaming up for thirteen successful years; along with his wife, Alice, Tom adopted Bert as a surrogate uncle.

Wheeler possessed a rare talent for winning new friends, an ability that often surprised Bert himself. "I can walk into a bar in Omaha or Des Moines," he reflected in 1960, "and in no time at all somebody recognizes me. The next thing you know, we're having a party." Colleagues from Bert's Hollywood heyday recall him as gregarious and happy, the first to laugh at other people's jokes. Bert's dressing room at RKO was the studio locale for nonstop partying; he socialized indiscriminately, mixing with everyone from the studio brass to bit players and stagehands.

An associate once remarked that "Bert would give you the shirt off of his back. Anybody who told him a hard luck story would get whatever they needed." He was also a man of strong loyalties. Wheeler worked with a vaudevillian named Donald Kerr for three weeks in 1921; fourteen years later, when Kerr found it impossible to get established in Hollywood, Bert hired him as his stand-in for *The Nitwits*. Joe Smith commented, "You can't find anybody who can say a nasty thing about Bert Wheeler. He was the sweetest little guy in the world." His perennial leading lady in films, Dorothy Lee, perhaps summed Bert up best when she reflected, "He was such a wonderful guy, easy to get to know and to like. If Bert were still alive

Bert Wheeler and Dorothy Lee, December 1930 (photo courtesy Dorothy Lee, reproduced by Maurice Terenzio).

and talking to us now, within ten minutes you'd feel like you'd known him for years."

As wonderful as the comedy can be in a good Wheeler and Woolsey film, the musical numbers performed by Bert with Dorothy Lee are altogether enchanting. Unlike the song-and-dance duets of RKO's other musical partners, Fred Astaire and Ginger Rogers, the Wheeler-Lee "turns" lack sophistication and luster but compensate with zest and the magnetism between two people who obviously care about each other. The lyrics were occasionally hokey and the choreography was usually regulation "tap," but Bert and Dottie's performances conveyed a type of young and innocent exhilaration, strangely captivating, that recalled a lost world of 1920s musical comedy. Few Hollywood musicals of the 1930s possess this same charm, and since then not many other films have successfully revived it.

Dorothy Lee and the Dillons were among Bert's dearest friends. Dottie's professional relationship with Bert began when he personally selected her to play opposite him in the first screen version of *Rio Rita* in 1929. They went on to appear in fourteen films together over the next seven years, but their friendship continued for the rest of Wheeler's life.

Bert always called her "my little leading lady," while Wheeler is still affectionately recalled as "Uncle Bert" by her grown children. "I almost can't believe he's gone," Dorothy says. "He was so full of life, just an incredibly fantastic person. Show business kept him young."

Albert Jerome Wheeler was born at 10 Ward Street in Paterson, New Jersey, on April 7, 1895. His father, James Wheeler, was a weaver in a silk mill; his mother, Katharine Foley Wheeler, died at the age of seventeen, while Bert was still an infant. "My people were all Irish, but Wheeler really is an English name," Bert noted. "My grandmother and grandfather came from Ireland." Consequently, young Albert Jerome was duly baptized into the rite of the Roman Catholic faith on May 5, 1895, in Paterson's Cathedral of St. John the Baptist. Bert was raised by a grandfather and an aunt, Margaret Wheeler McAveny, who futilely sent the boy to Public School No. 6 for his education. "I was a grammar school dropout," Bert would recall somewhat sheepishly, adding, "I can't count to ten in any language." It was Aunt Margaret who informally rechristened Bert: "She never liked the name of Albert. I've been known as Bert since I was a little bit of a kid."

Show business beckoned Bert in spite of his father's objections. Bert recalled, "I might have gotten stagestruck as a young kid, because I turned out to be a very fine roller skater when I was a kid and got a lot of publicity. Outdoors, I think I was on my way to the championship of the world. Then I went in show business." By the age of twelve Wheeler was already sneaking into theaters via the fire exits. Aware of Bert's furtive proclivities, the elder Wheeler warned his son not to attend burlesque shows. "Despite his warning me that I'd see something I shouldn't see, I went to a burlesque and I saw something I shouldn't see," Bert said. "I saw my father sitting in the seat in front of me."

When he was thirteen Bert finally became a property boy at the Paterson Opera House. One day the head property man requested cedar trees to be used as props. In spite of his diminutive stature, Bert obligingly trudged up nearby Garret Mountain and chopped down two trees a day, dragging them back downtown to the theater. His zeal eventually paid off: "I was lucky. Before long I was doing bit parts."

A career in comedy was not Bert's original ambition:

> In those days, I wanted to be a dramatic actor. Even before I ever got that job, I remember I had my choice a lot of times of seeing a baseball game or going to a stock company, repertoire, where they'd play different shows every day—and the shows always won out as far as I was concerned. There was nothing in my life that I ever loved like the stage—from the very beginning—and I still love it like a kid.

Bert always maintained that his acting debut came in a revival of George M. Cohan's stage farce *Forty-Five Minutes from Broadway*. The event occurred on April 17, 1911, at the Paterson Opera House. Bert had turned sixteen just ten days before and was no longer hampered by New Jersey's strict child-labor laws. His debut was inauspicious enough— Wheeler was a member of the chorus and handled a bit as a bellboy—but the next day the *Paterson Press* acknowledged that "the chorus was excellent," which was all the encouragement he required to continue on the stage. For a while, though, that was all the encouragement young Wheeler would get.

"My father used to kid me when I finally got going," Bert would playfully recall in later years. "He'd say, 'You got all your talent from me.' He was an usher at the Opera House in Paterson. That's as far as the theatrical strain went." Occasionally Bert would oversimplify the story about his show-business debut: "As a matter of fact, my folks were both dead ... and I was being raised then by my aunts. So there wasn't any serious objection to me going into show business." In truth, the elder Wheeler was alive, kicking, and dead set against his son's histrionic inclinations. A major argument between father and son ensued, culminating in Bert's decision to run away to New York City. Much to his surprise, Aunt Margaret bestowed her blessings upon Bert, packed his trunk, and gave the boy what meager savings she could spare. Bert never forgot her kindness and was deeply devoted to his aunt for the rest of her life.

Paterson is a mere fifteen miles northwest of Manhattan Island, or about forty-five minutes from Broadway via the Erie-Lackawana railroad and a Jersey City ferryboat ride. Bert arrived in New York with plenty of enthusiasm but no immediate prospects. "For a few days I just wandered Broadway, marveling at everything I saw," he recalled to Tom Dillon. "I'd stick my nose to the windows of those fancy restaurants, looking at all those swell steaks and good food. Today when I can afford a good steak I haven't got good teeth." Eventually Bert obtained an audition with Gus Edwards, an impresario who promoted popular children's acts such as *School Days* and *Kid Kabaret*. His talent roster of tyro performers was an impressive one and included at one time or another Groucho Marx, Larry Fine, Hildegarde, Eleanor Powell, George Jessel, and Eddie Cantor. Bert's pure tenor voice, cultivated in the parish choir and at Paterson socials, assured him a place with Edwards, who hired Wheeler on the spot at twenty dollars a week. But the association was destined to be an unhappy one—Edwards had not reckoned on Bert's pugilistic tendencies. Mrs. Gus Edwards recalled in the 1950s that Bert had been "our lovable 'bad' boy, who caused many a black eye with his backstage scuffles." Gus Edwards's own estimation of Bert wasn't nearly so paternal; he once quipped that Wheeler had been "the original Dead End Kid."

A number of apocryphal stories have sprung up regarding Bert's association with the Edwards troupe. One of the yarns places Bert in Edwards's *Postal Telegraph Boys* act, together with Groucho and Harpo Marx, George Jessel, and Walter Winchell, performing a benefit for the San Francisco earthquake survivors in 1906. Leo Edwards, Gus's younger brother, first told this anecdote in 1968 to a reporter for the show-business publication *Variety*. The truth of the matter is that at no time were Groucho, Harpo, and Winchell in the act together with Wheeler, who did not join Edwards until 1911. Yet an elderly Groucho Marx "confirmed" Bert's presence in a 1976 interview with his biographer, Hector Arce. More annoying is a 1930s press release that "quotes" a juvenile Georgie Jessel admonishing Wheeler, "You had better quit licking us Jewish boys, Bert. You know you are sure to be working for one of us some day." Such fabrications resulted in good newspaper copy for the trade press but present a curve ball to latter-day historians in pursuit of the facts. "I was with an act called *The Newsboy's Sextette*, with Georgie Jessel," Bert recalled in 1958. "Winchell was with another act, but he was with them at the same time." Out of Bert's brief sojourn with the Gus Edwards troupe, only one other event is incontestable: because of his rowdy behavior, Wheeler was fired.

Contrite and wiser, Bert landed work with a local stock company at the Onondaga Theatre in Syracuse, New York. He appeared in Harry Gribbon's comedy production *The Gingerbread Man* (1912), and depending upon whose account you are reading, Bert either understudied Gribbon or actually took over the comedy lead when Gribbon took ill. Next Bert appeared with the Gus Hill Company in *Mutt and Jeff* (1912), a "cartoon comedy" tabloid revue featuring real-life counterparts of comic-strip characters. "I'm not exaggerating," Bert recalled. "Forty-seven weeks that we didn't have a two-day stand. They were all one-night stands. There were a lot of shows in those days. You'd get great, big, long seasons. Of course, as a kid I loved those one-night stands; that was the real show business." The constant grind was agony, but Wheeler was honing his skills as a comedian: "This was just the kind of training that I needed to take some of the assurance out of me and to teach me the fundamentals of stage work."

After leaving Hill, Bert had supporting roles in the comic opera *The Firefly* (1913) and the musical *When Dreams Come True* (1914). During the run of the latter play, Bert met Margaret Bruce Kudner Grae, a doe-eyed brunette chorine. Bert would regale her with plans for a proposed vaudeville act, an open invitation to share his dream. The troupe disbanded in New York City; Bert and Margaret married there in the municipal courthouse on April 27, 1915. They immediately set about rehearsing some songs and patter for a fifteen-minute vaudeville act.

Initially calling themselves Gray and Wheeler, their debut took place at the Crotona Theatre in the Bronx. *Billboard* magazine (May 29, 1915) bestowed a favorable nod upon these youngsters, although the critic had trouble discerning who was who:

> Gray and Wheeler sang "Somebody Knows" very successfully. This number is proving a winner for doubles. Gray also does a Charlie Chaplin stunt that has attracted favorable comment.

An appearance the following week at William Fox's City Theatre garnered the team its first *Variety* notice (May 28, 1915). Under the headline "New Acts Next Week," *Variety* furnished a glimpse of the Wheeler's earliest attempt in vaudeville:

> To Charlie Chaplin this couple owe the success of their present act. The boy is a dead ringer for the picture comedian and makes the most of it. ... The stereotyped opening with a song is done with the boy in evening dress and the girl in an evening gown. A ballad is used by her, giving him the opportunity to change into the Chaplin makeup. This is most minutely looked after and his appearance is exact. The usual by-play employed by the picture comedian is gone through. The girl comes in for some of the rough comedy. While the Chaplin craze is on, this turn will prosper and should stand a chance of getting a big time booking, but the death knell of this sort of impersonation may be sounded shortly.

By 1915 Charlie Chaplin was the yardstick by which all new comedians were measured. Audiences craved Chaplin's brand of hijinks; if a Chaplin film were not available, any reasonable facsimile was nearly as welcome. Stan Laurel, Harold Lloyd, Billy West, and Billie Ritchie were all trotting out Chaplinesque derivations either onstage or in the movies. A struggling young comic was guaranteed immediate public acceptance if his Chaplin imitation was good. From all accounts, Bert's "tramp" was sensational. Changing the name of the act (and Margaret's first name in the process), the team became Bert and Betty Wheeler. The alliterative cadence sounded friendly, and besides, there would be no more mistaking who was who. Joe Smith remembered the earliest days of the Wheelers' first act:

> Charlie Dale and I were part of the Avon Comedy Four, and we'd occasionally appear at the same Keith Theatre with the Wheelers. This must've been 1915 or '16. They were very young, and very tiny, so you'd get the effect of two kids horsing around. Bert was really an eccentric dancer in those days; he'd do some kidding with Betty and maybe a song or two. He used to do a Chaplin imitation, the best I've ever seen.

Just two little kids horsing around: twenty-year-old Bert Wheeler and his eighteen-year-old bride, Betty, in 1915.

Soon the Wheelers were booked into New York's Palace Theatre, barely two years old and already regarded as the mecca of big-time vaudeville. *Variety* (July 16, 1915) favorably reported that "as an impersonator of the film comedian [Chaplin], Bert Wheeler has something on a great number of impersonators. As a matter of fact, his impersonation is the one

Bert doing his Charlie Chaplin routine onstage, 1915. After Chaplin witnessed the act, he inscribed this photograph "To my worthy imitator, Mr. Wheeler."

big thing in the act at present." Following their success at the Palace, Bert and Betty obtained coast-to-coast bookings. When they appeared at the Los Angeles Orpheum, Hollywood's sprouting movie colony came out to see the show. So did Charlie Chaplin. Surprisingly enough, he enjoyed Wheeler's imitation tremendously and autographed a photo of Bert in tramp costume: "To my worthy imitator, Mr. Wheeler. I cannot tell myself from you. Sincerely yours, Charlie Chaplin." Chaplin's testimonial was uncharacteristic and extremely generous. This endorsement became the focal point of a half-page ad the Wheelers ran in *Variety* (March 10, 1916). Bert even had handbills of the photo printed up as promotional flyers. Even though Bert and Betty were experiencing their first brush with fame, the glamour of show business was replaced by the necessity of survival whenever the newlyweds left the stage. Bert reminisced,

> I can remember this—that I was getting $35 a week and I could save a nice sum out of that $35. We could stop at the best hotels in town—$1.25 a day, with three meals a day. It's amazing. We'd travel through storms and blizzards. We practically lived on the train. Most of the time we'd get up at five or six o'clock in the morning. Lots of times, we would never get to the hotel. We'd go right down and get on our sleeper.

Bert and Betty had been in vaudeville for less than a year, yet they felt confident that the pinnacle of success was within their grasp. All this had occurred before Bert's twenty-first birthday. But their luck had run its course. To their amazement and horror, the next year would find the team trapped in a vaudevillian's nightmare.

Seemingly overnight, the Chaplin craze ended. Enthusiasm for the genuine article had not abated one iota—if anything, Charlie Chaplin's own extraordinary popularity would peak after the First World War—but the strong of Chaplin impersonators was too formidable a competition for the Wheelers. Bert and Betty desperately clung to the Chaplin motif for another year. Worse than becoming old hat, their act became stale. Somehow they did manage to secure a playdate at the Palace again. *Billboard* (February 10, 1917) reported that

> Bert and Betty Wheeler did not succeed in putting their comedy and songs over. Bert's dancing was the only thing worthwhile in the act. The pair had done much better on their previous visit, but after this afternoon's performance it was rumored that they would be out of the bill.

The *New York Star* (February 14, 1917) charitably called the performance "unsuited" and excused the actors: "Bert Wheeler wasn't feeling very good and I guess we'll get another act for tonight." *Variety* (February 9, 1917) simply stated that "Bert & Betty Wheeler were out of the bill." Bert's rationale seems as good as any: "The first time at the Palace one bit was imitating Charlie Chaplin. Great. I come back [two years] later and the kids on the street were doing it better than I was."

The pair next ended up at the Olympic, a Brooklyn vaudeville house that catered to a nondiscriminating clientele. Unlike the better theaters that required only two performances a day from its actors, the Olympic commanded a grueling four shows every day. The Wheelers likewise flopped here, once again after their very first appearance. That night in his attic dressing room, angry and frustrated, Bert collected every piece of his wardrobe and makeup and threw it out the window.

The Wheelers sought refuge at the Bartholdi Inn, a roosting place for out-of-work actors located at 173 West Forty-fifth Street. "It was kind of a hard struggle for a while," Bert later reflected, but success was around the proverbial corner. Bert and Betty made the acquaintance of Tom Moran, one of the hotel's semipermanent boarders who had recently been a singing messenger boy in an act called The Telegraph Four. Bert and Tom took to each other immediately and devised a routine that served as a last-minute replacement at a tough vaudeville house on Fourteenth Street. Figuring that they had little to lose, Bert shed all his inhibitions about ad-libbing. Once onstage, he began improvising bits of business like mad. To his utter amazement, the calloused audience was ecstatic about the comedy. Booking agents who had ignored Bert and Betty were suddenly anxious to sign up this "hot new item." Packing Betty off to her parents' home in Chicago, Bert and Tom christened their act *Me and Mickey* and set off on a season of engagements. Bert was finally on the threshold of "finding himself" as a unique and gifted comedian. From then on, there would be no need for Wheeler to portray anybody but himself.

Eyewitnesses to the Wheeler and Moran act are difficult to come by, but the original, glowing accounts from trade journals, such as this chronicle from *Billboard* (June 22, 1918), can still be read.

> *Majestic Theatre, Chicago:* Bert Wheeler and Tom Moran are as good a duo of entertainers as can be found in vaudeville. Wheeler cuts up constantly in a most amusing and natural manner with confidential asides, which are relished by the audience. Moran has a splendid singing voice, the effect of which even Wheeler's incessant interruptions can't completely spoil. Exceptionally clever dancing is not the least point in this most meritorious act.

The *New York Star* (June 26, 1918) reported that "Wheeler and Moran, singing, talking, and dancing comedians, got a lot of laughs with the comedy talk and hands for the extremely good dancing." *Variety* (June 21, 1918) simply stated that "Wheeler and Moran are a couple of nuts.

This extremely rare still of Bert is the only surviving evidence of an unfinished silent comedy shot in San Francisco, 1918, while Wheeler was touring the Orpheum Vaudeville circuit with Tom Moran.

They're as good nuts as one usually finds on a vaudeville bill." From Bert's account, the "clever dancing" was virtually a gymnastic exhibition:

> A great piece of fate happened to me. I'm known [for it] in show business today even. I was the first person who ever came out for twenty-five minutes and lay on my stomach and did an entire act without getting up.

That happened to be an accident. I was playing in Omaha, Nebraska, and I was rehearsing after a matinee to do a dance, and I broke my ankle. There was no possible way of getting a replacement act there. This manager was so mad at me, he said, "You gotta do something!"

Bert assured the manager that *Me and Mickey* would go on that night with both partners performing. In the meantime he had to conjure up something, somehow. "At the next show," Bert recalled, "I crawled out through the curtain and did the whole act lying on my stomach." The idea was an inspiration, and it became a classic piece of vaudeville *lazzi*. "That's the only way I could do this act—and the act turned out better than it was at the matinee, standing up!" Fifty years later, *Variety* (January 24, 1968) recalled the moment that evolved into a Bert Wheeler trademark:

> Wheeler would lie on the stage, supinely munching a sandwich while his partner went through legmania and kindred business. When Wheeler cracked, "Next time I think I'll telephone in my act," it broke up the house.

Unfortunately, *Me and Mickey* was destined for a brief partnership. Tom Moran was a heavy social drinker; Bert was not. "Bert couldn't drink, so he almost never did," Dorothy Lee remembers. "If he had two drinks he'd be under the table, fast asleep." Bert needed a partner who would live for the act, to keep it fresh and funny. It was time to reenlist Betty. Reuniting in Chicago, the Wheelers spent the winter of 1918-19 devising a routine comprised of some of the *Me and Mickey* material but also much that was new and witty. The key novelty was Bert's adroit delivery when conversing with the audience. Joe Smith marveled at how Bert would "start talking to the crowd as though he knew them his entire life. The guy could actually thaw out a 'cold' audience in very little time. He was an irresistible little comic." Bert himself recalled, "There isn't an old-timer around who doesn't remember our act. Every day I'll meet somebody who'll pick out some different thing, because in those days there was no stealing." Wheeler went on to describe the craftsmanship that was polished so carefully during this early period:

> You didn't really write your act, you made it great by constantly playing it. We didn't have the money to go to a writer and say, "Write me ten minutes." You had to get that material through work, a lot of bitter work, too, and a lot of hard work. And if anybody ever stole it on you, you would either give them so much bad publicity or wait for them with a baseball bat, if they were too big. We scared people from stealing our stuff in those days.

The Wheelers called their new act *Bits of Everything*, the same title they had used throughout 1916-17. Recharged and ready, Bert and Betty arrived in New York during the spring of 1919; big-time vaudeville was not the same thereafter. Their rapid ascent can be gleaned from the following reviews:

The 81st Street Theatre, NYC: Bert and Betty Wheeler offered *Bits of Everything*. They started slowly, but worked up quickly. Bert, with a "nut" method, is good and went over well. Betty proved to be a valuable foil and looks good in her gowns of excellent taste. [*New York Star*, April 30, 1919]

Colonial Theatre, NYC: Bert and Betty Wheeler are cleaning up the first half [of the program]. [The team] received the Colonial's hallmark of approval, the long drawn out, sustained unison applause, which has become famous as the "Colonial Clap." [*Variety*, March 25, 1920]

The Alhambra, NYC: Funny Bert with his pretty little wife, Betty Wheeler, scored one of the biggest hits of the evening with their pitter-patter. Bert is a versatile chap, who can do most anything in a way that will make any audience sit up and take notice. Betty's singing brings keen delight to the throng. It was a pandemonium of handclapping that followed the termination of their act on Monday evening. [*New York Dramatic Mirror*, April 17, 1920]

The 81st Street Theatre, NYC: Bert and Betty Wheeler took "in one" and they held it down, although not programmed for anything in particular. This is another disconnected revelry of song, dance, comedy, bum acrobatics and a serious attempt at ballad singing as a duo for the finish. It's all their own, this Bert and Betty act, and they almost held up the show to a kind of hit that will in the future prevent them from being strangers here. [Bert] does a cane dance, walks in the trough, and juggles a once white derby. That's good, too. [*Billboard*, December 25, 1920]

Colonial Theatre, NYC: Bert and Betty Wheeler ... are a hit. Bert, however, lies down. Lies down through most of the act when personality is hard to put over. Saw Victor Moore once in an act—Vic lay in bed the whole time the act was on and it flopped. Bert, however, lies half on the piano where he delivers some snappy material.... Bert says the act is a "wow." Let it go at that. [*New York Star*, October 8, 1921]

B. F. Keith's Riverside, NYC: The show is brought to a close by Bert and Betty Wheeler. It looked like tough going for this pair in this spot, but Bert Wheeler's clowning soon won the admiration of the crowd and everybody stuck.... Bert and Betty deserve a lot of additional credit for holding the audience with their tomfoolery in this position. [*New York Star*, October 15, 1921]

The Wheelers at the threshold of their greatest success, in 1920.

The Palace, NYC: Bert and Betty Wheeler, taking no chances on trick introductions, tore on and went to it and almost made the house forget the rest of the show. It pyramided to a smashing comedy, singing, and dancing triumph, holding in the mass far past 11 o'clock and taking in enough glory for any act in any spot. [*Variety,* December 2, 1921]

Colonial Theatre, NYC: Bert Wheeler, with his "intimate" start with the audience, has things pretty nearly his own way throughout. The pair are pulling down a big hit. [*New York Star,* October 21, 1922]

The Alhambra, NYC: Young Wheeler is a great natural comedian and clown. The wonder is somebody hasn't grabbed him off for a revue production. His knack for ad libbing would make him valuable for such an entertainment. He has a lot of new stuff in the Wheelers' specialty, all of it smooth, casual nonsense. The comedy revel of the Wheelers [is] the high point of the show. [*Variety*, November 3, 1922]

The Palace, NYC: Bert and Betty Wheeler, next to shut, put it over again, as they always do. The higher the game, the more they win, it seems, and this with what goes as "low" comedy. But, there is something about Bert that is far from low, even though he does most of his work on the floor. The little chap is penetratingly human as well as shrewdly sly. Miss Betty is nobody's little lame sister, either, before the customers. She has opera pipes and a rare sense of timing laugh points. Great act. [*Variety*, July 26, 1923]

The above praise is just a sampling of the uniformly excellent reviews that the Wheelers received from major show-business publications. Only one dissenting voice cried out, rather pathetically at that: Mark Henry in *Billboard*. His prudish sensibilities are as amusing to read as the rave reviews.

The Palace, NYC: Bert and Betty Wheeler did essentially the same act they have shown around New York for several years. The same low comedy, the same uncouthness of costuming on Bert's part, the shirt out in front, the bare legs and a lot of other unrefined business that may bring laughs and enable them to say "We were a riot," but none of which either adds to or advances the art of entertainment one iota. [November 11, 1922]

The Palace, NYC: If anyone in a normal frame of mind can see anything entertaining or even slightly refined in a man in misfit, ragged clothes, lying around the stage, eating a sandwich and remarking, "If I sneeze, every man for himself," and a lot of other inane, impossible and unnecessary banalities, this writer cannot, neither can he witness this act of the Wheelers without a serious disturbance of the gustatory nerve. [July 28, 1923]

Bert's contemporaries apparently had stronger stomachs than Mark Henry's, because they loved the Wheelers' routines. Joe Smith remembered that "in the 1920s, Bert and Betty had a great act. He was a cute little guy and she looked like a living doll. Together they were unbeatable." Actress Esther Muir commented, "Bert was wonderful. I was so surprised, because he had a very good singing voice. And Betty Wheeler was very, very pretty." Veteran comedian Eddie Quillan called the act "pure magic. When Bert and Betty played the Long Beach Theatre in California, Harold Lloyd wanted to sign Bert up for silent pictures, he was so good. But Bert wouldn't split the act for anyone." Actress June Havoc, immortalized as Gypsy Rose Lee's sister in the musical *Gypsy*, still considers the Wheelers' routine to have been one of vaudeville's greatest.

> I played on the bill with Bert and Betty Wheeler when I was a very small child, Baby June. I remember the act because Bert was so wonderful. He sat with his legs dangling into the orchestra pit while Betty sang a lovely song. After listening a while, he extracted a ham sandwich from his pocket and began eating; but the emotion of the song overtook him and he began to weep. At first the tears just slid down his face, but then they began to flow, and then they gushed—it was hilarious! He sobbed as he wept, and the audience was in hysterics. [The gag] was his secret trick, belonging to him—he invented it. It had to do with a large handkerchief and the ham sandwich, but don't ask me how. He never stopped rehearsing between shows, or trying to learn to play a saxophone or a clarinet or something. He was an inspiration.

Tom Dillon explains how Bert achieved the effect of a bawling Niagara: "Bert told me that he had glycerin on the handkerchief. He'd rub it into his face when he simulated crying. Bert once remarked that more people remembered that bit than anything else he ever did." "I'll tell you another thing," Bert added, "I always ate an apple and ate a sandwich during the act." Food munching became a familiar Bert Wheeler staple, carried over into his movie career. Bananas, lemons, peanuts—even candlesticks, shrubbery, and glass earrings—were not safe from this human intake valve. However outrageous, there was a blissfully innocent edge to Bert's comedy:

> I was eating this apple and a sandwich, and I had a paper bag in my hand. My wife grabbed this paper bag, and she reached in and pulled out some powder puffs. She said, "What are you doing with these powder puffs?" I said, "My God, I've been eating them all day, I thought they were marshmallows." That was a big joke. I paid fifty dollars for that joke. Now, you can imagine, if anybody had stolen it, I would have committed murder!

Bert described another bit that reveals just how intimate the rapport was between comedian and audience:

> I was lying on my stomach and talking about my wife, and I told that she had a gold tooth. I said she was very self-conscious of this gold tooth. I said when she walked out I'd ask her to show the tooth, but I begged the audience not to laugh, "because if you laugh she'll get mad and she won't show it." I had made such a big to-do about it that I had them screaming, just telling about the tooth.
>
> Now, psychology's a funny thing. When she walked out in the spotlight and she stood there, there was not a word mentioned. I would look around

> at her, and then I'd look back at the audience, and I said, "I'll ask her to show it." I'd say, "Would you show it?" She'd say, "No." I'd say, "She won't show it"—you know, crying.
>
> As she was singing, I'd get up and I'd walk around her, and all of a sudden she took a high note, and the light would shine on this gold tooth, and I'd scream at the top of my lungs, "There it is!" Now, that doesn't sound funny, me explaining it, but it was a real funny situation. I mean, I had a whole monologue—I kept them screaming telling about her gold tooth. I had a lot of funny gags. I just can't recall the gags, but that was the situation.

Bert once described Betty as "kind of a stunning-looking girl, [who] wore beautiful clothes, and she did straight for my jokes." The Wheelers, like most married couples, had their share of squabbles; their differences of opinion usually centered around the vaudeville act. Bert remarked that Betty "was not too good a singer—no. Many a fight we had about that. For instance, she'd sing a song like 'Love Brings a Little Gift of Roses'—many a fight we had, as I did everything to detract."

For Bert, even domestic discord could prove a ready source of comedy:

> I found a rubber chicken I bought from a man on the street. It had feathers on it. It was a balloon. And I had this chicken timed so just at the high note Betty took at the finish of this song, the chicken would "die." Did you ever see the air go out of a balloon? Well, if you saw a balloon die, you know the funny quirk it takes? Well, that was one of the bits.

One of the people who remembered "the bits" was Ned Wayburn, a talent scout for the leading theatrical showman of the 1920s, Florenz Ziegfeld. Wayburn had discovered future luminaries Will Rogers and Eddie Cantor for the opulent *Ziegfeld Follies* revues, and he recommended Bert and Betty to Ziegfeld, too. Years afterward Bert recalled the moment Ziegfeld first laid eyes upon him:

> Flo Ziegfeld picked me up at the Palace, New York. I was the first one to do one of the great, great afterpieces in big-time vaudeville. There was another famous act in vaudeville called the Mandel Brothers, great comedy acrobats, and a fellow by the name of Dotson, a famous dancer. There was an actor in vaudeville named Owen McGiveny and he played *Oliver Twist*. He did all the characters himself; he made all these changes. And it was a sensation.
>
> The Mandel Brothers, Dotson, and I were on this show with McGiveny one week, and we got kidding around. We thought of this burlesque, and we asked the manager to let us do [it]. Well, it was an absolute sensation. So we played this for nearly two years. And I was

Bert goes into his famous crying bit for Betty at the Hippodrome, New York City, 1924.

doing this burlesque when Ziegfeld saw me at the Palace. I went right from the Palace into the *Ziegfeld Follies*.

Owen McGiveny was a "protean actor," or quick-change artist, who would scurry behind a curtain and, within seconds, miraculously emerge as a different Dickensian character. Bert and his cronies devised a sketch entitled "The Wager" that spoofed McGiveny's lightning transformations. Bert would make an announcement to the audience that he has a wager on with McGiveny to perform the latter's act and make all of the changes in less time. McGiveny would come onstage and tell Bert that he had a lot of nerve attempting to duplicate his successes. Bert would then employ Betty, Dotson, and Willie and Joe Mandel to hide behind the curtain and emerge all over McGiveny's set, pretending to be Wheeler in disguise. Timing was everything; the cast was choreographed at breakneck speed. At one point, Bert would walk past a column eating an apple, "emerge" as the black Dotson still eating the same fruit, pass another column and appear again as Bert, left with an apple core. According to the *New York Star* (November 11, 1922), "the affair turns out to be one of the biggest laughing satires that vaudeville has ever seen. We have heard Palace audiences laugh, but we have never heard them scream as they are doing this week. "The Wager" never lost a customer."

Ziegfeld liked what he saw; Bert and Betty were hired to appear in the star-studded and lavish *Ziegfeld Follies of 1923*. To Bert, Ziegfeld's selection meant success, prestige, everything: "Any actor in my period would say that with Ziegfeld you've really made it. I made a lot more money in pictures, but, boy, my real pride and joy—and I have to stick my chest out—is when I think of my Ziegfeld days."

Fannie Brice, Ann Pennington, "Gentleman Jim" Corbett, and the Paul Whiteman Orchestra were also featured in a production already loaded with top-flight personnel. Opening night (October 20, 1923) tickets sold for a hefty twenty-two dollars from the box office, while the scalpers received considerably more. For the first time, the cream of Manhattan's critics would appraise Bert and Betty. The outcome was wholly predictable: "Our favorite act was Bert and Betty Wheeler.... The comedy of this particular turn is all low, broad, enormously inventive and delightful!" (Heywood Broun in the *New York World*); "By long odds the funniest event of the evening is Bert Wheeler, who blew in from vaudeville and ran right off with Mr. Ziegfeld's show" (James Craig in the *New York Mail*); "We counsel him [Ziegfeld] to keep the Wheelers in his show" (Percy Hammond in the *New York Tribune*). Best of all was Alexander Woollcott's eloquent assessment in the *New York Herald*:

> After due reflection we found that the American Girl was most glorified by ... a round faced little comedian named Bert Wheeler who has come out of vaudeville and who threatened on Saturday night to take the new Follies and, for all the hot rivalry all around him, make it his oyster.

Five days after the Wheelers' acclaimed debut, trouble struck. Bert was performing one of the show's sketchbook routines when his pursuit of laughter got the better of him:

Irish-American Bert performs a Russian jig in *The Ziegfeld Follies of 1923*, the revue that made him a major star.

I'm doing a comedy scene with Fannie Brice where I'm on top of a roof fixing a radio antenna. I slide down the roof and catch myself—I was quite athletic in those days. The audience is laughing so hard that I forgot to hold on. I fell off that roof. It knocked me out and fractured my elbow. Just as I was passing out, I heard somebody say, "He'll be out of the show for a long time." I was only out of it a week. After waiting all of my life to get with Ziegfeld, I had to have that accident.... I thought, "Ohhh—my life is gone!"

During Bert's brief hiatus, Ziegfeld had his top comedian, Eddie Cantor, substitute for Wheeler—a telling sign of the importance that Ziegfeld attached to his new "discovery." *The Ziegfeld Follies of 1923* chalked up an impressive run of 233 performances at the New Amsterdam Theatre before going on a nationwide tour. Forty years later Bert recalled his Ziegfeld days with glowing affection:

> In those days you just felt that you couldn't get any higher than the Ziegfeld Follies. Once you reached Ziegfeld, that was it. That was more than being in any other Broadway show. To be a Ziegfeld star was just like being president of the United States—you just couldn't go any higher.

During layoff periods the Wheelers resided in a modish bungalow on Long Island and appeared in only the most prestigious of the New York vaudeville houses—the Palace or the Hippodrome. Bert and Betty Wheeler had reached the pinnacle of their success as a team. "We were one of the high-paid comedy acts of our time," Bert recalled. "I was quite a name—a headliner—but not a big box-office smash. When we split up [in 1926] we were getting $1,500 a week. Today [1966] you're really a bum getting $1,500 a week!"

Although Bert downplayed his importance in vaudeville, he was greatly exaggerating the team's wages at this time. An examination of the Ziegfeld salary lists preserved at the Theater Collection of the New York Public Library reveals that Bert and Betty were grossly underpaid by Ziegfeld's organization. The Ziegfeld payroll ledger for March 1925 is quite an eye-opener. Although Bert and Betty Wheeler were the principal attraction of the *Ziegfeld Follies* on tour, they were receiving $650 a week for the team—a considerable sum in those preinflation days, but nowhere near the figure that Bert remembered. Conversely, singer Charles King was only a featured player in the same show but received $600 a week. Comedienne Hazel Dawn was likewise only featured on the tour yet received $1,000 a week. Ziegfeld's older, longer-established comics were receiving munificent fees in comparison to the Wheelers. W. C. Fields's salary was $1,531.25; Leon Errol earned $2,500; and Will Rogers took home $2,712.50. Most impressive of all was Eddie Cantor's arrangement; as the star of Ziegfeld's musical comedy *Kid Boots,* he raked in 10 percent of all gross profits. This averaged anywhere from $3,000 to $3,500 a week. If Bert was truly honored to be working for Ziegfeld, Ziegfeld was truly lucky to have an ignorant businessman like Wheeler working for him.

More importantly than the money, Bert idolized Ziegfeld. "Ziggy was swell," Bert recalled fondly. "He had this great class. He was elegant. Used a private railroad car to go fishing." Bert especially valued Ziegfeld's equanimity as an employer:

I could have my arguments and fights with him, where some smaller man would have fired you for it—but not him. He was really a big man, in every way. I think he liked me personally, too, as much as he liked me as an actor. He was just that kind of a man, too—a wonderful man. As far as I was concerned, [he] was the greatest.

The Ziegfeld Follies of 1923 toured the country until the spring of 1925, during which time Bert and Betty returned to New York. The *Follies* of 1925 included in its cast both Will Rogers and W. C. Fields; Bert remembered that "W. C. Fields was taken sick, and for five weeks I jumped in and took his place. I didn't do any of his scenes, but I took his place and was in the same *Follies* with Will Rogers." After his recovery, Fields appeared on the same bill with the Wheelers at several actors' charity benefits. "He was a very peculiar man," Bert noted. "Lived alone. He had a certain amount of friends. He liked very few people, but he liked me. I think, in my time, Fields was the greatest comedian who ever lived."

Vaudeville's reviews of the Wheelers' act at this time reveal them at the height of their powers, operating with precision and assurance. They parted company with Ziegfeld and went on a national tour in the late autumn of 1925. By now the critics welcomed Bert and Betty back as long-lost kin:

> *E. F. Albee Theatre, Brooklyn:* Bert and Betty Wheeler are back from the ranks of musical comedy—back home among those who love them and thoroughly enjoy their efforts.... The Wheelers know that vaudeville lovers admire them—if they didn't know before Monday evening, they sure know now. They registered for a distinct hit.... The audience just seemed to be partakers of a get-together event, judging from the way they laughed and applauded. [*New York Star*, December 11, 1925]

> *The Hippodrome, NYC:* Bert and Betty Wheeler worked a bit to get started, but after Bert had gone into the audience, munching an apple, the audience started warming up.... The Wheelers are real artists and they know vaudeville and its requirements.... Bert served some big portions of digestible and wholesome comedy. There was no trouble digesting it and it was most relishable. They registered distinctly with a Charleston finish in which Bert did a tap Charleston ... ending proceedings with a thunderous din of applause. [*New York Star*, December 18, 1925]

> *B. F. Keith's Riverside, NYC:* The Wheelers were forced to follow, so Bert flopped into the trough without delay and went to work. New wrinkles and quips plentifully amused the gathering, which donated a reception upon the flash of the name cards. Miss Wheeler is splendidly gowned, while the comedy of Bert is as sure-fire as ever. The Wheelers closed to applause from all corners. [*Variety*, January 13, 1926]

The Wheelers then proceeded to tour the country's vaudeville houses before returning to New York in the summer of 1926. Back in Manhattan, Bert had a run-in with the popular monologist Frank Fay when he and Betty played the Palace (week ending July 26). Fay had been programmed to act as the Palace's master of ceremonies for one week; instead, his raconteur style of delivery proved to be so popular that he was held over for eight weeks. Forty years later Bert was still laughing at the incident that cemented their friendship:

> Frank Fay was at the height of his career when he played the Palace. Practically every act or actor that played the Palace had to do a bit with him. I get in from out of town. I had been out of New York a number of weeks on the Orpheum circuit. Fay said to me, "You and I are going to do a bit together." I said, "That's fine. What is the bit?" He said, "We're going to tell the audience to stay after the show. You and I will do the afterpiece." That was all right with me because I had done that afterpiece with Fay before. But I asked, "Why does it take two people to go out there and tell them about that? Let's rehearse something. We know a lot of bits." Fay says, "Don't you know I'm probably the busiest man and the most popular man in this town? I haven't got time."
>
> I knew what I was in for. I get out on the stage with him and he starts in on me. I tell you, he must've popped nine or ten gags off my head. The people are falling off their seats, laughing at this man. Now that burned Fay up, he expected me to answer him. If I'd have answered him, he'd have killed me double. He was just laying for me to answer him. For once in my whole life I got very smart. I let Fay run out of material, like a fighter does, out of steam.
>
> Finally he got so mad because I wouldn't answer him. He asked me, "Aren't you going to say something to the folks?" I said, "Yes, when you're through getting those titters"—a titter, you know, is a snicker. Fay says, "Titters!" I said, "Fay, let's face it, you're a light comedian." That got a yell, too. Fay asked, "Whaddya mean, 'light comedian'?" I said, "Fay, you have your method of getting laughs, I have mine. What you consider a big laugh would be a snicker to me." He said, "Well, go ahead, the hall is yours!" I said, "Now, would you like to see me get a laugh like you've probably never gotten in your whole life?" He said, "I'd love it." And I smacked him right in the puss.
>
> After I smacked him he just stood there with that audience yelling. When they stopped laughing he looked out and said, "That's what you get for mixing up with 'low' comedians." That was one of his standby cracks.
>
> You know what happened? Bill McCaffrey, who was the booker at the Palace at that time, came running backstage to compliment us. He thought that we had rehearsed that bit. But I'll tell you one thing about Fay—he did that thing with me all week, it caused such talk. He took that smack and by Saturday night I was bringing 'em up from the floor! But he was game.

Bert and Betty Wheeler at the height of their popularity in 1925.

Shortly after this sojourn the Wheelers were on the road again, touring the midwestern and southern states. On the same route were Claude and Clarence Stroud, twin brothers breaking in a dancing and acrobatic act. A *Variety* review (June 16, 1926) described them as "two well appearing, tall boys with an idea, bound to put them across." Two months into the interstate tour, disaster struck: Betty told Bert that she loved Clarence Stroud and wanted to marry him. Bert was devastated. The act split in

New Orleans during September 1926. Betty returned to her parents' home in Chicago to secure a divorce, while Bert hied himself away to a New York hotel. Within days after the breakup, Bert received three separate offers to star in musical comedy shows destined for Broadway. He quietly accepted Florenz Ziegfeld's proposal, then retired behind a curtain of silence.

Betty's decree was granted on November 15, 1926. Bert did not protest. There was no alimony; Bert made a $34,000 settlement of joint cash and property out of the couple's $50,000 savings. Betty wed Clarence Stroud in Chicago the next day and joined the Stroud twins' act. Betty's move, as the *New York Times* noted, "marked her descent into small-time vaudeville." Within four years, her marriage to Clarence Stroud was over (afterward Stroud confided that Betty regretted having left Bert). By the 1930s Betty Wheeler was a pleasant memory from a vanishing form of show business while Bert was an internationally known and beloved movie star. Bert soon regained his sense of humor, but the hurt stayed with him a long time. In later years Bert would only state that "a personal thing happened so that we split up and she got married again." In 1951, when he was a guest on Bing Crosby's radio show, Wheeler startled Bing with an ad-libbed quip in the following exchange:

> BING: You know, Bert, I can still remember the vaudeville act you used to do: "Bert and Betty Wheeler"—
> BERT: Was that her name?

Though Bert was temporarily in the doldrums, his career was about to start a dizzying ascent. Joe Smith philosophically considered the Wheelers' split to be a blessing in disguise for Bert: "Betty left him for another fellow. Bert teamed up with Robert Woolsey, went to Hollywood, and became a bigger success. He traded one partner for a better one."

2
Robert Woolsey

Comedy duos usually accentuate the differences between team partners for laugh effect, and the Wheeler-Woolsey combination was no exception to this rule. Bert Wheeler always portrayed a dreamer; Robert Woolsey was all business, a 78 rpm metabolism spinning through a 33⅓ world. Wheeler's face was expressive; Woolsey's countenance was inscrutable. Wheeler was athletic and young; Woolsey was gaunt and appeared superannuated. Wheeler was good looking; Woolsey was, to be blunt, homely. Put a pitchfork in his hand and he was an austere rustic out of the painting *American Gothic*. In movies, Wheeler always got the girl; Woolsey was born to watch from the sidelines and crack jokes.

Yet Bob Woolsey had a wicked way of delivering his lines and the ease and assurance of an accomplished comedian. His beady brown eyes focused in on an object worthy of ridicule—a snobby dowager or a pompous businessman—and within moments, Woolsey would adroitly slay the enemy. Faced with imminent danger, he'd blink nervously, swallow hard, and let loose with his war whoop "Whoooah!" a trademark as familiar to 1930s moviegoers as Groucho Marx's wiggling eyebrows or Stan Laurel's frightened tears. A pair of slightly oversized horn-rimmed glasses and a perpetually lit cigar were the standard Woolsey accoutrements. "Woolsey was the cigar smoker," Bert Wheeler recalled for the benefit of the uninitiated. "He never appeared in a scene—even in bed—without smoking a cigar."

Both Bert Wheeler and Bob Woolsey found humor in their daily lives, but Woolsey's approach to comedy was diametrically opposed to Wheeler's. Bert was an intuitive comedian whose freshest inspirations stemmed from a living, breathing, laughing audience's reaction. "There's nothing more satisfying to me than to hear people laugh," Wheeler noted in a newspaper interview. "I prefer the stage, or a variety of the medium where I can play to a live audience. . . . Bob and I hated moviemaking. If we could have had a live audience, our movies would have been much better." Wheeler's bitterest comments about the team's pictures were made long after Woolsey's passing; for years Bert's observations were taken as the duo's collective opinion. It comes as no small surprise, then, to discover that Woolsey actually enjoyed filmmaking and the Hollywood scene. Bert privately told Tom Dillon that

> I hated making pictures, but Woolsey kind of enjoyed it. He liked to argue with those big-shot moguls, and living in Malibu on the beach appealed to him. As soon as I finished a picture, I'd get the hell back to New York as fast as I could.

Why would Bert tell reporters that he and Woolsey hated moviemaking yet confide differently to Tom Dillon? Tom believes today that Bert did not want to churn up any unkind memories about past associates; by Dillon's own account, several film producers had treated Bert unfairly, yet Wheeler was never one to criticize others (not even those who damaged his movie career). Tom says, "It was easier for Bert to write off Hollywood as an unpleasant place for Wheeler and Woolsey, instead of singling out those individuals who made Hollywood unpleasant for Bert Wheeler." (Woolsey made his own feelings about New York clear in a 1932 interview. "I haven't anything against Broadway except it's just one street.")

Whereas Bert lived comedy, Bob studied it. Coworkers recall Woolsey's relentless determination to add gags or improve the quality of a script. Esther Muir, who appeared twice with the team, remembered Woolsey as being "a very good technician. He may not have been the funniest man in the world, but he *knew* what was funny. He was very impatient and couldn't tolerate anyone who didn't know their craft." Edward Bernds, a sound mixer on Wheeler and Woolsey's *So This Is Africa* (1933), said of Woolsey, "That man treated comedy as a serious business. He kept to himself on the set and always seemed to have his nose in a book, possibly looking for ideas he could use in the picture." Buster Libott, who was the boom man on the same film, recalled Woolsey as being "a sourpuss all the time. I don't think I ever saw Woolsey smile. He was always glum." Dorothy Lee recalled Bob as being a "feisty fighter" when arguing about how to execute a gag, while Bert commented, "He was a tough little guy—didn't look it, but he was."

Besides trying to bolster the script, Woolsey was preoccupied with dominating the footage. He would work furiously to incorporate a nuance that distracted from the other players' performances. Eddie Quillan was working with the team in *Girl Crazy* (1932) when his brother Johnny visited the set:

> Bob Woolsey always had this cigar in his hand. Johnny would come with me and watch the filming. After several days of this Johnny said to me, "Gee, that Woolsey's got two great expressions." I asked, "He has? What are they?" And Johnny very deliberately tapped the ashes off his cigar—twice. Of course, Woolsey didn't have any expressions at all; he was

always "dry." The business with the cigar was Woolsey's manner of making you notice him on the screen at all times.

Woolsey's scene-stealing tendencies backfired on him once, during the shooting of *Rio Rita* (1929). Dorothy Lee recalls her first screen encounter with the inveterate ham:

> It didn't take me long to learn about upstaging people. Bert Wheeler taught me about that. He said, "Now when you work with Woolsey, he'll back up, or he'll go forward so that he'll back you up. You just start to go forward or backward—you walk right with him to make sure that he can't upstage you." See, I didn't know what *upstaging* meant. How would you know? 'Cause if we're doing a scene face to face, we'd look at each other. If I were doing a scene with Woolsey, he'd have me so that the back of my head would be to the camera—and *his* face would be toward the camera!
>
> Bert tipped me off to that. So Bert and I fooled Woolsey. Whenever he'd take a step back, we'd take two steps back! Woolsey got pretty angry at us—but we cured him of pulling that stunt!

Robert Woolsey is not remembered in the reverential fashion reserved for Bert Wheeler. Woolsey died in 1938, a comparatively young man at the height of his popularity. Surprisingly, contemporaries like George Burns and Bob Hope barely recall him at all. Yet in his lifetime Woolsey earned a fortune and, unlike Wheeler, he stayed rich. Although both comedians came from poverty-stricken, single-parent households, their reactions to sudden wealth were as dissimilar as everything else in their personalities. "Bert would give you his last dime," Dorothy Lee remembers, "but Woolsey was a cheap, stingy tightwad." Bob had a happy, enduring union as opposed to Bert's four failed marriages. "Woolsey even thought himself to be a ladies' man," Dottie says, "although God only knows why!" Woolsey was no comedic genius, but his talent was impressive enough to share the spotlight with a great clown. And with the right material, Bob Woolsey was half of a great team.

Robert Woolsey was born in Oakland, California, on August 14, 1889. When he was five, his family moved to Carbondale, Illinois, a railroad and mining community. Bob's father, Thomas, died in 1896, leaving his widow, Sarah, in dire poverty with six children to feed. With the exception of Bob's youngest brother, Charles, all of the Woolsey siblings passed on due to childhood illnesses. Bob and Charlie supported their mother through a variety of part-time jobs: newsboy, messenger, butcher boy, errand boy, stablehand. Bob was pitching hay in East St. Louis when a jockey nicknamed Wee-Wee Higgins took note of the spindly youth's glib manner and brash enthusiasm. Higgins introduced Bob to the owner of a horse breeding farm at St. Charles, Missouri. Woolsey alternated there as a stablemate in the winter and a jockey during the summer months. "I rode all the old nags, but I didn't mind," Bob recalled. "I was always crazy about horses. I discovered that good horses make good jockeys, just like good roles make good actors." First-prize money was usually $5; losers received $2.50 for their efforts. (Years later Woolsey admitted, "I never won!")

A fall off a horse in 1904 permanently sidetracked Woolsey's equestrian ambitions. Recuperating in bed with a broken leg, Bob ventured that acting might be a less hazardous way to make "easy money." After a few false starts, Woolsey was out rusticating on the county fair circuit, trouping with itinerant performers: the Reynolds Stock Company, the Duckworth Players, Captain Maywood's Repertoire Company's Floating Palace. With a few dollars that he had managed to stash away, Bob organized an acting company of his own, Woolsey's Comedians, in 1908. The troupe toured the Midwest and profited from Bob's enterprising tactics. He later boasted, "I gave a live baby away. Did that bait bring them in? I'll say it did. A coupon representing a chance on a live baby went with every seat. The live baby was a little pig."

Bob eventually worked his way back to the West Coast, joining the Alcazar Stock Company in San Francisco. "In his lifetime," Bert Wheeler once speculated, "I'll bet he played seventy or eighty parts in different shows. He was what they call a Coast Defender out in California." In San Francisco, Bob met Gilbert M. Anderson, a pioneer movie producer (he cofounded the Essanay Film Company in 1907) and the screen's first cowboy hero, "Broncho Billy" Anderson. Coincidentally, Anderson dabbled in live musical comedies along the Pacific Gold Coast and had a fine eye for recognizing fresh talent. Anderson enticed Woolsey into working for him via some sweet flattery, telling Bob that "as an actor, you're a swell comic!" Anderson's Essanay Company proclaimed an industry coup when it hired Charlie Chaplin in December 1914. Chaplin proceeded to make one film at the studio's Chicago headquarters before deciding to move to Essanay's facilities in Niles, California, near San Francisco. Broncho Billy asked Bob if he would like to audition for Chaplin. Woolsey's reply was abrupt and adamant: "What, me go down there and let some comic hit me in the face with a lot of pies?" One can only speculate as to how Bob's preconceived comedic notions would have fared against Chaplin's; Chaplin possessed a ballooning ego that Woolsey would have been only too happy to puncture. Instead Bob trekked back east, closer to the bright lights of Broadway. It would be fourteen years before Woolsey again would grace the movies.

In 1916 Bob joined Rorick's Company, a repertory unit that was not very different from the sundry acting troupes he had been affiliated with. But as far as Woolsey was concerned, two significant factors distinguished the Rorick outfit: its proximity to Manhattan (stamping grounds were in Elmira, New York) and, more importantly, the ambitions of his fellow thespians, ex–Broadwayites anticipating their return engagements to the Great White Way. The Rorick's star comedian was a bespectacled native of San Francisco, Walter Catlett. Although he and Woolsey were the same age, Catlett had already beaten Bob to the punch with a Broadway featured role in *The Prince of Pilsen* in 1910. Described by the *New York Star* (March 1, 1916) as a "very clever comedian" capable of "running away with the show," Catlett shared his dressing room with Woolsey, and the pair became fast friends. They respected each other's talents, Catlett becoming teacher to Woolsey's pupil.

Although Walter Catlett was only twenty-seven at the time, his prop eyeglasses and big black cigar created the stage illusion of a middle-aged, bourgeois businessman. Filled with a boundless energy that reflected across the footlights, Catlett earned laughs by belying his stuffy appearance with outrageous antics and eccentric dancing. Woolsey learned from a master. "As a matter of fact," Bert Wheeler recalled in 1958, "Woolsey used to admit that he was a copy of Catlett, practically. He admitted it. He was a little guy and he looked different. Catlett was a big tall guy. But Woolsey carried himself like a big fellow." Shortly thereafter Catlett went on to major Broadway stardom, costarring with Charlotte Greenwood in *So Long, Letty* (1916) and reaching the pinnacle with Florenz Ziegfeld's *Follies of 1917*. Envious of his friend's success, Woolsey remained mired in a dreary routine of one-night stands in one-horse towns. "At that point in time," he remarked in the 1930s, "I was determined that if I ever landed on Broadway, I'd never leave it."

Before arriving at his destination, Woolsey met Mignone Park Reed, a former dancer in a musical stock company. They wed in 1917 and, according to Dorothy Lee, the pair made an ideal couple if for just one reason:

> Minnie Woolsey was as homely looking as Bob was—the poor woman! She was pleasant and quiet, but if she got a little drunk at a party she'd get up and start doing these high kicks. She thought she was a chorus girl again. Bob would nudge us and mutter, "Uh-oh, better look out—the old girl's stewed to the gills!"

Bob eventually got to Broadway in 1919, when he landed a supporting role in a lightweight musical comedy entitled *Nothing but Love* at the Lyric Theatre. The stars of the show were Ruby Norton and Andrew Tombes; what laughs the affair had were divided between the principals, with crumbs scattered between Donald Meek and Woolsey. Reviews were indifferent, with Alan Dale of the *New York American* (October 15, 1919) noting that Robert Woolsey might be an amusing comedian if given a chance.

Bob's big chance continued to elude him. Woolsey had a larger role in a comedy titled *Dere Mable* (1920), which circled around the metropolitan region before flopping out of town. Bob then devised a forty-minute stage act known as *The Bubbles Revue,* in which he appeared along with Queenie Smith, Robert Emmet O'Connor, and Marjorie Leach. The *New York Star* (February 23, 1921) declared the performance "full of good, clean comedy and well presented." This ensemble appeared in New York vaudeville houses, giving Bob both a rare foray into that medium plus exposure to prospective employers. Finally his doggedness paid off: Woolsey was spotted by Gleerich Productions, which hired him as lead comic in *Maid to Love.* The script was full of holes and the production was underfinanced, but Woolsey turned these liabilities to his advantage. He offered his services free of charge to "doctor" the play, citing his many years' theatrical experience as his credentials. The producers gladly accepted Bob's assistance, allowing him to take liberties with the piece. Woolsey shrewdly enlarged his own role, trotting out every surefire piece of comedy business and cramming it into the play.

Maid to Love, rechristened *The Right Girl,* opened at the Times Square Theatre on March 14, 1921. The critics couldn't have cared less about the play, but they were ecstatic about Robert Woolsey, "Broadway's newest musical comedy star." Bob had purloined Walter Catlett's trademark cigar and glasses, but the smooth professionalism that Woolsey projected was entirely his own. Woolsey would always remember opening night as "my greatest thrill in the theater." The reviews give some indication of his success; *Billboard* (March 26, 1921) proclaimed that

> *The Right Girl* is conspicuous for nothing in particular save the giving a chance on Broadway to a new comedian. Woolsey dances well and does wonders with the commonplace material of which his part is composed. He knows all the tricks, and doesn't laugh at his own stuff. Mr. Woolsey can go far, if he wants to.

Variety (March 18, 1921) acknowledged that Bob "practically walked away with both the book and score." The *New York Journal* (March 16, 1921) declared that Woolsey "has all the meat of the play; his is a genuine comedy role with plenty of fat lines, and he makes the most of them." Even prissy Alexander Woollcott, the *enfant terrible* of theater critics, sniffishly conceded in his *New York Times* review (March 16, 1921) that

Bob and chorines in *The Right Girl* (1921), performing his showstopper, "Things I Learned in Jersey."

the life of this somewhat dead party is unquestionably Robert Woolsey, who accomplishes a great deal with a pair of horn-rimmed spectacles and about two jokes. His amusing legs and comic effervescence carried several licenses to triumph last evening.

Prior to the play's opening, a photographer from the White Studios took pictures of the various cast members enacting scenes from *The Right Girl*, a standard practice then as now. Woolsey is featured in two of these photographs. After Bob's skyrocketing success, the show's producers had the White Studios take a new series of pictures exclusively featuring Woolsey with the chorus girls. Overnight Bob had willingly become an exploitable commodity, the utility comic, eagerly enriching the play as he bettered his part. As a footnote to this acclaim and attention, Woolsey received the following "congratulatory" telegram:

DON'T BE SO FUNNY, PLEASE. HEARD OF YOUR GREAT SUCCESS WITH GREAT REGRETS. PLEASE CUT OUT GLASSES AND ALL LAUGHS. COMPETITION TOO KEEN NOW. CAN PLACE YOU IN STOCK IN MANILA.

MOURNFULLY YOURS,
WALTER CATLETT

Woolsey jockeys for position with Victor Morley, Joseph Cawthorn, Marion Sunshine, Lillian Lorraine and Douglas Stevenson in *The Blue Kitten* (1922).

Catlett's tidings confirmed all Bob's hopes and dreams. The teacher applauded his pupil; Robert Woolsey had indisputably "arrived."

Bob became a Broadway fixture over the next six seasons. He worked steadily, although the ideal vehicle to showcase his talents eluded him. Woolsey was either swallowed up in shows that were brimming with comedians or the sole bright light in a turgid production desperately in need of laughs. The star of *The Blue Kitten* was Joseph Cawthorn, a veteran of musical comedy whose career stemmed from the 1890s. Woolsey vied for attention with four other comics in this cream-puff adaptation of a naughty French farce; few reviewers even took note of his presence. Alan Dale, who had championed Bob in his earlier Broadway appearances, regretfully reported in the *New York American* (January 14, 1922) that "some day [Woolsey] will get a role worthy of him, and then he'll be—as they say in vaudeville—'a riot.' But not last night."

Woolsey's material was soundly panned by most critics reviewing *The Lady in Ermine*. The *Evening World* (October 5, 1922) stated that "Woolsey is loaded with so many bad jokes that he has no chance to be funny." The *New York Tribune* (October 3, 1922) assumed an apologetic tone:

> Robert Woolsey, excellent comedian that he is, found it difficult to rise above the material which fell to his lot. His antic feet and facile expression helped him create amusement where his lines did not. Even that old one, "What is the saddest thing in the world? A Sunday in Philadelphia," cropped up during the course of the proceedings.

Alan Dale came to Bob's defense in his cogent review for the *New York American* (October 5, 1922):

> Woolsey does not horse play. He has no "topical" allusions to the subway, to the World Series and to politics. He does what he has to do in a singularly agreeable manner, and scores. They'll tell you he is "lacking in humor" because he isn't rowdy and a stage-holder-up. Do not believe this. Woolsey is most amusing and not in the least imitating. These flannel-voiced gentlemen usually get my goat. It is a pleasure to meet a comedian whom the low-brows will call "too quiet."

Woolsey next appeared in *Poppy*, where he was barely noticed by the press at all—primarily because he was sharing the stage with W. C. Fields. Fields's characterization of carnival pitchman Eustace McGargle dominated the proceedings; it was his show, deservedly so, and the magnificent W.C. made the most of his debut into musical comedy. Madge Kennedy, who essayed the title role, recalled (in 1985) absolutely nothing of Woolsey save that he was a member of the supporting cast. Those reviewers who acknowledged Bob's contributions seemed indignant at his appearance in Fields's play. The *New York Herald* (September 5, 1923) offhandedly remarked, "Miss [Luella] Gear was helped enormously through the 'Mary' song by Robert Woolsey, one of those complacent, sledge-hammer comics whom, up to then, a good many of us had rather intended to kill." The *New York Times* (September 4, 1923) was equally vitriolic:

> Members of the cast mainly furnish additional proof of the skill of Mr. Fields, for the barrenness of the book is never quite so evident as when Mr. Woolsey, for example, is performing. Nevertheless, *Poppy* emerges as an exceptional musical comedy.

Woolsey endured all criticisms hurtled at him with cool detachment. His rationale was that even a negative reaction from reviewers was better than no reaction at all. Besides, *Poppy* guaranteed Bob a healthy Broadway run and afforded him the vantage point of studying W. C. Fields at close range, eight times a week, for over a year. When not performing onstage Woolsey stood in the wings and observed Fields's consummate skill at ad-libbing, juggling, or just being outrageously funny. Bob wisely watched the

Decomposition has all but destroyed the only surviving photograph of Robert Woolsey and W. C. Fields in *Poppy* (1923).

maestro and apparently made valuable mental notes, for the lovable carnival rogue depicted by Fields was a close cousin to Woolsey's own movie shysters of the 1930s.

"Woolsey used to tell me a lot of stories about Fields," Bert Wheeler recollected in 1958.

> Fields had a little stooge in those days named Shorty, a little guy. So this is the night before the dress rehearsal; he says, "Shorty, this is where I shoot the shotgun off and it goes through the roof and a swan comes through." The woman [Dorothy Donnelly] who wrote this play says, "What do you mean, swan?" He says, "Well, I shoot a gun, it goes through the roof and a swan comes through." This woman walked out saying, "You can't do this to my beautiful play!" Bobby Woolsey told me, "This'll ruin the thing. You know, it's all right in a sketch but not in a real dramatic play." Woolsey told me, "That swan came through the roof and the audience laughed for five minutes. It never hurt the play."

Effects of Bob's Fieldsian apprenticeship were evident by the time of his next Broadway sojourn in *Mayflowers*, an operetta-comedy with Woolsey as sole comic relief. Critics executed an about-face assessment, with the *Evening World* (November 25, 1925) declaring that "Robert Woolsey was the master comic, able enough in view of his modest material." The *New York American* (November 26, 1925) indicated that "Woolsey was that ever-chastised character—the comedian. Oh, is it hard to be a comedian. What a lot! Mr. Woolsey made the most of everything."

Woolsey next became a Broadway angel, coproducing (and starring in) *Honest Liars*, a three-act farce. The *Evening World* (July 20, 1926) gave a perceptive analysis of Bob's talents under the guise of a critique:

> The only dues to *Honest Liars* is Robert Woolsey. The baffled reviewer, casting about for some explanation as to how this piece ever saw the footlights, can only cling to the memory of this valiant little figure, working against all odds in the principal role. For Mr. Woolsey is a musical comedy comedian and as such is probably familiar with the most hopeless plots that the human mind can invent. He has even been known to pull them out of their deepest gloom by the sheer force of his amiable idiocies.

At this juncture Bob was selected for Florenz Ziegfeld's *Rio Rita*, which finally led to major stardom, Hollywood success, and, naturally, Bert Wheeler. But an overlooked episode in the Woolsey chronology is his participation in *My Princess*. Six months into *Rio Rita*'s triumphant run, Woolsey was lured over to the Schubert organization. Bert Wheeler tells the story:

> Something a lot of people don't know: Woolsey opened with me in New York, and he was a smash hit, but Ziegfeld let him go. Nobody'll ever know why. And he put Walter Catlett in his place. He must have gotten mad at Woolsey for something. [In 1927] I knew Walter better than I did Woolsey. I was over in England with Walter [in 1919]. Walter was a terrific man. I'm in the middle, between these two guys, because I'm very fond of both of them, and they were both great in the part. Catlett played it the rest of the year. Then he didn't want to go on the road, and Woolsey went on the road—went back into the show—and that's when the pictures grabbed it.
>
> Now, if Catlett had stayed in it, he and I would have done it in the movies, and instead of Wheeler and Woolsey it would have been Wheeler and Catlett. Catlett was great in the role—and so was Woolsey. Each did it his own way, but they were both something alike.

Newspaper notices for *My Princess* present Woolsey as an accomplished, assured, and highly respected jokester. If contemporary reviews are any indication, the Woolsey persona later projected in the movies was fully developed and ripe for Hollywood. The *New York Herald Tribune* (October 7, 1927) tendered Bob numerous compliments and gleefully described a "hokum" exchange:

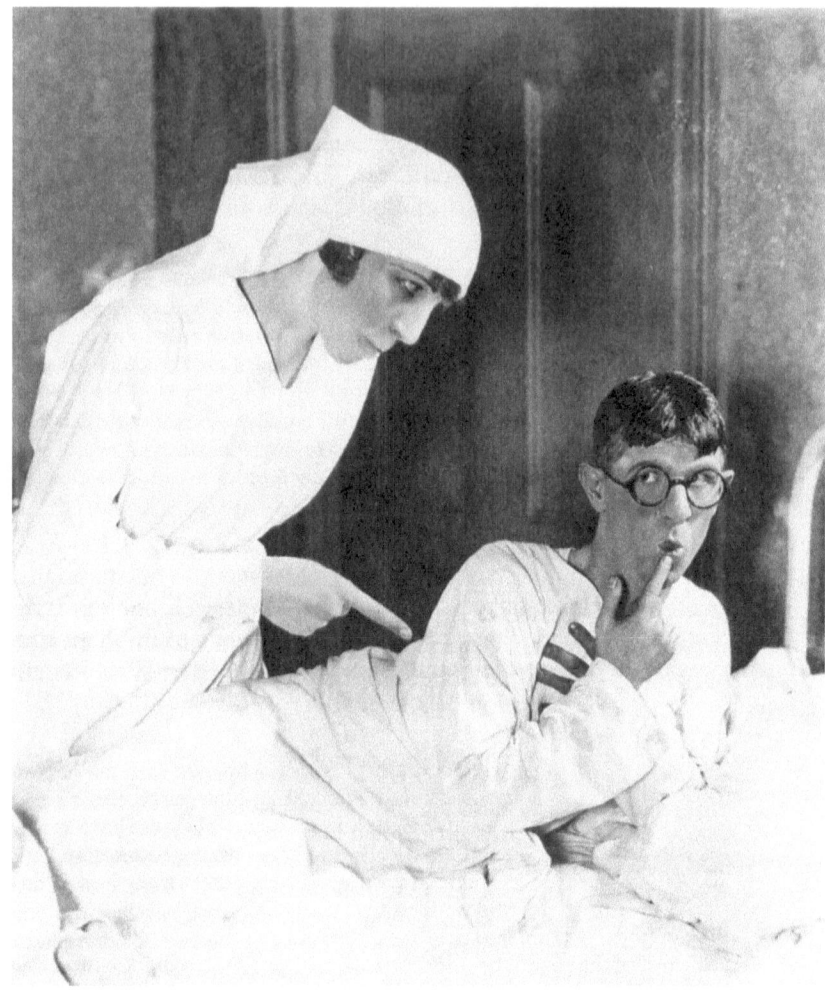

Nurse Harriet Harbaugh scolds patient Woolsey in *Honest Liars* (1926).

>Woolsey ... was present long enough to say that he lived in Minute Street. On being asked the location of Minute Street, he replied, "Sixty-second." Donald Meek at another time was complaining that Mr. Woolsey had worsted him in a real estate deal. "You told me that I could grow nuts on that land," said he. "No, I didn't," answered the merry fellow. "I said you could go nuts on it."

Bum jokes? No doubt, but Groucho Marx was impressed enough by Woolsey's delivery of the latter gag that he borrowed it for the Marx Brothers' 1928 musical comedy hit, *Animal Crackers*.

The first meeting: Ada May, Bert, Bob and Noel Francis in the 1927 stage version of *Rio Rita*.

Woolsey wrote the book for the 1928 musical *Tell Me Again* (a non-success) and appeared in one last solo venture, *Excess Baggage* (it never made it to Broadway) before once again taking his rightful place in the cast of *Rio Rita*.

Robert Woolsey's road to stage success was rather placid in comparison to Bert Wheeler's rocky path. Real stardom came comparatively late to Woolsey (he was thirty-seven when *Rio Rita* made him a full-fledged star; Bert was twenty-eight when he conquered the *Follies*). Once they joined forces, Wheeler and Woolsey would discover international fame as one of the 1930s' best-loved comedy teams—an unforeseen by-product of Ziegfeld's coupling.

3
Rio Rita (1929)

Adapted and directed by Luther Reed. Produced by William LeBaron. Based on the musical *Rio Rita*, by Guy Bolton and Fred Thompson. Music by Harry Tierney. Lyrics by Joseph McCarthy. Dialogue directed by Russell Mack. Costumes by Max Ree and (uncredited) John W. Harkrider. Photographed by Robert Kurrle. Photographic effects by Lloyd Knechtel. Color photography by Technicolor process. Musical direction by Victor Baravalle. Sound recording by Hugh McDowell Jr. Music associate, Max Steiner. Dances staged by Pearl Eaton. Chorus directed by Pietro Cimini. Film editing by William Hamilton. Associate editor, Pandro Berman. Dates of production: June 26 to July 20, 1929. Released by RKO on October 6, 1929. 135 minutes.

Cast: Bebe Daniels (Rita Ferguson), John Boles (Captain Jim Stewart), Bert Wheeler (Chick Bean), Robert Woolsey (Ed "Woody" Lovett), Dorothy Lee (Dolly Bean), Don Alvarado (Roberto Ferguson), Georges Renevant (General Ravenoff, alias the Kinkajou), Helen Kaiser (Katie Bean), Tiny Sandford (Louie Davalos), Clyde McClary (Louie's Henchman), Nick De Ruiz (Padrone), Sam Nelson (Ranger McGinn), Fred Burns (Ranger Wilkins), Eva Rosita (Carmen), Sam Blum (Café Owner), Benny Corbett, Tom Smith, Bud Osborne, Bud McClure, Hank Bell (Rangers), Fred Scott (Ranger Soloist), Blue Washington (Bank Robber), Richard Alexander (Gonzales, Ravenoff's Aide), Charles Stevens (José, Rita's Indian Servant), Elias Gamboa (Mexican Extra), Robert Livingston (Dance Extra at Ball), the Pearl Eaton Girls, the Pietro Cimini Grand Chorus.

Synopsis: Jim Stewart (John Boles), captain of the Texas Rangers, stalks a fearsome bandit terrorizing the Rio Grande who is known only as the Kinkajou. Jim suspects Roberto Ferguson (Don Alvarado) to be the mysterious outlaw, but since the Ranger is in love with Ferguson's sister, Rita (Bebe Daniels), Jim refrains from making hasty accusations. The situation is further complicated by the presence of General Ravenoff (Georges Renevant), an oily Russian expatriate whose wealth and army of thugs controls the Mexican border town of San Lucas. Ravenoff likewise has amatory interests in lovely Rita, but the General is thwarted at every turn by Ranger Jim. Ravenoff vows to eliminate Jim and claim Rita as his bride.

Meanwhile, New York bootlegger Chick Bean (Bert Wheeler) is obtaining a Mexican divorce so that he can marry his new sweetie, Dolly (Dorothy Lee), a local showgirl. After Chick and Dolly wed, Ed Lovett (Robert Woolsey), Chick's lawyer, informs his client that the divorce decree was invalid. Chick is advised to stay away from Dolly until the messy entanglements can be straightened out.

Ravenoff tricks Rita into believing that Jim is going to arrest her brother; she spurns the Texas Ranger but refuses to let Ravenoff shoot her beloved Jim. Rita sorrowfully agrees to marry the General, fearing that Ravenoff would otherwise expose her brother as the Kinkajou.

The subplot has not been idle, either. Chick's first wife, Katie (Helen Kaiser), arrives in San Lucas to accuse Chick of bigamy. Instead, she falls for Lovett in a big way.

Ravenoff plans an elaborate wedding for himself and Rita on his old pirate barge, situated on the Mexican side of the Rio Grande. Jim stealthily cuts the ropes mooring the vessel, which drifts over to the U.S. border. Just as Rita is about to marry Ravenoff, Jim's Texas Rangers board the barge, arresting the Russian villain as the real Kinkajou. Roberto is revealed to be a member of the Mexican Secret Service; Jim extradites Ravenoff to Roberto's care in exchange for Rita's hand in marriage.

★ ★ ★

Rio Rita is the granddad (or should that be grandma?) of all blockbuster Hollywood musicals. It's a weather-beaten relic, as befits its age, but while *Rita* creaks (loudly at times), it seldom sags. The film's performances are still delightful, the score is tuneful, and the outdoor locations are invigorating. Best of all, the Wheeler and Woolsey sequences are so enjoyable that the film comes alive whenever they appear. Every one of the team's routines is a flawless, wonderfully constructed little gem.

Rio Rita was first a smash hit musical on Broadway, debuting before *The Jazz Singer* ushered in successful talking films. Flo Ziegfeld established a trend for extravagant stage spectaculars with his annual editions of the *Ziegfeld Follies*, begun in 1907. By 1927 the *Follies* were proclaimed "a national institution," but the format had grown stale with overuse. Challenging himself, Ziegfeld erected a palatial theater to reflect his princely status in the theatrical world. The Ziegfeld Theater was conceived to house elaborate musical comedies, operettas, and revues, and the hall's first planned attraction would be the showman's most elaborate production to date, *Rio Rita*.

Ziegfeld's monument was completed just in time for *Rio Rita* rehearsals to commence on November 24, 1926. The theater's location (Sixth Avenue and Fifty-fourth Street) was a daring gamble on Ziggy's part, since it was several blocks removed from the glitter of the theater district. Ziegfeld confidently oversaw every aspect of the massive show he was nurturing. But Bert Wheeler felt the crunch from Ziggy's working methods:

> Ziegfeld didn't know anything about comedy. He wouldn't take a chance on a young comedian. You had to have arrived before. He said, "I don't know anything about comedy. I just hire the guys that do."
> But the comedians needed the stage to get out their work. You'd have to go down and rehearse anyplace you could find, in the alley or closet or anyplace, because he was draping those girls on the stage, fixing their costumes and adjusting the lighting on them.

No expense was spared in making *Rio Rita* Ziegfeld's most opulent showpiece. The lavishness dripped into the players' increased salaries—both Bert and Bob took home $750 a week. Ziegfeld assembled a roster of eight leading stars, seventeen supporting players, sixteen dancers of the Albertina Rasch ballet troupe, twenty-three "Texas Rangers," and fifty-four Ziegfeld Girls. Bert never forgot the last ensemble:

> Gosh, I remember in those days he'd pay girls that couldn't open their mouths $200, but they were beautiful. [An average salary was $25 a week at the time.] They were always tall girls. He liked the tall girls for himself. Wanted us [comics] to go out with the little gals, the hoofers. Well, being five-four I defied him!

Little time was wasted. Rehearsals over, the show went into tryouts immediately after the Christmas holidays. "When I opened in Boston in *Rio Rita*," Bert recalled, "I wasn't very happy with my part, and neither was Ziegfeld happy with me. But that's what happened in those days with comedians." Wheeler continued:

> Ziegfeld had plenty of confidence in me. There were a couple of guys that worried me. Ziegfeld said, "Don't worry about him. Worry about the rest of the show. He'll take care of himself." Even when I was not doing well, he knew that I would come through, and by the time I got to Philadelphia, after being in Boston two or three weeks, I had myself a part. By the time I got to New York, I had a great part, and it wasn't a cinch. We worked every night on it.

Composer Harry Tierney's copy of the 1926 script indicates that Bert and Bob's roles were enlarged and expanded prior to the New York premiere. Bert reminisced about his working methods:

> Did I use material that was written in my part? Well, I put a lot of it in myself, I really did. In those days it was expected of us, both by the author and the rest. When you were a star comedian, you were expected to practically write your own part.

Although Bert and Bob had both worked on Broadway throughout the 1920s, their paths had never crossed before:

> When I was in *Rio Rita,* I met Bobby Woolsey for the first time. I met him as just another comedian in this show. He was a hard guy to know at first, but we got to be quite friendly. We never dreamed we'd ever be partners. We were just two comedians hired for that show. That's how we became a team.

While Bert experienced a bad case of first-night jitters, Bob seemed to thrive under the pressure of being funny. "Bobby Woolsey was a guy who never worried about an opening night on the road," Bert remarked. "He had a lot of experiences in shows, and I'd had mine in vaudeville and revues. He was in all those stock companies out west." Bob worked with the same relentless determination as his teammate, polishing his material, even revamping his comedy style to play opposite Wheeler: "When I first met Bert in *Rio Rita,* I adapted my cocky, bragging type of comic as a contrast to Bert's more sympathetic personality." Or as Bert simply put it, "In *Rio Rita,* he was the wise guy and I was the sap!"

Rio Rita opened at the Ziegfeld Theater on February 2, 1927. Ziegfeld's magnificent showplace, the sets, costumes, and showgirls all received high praise, but Wheeler and Woolsey's smooth chemistry walked off with the top honors. The tough-as-nails New York press fell over themselves, scrambling for superlatives to praise the new team. "The pair of comedians quite won the hearts of the big crowd," wrote the *New York Telegraph.* The *Daily Mirror* felt that Wheeler and Woolsey "have few equals at the art of provoking laughs," while the *New York American* observed, "Robert Woolsey and Bert Wheeler merely made merry with none of the hoggishness of the cut and dried comedians who hold up stages and glory in it." *Variety* called the show "brilliant musical comedy" and observed that

> Woolsey handled himself like an old-timer. No laughing at his own jokes, not he. Wheeler is a funny fellow, and a hoofer, too. Wheeler put over a fast one, unexpectedly. In a drinking den, a heavy piece for the next scene fell loudly. Bert remarked, "It's the mice," and worked in an extra laugh.
>
> Then with Woolsey for next to closing was the face-slapping bit, with both boys spoiling their dinner jackets. It was a panic, the house forgetting that Noel Francis was warbling beside them.

The Good Neighbor Policy (and Bert Wheeler) take a beating from a dusky assailant in the stage *Rio Rita*.

The Wheeler-Woolsey scenes were, it should not be forgotten, a subplot to the romance between a dashing Texas Ranger and the beautiful Mexican woman. But Bert and Bob emerged as major stars in their own right. "A funny thing," Wheeler confided to an interviewer, "after the show opened and it was a smash, somebody said, 'Gee whizz, we ought to do something about this. There were two complete stories going on in *Rio Rita*, and nobody ever knew it.'" Bert continued,

> We had another story going along with us. I never met Rita or anybody connected with the other story. Isn't that funny? And the show was a very big hit. They asked Ziegfeld, "Well, don't you think you should tie it up?" He said, "Why monkey with success?" They were both important stories, and nobody realized it.

Rio Rita scored a solid run of 494 performances, a lengthy stint and ultimately a nomadic one. *Rita* shuttled from the Ziegfeld Theater to the Lyric on December 26, 1927 (to make room for Ziggy's most important production, the classic *Show Boat*); on March 12, 1928, the play shifted to the Majestic so that *The Three Musketeers* could occupy its berth. Other changes were in the wind. Walter Catlett stepped into Woolsey's role on October 17, 1927; Bob returned to the cast only when *Rita* went out on the road, rejoining the show January 21, 1929, in St. Louis, Missouri.

And Bert got married again—to Bernice Speer, a tap dancer appearing at a New York nitery, the Silver Slipper. The couple secretly wed in Jersey City, New Jersey, on April 15, 1928, just as *Rio Rita* went into a layoff period. "I was the only member of the cast who never missed a performance," Bert explained at the time. "All of us couldn't stand playing anymore. We've all signed for next year, and in the meantime I'm leaving for California to do some vaudeville and fool around with pictures." Bert indicated that the movies had made him firm offers (including a tempting proposition from Harold Lloyd), "but I couldn't accept, on account of my contract with Ziegfeld."

Just in case Bert planned to do more than just "fool around" with pictures, Ziggy asked *Variety*'s editor in chief, Sime Silverman, to issue a little statement on his behalf:

> May 30, 1928: Bert Wheeler will be enjoined by Ziegfeld if he [Wheeler] attempts to make a Vitaphone picture upon the occasion of his upcoming visit to the West Coast.
>
> Ziegfeld has Wheeler on a long-term contract and is protected by an anti–talking picture clause, reported as in all Ziegfeld contracts issued during the past two years.

Ziggy's concern was not unfounded—on February 28 of that year Bert was ready to sign a contract with the Vitaphone Corporation (a Warner Brothers subsidiary) to star in "three complete acts or numbers, each of not less than ten minutes duration." For his services, Wheeler would receive fifteen hundred dollars "to be paid at the time the said three records and motion picture films are approved by Vitaphone." Although

Bert did not sign the agreement, Ziegfeld realized that once Wheeler trekked west, the temptation might prove irresistible to the spunky comic. "Knowing Bert as well as I do," Tom Dillon comments, "I could see him defying Flo Ziegfeld and making those films. Bert was a wonderful fellow, but he could do something arbitrary that hurt his best interests."

Bert forgot all about talkies when his agent, Leo Fitzgerald, announced the terms he had secured for Wheeler's vaudeville dates: fifteen hundred dollars a week—double Bert's current Ziegfeld salary. Without further ado, Bert, Bernice, and the act's straight man, Al Clair, took the gravy train west to the land of perpetual sunshine. "I loved Hollywood," Bert recalled in 1958. "I loved it then [in 1928] better than I did later on. I knew Hollywood pretty well before I went out there to make a picture, so Hollywood was nothing new to me."

When the trio appeared at Los Angeles's Orpheum Theater, an eye-popping array of screen stars turned out to greet Bert. "I've seldom seen anything like it," Eddie Quillan remembers. "It was a who's who of comedians in attendance: Harold Lloyd, Stan Laurel, Buster Keaton, Lloyd Hamilton, Mack Sennett—I forget who else—and gosh yes, myself." *Variety* (July 11) noted that "'Bits of Everything' [were] offered by the Wheeler trio with the stellar member getting over as big as a bass drum. Wheeler, always well liked here, just pushed 'em over." The three troupers were summer guests at Harold Lloyd's estate, Greenacres, so enormous that after two years of construction it was still unfinished. "I knew Harold Lloyd very well," Bert said later. "He made me this offer in pictures long before [the movie] *Rio Rita*." Wheeler explained Ziegfeld's "anti–motion picture clause" to his amiable host, but the generous Lloyd shot screen tests of Bert anyway, presenting the footage to Wheeler as a gift. "You never know when you could use it," Lloyd informed his friend.

It was not until the spring of 1929 that Ziegfeld allowed Bert to make a talkie for Vitaphone—and that was only because Ziggy decided to close *Rio Rita* on May 11, 1929, at the Chicago Civic Auditorium. Up to May 4, *Rita* earned the maestro $243,069.31 (as compared to *Show Boat*, at $299,409.17, Ziegfeld's topper). *Rio Rita* could have toured another year, except that Ziegfeld sold his movie rights to RKO-Radio Pictures for $85,000. RKO president Joseph Schnitzler personally requested the services of only two performers out of the entire Broadway cast—Bert Wheeler and Robert Woolsey. Ziggy gave his blessing on April 10, as long as "their services are to commence by the 15th of June for a period of five weeks." The Great Showman's words almost take on a parental tone: "Further retakes are subject to such time that will not interfere with their Ziegfeld rehearsals." Stage-bound *Rio Rita* would be filmed outdoors, in the airy vistas of southern California.

Happily, for once Bert's personal life was going well, too. During the

Chicago run of *Rita*, Bernice gave birth to a daughter, Patricia Dolores, who "very considerately waited until after her father came off stage Saturday night to make her entrance," according to an anonymous press clipping.

Wheeler finally filmed his long overdue Vitaphone short, *Small Timers*, on May 17 in the old Brooklyn Vitagraph Studio. *Old Home Week* might have been a more suitable title—Bernice, Al Clair, and Sam Silverbush appeared with Bert for director Bryan Foy, a friend from vaudeville days, while Eddie Welch, another Wheeler crony, wrote the gags. The ten-minute vignette was shot in nine hours, for which Bert was paid fifteen hundred dollars—three times the amount that Vitaphone would have paid him only a year before. Bert, Bob, their wives, and little Patricia then proceeded to head west for a rendezvous with RKO.

If Bert and Bob felt like rookies in the movie colony, they were not alone. Dozens of former Broadwayites were making their screen debuts about the same time—including the Marx Brothers, Humphrey Bogart, Helen Morgan, Fanny Brice, Frederic March, and James Cagney, to name a few. There were many new faces on the block when Bert and Bob reported to the studio on June 15. Wheeler, Woolsey, and RKO itself were all newcomers to the picture business.

Radio-Keith-Orpheum, better known as RKO, was founded in late 1928 by General David Sarnoff, president of the fledgling Radio Corporation of America. The ambitious Sarnoff sought to merge RCA with a movie studio that would produce prestigious sound films to be shown on a circuit of important theaters. The established Hollywood powers—MGM, Paramount, Fox, Warners, and Universal—were not about to relinquish their holdings. General Sarnoff needed to forge an unholy alliance with a Hollywood insider cunning enough to orchestrate such a deal. Through the Machiavellian connivance of banking wizard Joe Kennedy, Sarnoff's dream came true.

Kennedy assembled a package deal that the drooling Sarnoff found irresistible. The General wanted a movie studio? Kennedy sold Sarnoff his own. RCA found itself the proud owner of rickety FBO, built in 1920 on land purchased from the Hollywood cemetery. Of course, it needed modernization, but to a novice like Sarnoff, those were minor considerations. The General wanted a theater chain? Kennedy happened to have one of those on the auction block, too. The Keith-Albee-Orpheum circuit offered a batch of decrepit vaudeville houses, which, after overhaul and a conversion that would allow them to show talkies, would suit Sarnoff's purposes. For these manipulations Kennedy pocketed $5 million in bonuses, stock options, and commissions before beating a wise retreat out of the motion-picture racket.

General Sarnoff was so blinded by showbiz searchlights that he was

Rio Rita (1929)

undaunted by the tremendous financial outlay required to stimulate his sleeping dinosaur. In 1929 RKO pledged $4 million for studio expansion and the construction of soundstages. It was an awful lot of money, but then this was the 1920s, the boom era: the stock market was soaring and the economy was expanding. What, Sarnoff reasoned, could possibly go wrong?

For a while everything went just right. *Rio Rita*, budgeted at $675,000 with music and Technicolor sequences, would be an eye-catching standout on any studio's schedule. Tiny RKO slowly began expanding while *Rita* was in preproduction. For a time it was open to debate which was bigger—RKO or *Rio Rita*. "When I went out to Hollywood in 1929," Bert said, "they didn't even have a restaurant on that lot—just a hot-dog stand. The streets were all mud—they didn't even have asphalt—and they only had two soundstages." RKO's sleepy locale at 780 Gower Street was dwarfed by its mighty next door neighbor, Paramount, but the proximity of the powerful giant had distinct advantages. When Paramount's studio chief, B. P. Schulberg, dropped silent star Bebe Daniels from their roster, she impetuously paid a visit to RKO. Production head William LeBaron eagerly signed Daniels, one of Hollywood's biggest stars, to play the title role in *Rio Rita*, her first sound film.

Ideally cast as Rita, the brunette beauty shrewdly forfeited her salary for a share of the gross profits. Playing opposite her was the ideally rugged John Boles, borrowed from Universal at $5,000 weekly. The film industry could dole out salaries that even a showman like Ziegfeld could ill afford. Bert and Bob each received five-week guarantees at $2,750 per week, while an eighteen-year-old native of Los Angeles named Dorothy Lee was hired to portray Wheeler's pert vis-à-vis. For Bert and Dorothy, it was the start of their forty-year friendship.

Born Marjorie Millsap on May 23, 1911, Dottie attended Westlake School for Girls ("They tried to turn me into a snob, but I outfoxed them") before traveling to New York, where she auditioned for bandleader Fred Waring. Dottie performed an energetic Charleston and sang some jazzy tunes. "Waring thought that I had personality," Dorothy relates, "even though I couldn't sing." Waring liked what he saw, signing Dottie for his Broadway hit *Hello Yourself* (1928), a spoof about campus life. At five feet, one inch with a pouty face, bewitching eyes, and squeaky, babylike voice, she made an adorable flapper. While appearing with Waring she made her first talkie, *Syncopation* (1929). The film was shot in Manhattan during the daytime while Dottie appeared in *Hello Yourself* at night. Indirectly, *Syncopation* brought Bert and Dorothy together. Dottie recalls,

> I was playing in *Hello Yourself* with Fred Waring, and Bert was playing in *Rio Rita*. He had seen me in *Syncopation*; he sat through it and caught

the name Dorothy Lee in the credits. He had just signed with RKO and he thought, "I've got to find this girl Dorothy Lee to play opposite me in the show!" So he can't find me and was trying to figure out how to go about it. One day he's standing at some bar that was an actor's hangout, and he says to the fellow he's with, "God, I've just seen this movie with Dorothy Lee. She'd be perfect for my film, but I can't locate her." The guy with him said, "Oh, for God's sakes, I'm appearing opposite her in the Fred Waring show."

Dorothy was signed by RKO for five weeks at a weekly salary of $450. "That's like giving a teenager $4,500 a week today and telling the kid, 'Just spend it,'" Dottie notes.

No investiture was too costly in those last prosperous days of the twenties. RKO did not own a back lot to construct a Mexican village, so an unusual arrangement was struck with *Tarzan* author Edgar Rice Burroughs. Burroughs agreed to rent his Tarzana Ranch to RKO for the building and photographing of motion picture sets. Burroughs would receive $500 per day during shooting, $15 per day during preparations, and the right to keep "all sets, dressings, movable foliage and scenery" once the shooting was finished. A year later, RKO's acquisition of its Encino ranch eliminated the need for such extravagant pacts.

Production got underway on June 26, 1929. The newfangled sound equipment challenged the patience of cast and crew; shooting outdoors presented nearly insurmountable problems. "It seemed to me that the sound cameras picked up every noise except the actors' voices," Bert remarked. Dubbing was nearly impossible to achieve; Bert never tired of recounting how thirty musicians would sit off-camera in the blazing sun, accompanying an "intimate" love scene between Bebe Daniels and John Boles. "It really cost them a fortune with those musicians sitting out there, waiting."

Luther Reed was selected to direct *Rio Rita*. A former scenario writer and director in silent days, Reed's outdoor footage looked alive and fluid compared to that of most other 1929 talkies. Even more important to the picture's success was the guiding hand of William LeBaron, RKO's paternal production chief. LeBaron had an extensive background in Broadway theater, and had been one-time supervisor of Paramount's East Coast studio. "He was a fantastic guy," Dorothy remembers. "Bill LeBaron had a special fondness for stage comedians like Bert and Bob. He was a boss who looked out for you."

Filming wrapped on July 20 — a surprisingly fast and efficient shoot for such a tremendous spectacle. Postproduction work was completed in little over a month. Private screenings were arranged for all employees on September 5: studio personnel knew they had a hit of gigantic proportions on their hands. One month later, the public would find out for themselves.

Rio Rita (1929)

The film opens at a border café in Fremont, Texas. Inside, two Texas Rangers are nailing posters to the wall: "$10,000 REWARD—For the Bandit Known as THE KINKAJOU—DEAD OR ALIVE." A flapper asks her date who the Kinkajou is. She is told that "'Kinkajou' is Mexican for *wildcat*, and this bandit is all of that. He's been making monkeys out of the Rangers." (Incidentally, the encyclopedia identifies the kinkajou as a "nocturnal foraging mammal of the raccoon family, primarily a fruit and insect eater.")

Bert and Bob are introduced while watching Dorothy dance with the showgirls. It's a fairly straight expository scene, as lawyer Bob lets Bert know that his Mexican divorce was granted by the courts. The Rangers tap Wheeler on the shoulder, causing Bert to throw his arms up in surrender fashion. One Ranger cheerfully informs Bert that they are "not looking for bootleggers tonight." Wheeler smokes a cigarette during the sequence, something his child-man character would never do in subsequent films. Bert's smoking, the bootlegging reference, and divorce allusions are out of line with the innocent persona he projected later. For all its hokey nonsense, *Rio Rita* was initially geared toward an "adult" audience of sophisticates. In the movies, W & W's patronage rapidly switched to the common people, foreign audiences, and the most devout fans of all, kids.

Woolsey next appears (in a beautifully photographed outdoor sequence) at the Mesa Francisca. Resplendent in a crisp white suit, Bob is besieged by local peddlers. Pretty soon he is the unhappy owner of a giant sombrero; flirting with a señorita, he is thrown to the ground by a jealous hombre, causing a sympathetic flower girl to hand him a rose. The sequence was filmed silently, allowing the camera to glide between the players. Music, singing, and sound effects (a bass drum for Bob's "thump" to earth) were expertly dubbed in afterward.

Bert and Dottie drive up with a Just Married sign on their motorcycle, Bert nattily attired in a sleek top hat. "Who gave you away?" someone asks Dot. "Nobody said a word," she replies. The innkeeper expresses concern that the honeymoon suite might be too expensive for Wheeler. Dorothy informs the man that Bert "always stops in the best hotels." "Yes," Wheeler snorts contemptuously, "and I've got the towels to prove it!" At this tactful moment Bob comes forward to confer with his client.

BOB: How's things, how's things?
BERT: Great, thanks to you, and today I'm starting fifty years of billing and cooing.
BOB: Heh, heh, listen, my boy, let me set you straight: the cooing stops when the honeymoon is over, but the billing goes on forever! When did you get married?
BERT: About fifteen minutes ago, and I'm still happy.
BOB: You are? Well, let me tell you something, that you had no right

> getting married without my consent. I'm your legal adviser, and I'm afraid I've got to hand you an awful shock—
> BERT: I know, it's your bill!
> BOB: How would you like it if I told you your Mexican divorce is no good?
> BERT: Yesterday you told me that it was good!
> BOB: Yeah, but that was yesterday, today is Friday.
> BERT: What are you talkin' about?
> BOB: I have just learned that the United States does not recognize Mexican divorces. I hate to tell you this, but you'll probably have to do five years in jail!
> BERT: [*nervously*] You know that I'm sick—I'd never be able to do that long—
> BOB: Well, do the best you can, kid, do the best you can!

The repartee is expertly timed, Bob's rat-a-tat-tat delivery contrasting nicely with Bert's good-natured innocence. Bob is glib, sardonic, and assured; Bert is naive, trusting, and childlike. The interplay between them is impeccable. For the duration of the film, Bert reluctantly schemes to stay as far away from his wife as possible—at least until his divorce is recognized. Dorothy returns to the scene and wonders what the boys were discussing:

> BERT: He [Bob] wants me to go on a hunting trip with him and some of the boys.
> DOT: Lovely! When?
> BERT: Tonight.
> DOT: On our wedding night you're going hunting?
> BERT: [*sheepishly*] Well, it would be original, wouldn't it?

Next up comes the film's famous drinking scene, where the duo gets sloshed on "old Aztec wine" and proceeds to hallucinate. Bob pours a little into a shotglass (the glass disintegrates) so the boys decide to sample it from the bottle. Bert warns, "One little sip is all I'm gonna have." One little sip does it—Wheeler begins to yap like a dog before lapsing into a baby's voice. Listening to Bert's babbling, Bob comments, "Now that's what I call whiskey!" Bert imagines that a beautiful woman enters the room. "Hey," he tells Bob, "she shouldn't take off her clothes—not here." "Gimme a drink of that stuff!" Woolsey responds. Once Bob takes a sip, recognition sets in: "Why, I *know* the girl!" The drunken partners attempt to flirt with their invisible woman.

The innkeeper enters and informs the boys that nobody else is in the room with them. "He's drunk!" Bert advises Bob. "Wait a minute," Bob decides. "I'll find out if she's there—I'll pass my hat right through her." Bob swings his hat through the air. "Boy, he's right," Woolsey decides, "there's no girl there." When a real señorita enters, the boys think she's another mirage. "Hey," Wheeler says. "I'll pass my hat through this one." Bert's topper smacks the poor woman squarely in the derriere. Her ferocious husband (behemoth Tiny Sandford) suddenly storms into the room with his gang. "Hey," Bob instructs Bert, "pass your hat through them!" Bert and Tiny wrestle for possession of a shotgun while Bob faces the gun's barrel no matter which way he turns (shades of Chaplin's *Gold Rush*). Woolsey distracts Tiny by kicking him in the behind, leaving Bert in control of the weapon. Bert marches Tiny out of the room, keeping the shotgun aimed at the big lug's rear end. Bert's ad-libbed exit, "I'll be right back!" closes the skit on huge laughs.

Wheeler and Woolsey are invited to a magnificent fiesta being held at General Ravenoff's hacienda. Bert is mistaken for the Kinkajou, an identity that the female guests find rather sexy. Bert enjoys the fuss, except that each girl has clipped a button off his tuxedo trousers as a souvenir. In a variation on his beloved vaudeville act, Wheeler lolls about on the staircase and flirts with a pretty girl:

> BERT: [*coyly*] You know, honey, as a rule I don't go around saying these things, but would you believe me if I tell you something—you really are beautiful! Do you believe me?
> CARMEN: I would like to believe you—but my mother say the men are liars.
> BERT: Your mother say the men are liars?
> CARMEN: My mother say that *all* the men are liars!
> BERT: [*amused*] Your mother says all the men are liars? Gosh, your mother's been around, hasn't she?
> CARMEN: I must have just one kiss!
> BERT Oh, gosh, why was I ever cursed with this appeal! Now, Carmen, before I give in, do you know anything about kissing?
> CARMEN: I am the best in Mexico!
> [*Carmen kisses Bert; he reacts*]
> BERT: Whoever told you you're the best in Mexico?
> CARMEN: All the men tell me I am the best!
> BERT: All the men tell you you're the best? Well, don't forget what your mother told you!

Bert performs an exhilarating song and dance number with the chorus girls, "Out on the Loose." This includes an a capella tap dance from Wheeler, who midway instructs the orchestra, "Faster!" In hindsight there is something autobiographical about the number that is both ironic and touching. At this point in the film, Bert believes that his second wife (Dorothy) has left him. Although saddened and hurt, he resolves to cheer himself up and continue living: "I've a few oats to sow, and I don't care where they grow." In real life Wheeler's matrimonial woes were nearly devastating, yet each time he pulled himself up by his bootstraps, rekindling

"Why, I *know* the girl!"—Bob and Bert in a pose from their famous drunk scene from the movie version of *Rio Rita*.

his zest for life, making people laugh. Surrounded by young lovelies at the start of the number, Bert finishes up alone, happily dancing off into the sunset—as he loses his trousers.

The film's last half-hour (shot in Technicolor) is set on Ravenoff's gambling barge and features the first of Bert and Dottie's love duets, "Sweetheart, We Need Each Other." The contrite lovers kiss and make up, then celebrate with a delightful bit of hoofing. "Bert taught me the steps for that number," Dorothy recalls. "It might've been something that Bert performed onstage in *Rio Rita*, but we devised the finale ourselves." As the sequence ends, Bert and Dottie tumble over each other, Bert leaps on Dorothy's back, and she supports him for the last line of the song. "It's one of the cutest bits we ever did, don't you think?" Modern audiences agree with Dottie's assessment, applauding the scene at the film's infrequent revivals.

The last major comedy vignette is the film's finest: with Bert and Dorothy reconciled, Bob wins the hand of Bert's ex-wife, Katie (Helen Kaiser), who conveniently just inherited a fortune. Bert and Dorothy join Bob and Helen Kaiser, who are sitting on the railing of the ship. Woolsey can't wait to share the good news:

> BOB: Boy, congratulate me!
> BERT: About what?
> BOB: Katie and I are gonna be married!
> BERT: Aw, you darn fool!
> BOB: Darn fool? Katie's uncle just died and left her three million dollars!
> BERT: Well, you'll earn it!

Wheeler's last crack offends his teammate; in a series of retaliations, the boys smile as they methodically destroy each other's carnation, cigar, and bow tie. They playfully pat each other's cheeks, the pats gradually turning into a face-slapping game. "You're gettin' sore at me!" Bert sweetly mutters. "Aw, no!" Bob cheerfully replies. The girls provide musical accompaniment, singing "Sweetheart, We Need Each Other," oblivious to the team's feuding. Pain from all the slapping changes the boys' laughter into tears. Bert and Bob warble the song's final line. The crybabies embrace, falling over backward into the water; a moment later, the girls join them for a dunking. It is a beautifully played, deliciously funny sequence, executed in a single two-minute take. Comic perfection was not achieved without great price, as Dottie recalls:

> Warner Brothers owned the first color cameras, you see. They would use it in the daytime. From Warners' lot in Burbank to RKO would be about fifteen miles. Warners would use the camera when they wanted it; then RKO would rent it. RKO would have to bring it to the studio on Gower Street, which is right in the middle of Hollywood.
>
> So we would have to work from eight o'clock until six o'clock in the morning. We always worked all night, and I will never forget the scene. It was four o'clock in the morning, and brother, it was very cold. I remember the scene so well because I know every time I hit that water I felt I never was going to live, except that I was eighteen years old!

It's four o'clock in the morning and they had four costumes made, so that if the thing didn't take, they would dry us off and put us back on that board. And I think they filmed it four times! The water was thirty-five or forty degrees. It was on the back lot; why they had to take it outside I will never know, but in those days you didn't question things. We knew we had to use Warners' color camera at night. It was freezing; each time we'd say, "Oh my God, here we go again!"

The end results were justified when *Rio Rita* became the smashing success everyone had predicted. While Bebe Daniels and John Boles were the nominal stars, Bert and Bob ultimately reaped the highest dividends. *Variety* reported, "In comedy it's Bert Wheeler, first, with Robert Woolsey next. . . .

Wheeler and Woolsey split up the comedy, from crossfire to slapstick and Wheeler the 80 of the 80-20 with Woolsey on the short end." *Rio Rita* was selected by *Film Daily* as one of 1929's ten best films and went on to gross $2.4 million for RKO.

The film's tremendous popularity nearly led to its own extinction. When *Rita* was to be reissued in 1932, David O. Selznick instructed production assistant Pandro Berman to "cut *Rio Rita* not less than 8,000 feet, not more than 8,300 feet." This would reduce the film's length by a third, from 135 to approximately 90 minutes. On April 12, 1932, Katharine Brown, RKO's New York representative, informed Selznick that the "*Rio Rita* recut print [is] in very bad condition, and as domestic negative is too worn for future printing, think it advisable we recut foreign negative." The following day Selznick agreed with her suggestion. When RKO sold MGM its rights to *Rita* for an Abbott and Costello remake (1942), Metro inherited the edited negative. The sole 35 mm print of *Rita* circulating today is this truncated version. It is longer than Selznick's original intentions: in 1978, the film was 105 minutes when presented in New York City. But for a 1983 Los Angeles showing, the print ran 101 minutes. An entire Technicolor number (fortunately, not involving the principals) had been removed. Why?

What is frustrating is that a battered 16 mm print of the deleted footage *has* resurfaced, although to date nobody has tried to reassemble a complete *Rio Rita*.

Reconstruction is painstaking and costly, particularly when the restored product is not likely to generate significant revenue. If *Rita* is rejuvenated, the work will most likely be sponsored by Turner Entertainment. Ted Turner not only owns the rights to RKO and MGM properties, he also has a deep commitment to saving the cinema's past. Until that time, we can only wait.

Abbott and Costello's bowdlerized remake is hardly a remake at all. Apart from two songs and a sliver of Wheeler and Woolsey's drunk

Rio Rita (1929)

Dorothy Lee and Bert performing "Are You There?" a number cut from the 1932 reissue of *Rio Rita*.

Nick DeRuiz (arms akimbo), Bob and Eva Rosita in another number deleted from *Rio Rita*'s reissue, "I Can Speak Espagnol."

routine, the A & C *Rio Rita* is a different picture, involving Bud and Lou with Nazi spies in wartime Mexico. But A & C's first movie, *One Night in the Tropics* (Universal, 1940), with the boys in support, is a suspiciously close cousin to the 1929 *Rita*—but that story is a chapter for someone else's book.

4
The Cuckoos (1930)

Directed by Paul Sloane. Produced by William LeBaron. Associate producer, Louis Sarecky. Adapted for the screen by Cyrus Wood. Additional material (uncredited) by Roscoe Arbuckle. Based on the musical *The Ramblers*; book, music, and lyrics by Guy Bolton, Bert Kalmar, and Harry Ruby. Art direction by Max Ree. Photographed by Nick Musuraca. Photographic effects by Lloyd Knechtel. Color photography by Technicolor process. Musical direction by Victor Baravalle. Sound recording by John Tribby. Dances staged by Pearl Eaton. Film editing by Arthur Roberts. Dates of production: January 27 to February 28, 1930. Released by RKO on May 4, 1930. 90 minutes.

Cast: Bert Wheeler (Sparrow), Robert Woolsey (Professor Cunningham), Dorothy Lee (Anita), Jobyna Howland (Fannie Furst), Hugh Trevor (Billy Shannon), June Clyde (Ruth Chester), Ivan Lebedeff (Baron de Camp), Marguerita Padula (Gypsy Queen), Mitchell Lewis (Julius, the Gypsy King), Raymond Maurel (Singer), Harry Semels, Bob Kortman (Gypsies), Hector V. Sarno (Tamale Vendor), Kalla Pasha (Hotheaded Cowboy).

Synopsis: Professor Cunningham (Robert Woolsey) and his assistant, Sparrow (Bert Wheeler), are bogus fortune-tellers who find themselves penniless at a Mexican resort. Sparrow has fallen in love with Anita (Dorothy Lee), an American who has lived with a band of Gypsies since childhood. Julius (Mitchell Lewis), the leader of the band, also has designs on Anita, and swears that he will kill the pair of quack mystics.

Baron de Camp (Ivan Lebedeff) hires Julius and the Gypsies for $10,000 to remain under his command. The baron desires to marry Ruth Chester (June Clyde), who has been brought there by her aunt, Fannie Furst (Jobyna Howland), to separate Ruth from Billy Shannon (Hugh Trevor), an aviator. Billy, however, tracks Ruth down and flies to Mexico. Meanwhile, the professor and Sparrow have conned Fannie into believing they are genuine mystics and are invited to a swank party at Fannie's San Diego estate. At the baron's behest, Julius and the Gypsies kidnap Ruth; the fortune-tellers assure Fannie that they will rescue her niece.

The boys give pursuit on a swaybacked horse, engaging a room south of the Mexican border near the gypsy camp. Billy locates Ruth, and with the assistance of the professor and Sparrow, manages to overcome the Baron and his gang. Billy, Ruth, Anita, Sparrow, and the professor hurry off to Billy's plane. The happy group returns to San Diego, crash-landing on the penthouse of a hotel. The hotel's jazz orchestra obliges the downed flyers with a medley of the movie's songs as the film fades out.

★   ★   ★

Bert and Bob headed east upon completion of *Rio Rita,* ready to start their Ziegfeld rehearsals, only to discover that Ziegfeld had nothing for them to rehearse. Nor did the Great Showman have salaries to pay them — or any other members of his organization not already involved in a show. In short, Ziggy was broke.

"Poor Mr. Ziegfeld lost a fortune speculating in the stock market," Bert recalled. "This was even before the market crashed. He lost the lease on the New Amsterdam Theater, where I starred in my first *Follies.* And he had to let most of us go." Drained of funds, Ziegfeld trekked west himself, collaborating with Sam Goldwyn on a movie adaptation of his final stage success, *Whoopee.*

Executives at RKO regarded these developments — or setbacks — with keen interest. In August 1929, a rough cut of *Rio Rita* was assembled for the studio bigwigs. Bebe Daniels was splendid, they agreed, but the subplot — with its "comedy relief," particularly Bert Wheeler's contributions — dazzled the moguls. Florenz Ziegfeld's misfortune was a boon to RKO, if they could act quickly on this insider information. A decision was reached to snatch this "Wheeler boy" without further delay. On August 20, Bert, Bernice, and Patricia headed back on the train to California. "Now that I was a daddy and could afford to settle down," Bert told a friend, "we became cross-country marathon racers. New York to Hollywood is a hell of a jump between engagements."

In later years, Wheeler always reminded interviewers that he and Woolsey never planned on remaining a team. "We thought we'd go our separate ways after shooting *Rio Rita,*" Bert told Tom Dillon in the 1960s. "But the studio had other ideas, so Bob and I stayed around for twenty more pictures." Bert's account is basically correct, but RKO's initial intent was different. Following *Rio Rita,* RKO rolled out the red carpet for Bert Wheeler, foreseeing a profitable association with a comedian who had star potential. But the door was shut tight on Robert Woolsey, who was not considered a "unique talent." That was mistake number one; a few more would follow.

On Monday, September 9, Bert signed an exclusive RKO contract for one year at $2,403.84 a week (thirty-two cents short of $125,000). The

RKO reader's department began pouring over literary properties, searching for the ideal Wheeler vehicle. None of the scripts consulted suited Bert's screen personality, so staff writer James Ashmore Creelman drafted an original story entitled *The Cake Eater*. Creelman's fluffy yarn might have proved suitable for a light comedian like Reginald Denny or even Edward Everett Horton, but Bert was too energetic and earthy to be mired in this tea-and-crumpets tale. *The Cake Eater* was shelved while RKO executives drummed their desktops.

Meanwhile, *Rio Rita* was released, proving to be a box-office bonanza for the flourishing little studio. Even the stock market crash of infamous Black Tuesday (October 29) could not put a stranglehold on the musical's unprecedented success. Surveying the public's wild enthusiasm, production chief Bill LeBaron sagely recommended that they rework *Rita*'s subplot, expanding it into a full-length story for Bert Wheeler. Suddenly the discarded Woolsey became an essential ingredient to the formula; ditto Dorothy Lee, who was on the road again with Fred Waring's band.

Both Dottie and Bob were eager to return to the movies. On November 20, amid little fanfare, Dorothy signed a one-year contract with RKO for $500 a week. Woolsey signed a $2,000 weekly pact on December 23—$400 less than Bert was receiving—mistake number two. "Bob resented being considered inferior to Bert," Dottie recounts, "and he felt that the studio regarded him as a second banana. The lower salary drove home that notion, and I think it made Woolsey very bitter."

Even more damaging to Bob's pride was the period of his employment: a scant five weeks. Mistake number three: RKO effectively told Bob that once he finished the film, RKO would be finished with him.

"RKO humiliated Bobby," Wheeler reminisced in later years. Bert empathized with his partner's plight:

> I knew it, but what do you say to the poor guy? The studio felt there were a lot of comedians around exactly like Woolsey—Walter Catlett, Tommy Howard, Andy Tombes—and that they could always sign up one of those fellas when we needed 'em. It didn't occur to whoever at RKO that maybe those guys were already under contract someplace else.

Eventually the studio came to its senses, hiring Bob on a long-term basis (March 1, 1930) at his $2,000 weekly salary. The wound healed, but RKO would ultimately feel the cigar-chomping comic's backlash. In the mid–1930s, Woolsey engaged in heated salary negotiations with RKO management, fighting like a demon to fetch the best possible terms for the team—and this time Woolsey won the match.

Amid the contractual connivances, a movie had to be made, and a usable property was finally found: *The Ramblers*, a 1926 musical hit about a

Paul McCullough and Bobby Clark performing "Oh! How We Love Our Alma Mater" in their stage success, *The Ramblers*.

pair of wandering fortune-tellers. *The Ramblers* had a flimsy plot but some good comedy blackout scenes plus a fine score by Bert Kalmar and Harry Ruby. On Broadway it had starred the former burlesque team of Bobby Clark and Paul McCullough, who were currently starring in a series of Fox featurettes.

Late in the twenties, Clark and McCullough were considered the wackiest stage team this side of the Marx Brothers, although, if possible, they had even less of a hold on reality. Clark portrayed a surreal buffoon (his trademark was painted-on eyeglasses, adding to his weirdness), while McCullough was the do-nothing straight man. The Fox films of Clark and McCullough are unavailable today, but contemporary accounts do not encourage their exhumation. The duo's Fox pictures ran from twenty to fifty minutes each and were based on original stories hammered out by the brains of the act, Bobby Clark. In 1929 alone, the team ground out twelve such pictures; a typical *Variety* review for the team's *Waltzing Around* labeled it "a long 28 minutes . . . tiresome." Clark and McCullough were only too happy to leave talkies and return to their beloved theater, where they scored a direct hit in Gershwin's *Strike Up the Band* (1930).

The Ramblers adapted itself easily to Bert and Bob's established characters. Woolsey naturally assumed Clark's role of the take-charge character, while Wheeler tossed aside McCullough's straight-man part and instilled his own sweetly outrageous wit into the shenanigans. Once screenwriter Cyrus Wood's adaptation was completed, the roles of shady Dr. Cunningham and his gullible boy Sparrow fit the team like kid gloves. Retitling the film first *Radio Ramblers*, then *Radio Revels*, RKO finally settled on *The Cuckoos*, which South American aficionados chose as their nickname for the boys.

A most unlikely collaborator on *The Cuckoos* was former silent-comedy star Roscoe "Fatty" Arbuckle. RKO hired the heavyweight comic on January 21, 1930, as a gag writer, a capacity he kept for the next three months. Arbuckle, who in 1921 was second only to Chaplin in the pantheon of screen comedians, had been reduced to working anonymously on the other side of the camera. A lurid 1922 court trial, in which he was wrongfully accused of raping actress Virginia Rappe, destroyed his career even though he was subsequently found innocent of any wrongdoing. Bert Wheeler, who valued Arbuckle's friendship and welcomed his tutelage, had only the greatest admiration for the tragic clown:

> I think Fatty Arbuckle was three-quarters responsible for Wheeler and Woolsey's success. Our second picture [*The Cuckoos*] really set Wheeler and Woolsey up. We had another director, but Arbuckle worked on all our scenes. Sure, he *was* washed up, or he wouldn't have been "directing" us—and he wasn't even getting billed for it.
>
> Arbuckle was on the RKO payroll as what might be called a dialogue director. That man was really a clever man, and one of the sweetest men I've ever known in my life. He wasn't a pathetic, sad character—never—even when it was the toughest. He had the greatest sense of comedy—just loved to laugh, and loved to live, and loved people. It's a sad thing, that anything like [that scandal] had to happen to him—to a fine man like that. I always loved him.

The Cuckoos went before the cameras on January 27 under Paul Sloane's direction. Sloane was a competent director of stolid melodramas, but the realm of musical comedy was out of his league. Ironically, his most promising film, *The Lost Squadron* (1932), with Erich Von Stroheim, was finished by George Archainbaud when Sloane became ill during shooting. Sloane was later responsible for the musical branded the worst in RKO history, *Down to Their Last Yacht* (1934); it proved to be his swan song for the studio. Sloane's *Cuckoos* coworkers did not appreciate his mortician-like demeanor, either. "Paul Sloane was a real stiff," Dorothy Lee recalls. "You had to say your lines *exactly* as written for him." Bert commented, "He could rob you of your spontaneity. We'd rehearse little things over and over. Many a time I felt like telling him, 'You know, Paul, this stuff isn't Shakespeare!'"

Technically, *The Cuckoos* is a throwback to the first talkie films. It is almost entirely stage-bound, a primitively photographed transcript of a broadway musical. The earlier *Rio Rita,* with its invigorating camera work and alfresco location scenes, is far more imaginative than this follow-up. *The Cuckoos* looks as though it were shot in a week at the high-school gym, despite the fact that it was in production longer than *Rio Rita. The Cuckoos'* crudities offer a few derisive yuks: June Clyde, in an obviously phony garden setting, "calls" to her sweetheart, Billy (Hugh Trevor), who has just landed his airplane in a genuine exterior shot. Although Billy appears to be a mile away (June uses binoculars to spot him), her feeble cry, "Oh, Billy!" immediately gets his attention.

Filming wrapped February 28 on a trouble-free shoot. Plucky Dottie's antics, however, did jeopardize the schedule—and her life:

> *The Cuckoos* was about Gypsies, so of course they had this professional knife thrower on the set. He said, "I'll bet you're afraid to let me throw these knives at you." Well, honey, I've never turned down a dare. I stood in front of this wall, and this guy threw his knives. Our producer, Bill LeBaron, came along, saw what was going on, and gave me hell. P.S.— The knives never touched me!

Total budget outlay for *The Cuckoos,* including Technicolor sequences, was $240,115.29—only about one-third the cost of *Rio Rita.* Still, RKO's hype-happy publicity boys could not resist telling the trade papers that $750,000 was spent on this film ("Where?" exhibitors could rightfully ask). Billed as RKO's "Mighty Juggernaut of Joy," *The Cuckoos* became a smash hit with the public, doing tremendous repeat business (audiences came back to catch the wisecracks they missed the first time around) and firmly cementing the Wheeler-Woolsey-Lee alliance. Bert remembered *The Cuckoos* as "the picture that really got us off to the races." Sadly, the film was put out to pasture many years ago—it has not even resurfaced on cable television. The comedy seems shaky today, but sixty years have not dimmed Bert, Bob, and Dottie's electrifying musical numbers. For those moments alone, *The Cuckoos* is a jewel.

Under superimposed opening credits comes the film's first scene, a no-nonsense production number with the guys and gals of the chorus called "Down in Mexico." In an age when cellulite was considered sexy, flat-chested chorines with plump thighs swirl, pivot, and kick (the better to display their gartered legs). The stage, cluttered with potted palms, looks like Woolworth's basement on supersaver days, but the chorus boys are sporting sombreros and sing that they're "the best damn caballeros" (it is almost shocking to hear any expletive in a 1930 film). For the next ninety minutes the cheesy sets represent sunny Mexico, much the same way that

The Cuckoos (1930)

Bob and Bert's version of "Alma Mater," sung in their screen adaptation, *The Cuckoos*.

Astoria, Queens, interiors double for Florida beaches in the Marx Brothers' *Cocoanuts* (1929).

Bert and Bob are introduced soon afterward. They are on the lam from a knife-throwing Gypsy (Mitchell Lewis) who vows to kill anyone who falls in love with "his" girl, Dorothy. The boys are chased into the restaurant of a nearby casino; short of funds, they casually sit down and begin to devour the meals of two flappers. "Well, I like that!" one of the women says indignantly to Bert. "It's very good," he agrees between mouthfuls. The other girl asks, "You're Americans, aren't you?" "Yes, yes," Bob cheerfully replies, "but we can't lend you any money."

During this interlude the team performs a rollicking specialty number, "Oh! How We Love Our Alma Mater." It's a tongue-in-cheek parody of bootleggers; the delightful lyrics inform us that Bert and Bob "have been studious from birth," that they have "been to dear old Joliet and Ossining," and even "spent a term or two in Leavenworth." The boys go into a toe-tapping dance that's probably the most endearing skit they ever committed to celluloid, finishing with a patty-cake face-slapping routine. The comedy looks deceptively simple; Woolsey rhythmically whacks Wheeler's kisser in time to the music, while Bert never gets a chance to retaliate. It is a sheer delight, meticulously choreographed and seamlessly executed by the team. Filmed in a simple full-length shot, the scene's rough edges only add to its charm (without the advantage of redubbing, we hear Bert and Bob's shoes "squeak" on the polished floor). "Oh! How We Love Our Alma Mater" was performed by Clark and McCullough in *The Ramblers*. A 1926 recording of "Alma Mater," featuring Billy Murray and Monroe Silver, is enjoyable, but it is impossible to imagine anyone else in the roles after witnessing Bert and Bob's interpretation.

The "straight" comedy scenes are not nearly as surefooted. A protracted sequence involving Bert, Bob and a temperamental slot machine should have been a standout, but it is ruined by director Sloane's sluggish pacing, which allows too much dead space between punch lines. Individual gags here are occasionally outstanding: a señorita explains to the boys she's won so much money that she can hardly cram it into her stocking top. As she raises her skirt, exposing a shapely leg, Woolsey comments, "Keep that up and you'll make a lot of money!" Later on, a variation on the burlesque chestnut "Crazy House," where Bert and Bob spend a night in a hotel bedroom populated by zanies, falls flat due to ponderous editing.

Some of the team's best lines emerge in their encounters with Amazonian actress Jobyna Howland, who was adept at playing imperial dowagers. Learning that the boys are fortune-tellers, she can't resist holding a seance:

> JOBYNA: Can he [Bob] really speak with the dead?
> BERT: Lady, he could talk to you by the hour!
> JOBYNA: I was going to entertain my guests by singing tonight.
> BERT: I wouldn't do that if I were you.
> JOBYNA: Why not?
> BERT: They're still sober.
> JOBYNA: [*pointing to Bert's instrument*] Have you always played the flute?
> BERT: Oh, dear me, no. You know, I used to play the organ — [*sadly*] but I had to give it up.
> JOBYNA: Why?
> BERT: My monkey died.
> JOBYNA: [*attempting to sing*] YYI-I-I-PPP!
> BERT: What's the matter, what's the matter?
> JOBYNA: I'm just a little hoarse.
>   [*Bert takes this in, staring at her behemoth bulk*]
> BERT: Heh! Well, uh, we won't go into that!

The stately Howland makes an ideal comic foil for impish Bert, whose mischievous behavior is more lovable than exasperating. Bert's pranks allow him to trot out a tantalizingly brief array of tricks from his vaudeville days (twirling his flute like a cane, kicking it up with his leg, and catching

The Cuckoos (1930) 81

it in midair). Trademarks don't die, either—Bert becomes so bored waiting for his musical cue that he sits atop the piano, blissfully eating a sandwich.

Jobyna Howland foils beautifully for Woolsey, too; once Bob learns that the overstuffed matron has inherited $6 million, he's out to win her hand and pocketbook. Woolsey's backhanded marriage proposal ranks on a par with the classic Groucho Marx/Margaret Dumont love scenes:

> BOB: Will you marry me, or must I go on workin'?
> JOBYNA: Oh, Professor—do you think that you will love me till I die?
> BOB: Well, that depends on how long you live.
> JOBYNA: [*flirtatiously*] You know—
> BOB: What?
> JOBYNA: I feel so give-in-y!
> BOB: You feel so what?
> JOBYNA: I feel so *give-in-y*!
> BOB: [*pretending to comprehend*] GUVINNY! Oh, ha-ha-hah! Guvinny! Well, I can always hold my own with anybody with a Guvinny! Do you know why I love you?
> JOBYNA: No—
> BOB: It's because you smell so sweet.
> JOBYNA: That's because I always have violets in my bath. You should, too.
> BOB: I would—but I don't know Violet!

Bob and Jobyna then perform another riotous number, "I'm a Gypsy." Composers Kalmar and Ruby's lyrics are among their all-time best, with Woolsey giving a standout performance. Looking like a Park Avenue scarecrow in his form-fitting tux, skinny Bob glides across the stage, serenading his grande dame sweetheart. "I'll always be very attentive, of course," Bob croons. "Each year for your birthday I'll steal you a horse!" Bob attempts to elevate his jumbo-sized girlfriend (he really needs a forklift); instead, she lifts Bob, using him as a human dumbbell.

A pointless (and witless) comedy sequence follows at the U.S.-Mexico customs station. Bob attempts to bore open a keg of confiscated beer (Prohibition, you know) and drink the contents. In order to remain undetected, he hides underneath a crate and places the keg above him, drilling from below. Unfortunately, Woolsey's bright idea is thwarted when an ornery, loudmouthed cowpoke (former silent comedy villain Kalla Pasha, a heavy among heavies) moves the keg and plunks himself down. Bert, knowing that a sharp implement is about to make contact with an ample posterior, only infuriates the roughneck when he suggests that the hothead move over. "Are you tryin' to make me sore?" he shouts at the shivering Wheeler. "Don't do it!" he warns Bert, adding, "I've knocked off many a guy in my time, and I expect to get mine someday, but I don't know where!" (Kalla Pasha didn't have to wait very long to "get his"; in

Dorothy Lee almost always played the innocent ingenue, but in publicity poses she often appeared a femme fatale. From *The Cuckoos*.

1931 he boarded a Los Angeles trolley and, refusing to pay his fare, smashed an ink bottle over the conductor's head. Pasha was subsequently ruled insane and committed to a southern California sanitarium, where he died in 1933.)

Dorothy Lee has very little footage in the film, but she does display her high-kicking athletics in the showstopping Technicolor number,

"Dancing the Devil Away." While Dottie dances in repentance of her "sins" (i.e., associating with Wheeler and Woolsey), a succession of red-gowned showgirls graces a shimmering icy-blue stage in eye-popping splendor. Dottie's duet with Bert Wheeler, "I Love You So Much," is one of the loveliest songs they shared on film. "Whenever Dorothy Lee and I meet," Bert reminisced to Richard Lamparski, "somebody will always ask me about this song. It was a very big hit."

As the nominal love interests, June Clyde and Hugh Trevor are barely memorable at all. Clyde went on to make some fine musicals in the mid–1930s, but her renditions of "All Alone Monday" and "Wherever You Are" in *The Cuckoos* were not harbingers of things to come. Gangly Hugh Trevor was neither handsome nor virile nor talented, but that hardly mattered; his aunt was the wife of studio chief William LeBaron.

Film critics of 1930 overlooked *The Cuckoos*' claustrophobic sets, tolerated the botched comedy sequences, and raved over the outstanding musical interludes that brightened the film. *Variety*'s hard-boiled founder, Sime Silverman, declared it "a comedy laugh hit. It holds little besides the laughs, and doesn't need anything else. If comedy ever made a picture, it does here." Silverman had nothing but praise for the cast, particularly Bert Wheeler: "This Wheeler boy looks like one of the biggest prospects in pictures. He can comede, mugg, sing, dance, act, is a low as well as a light comedian, and looks as well as the best juve, making him a love interest all by himself." *Hollywood Magazine* found Bert and Bob "as low a pair of comics as you could wish for," while *Photoplay* termed it "a big show with all the trimmings. But oh, what laughs! Great for spring fever." *Film Spectator* enjoyed the team's hijinks and found Dorothy Lee to be "the hit of the picture. Her personality is such a compelling one that she is an outstanding member of the cast." The one voice in the wilderness was *New Movie Magazine*: "this is an irrational musical film full of the most elderly hokum and not over-funny anywhere. The film shows hurry and inexpertness in its production, but it has Dorothy Lee, who possesses real attractiveness."

Apart from "Dancing the Devil Away," *The Cuckoos*' Technicolor footage amounted to one additional scene, the finale, which reprised all of the film's tunes in a brief medley. For some reason the Technicolor reels of *Cuckoos* were shipped to RKO in New York City on August 9, 1933. This finale footage has not seen light of day since *The Cuckoos*' original release. While the missing portions are slight in comparison to *Rio Rita*'s deleted sequences, diehard movie fans would welcome the rediscovery of lost footage.

5
Dixiana (1930)

Adapted and directed by Luther Reed. Produced by William LeBaron. Story, dialogue, and lyrics by Anne Caldwell. Music by Harry Tierney. Scenery and costumes by Max Ree. Photographed by J. Roy Hunt. Photographic effects by Lloyd Knechtel. Color photography by Technicolor process. Musical direction by Victor Baravalle. Sound recording by Hugh McDowell Jr. Orchestrations by Max Steiner. Dances staged by Pearl Eaton. Film editing by William Hamilton. Dates of production: March 24 to April 26, 1930. Released by RKO on September 4, 1930. 100 minutes.

Cast: Bebe Daniels (Dixiana), Everett Marshall (Carl Van Horn), Bert Wheeler (Pee Wee), Robert Woolsey (Ginger Dandy), Joseph Cawthorn (Cornelius Van Horn), Jobyna Howland (Madame Van Horn), Dorothy Lee (Nanny), Ralf Harolde (Royal Montague), Bill Robinson (Specialty Dancer), Edward Chandler (Blondell), George Herman (Contortionist), Raymond Maurel (Cayetano), Bruce Covington (Colonel Porter), Eugene Jackson (Cupid), Robert Livingston (Extra).

Synopsis: Carl Van Horn (Everett Marshall), son of a Louisiana planter, falls in love with Dixiana (Bebe Daniels), a circus entertainer of New Orleans in 1840. They become engaged, much to the displeasure of Royal Montague (Ralf Harolde), a big-time gambler who is also in love with her. Dixiana agrees to relinquish her circus career and accompany her fiancé to meet his parents. Carl invites her circus partners, Pee Wee and Ginger Dandy (Bert Wheeler and Robert Woolsey) to stay as guests at the old plantation home. The Cornelius Van Horns (Joseph Cawthorn and Jobyna Howland) know nothing of Dixiana's circus background and prepare to welcome her with true southern hospitality.

Dixiana captivates the parents and guests with her charm. Pee Wee entertains the guests with his juggling, using the best Van Horn glassware with smashing results. Amid the ruckus, Ginger admonishes Pee Wee: "You should've let Dixiana do it—it's her famous trick in the circus!"

Mrs. Van Horn is furious and orders this "New Orleans scum" from the house. Carl allows them to depart, but secretly follows them back to the big city. Cayetano (Raymond Maurel), the circus impresario, refuses, at Montague's instigation, to take the trio back. They are compelled to work for Montague in his gambling house. Dixiana is bitter toward the Van Horns—Carl included—so she connives with Montague to ruin Carl at the gambling tables.

The plan is to "break" Carl, then force him to forge his father's name to IOUs. Montague promises to see that Dixiana will reign as Mardi Gras Queen for her troubles.

Carl falls into the trap. Realizing it almost immediately, he denounces Dixiana and flees from the gambling hall in bitter anguish. Dixiana laughs—then turns to Montague, tears up the IOUs, and throws the paper in the gambler's face.

Dixiana speeds off to the coronation while Montague vows revenge for her duplicity. He kidnaps her and carries her to his apartment. Carl follows and rescues Dixiana, challenging Montague to a duel.

In an effort to save Carl from what she considers certain death, Dixiana locks him in her room, dons his Mardi Gras disguise, and reports to the dueling field. Here she discovers that Montague arranged to have but one loaded pistol. She exposes the treachery in the midst of a crowd of onlookers. Montague believes that his toady, Blondell (Edward Chandler), has squealed on him. In a fit of anger, Montague shoots Blondell and is subdued by the angry crowd. Carl arrives at the field to witness Dixiana's devotion. They are reunited as Dixiana is rightfully crowned Mardi Gras Queen.

★   ★   ★

"*Dixiana*—that was a bomb!" Dorothy Lee rarely has a charitable word for her early Wheeler and Woolsey films, but the unkindest words are meted out to *Dixiana*. Says Dottie today:

> It was supposed to be a lavish follow-up to *Rio Rita*, which is why Bebe Daniels, Wheeler and Woolsey and I were in it. But instead of getting John Boles again from Universal, RKO imported Everett Marshall from the New York Metropolitan Opera. He had a magnificent voice but all the charm of a cigar store Indian. Nobody took him on the side to give him a few tips about acting in front of the cameras. His role was really important—I mean, he was only the male love interest! And he blew it in a big way. So that's the seat of the problem, and the reason why that film was ruined.

As bad as his performance is, Everett Marshall is only one of many pitfalls that conspired to ambush this overblown mishmash of a musical. Most 1930 movies look dull and draggy by today's standards, but *Dixiana* was branded a squashed soufflé from the moment it premiered. Modern

Dixiana (1930)

audiences expect early talkies to be claustrophobic and creaky; *Dixiana* supplements those expectations with a host of other ailments, among them anemic comedy, weak songs, and a puerile plot. Wheeler and Woolsey furnish the alleged comic relief, which is innocuous compared to the dreary shenanigans making up the main story line. Bert and Bob's own lucky stars were ascending, and their appearance in this all-talking, all-singing, all-boring flop did not hurt their popularity among comedy fans.

The moment that *Rio Rita* was out and coining money, RKO was busy shaping a second monumental musical cut from the same cloth as the Ziegfeld adaptation. *Dixiana* reduces *Rio Rita*'s ingredients for success into a predictable formula, paralleling, without ingenuity, the hill-and-dale plot twists. Besides the ensemble cast of Bebe Daniels, Wheeler and Woolsey, and Dorothy Lee, both films have the same director (Luther Reed) and songwriter (Harry Tierney), plus Technicolor finales. The studio concocted a "rough scenario" of *Dixiana* by November 15, 1929, five weeks after *Rio Rita*'s world premiere. Four additional treatments were drafted before the final script was approved on March 24, 1930, the very day that the picture went into production.

As with *Rio Rita*, Wheeler and Woolsey's sequences function as comedy relief, independent of the main story line. Unlike in the earlier musical, Bert and Bob's scenes in *Dixiana* do not offer a counterpoint to the melodrama. *Dixiana*'s comedy "turns" are just that—a string of meandering routines bogging down an already ponderous production. Fortunately, the team's exposure is severely limited here, while Dorothy Lee's role is reduced to a duet with Wheeler and two brief scenes (viewing the movie for the first time in sixty years, Dottie remarked, "I was surprised at how little I had to do in the film"). The team does manage to inject life into woebegone material, but it would have been wiser to scrap the Technicolor, eliminate two or three songs, and scuttle half the plot. Instead, RKO learned the hard way, reportedly losing $300,000 on this film at the box office. Mercifully, plans to shoot *Dixiana* in the Spoor-Berggren process (a cumbersome ancestor of wide-screen) were scrapped.

Bert and Bob's first scene is a cute one, though, as they perform their "circus" routine with partner Bebe Daniels. (It looks more like high-toned vaudeville than a circus, but vaudeville did not exist in 1840; RKO, no doubt wanting to avoid the wrath of *Variety*'s "wise" film critics, who in 1930 knew everything about "showbiz," possibly may have accurately depicted an early circus.) The boys are costumed as ostriches, performing a simple step dance with their "trainer," Bebe. Pulling off the ostrich heads, Wheeler and Woolsey are each awarded their own close-ups: Bert characteristically has something in his mouth (ostrich feathers) while Bob happily puffs away on a cigar. There is not much more to the sequence, but it is pleasant enough and a promising start.

Comedy expectations are abruptly scuttled the moment that Bert, Bob, and Bebe arrive at the Van Horn plantation (actually the Shelby mansion, situated among the sprawling hills of Universal City). Questionable humor is derived from a protracted sequence concerning an unmentionable item that Bert finds hidden beneath a bed. Bert and Bob periodically lift the bedspread to gawk at the enormity of the object, which the viewer is duped into believing is a chamber pot. Finally, the plantation owner (Joe Cawthorn) saunters in, informing the boys that the unseen artifact belonged to his late Aunt Sophie. "She must've been a very nervous woman," Bert observes. The object is dragged out from under the bed—it is a giant mousetrap.

The team resurrects an ancient practical joke whereby a sucker accepts a bet to pick up three cigars without saying "Ouch!" Upon picking up the third cigar, the victim is soundly kicked in the pants. *Variety* reproachfully noted, "Burlesque threw that out years ago." *Dixiana* takes place in 1840, but that is a lame excuse for employing pre–Civil War gags in the script.

Dorothy Lee makes her debut halfway through the film, charmingly cast as a fickle coquette with a deep-fried southern accent. After she pledges her devotion to Bert and Bob—separately—the boys combat in a duel of honor over her affections. What should have been an invigorating comedy episode is ruined by Luther Reed's placid direction: a series of slow dissolves reveals bric-a-brac smashed to pieces as Wheeler and Woolsey clumsily swashbuckle indoors. The boys soon tire of house wrecking and become distracted by a tray of food. The scene concludes with the team happily munching away, with Bert using his rapier to butter the bread.

Bert and Dorothy get to sing "My One Ambition Is You," one of Dottie's two all-time favorite duets (the other being "Sweetheart, We Need Each Other" from *Rio Rita*). "The song and dance are presented in a unique way, but that's not the reason why the scene is one of my favorites. I just love the song so much, period." Dottie did a test recording of the song for RCA Victor on August 11, 1930, accompanied by the song's composer, Harry Tierney, on piano, apparently her only attempt at a commercial recording She also sang the song in the late 1930s on ex-husband Jimmie Fidler's radio show. Dorothy further recalled that

> Bert came up with the staging himself. In those early days they [RKO] let you do a lot on your own. Bert and I were on this staircase; he was outside the banister while I was on the inside. When we came down the steps we performed a little dance. Meanwhile, Bob Woolsey's hiding behind a curtain. Every time Bert bows to me, Bob boots him in the fanny. Finally, Bert and I switch places and Bob accidentally kicks *me* in

Dixiana (1930)

Dorothy Lee relaxing at the beach shortly after filming *Dixiana*.

the behind. I think that Bert did it and slap his face. Bert retaliates by pushing me—I fall, and when he helps me up, my hoop skirt falls off. Neither Bert nor I notice this, so we dance off together. We must've taken four takes at the end of the scene where I had to unhook my skirt. We had to make it look like the skirt simply fell off of me. But each time you could tell I was unfastening it. It gave you the wrong idea when Bert and I danced out of the room, all smiles and arm in arm.

The rest of the film is a disaster. For an actress who spent most of the silent film era in frothy entertainments, Bebe Daniels seemed destined to become the soap opera queen of the talkies. Perpetually on the verge of tears, wringing her hands, suffering stoically from one emotional pitfall to the next, poor Bebe reprises all of the heartache she experienced in *Rio Rita*. Moviegoers were less inclined to empathize with the soulful-eyed beauty this time around. Dissatisfied with the four vehicles following *Rio Rita*, Daniels terminated her RKO contract and fled to Warner Brothers, where apart from landing a bitchy role in *Forty-second Street*, her luck failed to improve.

Everett Marshall was undoubtedly the "wonderful guy" Dorothy Lee remembers, but throughout *Dixiana* he grins, stares at his feet, breathes down other men's necks, and sings with the masculine aplomb of Jerry Lewis. Marshall's character registers as a dolt; when he appears at the Mardi Gras in costume, he is appropriately festooned as a clown and called a "schlemiel" by his own father. Dorothy Lee recalled that "RKO dumped Everett Marshall before the film finished unspooling." Marshall was dealt a second chance in Hollywood after *Dixiana* (Warner Brothers' *I Live for Love* in 1935). The baritone's bid for movie stardom dried up after a few parts; his film fling was even briefer than those of his fellow opera thespians Lawrence Tibbett and Dennis King.

Jobyna Howland, so well served as the society dowager in *The Cuckoos*, is boorish here at best, while Joe Cawthorn makes the first of two appearances with the team. Cawthorn had starred on Broadway in *The Blue Kitten* (1922); Robert Woolsey was a supporting member of that cast, but Cawthorn now foiled for Bob in several limp comedy vignettes. Cawthorn would contribute memorably to *Peach O' Reno* (1931), the first classic Wheeler and Woolsey movie. Ralf Harolde, as the slimy gambler Montague, dishes out menace in his meaty role, while the standout is Bill "Bojangles" Robinson, performing his famous staircase dance in a solo specialty as enjoyable as it is brief.

Critical opinion was split down the middle on *Dixiana*. *Photoplay* found the film "charming," calling it a "grand spectacle ... Everett Marshall adds voice and personality ... Bebe Daniels at her best." *Variety*'s Sime Silverman did not beat about the bush: "There is nothing to hang exploitation on; nothing in the story, comedy or songs. ... The whole affair runs along as though misjudged in every respect." Bert Wheeler's sole recorded comment was that "*Dixiana* wasn't much of a picture."

Dixiana is, ironically, one of the two Wheeler and Woolsey films that have lapsed into public domain, meaning that it is commonly available on videotape from any number of fly-by-night exploitation companies. Pity the comedy fan who purchases his duped copy of this prehistoric turkey, expecting a few honest laughs. Further damage was rendered when 16 mm prints of the film were issued to television without the climactic two reels of Technicolor footage. In 1948, the RKO laboratory noted that its color material "was found to have chemically disintegrated (two cans of dust) and accordingly was disposed of."

From 1956 through 1989, circulating copies of *Dixiana* were bereft of the climax and happy ending. Thanks largely to the preservation efforts of Marty Kearns, John Hall, and Richard May (in conjunction with the UCLA Film Archive, Turner Entertainment, and the David and Lucille Packard Foundation), a duplicate Technicolor negative was laboriously pieced together from several sources. The original, full-length *Dixiana* had its television premiere during April 1990 on the TNT cable station.

Although *Dixiana* is a bad film, its restoration leaves hope that the color footage from *The Cuckoos* will be snatched from the jaws of nitrate decomposition before it is too late. According to David Chierichetti, a former staffer at RKO General, color negatives exist on *The Cuckoos* but would cost at least ten thousand dollars to transfer onto safety stock. Perhaps it is too late, even as this book is published, although it would be nice to be able to revise this chapter with a happier ending.

6
Half Shot at Sunrise (1930)

Directed by Paul Sloane. Produced by William LeBaron. Associate producer, Henry Hobart. Story by James Ashmore Creelman. Dialogue by Anne Caldwell and Ralph Spence. Additional material (uncredited) by Roscoe Arbuckle. Lyrics by Anne Caldwell. Music by Harry Tierney. Scenery and costumes by Max Ree. Photographed by Nick Musuraca. Musical direction by Max Steiner. Sound recording by Hugh McDowell, Jr. Dances staged by Mary Read. Film editing by Arthur Roberts. Dates of production: June 30 to August 8, 1930. Released by RKO on October 4, 1930. 81 minutes.

Cast: Bert Wheeler (Tommy Tanner), Robert Woolsey (Gilbert Simpkins), Dorothy Lee (Annette Marshall), George MacFarlane (Colonel Marshall), Edna May Oliver (Mrs. Marshall), Leni Stengel (Olga), Hugh Trevor (Lieutenant James Reed), Roberta Robinson (Arlene Marshall), John Rutherford (MP Sergeant), Eddie de Lange (Military Policeman), Elisha H. Calvert (General Hale), Alan Roscoe (Captain Jones), Rolfe Sedan, Andre Cheron (Waiters), William Bechtel (Restaurant Patron), The Tiller Sunshine Girls (Dancers).

Synopsis: The setting: Paris, 1918. Colonel Marshall (George MacFarlane) of the U.S. Army, finds himself in a most embarrassing situation. His commanding general (Elisha H. Calvert) has charged him with the delivery of important orders pertaining to a major offensive, but all the Colonel receives are love letters from Olga (Leni Stengel), an exotic Russian flirt.

Furthermore, the Colonel has a wife (Edna May Oliver) who suspects him of infidelity; a daughter Arlene (Roberta Robinson), who loves Lieutenant James Reed (Hugh Trevor), whom the Colonel emphatically does not love; and another daughter, sixteen-year-old Annette (Dorothy Lee), who is boy crazy.

Tommy Tanner and Gilbert Simpkins (Bert Wheeler and Robert Woolsey), buck privates, go absent without leave from the Colonel's regiment to raise a little hell with the mademoiselles. Tommy shies behind the Colonel's staff car to escape the military police and discovers Annette inside the trunk, hiding from her father. She soon falls in love with Tommy while Olga tumbles for Gilbert.

Annette and Olga scheme to make heroes out of the boys in order to win them the Colonel's forgiveness. When the secret orders finally arrive, the Colonel commissions Lieutenant Reed to deliver them to the front line, but Annette steals the papers and sends Tommy and Gilbert on their mission.

Lieutenant Reed reports that the instructions were stolen from his pocket. Annette confesses to having palmed the papers for her would-be heroes. Colonel Marshall frantically demands that Tommy and Gilbert be captured at all costs.

Tommy and Gilbert proceed to the front in a motorcycle and sidecar, but a break in the lines means a volunteer must be sent crawling through no-man's-land. Gilbert quickly offers the services of Tommy, but then feels remorse when he realizes that the mission means certain death. Gilbert pleads with Tommy to switch places with him; instead, Tommy forgives his old buddy and scrambles "over the top."

As Tommy crawls on his stomach a shell bursts nearby; Gilbert runs to aid his stricken friend. Pulling Tommy out of the rubble, Gilbert also unearths the military policeman (John Rutherford) who has been chasing them throughout the picture. The MP gives pursuit as the boys seek refuge in a dugout.

On Armistice Day the captured duo are brought to Colonel Marshall's headquarters. The Colonel threatens to have them shot at sunrise. But the boys disclose that the Colonel, in a slightly confused state of mind, had tried to send General Hale one of Olga's perfumed love letters. Tommy and Gilbert blackmail the Colonel for his forgiveness, and all ends happily, with Tommy getting Annette, Gilbert getting Olga, Jim getting Arlene, and the Colonel—still stuck with his wife.

★ ★ ★

Half Shot at Sunrise was one of Bert Wheeler's favorite Wheeler and Woolsey comedies. Film critic Don Koll, who befriended Wheeler in the 1960s when both men were members of the Catholic Actors Guild, regularly ran an old-time-movie night at Guild headquarters in New York City. When Bert became president of the organization in 1966, the pièce de résistance on the bill was often a Wheeler and Woolsey film. Wheeler's generally low regard for the team's comedies led him to attend these screenings only occasionally. Few of Bert's impressions of his films are captured in print, but he let Koll know how much he enjoyed this particular comedy. Leonard Maltin recounts in his book *Movie Comedy Teams* that Wheeler told Koll he "was impressed by the fact that RKO built a French village set especially for [the team]." Or so Bert thought.

Actually, the elaborate Parisian town square that RKO erected on its

Encino back lot consisted of permanently built structures, designed to double for any number of European capitals. *Half Shot at Sunrise* simply happened to be the first film utilizing a newly erected set. It can be glimpsed in numerous RKO releases of the thirties and forties (including the team's own *Diplomaniacs*) and became a centerpiece for such major productions as Astaire and Rogers's *Story of Vernon and Irene Castle*. The studio would no more raze these "buildings" than they would dismantle the Western town built for *Cimarron* (1930), which was subsequently used in over a hundred RKO oater epics. Although Bert undoubtedly liked the film for other reasons, it does indicate the sense of importance he felt under William LeBaron's regime.

Sets or no sets, *Half Shot at Sunrise* is an uneven comedy, mixing some clever situations with less-than-luminous dialogue routines. While it is surprisingly cinematic for 1930, with invigorating outdoor photography work, *Half Shot* suffers most from the boys' delivery of their lines. Bert and Bob practically shout whenever they tell a gag, as though audiences needed to be cued for something funny. Portraying army cutups, the boys laugh uproariously at each other's jokes—an obnoxious penchant more suited to the likes of Clark and McCullough or Olsen and Johnson. Wheeler and Woolsey apparently still were not comfortable letting punch lines fall on dead air; their noisy yuks filled in the blanks where theater patrons should have been howling. Thirty years later Wheeler remarked, "If we could have had a live audience, our movies would have been much better."

Still, when the repartee is good, *Half Shot at Sunrise* can be rib-tickling fun. Two delightful musical numbers and some impressive visual stunts enliven the proceedings, which are several leagues in the right direction after the fiasco of *Dixiana*. Hollywood's newest comedy duo would eventually shed its stage-bound inhibitions and create some of the 1930s brightest films. But the team would pay its dues with shaky comedies for another year before Wheeler and Woolsey—and the movies—finally found each other.

While this stage-trained team became mired in dialogue skits, they adapted themselves to that movie phenomenon—the sight gag—with the greatest of ease. Bert and Bob's first visual joke comes early in *Half Shot at Sunrise*: masquerading as military policemen, the boys commandeer a car containing three mademoiselles. Bob takes the wheel and they are off on a joyride, until Bert whispers a question to one of the girls. Suddenly she begins hurling French expletives at Bert, smacking him on the head. "What did she say?" Bob inquires. "She said no!" Bert responds. With that, the boys hop out of the moving auto, leaving the irate women to regain control of the driverless car.

One reason for the film's improved visual humor was the return of an uncredited gagman on the studio payroll. Roscoe "Fatty" Arbuckle was

Bert and Bob share some fruit but not their trademark sandwich and cigar in *Half Shot at Sunrise*.

signed to an RKO contract on May 9, 1930, specifically to contribute material for *Half Shot at Sunrise*. According to Bert Wheeler, "Arbuckle was as responsible as anybody" for the film's success:

> He would work on our comedy scenes and direct them to us. He didn't actually do it on the set, but he told us what to do. Paul Sloane was the director. He was a darned good director, but he was smart enough to let Arbuckle, who knew us better than he did, work with us. He wrote,

too. He put a lot of great things in our pictures himself. We tried to keep Arbuckle. We would have had him with us the rest of our lives.

A certain crispness to the comedic byplay between the boys suggests Arbuckle's amiable presence throughout much of the film. Bert and Bob's smart military about-facing when reversing direction from adversaries was an Arbuckle standby from his Keystone days, although it is difficult to pinpoint with certitude what might be considered characteristic Fatty Arbuckle jokes. Still, his touch is more readily discernible here than in *The Cuckoos*.

When *Half Shot at Sunrise* is good, it is frequently hilarious. Bert gets a chance to flex his skills at mimicry when he flirts with a Parisian woman. Wheeler engages her in a lengthy tirade comprised of mock–French gibberish. Instead of being insulted, the woman coos in response, "Umm, what you say I like very much." "Ooooh," Bert exclaims excitedly, "I wonder what I said!"

The film's best sequence is Bert's introduction to Dorothy, done in typical musical comedy style: Wheeler is running away from the MPs when he hides behind Colonel Marshall's staff car. Dorothy, who has hitched a ride in the trunk, nearly steps on Bert's head as she clambers out. Foregoing social formalities, the two young people sit down to chat:

> BERT: [*looking at Dottie admiringly*] Ah—then there *is* a Santy Claus!
> DOTTIE: Snap out of it, soldier! What outfit?
> BERT: EK-2, A-W-O-L.
> DOTTIE: Well you better not let my dad catch ya!
> BERT: Awww! Who's your dad?
> DOTTIE: Colonel Marshall.
> BERT: [*frightened*] Are you sure?!
> DOTTIE: What!
> BERT: I mean—uh—whew! I mean, you flatter me.
> DOTTIE: Oh, have you ever met my dad?
> BERT: No, but, er—he's trying to meet me.
> DOTTIE: I'll fix it!
> BERT: No, no, don't do me any favors! Say, honey, I want to ask you something. It might sound a little personal, you know, at first.
> DOTTIE: What is it?
> BERT: Do you love me?
> DOTTIE: [*coyly*] Well, you'll have to give me a little time.
> BERT: Well, you better make up your mind, it's two-thirty now. You know, this Paris is a fast place.
> DOTTIE: Say, are you married?
> BERT: No, I just naturally look worried.
> DOTTIE: I think it's a shame they send cute little fellas like you to the front.
> BERT: That's what I said, but you can't tell these generals anything.

Dorothy Lee tries to make Bert jealous by flirting with Bob in *Half Shot at Sunrise*. Dottie's comment when she recently saw this photo: "It's really scary, isn't it?"

> DOTTIE: I think it's wonderful, us happening to meet this way.
> BERT: Gee—and I think it's wonderful to meet a girl who's beautiful enough to be dumb and doesn't take advantage of it!

Bert and Dorothy then perform a delightful song and dance number, "Whistling the Blues Away." Near the end of the specialty, Dorothy starts to undulate her hips, causing her fascinated partner to sit down transfixed and study her. "How old are you?" Bert inquires. "Sixteen," Dottie replies. "Oh, no," Bert says, "you couldn't learn *that* in sixteen years."

Shortly afterward, Bert, Dottie, and Bob execute a hysterically funny mock-ballet in a garden, climaxed by Dorothy jumping off the roof of a car to land in the arms of the boys—almost. The MPs arrive just as Dottie is about to leap from the roof—Bert and Bob dash away, leaving Dottie to jump, landing flat on her derriere. It is a painfully funny moment, but Dottie assures us that she was not injured. "They dug a hole where I was supposed to land. Netting was stretched across the hole and everything was covered with grass. You see, the studio didn't want its 'properties' to be damaged—generally speaking!"

Convinced that Bert and Bob have intentionally made a fool out of

Half Shot at Sunrise (1930)

her, Dorothy schemes to arrest them that night. Ensnaring the boys, Dottie informs them that she's collecting a five hundred dollar reward for their capture. Bert pledges his devotion to her, but Dottie will not hear of it:

> DOTTIE: [*Snaps her fingers in Bert's face*] This for you!
> [*Snaps her fingers in Bob's face*] And that for you!
> [*Sticks out her behind*] And this for your papa!
> BOB: Papa gets the best of everything!

Edna May Oliver made her Hollywood debut in *Half Shot at Sunrise*. The regal, storklike actress was a splendid foil for Bert and Bob's lowbrow antics, for instance, in a scene where the duo disguises themselves as waiters. Forced to wait upon Colonel Marshall's table, the boys flaunt their lack of serving etiquette, much to the consternation of the Colonel and his wife (Oliver). Some of the business is wonderfully amusing, as when Bert sets their table with all the aplomb of a two-bit hash slinger. Emerging later on roller skates, Wheeler circles a bald-headed patron who complains that his "cocoa is cold." Bert shoves the man's fedora on his head before gliding off. Woolsey scores with a passel of gags, too. The exasperated Colonel inquires why Bob is not in the army. "Well, it's a long story, Colonel," Woolsey begins. "You see, it's this way." He puts his booted foot atop the table, next to Edna May's dinner plate. "It's my feet." The Colonel asks, "Well, what's the matter with them? Flat?" "Cold!" Bob answers.

While the regal Oliver contributes excellent support with her subtle, acerbic wit, her screen spouse George MacFarlane chews apart the scenery to wearisome effect. MacFarlane was considered one of the "best" baritones in operettas of the 1910s and early 1920s (his basso-like delivery renders his commercial recordings unlistenable today). He later sank a great deal of money into two stage productions that wiped out his assets, one of which, *Honest Liars* (1926), starred Woolsey. Perhaps it is only fair play, then, that MacFarlane gets a chance to sabotage this production. While his silver-maned head and rotund physique are outwardly suitable for the role of the Colonel, MacFarlane's incessant blustering and hammy overacting reduces him to a flatulent, pompous windbag just waiting to be skewered.

Roberta Robinson and Hugh Trevor as the young lovers have virtually nothing to do; their parts seem to have been pruned in postproduction editing. Despite nepotism that guaranteed Trevor screen work for as long as Uncle Bill LeBaron was in charge, this one-dimensional "ingenue boy" soon quit show business to become an insurance agent. *Half Shot at Sunrise* was the last Wheeler and Woolsey film to carry a useless subplot; Bert and Dottie proved that they were more capable of handling the "love interest" themselves.

Leni Stengel lends an exotic air to the proceedings as the Russian coquette, Olga. The German-born international beauty spent years studying music in Milan (she was the grand-niece of Von Flotow, composer of the opera *Martha*) before making her dancing and singing debut in Riga, Latvia. Producer LeBaron spotted her singing in a Manhattan nightclub and signed her up as Woolsey's on-screen paramour.

As the Colonel's irrepressible daughter, Dorothy Lee gave a spirited performance well suited to the film's hijinks. Spunky, sexy, and on the prowl for anything in pants, Dottie virtually reprises her Dumb Dora role from her stage hit *Hello Yourself* with one marked difference—her Annette in *Half Shot* is an intelligent, no-nonsense woman shrewd enough to outwit the boys at every gyration of the plot. Garbed as a Mata Hari–type spy in trenchcoat and with pistol, she announces that she is capturing the AWOL doughboys for the five hundred dollar reward. Bert proposes a counteroffer: "I'll tell ya what to do. Just turn him [Woolsey] in and take two-fifty!"

The film's finale features a realistic depiction of no-man's-land, adorned with barbed wire, foxholes, trenches, and explosions. "They didn't know a thing about putting in the sound later on," Bert recalled. "We were out there with bombs going off, and this was going on while we were trying to tell jokes, and the stuff was breaking and bursting all around us. Just a few months later, they would dub all that sound in later on in the studio, as you know." Though visually striking, the episode nearly falls flat. Not only is war too realistically depicted for this lighthearted comedy, but Bob cold-bloodedly volunteers Bert for a suicide detail. Bob's conscience nags him until he apologizes to Bert:

> BOB: Gee, kid, I'm sorry. I didn't mean to get you into this—
> BERT: Aw, gee—that's all right.
> BOB: Yeah, but—you know, something's liable to go wrong out there. You know—you might not come back. Now wait a minute—I'll go.
> BERT: I'll come back all right. It'll be OK.

Bert and Bob play the scene straight; their ability to convey deep affection for each other is touching, with Woolsey surprisingly the standout. This beautiful piece of acting makes one forgive the plethora of bad punning that came earlier, but the intrusion of reality just does not jibe. Worse, Bert appears to be struck by a shell. Bob crawls out to assist "his pal," only to find Wheeler half-buried amid the debris. The sight of Bert in apparent agony stuns the viewer; we have been watching a comedy, pure and simple, but the interjection of physical pain violates the form. The scene evolves into a joke borrowed from Harry Langdon's *All Night Long* (1924): Bob yanks Bert free from the dirt, revealing that Wheeler has been sitting on top of another soldier—who happens to be the MP who has been hounding the boys throughout the picture; he gives chase as the sequence fades out. Despite the quick wrap-up gag, this bleak battleground episode leaves an unpleasant aftertaste with most viewers, after the lighthearted frolics that had preceded it.

In spite of its uneasy mixture of mirth and melodrama, *Half Shot at Sunrise* was applauded by critics and made a mint for RKO. Army comedies were usually surefire hits with moviegoers during the early Depression years. *Photoplay* deemed *Half Shot* "the most rollicking nonsense ever devised." *Variety* placed the picture's success on its dialogue: "The cross fire and talk carry laughs throughout. This is pie for Wheeler and Woolsey, right in their comedy alley." Many of the punch lines considered hilarious in 1930 are hopelessly huskered cornballs today, but within a few years the team's films made tremendous leaps forward in quality.

7
Hook Line and Sinker (1930)

Directed by Edward Cline. Produced by William LeBaron. Associate producer, Myles Connolly. Story (uncredited) by Tim Whelan, James Ashmore Creelman, and Wallace Smith. Screenplay and dialogue by Tim Whelan and Ralph Spence. Assistant director, Frederick Fleck. Scenery and costumes by Max Ree. Photographed by Nick Musuraca. Sound recording by Hugh McDowell, Jr. Film editing by Archie F. Marshek. Dates of production: October 1 to November 4, 1930. Released by RKO on December 26, 1930. 77 minutes.

Cast: Bert Wheeler (Wilbur Boswell), Robert Woolsey (J. Addington Ganzy), Dorothy Lee (Mary Marsh), Ralf Harolde (John Blackwell, alias Buffalo Blackie), Jobyna Howland (Rebecca Marsh), Natalie Moorhead (Duchess Bessie Venessie), Hugh Herbert (House Detective), George F. Marion, Sr. (Bellboy), Stanley Fields (McKay), William B. Davidson (Duke of Winchester, alias Frank Dukette), Ben Hendricks, Jr. (Spudoni), G. Pat Collins (Motorcycle Cop), Robert MacKenzie (Detective), Ethan Laidlaw, Frank Mills, Larry McGrath, Bert Morihouse, Lynton Brent (Gangsters).

Synopsis: Impoverished socialite Mary Marsh (Dorothy Lee) runs away from her mother (Jobyna Howland), who wants her to marry attorney John Blackwell (Ralf Harolde), whom she detests. She meets insurance salesmen Wilbur Boswell and J. Addington Ganzy (Bert Wheeler and Robert Woolsey) astride their tandem bicycle. In no time at all Mary and Wilbur fall in love, and the boys agree to help her renovate a decrepit hotel left her by an uncle. The crumbling hostelry is inhabited by two people, a septuagenarian bellhop (George F. Marion, Sr.) and a frowsy house detective (Hugh Herbert).

Through a publicity stunt, Addington fills the hotel with high society and their jewels. Rebecca Marsh, Mary's mother, arrives unexpectedly with John Blackwell in tow. She takes an immediate dislike to Wilbur and swears that her daughter will never marry him. But Mama falls hopelessly head over heels for Addington. Blackwell, a smooth operator, sends for his toughs to take the boys "for a ride" and clear the field for himself.

Another gang of crooks, attracted by the jewelry of the wealthy visitors, registers as hotel guests. This enrages Blackwell's mugs, who resolve to combine murder with pleasure and steal the valuables for themselves.

On a dark and stormy night, the rival gangs launch their nefarious schemes. Their noise awakens Wilbur and Addington, who go downstairs to prowl around. Mary and her mother also awaken, just in time to hear Blackwell expound on how he is going to kill the boys.

A pitched battle ensues when the rival gangs meet in the lobby. Machine guns, hand grenades, and dynamite sticks are employed to wipe out Wilbur and Addington, who blithely survive unscathed and are unaffected by the carnage around them. Most of the gang members proceed to bump each other off in their attempts to annihilate the befuddled duo. The sheriff rushes in, the lights go on, and the boys are proclaimed heroes for saving the guests' jewels. Rebecca Marsh accepts Addington's marriage proposal. Addington, now Mary's prospective stepfather, graciously allows her to wed his buddy Wilbur. The two couples embrace for a double-kiss fadeout.

★ ★ ★

Hook Line and Sinker is one of those Wheeler and Woolsey films that a viewer approaches with low expectations and crossed fingers. It was churned out in that early sound period when a static camera and wisecracking script were the requisites for creating a rollicking evening's entertainment. Bert and Bob's two previous opuses creak so badly today that one might have expected *Hook* to be the third turkey hatched in a row. Fairly unavailable (even for a Wheeler and Woolsey film), *Hook Line and Sinker* has only recently resurfaced in a pristine video release from the Ted Turner organization. To be sure, the film is lesser Wheeler and Woolsey, and it has some dull stretches, but it is no musty antique, either. Lightweight yet likable, *Hook Line and Sinker* is a sporadically delightful comedy that stands as one of the team's best from their prolific 1930 output.

Hook's genesis literally took a year in the making, dating from the period immediately following *Rio Rita*, when RKO envisioned Bert as a solo, starring performer. On October 3, 1929, James Ashmore Creelman submitted a "Bert Wheeler story" entitled *The Cake Eater*, which formed the basic outline for the eventual film. At this early juncture the story was a carbon copy of RKO's *Vagabond Lover*, which, coincidentally, Creelman also penned. Wallace Smith followed up with a treatment on November 15; apart from character actor Robert Edeson, the only other cast member indicated was Marie Dressler (reprising her dowager role from *Vagabond Lover*). A pairing between the actress and Bert could have been memorable; other leading comics recognized Dressler's magnificent qualities as a foil

(Buster Keaton was itching to use Dressler at this same time, while Chaplin teamed with Marie way back during comedy's dark ages, in *Tillie's Punctured Romance* [1914]). Unfortunately for RKO, Dressler's runaway success in Metro's *Anna Christie* (1930) dashed any chances of their borrowing the veteran comedienne. By this time the Wheeler-Woolsey chemistry had gained momentum with *The Cuckoos*, so studio savants decided to reshape *The Cake Eater* into a team vehicle.

Screenwriter Tim Whelan revamped the Wheeler story to accommodate both funnymen. Whelan had been one of Harold Lloyd's top gagmen in the 1920s (his credits with Lloyd include *Safety Last*, *Why Worry?*, *Hot Water*, and *The Freshman*). Whelan also contributed to Harry Langdon's best feature comedies, *Tramp, Tramp, Tramp* and *The Strong Man*. He was one of the few silent comedy writers able to integrate dialogue and situational humor skillfully into the talkie medium. His best Wheeler and Woolsey work was yet to come (*Peach O'Reno* and *Girl Crazy* were made the next year), but this first screenplay showed bright promise. Whelan labored over the project (now christened *Sherlock and Holmes*) from January 22 to April 11, 1930. A complete script entitled *Hook Line and Sinker—Wheeler and Woolsey #1* was finished on September 15. Whelan kept on polishing, however, and a revised shooting script was submitted on September 30. Filming began the next day, October 1, and was completed on November 4.

Affable Eddie Cline directed *Hook Line and Sinker*, beginning a five-picture association with Wheeler and Woolsey that lasted over the next seven years. Big, beefy, slightly cross-eyed, and possessing a persistent giggle, the high-spirited thirty-eight-year-old director kept his set "in the mood" for comedy production. In a contemporary press release, Cline rationalized why he didn't mind spoiling scenes by laughing during a take: "I believe that this stamp of approval helps the actors by encouraging them, and more important than that, by enabling them to gauge the effectiveness of their scenes." Veteran comedian Eddie Quillan disagreed with Cline's rule of thumb. Cline directed Quillan's first film in 1926, and they worked together sporadically over the next twenty years. Quillan recalls:

> If you were a[n] established star, like W. C. Fields or Bert Wheeler, Cline would become hysterical, laughing at whatever you were doing on camera, to encourage you. You'd think the man was having a fit, he'd act so uncontrollably daffy. It'd be an understatement to call Eddie Cline's behavior a royal pain in the neck, because in Cline's opinion everything you did was brilliantly funny, even if it wasn't.

Despite Cline's delirious outbursts, his comedy résumé was impressive: cutting his teeth with Keystone Comedies during the teens, serving as Buster Keaton's assistant director in the early twenties, and helming

Wheeler and Woolsey suspiciously eye a new addition to the team. The grimly determined candidate is Eddie Cline, director of *Hook Line and Sinker* and four later W & W films.

numerous Mack Sennett shorts late in the silent era. Previous Wheeler and Woolsey directors (Luther Reed, Paul Sloane) had little experience with comedians, and it comes as no small surprise that Cline, too, might have been selected for skills other than his comedic slant. He had just finished directing *The Widow from Chicago* for Warner Brothers, a minor gangster melodrama with a quasi-comic shootout similar to *Hook*'s own climax. Edward G. Robinson, in his pre–*Little Caesar* days, appears in *The Widow from Chicago*, as does Frank McHugh as a character reminiscent of Bert Wheeler. *Hook Line and Sinker* shares a similar crimeland motif and spotlights several actors soon to be typecast as goons or hoods when gangster epics flourished, one year later at Warners.

While Eddie Cline's directorial style was palpably featherweight at best, he was an able technician, emphasizing pace, timing, and tempo during a period when stage-bound drawing room affairs became the rule of the day. Cline intercuts frequently from long shots to medium shots to close-ups; despite a talky script, the film bogs down only two or three times, a marked improvement over the faltering approach found in the team's earlier comedies.

Hook also features an impressive array of supporting talent: slinky blond Natalie Moorhead, tough Irish cop G. Pat Collins, slimy villain Ralf Harolde, and, best of all, Al Capone's lookalike, Stanley Fields. The fifty-year-old character actor barnstormed around the country for years (he was Frank Fay's foil in vaudeville) before the talkies capitalized on his uniquely gruff voice and astounding resemblance to Chicago's gang lord. Although Fields could play straight roles, he caricatured sleazy thugs beautifully in comedies like Harry Langdon's *See America Thirst* (1930), where he portrays Tar-Face Spumoni, a bald-faced allusion to "Scarface" Capone. In 1930 alone Fields appeared in at least thirteen bad guy roles; Wheeler and Woolsey would encounter his ugly mug again—memorably—in the future.

Bert and Bob are in command of their destiny on this picture, turning in subtle, delightful performances. Genuine wit dominates the proceedings, beginning with the opening scene when motorcycle cop G. Pat Collins stops the boys for speeding on their tandem bicycle:

> COP: Pull over there! Didn't you guys see me wave at ya?
> BERT: Well, we waved back, didn't we?
> BOB: Yeah, he did like this [*Bob waves*].
> COP: Shaddup! Don't you ever think of accidents?
> BOB: Accidents! My dear man, that's our business!
> COP: Insurance, eh? But I don't need any insurance!
> BOB: You are just the type that does need insurance! Why, do you realize that since 1910 they've discovered fifty-two new ways of dying?
> BERT: And you *don't* look well.
> BOB: Yes, why, uh—people are dying this year that have never died before!

Within moments, the boys sell Collins a policy and turn their attention toward Dorothy Lee, who has been waiting patiently by the roadside. In accordance with the dictates of musical comedy plots, Bert and Bob readily agree to help Dottie renovate the hotel she has just inherited. "Wait a minute," Dorothy inquires. "Do you boys know anything about hotels?" "Child," Bob responds, "there are several hotels looking for us right this very minute!"

The Hotel Ritz de la Riviera turns out to be a dilapidated dump more suitable as an Addams Family resort than a hostelry for paying guests. "Mother says that all the big bugs used to live there," Dottie comments. "They're probably still here," Bob responds. "Let's look around." The cobwebbed lobby is no better. Bert observes that "this looks like the place that fella King Tut was buried." Behind the front desk snores the world's oldest bellhop (George F. Marion), oblivious of the new owner and her retinue. Bert dusts off the guest book and starts reading names of the

Bob, Hugh Herbert, George Marion, Bert, and Dot Lee seem to be ready for something to happen in *Hook Line and Sinker*.

registrants: "General Grant, Lydia Pinkham, Buffalo Bill..." Dorothy innocently asks, "Do you think they're still here?" "They are if they left their call with *him*," Bob replies, pointing at the dozing Marion. Woolsey picks up a newspaper and scans the headline: "McKinley Elected by 500,000 Majority." "Oh, boy," Bob intones cheekily, "wait'll they hear what Dewey did at Manila Bay!" The elderly bellhop is finally aroused when Woolsey repeatedly shouts, "Boy, boy!" to the decrepit duffer (in succeeding films Bob addresses nearly every male as either "boy" or "son"; with the exception of old-time cowboy star Harry Carey, nobody else in the history of Hollywood purveyed this annoying—albeit hilarious—habit to such condescending perfection).

George Marion gradually wakes up, gazing contemptuously at the three strangers. Perhaps this animosity was heartfelt for the doddering thespian: Marion's acting career dated back to the 1880s, and by the teens he was a keenly applauded Broadway fixture. He scored his biggest (and longest-running) success with *Anna Christie* (1922), Eugene O'Neill's naturalistic stage drama. Marion's finely etched portrayal of an old Swedish barge captain was an artistic triumph that the crafty old pro parlayed into an acting monopoly, repeating the role three times: Thomas H. Ince's 1923 silent film version; MGM's definitive 1930 talkie edition with Greta Garbo; and a *Lux Radio Theater* adaptation for Cecil B. DeMille, in 1939. Although Metro signed Marion to a long-term contract in 1930, his one-note talent wore out its welcome at the Culver City gates within a year. Marion's acting was impeccable, but he played the same dullard from one film to the next. Described in *Anna Christie* as resembling a "baboon" and an "old ape," Marion lives up to those depictions in *Hook Line and Sinker*. Stoop-shouldered and somnambulistic, the simian-faced actor kills every comic line with his catatonic delivery, sabotaging a surfeit of funny situations. At one point Bert is contemplating suicide aloud. Marion rises off his duff and says in sepulchral tones, "That's the best idea you've had since you came here!"

Even more curious is Hugh Herbert's presence as a grimy house detective who rarely utters a word but whose inscrutable gaze instills guilt into the hearts of Bert, Bob, and Dorothy. Herbert's role, with his occasionally delivered non sequiturs, is a faint ancestor of his better-remembered detective zany from Olsen and Johnson's *Hellzapoppin'* (1942). But the comic who endeared (or possibly irritated) audiences of the mid-1930s had not established his familiar "hoo-hoo" business as yet. Herbert's enigmatic pantomiming is more didactic than it is amusing; Hugh would better serve Wheeler and Woolsey three years later as the maxim-spouting Chinaman "Chow Chow" in *Diplomaniacs*.

The film's biggest laughs come from the scenes between Bert, Bob, and their straight men—the gangsters. At one point the boys listen in on Ralf Harolde, Stanley Fields, and the other henchmen planning a double murder (our heroes', of course). Eavesdropping from next door, Bert and Bob innocently mistake the hoodlums' murderous remarks for expressions of friendship:

> FIELDS: I think we ought to take 'em for a ride!
> BOB: [*to Bert*] Hey—you know what they're going to do?
> BERT: What?
> BOB: Tomorrow they're gonna take us for a nice, long ride.
> BERT: They are?
> BOB: Yeah.
> BERT: [*excitedly*] I hope it don't rain!

One of the mugs sarcastically quips that he'll give the boys each "a nice, juicy pineapple" (underworld parlance for a hand grenade). Woolsey relays this misinformation to his partner:

> BOB: Guess what—they're gonna give us each a nice, juicy pineapple.
> BERT: They are? [*stifling his laughter*] Oh, and I just love pineapples!

Bert and Bob are told to stick 'em up in this atmospheric still from *Hook Line and Sinker*.

> BOB: I wonder if I could get 'em to change mine to a grapefruit? They're juicier.
> BERT: You could ask 'em.

Encountering gang leader Ralf Harolde in the lobby, Bert and Bob cannot resist teasing him about the racketeers' "thoughtful" intentions. Harolde, aghast at the boys' apparent mockery of his death threat, schemes to kill them that very night.

The climactic episode is really an eye-opener, a thirteen-minute tour de force brimming with noirish overtones—quite remarkable when one considers that film noir did not establish itself for at least another decade. When a raging storm disrupts the hotel's electricity that night, Bert and Bob encourage the guests to lock up their jewels in the hotel's "world famous" safe. The gangs prepare to annihilate each other in a shootout, with the victor seizing the valuables and either side assassinating Bert and Bob. Here director Eddie Cline pulls out all stops: darkened sets, menacing shadows, rapid cutting, verbal and visual wit conspire to make the sequence one of W & W's finest. Best of all, the boys toss off characteristic wisecracks during the shootout without getting mired in heedless slapstick.

Like the Marx Brothers, Wheeler and Woolsey were manifestly not slapstick comedians; later in their careers, both teams performed obligatory slapstick climaxes that did not always suit their established personalities. Bert and Bob hastily sidestep the roughhouse in *Hook Line and Sinker*, furnishing a high-spot finale as exciting as it is hilarious.

The sequence opens on a slow fade-in of the rival gangs plotting their dirty work. Suddenly we cut to Bert and Bob in bed (Bob is reading *Detective* magazine, wearing a woman's nightcap and smoking a cigar). The wary Wheeler claims to hear strange noises between the thunderclaps. "That's static!" Bob replies—an appropriate rationale if you're watching a dupe print of this early talkie. The duo decides to go downstairs and investigate, putting on their top hats and tuxedo jackets over their nightclothes.

The boys end up smack in the middle of the gunfire. Although not oblivious to the carnage, Bert and Bob are unperturbed by most of the byplay (caught in the crossfire, Bert coolly comments, "You know, I don't think it's safe here!"). A welcome touch of black humor also crops up; when a mobster is felled by a bullet in front of the boys, Woolsey's pragmatism prevails:

> BOB: [*to Bert*] See if he's got a cigar.
> [*Bert finds a cigar on the dead man and hands it to Woolsey. As Bob puts it in his mouth, another gunman shoots it out.*]
> BOB: [*very calmly*] Well, I'm smokin' too much, anyway.

A subtle yet whimsical bit occurs when Bob tells Bert to "get up and reconnoiter." "I don't have to!" Bert responds smugly, like a little boy avoiding a trip to the bathroom. Bert's insouciance and Bob's wit notwithstanding, one of the film's funniest moments is strictly unintentional. One of the bigger, uglier thugs "turns yellow" on boss Ralf Harolde. The slightly built, urbane Harolde deals with this revelation by shouting "Swine!" and clobbering his henchman into unconsciousness.

Bert and Bob clamber aboard a tea cart and scoot their way across the lobby toward the safe. Despite volleys of gunfire, house detective Hugh Herbert naps contentedly at his post. "Good man," Bob notes. "Yeah," Bert adds, "he's watching things, all right." The boys mistake a stick of dynamite for a candle. Bert places the lit stick in his mouth as he fumbles with the tumbler's combination. Stanley Fields charges over, angrily grabs the dynamite, makes a mad dash—and trips. The explosion's force wrecks the foyer and causes the chandelier to collapse, *Phantom of the Opera*–style.

Amid the settling dust, Bob is seen cradled in Bert's arms. Woolsey rationalizes that "somebody must've turned the gas on!" while the police round up the crooks.

Hook Line and Sinker is far from perfect; the glut of bad movie musicals flooding the market in 1930 caused an industrywide moratorium of the genre that lasted until 1933. This may be the reason Bert and Dorothy do not perform a single tune, although Kalmar and Ruby's hit "Three Little Words" is the background music during their love scene. Jobyna Howland, so effective in *The Cuckoos*, is a royal pain to Bert and, even worse, to the comedy itself. Woolsey snidely refers to the towering actress as "the Twentieth Century Limited," yet arbitrarily professes he could truly love the gargantuan dowager. Still, Bert and Bob's own performances are invigorating and fun, the punchlines punchier than before, and the direction much snappier than most 1930 films. *Hook* points the way to the vintage comedies that Bert and Bob were destined to begin filming before long.

Contemporary critics tore the film apart: they considered the production values negligible (they were), called Dorothy Lee's acting inadequate (what else was new?), and judged the gags to be moth-eaten at best (wrong this time). *Hook Line and Sinker* was one of RKO's top-grossing films of 1930. No one had time to rest on his or her laurels, however. Less than three weeks after filming was completed, Bert, Bob, Dottie, Stanley Fields, and Eddie Cline were giving their all, once again, for old RKO.

8
Cracked Nuts (1931)

Directed by Edward Cline. Produced by William LeBaron. Associate producer, Douglas MacLean. Screenplay by Douglas MacLean and Al Boasberg. Dialogue by Ralph Spence and Al Boasberg. Based on the short story "A Growing Concern" by Welford Beaton. Scenery and costumes by Max Ree. Photographed by Nick Musuraca. Sound recording by Hugh McDowell, Jr. Film editing by Arthur Roberts. Dates of production, November 24 to December 23, 1930. Retakes filmed January 16–17, 1931. Released by RKO on April 18, 1931. 66 minutes.

Cast: Bert Wheeler (Wendell Graham), Robert Woolsey (Zander Ulysses Parkhurst), Dorothy Lee (Betty Harrington), Edna May Oliver (Minnie Van Arden), Leni Stengel (Carlotta), Stanley Fields (General Bogardus), Boris Karloff (Boris the Anarchist), Frank Thornton (Revolutionist), Harvey Clark (King Oscar), Ben Turpin (Ben), Frank Lackteen (Assassin), Wilfred Lucas (Reverend), Nikolai Bolin (Orchestra Leader), Erick Mack (Royal Ashtray), Robert Thurston (Royal Lighter), Buster Brodie (Royal Humidor), George Perloit (Royal Adviser), Eugene Burr (Royal Toothpick), Edward Peil, Sr. (King's Officer), Maine "Bud" Geary (Footman).

Synopsis: Dilatory spendthrift Wendell Graham (Bert Wheeler) is smitten with Betty Harrington (Dorothy Lee), but her Aunt Minnie (Edna May Oliver) regards him as a wastrel and an idiot. Determined to prove himself prudent and worthy of marrying Betty, Wendell invests $100,000 in a revolution in the faraway kingdom of El Dorania. If the coup d'etat succeeds, Boris (Boris Karloff), a political agitator, guarantees that Wendell will be proclaimed the next king.

At the same time, Zander Ulysses Parkhurst (Robert Woolsey), known as Zup for short, engages the present ruler of El Dorania, King Oscar (Harvey Clark), in a crap game, winning both the kingdom and the leader's sweetheart, Carlotta (Leni Stengel). Unbeknownst to Zup, King Oscar has orchestrated his own getaway, since whoever rules El Dorania is earmarked for death by the insurgents.

Aunt Minnie coincidentally takes Betty on a cruise to El Dorania, where the matron maintains considerable property holdings. Aboard the same boat are Wendell and Boris; the boat docks and is greeted regally by Zup, who is amazed to see Wendell, an old pal from Brooklyn. The nefarious General Bogardus (Stanley Fields), one of Boris's confederates, threatens to kill Wendell unless the latter agrees to "eradicate" King Zup. Wendell reluctantly agrees to having his buddy annihilated.

Assassination day arrives, with Zup set to be killed by an aerial bomb. Zup is forced to sit on a coronation throne roped inside the danger zone. Wendell chuckles to Zup that he's removed the caps that make the bombs explode, but the assigned pilot, Cross-eyed Ben (Ben Turpin), has spent all night reinserting the caps. One of the bombs intended for Zup unexpectedly explodes off target, tearing a tremendous hole in the ground and bringing in an oil gusher.

Wendell and Zup call off the revolution and decide to form a republic. General Bogardus and Boris are tossed into the hoosegow, while Aunt Minnie wearily acquiesces to a marriage between Betty and the now-prominent Wendell.

★ ★ ★

Before the advent of VCRs and cable, when "Wheeler and Woolsey" meant about as much to the average film fan as Eadweard Muybridge and his zoetrope, movie buffs already had a hankering to see one comedy starring this disregarded duo: *Cracked Nuts*. During the early 1970s an unusual situation captured the imagination of film enthusiasts. Dyed-in-the-wool comedy pros knew the Abbott & Costello, Marx Brothers, Laurel and Hardy, W. C. Fields, and Three Stooges films by heart yet realized there also existed a cache of Depression-era comedy that television had not tapped. Some of these curios sounded as if they belonged in the junk pile; descriptions of others leaped off the printed page like buried treasures waiting to be unearthed. Good or bad, these comedic antiquities sounded intriguing. Then aficionados heard about *Cracked Nuts*.

The movie sounds like a textbook of comedy milestones: its zany plot unfolds like early Marx Brothers, anticipating the quintessential *Duck Soup* by two years. The title even *sounds* like a Marx Brothers film (*The Cocoanuts*; *Cracked Nuts*' working title was *Assorted Nuts*, while *Duck Soup*'s working title was *Cracked Ice*. In *Duck Soup*, Groucho sings a few bars of the song "El Manicero" [the peanut vendor], which *Cracked Nuts* uses under the opening titles). Al Boasberg, future gag writer on the Marxes' *A Night at the Opera* and *A Day at the Races*, cowrote *Cracked Nuts*' dialogue and screenplay. During the movie, Wheeler and Woolsey perform a crossfire dissertation about the town of "What" and "Which"—a missing link/precursor to Abbott and Costello's baseball classic, "Who's on First." As an added bonus, Boris Karloff, in his pre–*Frankenstein* days, appears prominently in *Cracked Nuts* as a comic villain (monikered Boris, no less). Numerous buffs who had heard about the movie were frantic to see it.

After the drooling anticipation and pent-up expectation, the god of comedy smiled down upon these Saturday matinee dilettantes and opened the floodgates. RKO movies began sprouting on the film collector's market during the mid-1970s. Pirated 16 mm television copies of *Cracked Nuts* began whizzing out of WOR-TV's film-storage facilities in Fort Lee, New Jersey. Prints that had been gathering dust for twenty years now experienced their first-ever unspooling. Imagine the moment of discovery: a triumphant film fan outbids the other unlucky beggars clamoring for *Cracked Nuts*. Perhaps this same collector had the pick of RKO's litter and bypassed choice classics like *King Kong*, *Top Hat*, or *Citizen Kane* in favor of this scarcer "unknown" quantity. Threading his projector, the collector prides himself on his good fortune in landing a print of this rare treasure, a veritable holy grail of the cinema.

Sixty-six minutes later, that same collector is now wondering how fast he can unload this bizarre little potboiler.

Cracked Nuts is not much weaker than the Wheeler and Woolsey starrers that preceded it. But the threat of great expectations (a danger of reading too many film books) makes this wispy satire appear worse than it actually is. *Cracked Nuts* has the earmarks of so many later movies that it is bound to compare unfavorably with comedies which followed. It might be argued that *Cracked Nuts* was a slippery stepping stone toward a better type of sound comedy in that primitive talkie era. The crazy political revolution motif had been presented in films before: Douglas Fairbanks's early silent pictures *His Majesty, the American* (1916) and *The Americano* (1917) ridiculed juntas and tinhorn political messiahs mercilessly. Harold Lloyd's *Why Worry?* (1923) was the best of these spoofs, mirroring a true-life counterpart in the South American revolutions of the 1920s. *Cracked Nuts* is the earliest talkie feature to simultaneously poke fun at the kitschy fairy-tale-kingdom plots that had been the domain of stage operettas (like Franz Lehar's the *Merry Widow* [1905]) and the films of Ernst Lubitsch (*The Love Parade* [1929] and *Monte Carlo* [1930]).

The following year Paramount offered an improved "crazy country" comedy with *Million Dollar Legs* (Eddie Cline directed both films), while 1933 saw the best entries into the genre, Wheeler and Woolsey's *Diplomaniacs* and the Marx Brothers' *Duck Soup*. Charlie Chaplin was heavily influenced by these political satires when he took his long-delayed plunge into talkies with the Hitler spoof, *The Great Dictator*, in 1940.

Cracked Nuts is an unsettling mixture of black humor, weird visual gags, and rambling dialogue routines. Yet this potluck gag bag offers Bert and Bob their strongest characterizations since *The Cuckoos*, and it is interesting to speculate on who had a hand in shaping their roles. Douglas MacLean, a breezy silent comedian whose two talkies knocked the acting winds out of him, served as an associate producer and screenwriter here. In *Cracked Nuts*' early scenes, Bert Wheeler hardly resembles the vaudeville loony of yore, behaving instead like MacLean's own dapper man about town. Bob Woolsey still has his share of clunker lines but he is no longer wrestling with the quips: his timing and delivery are impeccable. Most surprising of all is the development of the story: Bert and Bob do not meet until the film is half over. RKO was considering solo vehicles for both comedians, and the experiment here confirmed the studio's decision to split the duo.

The basis for *Cracked Nuts* was Welford Beaton's short story, "A Growing Concern." FBO Studios, RKO's forerunner, purchased the property in 1928 for a thousand dollars and in true Hollywood style suddenly wondered why they had. A reader's synopsis described the plot as a "wild farce comedy of an imaginary kingdom — expensive, not suitable to any one on our program, and hardly believable." Since FBO's stars at the time were Ranger the Wonder Dog and cowboy Tom Mix, the project was shelved. With the influx of RKO capital (and Wheeler and Woolsey), the property was revived and reworked by writer Al Boasberg under the draft title *Deuces Wild*. Ralph Spence, a title writer in silent days whose claim to fame was the hokey stage whodunit *The Gorilla* (1925), assisted Boasberg and producer MacLean throughout October 1930. Director Eddie Cline added a few touches of his own before the final script was submitted to the studio brass on November 15, 1930. Filming commenced just nine days later, making *Cracked Nuts* the fifth Wheeler and Woolsey feature produced during 1930. "It was tough doing five pictures in a year," Bert said in 1958. "I don't know how we did it. We raised the dickens afterward; we didn't want any part of that. It was too rough. We cut down to three [films a year], then two."

Sad to say, *Cracked Nuts* reveals the strain that went into its production. Typical of the film's level of wit is the opening gag, when it is revealed that Dorothy Lee is living at the Venus de Milo Arms. Song and dance numbers were usually the high point in Wheeler and Woolsey comedies; not so in *Cracked Nuts*. Despite Hollywood's moratorium on musicals, the film spotlights Bert and Dorothy Lee in an agonizing ditty called "Dance and Let the World Dance with You" (which no one received credit for composing). The pair briefly executes a limp tango, screeching the word "daaaance!" several times while stomping on each other's feet. When Edna May Oliver enters the scene, she indulges in a little foot-trampling of her own. "Bert knew how to make it look like he was stepping on your toes without really doing it," Dottie Lee recalls. "But that wasn't the case with Edna May Oliver. You see, she had big feet!"

Cracked Nuts (1931)

Cracked Nuts actually opens with a nifty little scene, a Bert Wheeler tour de force Harold Lloyd might have envied, played without dialogue. Bouquet in hand, Wheeler goes a-courtin' his sweetheart, Dorothy. While Bert waits at the elevator, a big bruiser enters and quickly grows impatient when an elevator doesn't materialize. Bert becomes nervous when the man gets physical, pounding on the elevator door with his walking stick. Breaking off the door's ornamentation, he disgustedly takes the stairs. The elevator finally arrives while Bert is blissfully sniffing his rose bouquet. Assuming that Bert wrecked his door, the angry elevator operator hurls Wheeler across the floor. The startled Wheeler gracefully slides through the revolving door out into the street. Bouquet still in hand, Bert blithely tips his hat and seeks an alternate route. (Al Boasberg's penciled notes on the script indicate that the floor was heavily polished and Wheeler's pants had roller skates sewn to them.) Once outside, Bert finds a convenient ladder that, coincidentally, leads to Dorothy's apartment. More precisely, it leads to the bathroom.

Bert hides behind the shower curtain, just in time to overhear Dorothy's aunt (Edna May Oliver) vivisect his character: "He's a wealthy idler who produces nothing, achieves nothing, and means nothing." Bert's facial reactions throughout the sequence are priceless. Edna May naturally turns the shower on while Bert is still in hiding; he nearly escapes detection, but Dorothy accidentally gives him away. The regal Oliver proceeds to verbally annihilate him:

> EDNA MAY: I have an idea you broke into this apartment.
> BERT: No man with any sense would do a thing like that!
> EDNA MAY: How do *you* know what a man with any sense would do?
> BERT: [*quietly*] Well, you've got me there.
> EDNA MAY: Don't stand there acting like a fool!
> BERT: [*plaintively*] I'm not acting.

Bert resolves to achieve great things; to that end, he solicits opportunities through the newspaper classifieds. Two mysterious characters (Boris Karloff and Frank Thornton) offer Bert an unusual proposition: purchase a revolution in the faraway kingdom of El Dorania, depose the present monarch, and be crowned king. Boris Karloff's first scene sets the tone for his entire performance: he's an obedient toady in Wheeler's presence and a scheming turncoat behind Bert's back. If Karloff's schmoozy monotone delivery and grim visage were not a harbinger of doom, his pallbearer's costume would tip off anyone—except Bert Wheeler. Karloff's acting here is overwrought and unctuous: he rubs his palms together while discussing money matters; cocks his head sideways while praising Bert; issues long innuendo glances to his confederates when conspiring. One cannot condemn Boris for his behavior, considering the dialogue he was expected to deliver. Consider these exchanges:

> BERT: If I bought this revolution, would it distinguish me?
> BORIS: Ah, that is just it! You will depose the present monarch, King Oscar, then you will automatically become king!
> BERT: You mean I'd have a crown and a specter and everything?
> BORIS: Everything! Ah-h, it'll take a man of your force, your aggressiveness, your leadership, to rattle the ancient bones of El Dorania!

Or later, onboard the boat:

> BORIS: Don't worry, Your Majesty—soon we shall have arrived in El Dorania.
> BERT: You mustn't call me "Your Majesty" until I'm king—I'm just Wendell to you.
> BORIS: Oh, thank you! Thank you, Your Majesty!

In later years Boris Karloff had great fun spoofing his horror-film image, both in movie romps and on television. Such flights of fancy could only occur after he had established his screen persona as filmdom's number-one boogeyman. At the time of *Cracked Nuts*, the $125-a-week actor was too preoccupied with hustling for film work to be concerned about the quality of his appearances; his role in this Wheeler and Woolsey opus was one of his showier bits to date. Ten years later, with Frankenstein's monster, Im-ho-tep, Dr. Fu Manchu, Mord, and the other great fiends behind him, canny Karloff mocked himself beautifully in the Broadway black-comedy hit *Arsenic and Old Lace* (1941).

In the hands of a less inhibited performer (Bela Lugosi's high-powered Hungarian bravura immediately comes to mind), the bad guy role of *Cracked Nuts* could have evolved into a comic villain's delight. Instead, Karloff in *Cracked Nuts* is neither amusing, sinister, nor memorable; film reviewers at the time ignored his gawky emoting with good reason. Several months after *Cracked Nuts'* release Karloff found his metier, contributing performances to *The Criminal Code* and *Frankenstein* that propelled him to the front ranks of movie stardom, where all good monsters belong.

In contrast to Karloff, Bob Woolsey struts his showiest performance to date. Resplendent in an admiral's regalia, furiously puffing on a cigar, Bob buoys the slight material with a sharp, clever portrayal. Not all of Woolsey's lines connect as knee-slapping wit ("I proposed to her by letter and she was so dumb, she accepted the mailman"), but the brio Bob exudes is first rate all the way. Woolsey's delivery doesn't disappoint when the material is behind him:

Top: Frank Thornton, Stanley Fields, Boris Karloff, Bob, and Bert spot an oil gusher in *Cracked Nuts*. Within a year, *Frankenstein* would make Karloff a star. *Bottom*: Bert brings out the heavy artillery, stumping Bob in *Cracked Nuts*.

> LENI: Have you never thought seriously of marriage?
> BOB: Certainly! That's why I'm single.
> LENI: Ah—love—love is intoxication—
> BOB: Yeah, and marriage is the hangover!

And:

> LENI: Your majesty . . . next week you will get your face on all coins of the realm!
> BOB: Never mind gettin' my face on 'em—what I want to do is get my *hands* on 'em!

Even at this early stage of the game, the Marx Brothers' first two movies inspired some of the dialogue and routines used by Wheeler and Woolsey. Take Groucho Marx's culinary non sequitur from *Animal Crackers* (1930): "If you take cranberries and stew them like applesauce, they taste much more like prunes than rhubarb does." In *Cracked Nuts*, Woolsey recites a similar recipe: "When cranberries are stewed, they make better applesauce than prunes any day." Not satisfied with this assault, Woolsey furnishes another variance on the gastronomic theme:

> There was a woman that could cook coffee! At first it was bad, but we found out what the trouble was—she was making it with tea. But later on she started making it with cocoa, and it tasted so much like clam broth, we froze it and made ice cream out of it!

This gag—if it is indeed a gag—was not especially funny when Groucho Marx uttered it, and Woolsey's repetition reinforces the lack of original material at hand.

Bert and Bob finally meet, twenty-nine minutes into the picture. Like an old (very old) vaudeville skit, the boys indulge in some aimless banter which, for sheer gall, is worth repeating:

> BERT: [*recognizing Bob*] Well, well!
> BOB: Well, well, well, well, well, well, well!
> BERT: How've you been?
> BOB: Well! And you?
> BERT: Well, I, uh—
> BOB: I know—you haven't been well. Hah, hah, hah, hah! Do you remember that day in your backyard when you fell into the—
> BERT: Well?
> BOB: Yeah!
> BERT: Very well!
> BOB: [*quietly*] Is there any chance of us getting out of this well at all?

Cracked Nuts (1931)

When Bert and Bob embark on something that could be considered a comedy routine, it turns out to be a pale imitation of Groucho and Chico's "Why-a-Duck?" from *The Cocoanuts* (1929). True, W & W present an embryonic version of Abbott and Costello's "Who's on First?" as they examine a map of the towns "What" and "Which," but the wordplay escalates only toward seething frustration, never genuine laughter. Having tapped everyone else's material, writer Al Boasberg even engages in self-plagiarism. Boasberg wrote a protracted sequence for Buster Keaton's first talkie, *Free and Easy* (1930), in which Keaton repeatedly ruins his MGM screen test by mangling the dialogue. Instead of exclaiming, "Woe is me, the Queen has swooned," Buster twists the line into "Woe is me, the Quoon has sweened," and similar unfunny malaprops. In *Cracked Nuts*, Bert and Bob double the dubious fun, taking turns getting tongue-tied over the phrase, "Twenty miles as the crow flies," which from their confused minds emerges as "Twenty miles as the cry flows" and similar inanities. Five years later, this exercise in banality would be repeated, word for word, in the weakest Wheeler and Woolsey vehicle of all, *Mummy's Boys*.

Bert and Bob trot out a few more limp routines, including a rehash of *Rio Rita*'s famous wine-cellar scene (for which retakes were required, a month after principal photography was completed on *Cracked Nuts*). A number of other sequences were filmed and later scrapped, including an escapade wherein Edna May Oliver and Dorothy Lee are pressed into El Dorania's secret service. At director Eddie Cline's behest, an interesting cast change occurred during filming. Stuttering comic Roscoe Ates was originally signed to portray an aerial bombardier. Cline thought it would be much funnier to have the cross-eyed Ben Turpin play the role, and producer MacLean agreed to the substitution. Eddie Cline had directed Turpin during silent days in Mack Sennett two-reelers, but Turpin's talkie work was limited to cameos and bit parts. Unhappily, this veteran slapsticker's surprise appearance in *Cracked Nuts* backfires: his cockeyed viewpoint is a one-joke idea, and worse, nobody bothered to rewrite Turpin's dialogue with an amusing slant. Ben is here without his trademark mustache; missing the outsized adornment, he's virtually incognito. Turpin's plain facial features are self-effacing, placing all the emphasis on his ocular disorder. The comedian's monotone delivery reveals why he did not remain a crowd pleaser when he had to open his mouth. Further troubles plagued the production. After Ben completed his cameo and collected an impressive thousand dollars for an easy day's work, the filmmakers realized that audiences were unlikely to recognize the once-famous Ben Turpin at all. Bert and Bob's dialogue was hastily rewritten so that they would reminisce—at great length—about good ol' "Cross-Eyed Ben," reassuring viewers that the frail-looking pilot was indeed the popular silent-screen comedian. (Eddie Cline no doubt realized his mistake; when he later directed Turpin in *Million Dollar Legs*, Ben sported a mustache and kept his mouth shut.)

The actual Assassination Day festivities are lifted directly out of Keaton's *Convict 13* (Eddie Cline was Buster's codirector), replete with cheering crowds and stadium vendors. An explosion entwines Bert in a coil of barbed wire, resulting in an unpleasant, painful gag. After one of Turpin's misguided missiles strikes an oil well, making them millionaires, Bert and Bob matter-of-factly have the villains arrested (why couldn't they do that before?). A brief coda wraps the film: Bert and Dottie marry while a resigned Edna May quips, "Oh, well, I'll take vanilla." Her scripted dialogue was "Oh, well, what the hell!" Both lines aptly convey the screenwriters' mounting desperation—and defeat.

Among the other players, Stanley Fields is ideally cast as the lead villain, General Bogardus (an early draft refers to his character as General Threat), but once his presence is established, he is never given anything menacing to do (shades of his gangster role in *Hook Line and Sinker*). Dorothy is hardly in the picture at all, while Leni Stengel disappears after a few early tête-à-têtes with her man Woolsey. Only Edna May Oliver, among supporting cast members, commands some pearly moments, although she is cast as the nastiest of old crows. "Edna May Oliver played these stuck-up society dames," Dorothy Lee recalls, "but in real life she was a warm, goodhearted person. A little shy, she was self-conscious about herself. But we eventually took to each other and became good friends."

There was a half-baked attempt to give this flimsy production a comic-epic grandeur; Al Boasberg specified that the film's occasional intertitles be handled "like the cards in *Cimarron*," the studio's most impressive film to date. When RKO selected its "best films" of 1931, *Cracked Nuts* was chosen by studio personnel, along with *Cimarron* and *Young Donovan's Kid*. In a dark Depression year when RKO films failed to click, *Cracked Nuts* was one of the few moneymakers for the firm. Audiences flocked to see their beloved team whether the product was good, bad, or indifferent.

Contemporary critics were less than thrilled with *Cracked Nuts* and blunt with their rationales. *Variety* noted the film's padding, observing that "long dissertations about nothing at all will wear down any fan." *Time* commented, "Bert Wheeler and Robert Woolsey go through their routines on the same set. Unfortunately, such gags as the long dialogue in which the word 'well,' used as an interjection, is dragged through every possible shade of meaning [was] not good even when it was new." Forty-five years later, a befuddled Pauline Kael reviewed the *Cracked Nuts*' revival for the *New Yorker*, and remarked, "It was often impossible to decide if [Wheeler and Woolsey] were wonderfully terrible or just plain terrible, but they were totally unpretentious." The team's luck was about to improve, though the ideal vehicle was still just a dream.

9
Wheeler and Woolsey, Split Asunder

"Wheeler and Woolsey are head and shoulders above any other featured draw on the Radio lot," *Variety* noted in its December 31, 1930, issue. "Much of the draw of the Radio musicals that would otherwise have suffered from the turn against musicals can be ascribed to the comedy of the pair. [Wheeler, Woolsey, and Dorothy Lee] are now slated for stardom on future product." Two months earlier, *Variety* remarked that "Radio execs have agreed that Wheeler should team up with Dorothy Lee, figuring the pair a natural," and that Woolsey "will be used individually and if clicking will stay that way."

Throughout 1929 and 1930, RKO continued to flex its fledgling muscles with ads referring to the studio as "the most spectacular show machine of all time!" In reality the "show machine" had produced little that was worth showing, with an even bleaker outlook for 1931. Corporate profits for RKO's second year (1930) were very good—nearly $3.4 million—but not in the same league as the established major studios: MGM, for instance, had profits of $14.6 million in 1930, while Paramount's ledger sheets were in the black with a staggering $25 million. "In the RKO houses," *Variety* soberly announced, "business was the poorest of 1930." RKO's most conspicuous problem was its lack of star power. Bebe Daniels defected to Warner Brothers after the *Dixiana* fiasco. Darlings of the airwaves Freeman Gosden and Charles Correll (Amos 'n' Andy) were a hit in RKO's *Check and Double Check*, but audiences came solely out of curiosity to view two white actors in blackface: on radio, Amos 'n' Andy were a delight; in movies they were a puzzlement, never starring in another RKO film. Richard Dix would eventually emerge as a perennial, but his early RKO days were marked by lackluster vehicles. Rounding out the studio-contract roster were has-beens Betty Compson and Jack Mulhall and nonstars Sue Carol and Lowell Sherman. With RKO's firmament of stars sputtering at best, Wheeler and Woolsey emerged as the studio's dazzling supernovas.

In the climate of a worsening Depression, the public wanted laughs and enjoyed the adventures of Bert, Bob, and their diminutive leading lady, Dorothy. By the autumn of 1930 RKO executives knew that Wheeler-Woolsey-Lee on a marquee would rake in badly needed profits. Why not split the team up, doubling their annual releases and, they hoped, their profits? This scatterbrained notion seemed like a good idea to somebody at RKO at the time.

Bert Wheeler later remarked that "we worked like hell that first year in Hollywood," but this wage-slave duo was handsomely paid for their efforts. Bob Woolsey's salary earnings for 1930 were $104,000, while Bert Wheeler's deal paid him $124,999.68 during that mutually remunerative year. With *The Cuckoos*, *Half Shot at Sunrise*, and *Hook Line and Sinker* coining a mint for the studio's depleted coffers, studio chief William LeBaron gladly approved new contracts for Bert and Bob on January 5, 1931. This time Wheeler and Woolsey signed pacts that ran concurrently for one year, guaranteeing each comic the same salary—$3,000 a week. The equal salaries were not an indication that Bert Wheeler had lost his favored status, but the studio's realization that Bert and Bob were both extremely valuable to RKO's future.

RKO dug into its trunk of stage plays inherited from FBO and dusted off *Too Many Cooks* as Bert and Dorothy's first starring vehicle. Adapted from a 1916 comedy written by and starring Frank Craven, *Too Many Cooks* was genteel entertainment onstage but a yawner's marathon on film. Douglas MacLean, the film's associate producer, had starred in a 1920 silent-film version deemed so poor that it never played New York City. For Dorothy Lee, the production was a grueling, miserable experience. "Bert and I played a young couple building our own little home in the country. The whole damn picture centered around us babbling away at this construction site. Our pushy relatives try to break us apart. That's all there was to the stupid movie."

Filming of *Cooks* was mercifully brief, from February 28 through March 22, 1931. Despite the tight shooting schedule, Dorothy recalls it as a hellish ordeal, since she and Bert were required to be in nearly every scene: "Every day I'd ask Bert, 'Why are we shooting this?' He'd shrug, smile at me and say, 'Yeah, it stinks, but they gotta pay us for doing *something*.'"

Although RKO inherited the property from its predecessor, talkies were considered a new medium, and all literary contracts had to be renegotiated. Broadway showman William A. Brady and playwright Craven divided $20,000 for the motion picture rights to *Too Many Cooks*. Curiously, their 1931 agreement with RKO specified that the "rights to reproduce the story by television with living actors from legitimate or spoken stage [were] reserved to owner." Not only were Brady and Craven outrageously optimistic about television's future in the Great Depression, they were crazy to believe that anybody might want to see *Cooks* on television after suffering through it on the big screen.

On the positive side, Bert and Dorothy are quite good, contributing sensitive, light-comedy performances. But it's all for naught, since Bert is completely miscast: Wheeler doesn't look or sound like a parlor-room comedian. His elfin stature, rubbery face, and Brooklyn accent belonged to the slightly off-center world of musical comedy. Instead of a carload of belly laughs, *Too Many Cooks* offers a soupçon of charm, with all its punches pulled.

This was Bert Wheeler's first collaboration with director William A. Seiter, an expert craftsman who was making his RKO debut. Seiter was paid a paltry $3,500 for directing *Too Many Cooks* but by the 1940s he would be earning $100,000 per feature film. A graduate of silent-comedy two-reelers (like nearly everybody else in Hollywood in the 1930s), Seiter went on to direct several of the great comedy teams—Laurel and Hardy (*Sons of the Desert*, 1933, for which Frank Craven wrote the original story), the Marx Brothers (*Room Service*, 1938), and Abbott and Costello (*Little Giant*, 1946)—in addition to major musicals like *Roberta* (1935), starring Fred Astaire and Ginger Rogers. Seiter helmed four Wheeler and Woolsey comedies in all with generally pleasing results. He brought the gentler side of their personalities to the fore, giving their roles greater depth while simultaneously integrating comedy routines into the story line. Three of Seiter's W & W vehicles—*Peach O'Reno*, *Girl Crazy*, and *Diplomaniacs*—rank among Bert and Bob's breeziest and all-time funniest films.

Bob Woolsey probably gulped hard when *Everything's Rosie* commenced filming on March 30. Studio wags were convinced that Wheeler would be a success as a solo but were not so sure about Woolsey. Now, with Bert's film a certified lemon and Bob saddled with an ameliorated script, Woolsey probably had second thoughts about his debut as a single.

Clyde Bruckman was borrowed from the prestigious Harold Lloyd Corporation on February 14, 1931, to work on the story and direct the film. Apparently RKO felt that yeoman services were required to buoy Bob's premiere solo effort. Bruckman's credentials were impressive; he codirected Buster Keaton's *The General* (1926) as well as Lloyd's first two talkies, *Welcome Danger* (1929) and *Feet First* (1930). Since Harold Lloyd's comedies were traditionally filmdom's funniest (and most profitable), it seemed a sensible choice to seek Lloyd's own helmsman to guide Woolsey through uncharted waters. However, RKO miscalculated Bruckman's true talents—he was not the miracle man they hoped for and needed. Bruckman was just another cog in the machine of Lloyd's Laugh Factory, and a rather small cog at that. Harold Lloyd comedies were crafted through a team effort: half-a-dozen gagmen, several assistant directors, Harold himself, and the nominal director all contributed to the shaping of a Lloyd comedy. As a writer, Bruckman was passable, but in a directorial capacity poor Clyde was worthless—a fondness for the bottle and a nasty habit of recycling other people's material eventually rendered him unemployable.

Everything's Rosie was adapted by Al Boasberg from his original story, *Going, Going, Gone!*, a tale that did not ignite much enthusiasm among RKO bigwigs. As he had done long before in *The Right Girl,* Bob was allowed to embellish the narrative with morsels of comic activity and a smattering of old stage routines.

Director Bruckman, himself an old hand at pilfering, encouraged Woolsey to purloin comedy business until *Everything's Rosie* was transformed into a thinly veiled rehash of *Poppy*, the 1923 W. C. Fields play in which Bob had had a supporting part. This time Woolsey essayed Fields's plum role of Dr. Eustace P. McGargle, the shifty yet lovable circus medicine man, rechristened and slightly transformed here into Dr. J. Dockweiller Droop. Incidentally, never once through *Rosie*'s production did RKO's legal department bother to investigate such trivial matters as a potential copyright infringement—instead, filming proceeded with "business as usual."

Bert was a regular visitor to the set, as was his daughter, Patricia. Like a doting stage mother, Bert talked the studio into giving Patty the microsized role of Rosie as a child. *Variety* (April 1, 1931) related the result:

> Bert Wheeler's two-year-old daughter's name is Patricia and she isn't old enough to tell a lie for a salary check. They wanted her to say "My Name is Rosie" for a scene in *Going, Going, Gone*. She persisted that "My name is Pat." So—out!

Everything's Rosie wrapped principal photography on April 13, a scant two weeks after filming began. It was rushed into release the following month, garnering Robert Woolsey's worst-ever reviews. *Variety*'s column "The Woman's Angle" (May 27, 1931) tersely summarized a common complaint: "Endless succession of gags recited by Bobby Woolsey, whose personality is not attractive enough to monopolize a film." *Everything's Rosie* is about as unappealing as an alleged comedy can be. Woolsey never shuts up for a minute; without partner, Bert, at his side, Bob starts talking to himself:

> BOB: What is your name, good woman?
> LADY: Olive.
> BOB: Give me your palm, Olive. And if you make a crack about "Not on your life, boy," I'll slug you!

The film is loaded with dialogue like this; no one ever answers Woolsey with a smart riposte, so he holds punning duels with himself. The effect is nerve-racking for most viewers—Woolsey's lunatic character cries out to be straitjacketed, yet this screwball evades incarceration at every turn of the plot.

Fortunately, wiser studio heads prevailed, canceling plans for subsequent solo outings (Wheeler and Lee were to have filmed *If I Were Rich*, although Woolsey had nothing pending on his agenda). The studio would never again consider splitting the team; Bert and Bob scampered back together in a hurry. Neither comedian had experienced a failure of this magnitude, but the boys treated their twin-turkey escapade lightly. Woolsey naturally had to have the last word, quipping to reporter Dan Thomas that he and Bert collected press reviews on each other's solo ventures. "Whenever I'm feeling low," Bob cracked, "I just look over those reviews of Bert's picture—they're like a tonic!"

10
The Stolen Jools (1931)

Directed by William McGann. Produced by Pat Casey. Supervised by E. K. Nadel. Story (uncredited) by Al Boasberg, Edwin Burke, Arthur Caesar, Edgar Allan Woolf, Percy Heath, Henry Meyers, and Howard Green. Filmed circa late February–March 7, 1931. Presented by the National Variety Artists by arrangement with Chesterfield Cigarettes. Released by Paramount April 4, 1931. British release title: *The Slippery Pearls*. 20 minutes.

A promotional short to benefit the National Variety Artists, with cameos by Wheeler and Woolsey, Dorothy Lee, Buster Keaton, Laurel and Hardy, Joe E. Brown, Barbara Stanwyck, Irene Dunne, Joan Crawford, Douglas Fairbanks, Jr., Maurice Chevalier, Gary Cooper, Norma Shearer, Victor McLaglen, Edmund Lowe, Fay Wray, Wallace Beery, Edward G. Robinson, George E. Stone, the "Our Gang" kids, Polly Moran, Hedda Hopper, George Sidney, Charlie Murray, Robert Ames, Bebe Daniels, Ben Lyon, Loretta Young, Frank Fay, FiFi D'Orsay, Warner Baxter, Winnie Lightner, Claudia Dell, El Brendel, Charles "Buddy" Rogers, Eugene Pallette, Skeets Gallagher, Stuart Erwin, William Haines, Charles Butterworth, Gabby Hayes, Wynne Gibson, Richard Dix, Lowell Sherman, Jack Oakie, Richard Barthelmess, Mitzi Green. Starring Eddie Kane as himself.

Synopsis: Detective Eddie Kane scours the backlots of Hollywood while searching for Norma Shearer's stolen necklace. Along the way he encounters some suspicious-looking (and suspicious-acting) movie stars.

★ ★ ★

There's no people like show people, so the song goes, and the movie industry has lived up to that maxim in many ways. By 1929, over fifteen thousand performers were registered members of the National Variety Artists, an organization founded primarily to benefit ailing, down-at-the-heel actors. Impresario Edward F. Albee, hailed as the Grand Old Man of vaudeville and founder of the NVA, died in 1930 just as the live entertainment *Variety* had dubbed "Big-Time Vaude" was desperately sick itself. Albee was adjudged somewhat less than grand when the terms of his will were made public: he left less than 1 percent of his $25 million estate to the actor's club he had nurtured. Simultaneously, talking pictures and a Depression that wouldn't quit crowded out hungry stage performers seeking employment. Their famous screen counterparts took matters into their own hands by staging live benefits and by appearing in this strange little film for the NVA relief fund.

The Stolen Jools is a whimsical pleasantry the first time through: its shower of stars whizzes by at breakneck pace—there is no time to be bored or distracted. With the second or third viewing, however, you realize just how ho-hum most of the film is. Several Hollywood studios generously contributed to the production of this short by lending their brightest stars. It is an academic point, but actors from prestigious MGM and Paramount come off the worst, while thespians from the faltering Fox camp and scruffy RKO are refreshing, at ease, and still funny.

Bert and Bob come off best of all: the necessity of cramming over forty stars into a bare twenty minutes accelerates the pace of their brief scene, while their dialogue remains sharp. Many of the players in *The Stolen Jools* treat their comic blackouts as one big joke; Wheeler and Woolsey take their comedy turn seriously, and are all the funnier for it. Their bit takes place at a diner counter. A mountain of empty coffee cups is piled high in front of Bert as the scene opens:

> BERT: [*apprehensively*] You know, I'm still nervous.
> BOB: What you need is a cup of coffee. [*to waiter*] Boy!
> BERT: Hey waiter, bring me a cup of coffee—
> WAITER: Just as soon as I can get to you.
> BERT: [*to Bob*] I don't like that guy. I don't think he's a waiter. At least he don't act like one.
> BOB: Oh, yes, he does!
> BERT: I think he's a crook!
> BOB: Yeah? Wait a minute, I'll ask him. [*to waiter*] Son—are you a crook? I mean, what is your business?
> WAITER: I'm Inspector Kane.
> BERT: What'd I tell ya?
> WAITER: What do you mean?
> BOB: Well, if you're an inspector, what're you doing here?
> WAITER: Shh! I'm looking for pearls!
> BERT: Why don't you try the oysters?
> BOB: Heh, heh, that's good!
> WAITER: Now wait a minute! Let me tell you something, this is serious! There was a ball given last night—
> BOB: Yeah, it's still on the menu.
> WAITER: What's on the menu?
> BOB: Codfish bowl, right—

WAITER: This is serious! The ball was given for ladies and gentlemen.
BERT: We weren't there, then.
BOB: No, we were not.
WAITER: Now, some jewels were stolen from Norma Shearer—
BOB: Does she work here?
WAITER: No, she don't, but I'm gonna get those jewels! Do you know anything about it?
BOB: Wait a minute. If there was a ball given last night and any jewels were stolen, had we been there [*points at Bert*], he would've gotten 'em!
BERT: Now why make a crack like that? I had nothin'—
WAITER: [*to Bert*] Hey, did you ever steal anything?
BOB: Wait a minute—better let me ask, waiter. [*Bob whispers something to Bert. Bert suddenly beams with delight.*]
BERT: [*asking Bob*] Now?
BOB: Now. [*Bert smacks the waiter's face.*]
WAITER: [*angrily*] Whaddya mean by doin' that?
BERT: He told me to do it!
WAITER: He did! [*Waiter smacks Bob's face.*]
BOB: [*to Bert*] You tell everything you know, don't ya? [*Bob smacks Bert.*]
BERT: Don't give me that! [*The boys alternate smacking each other's faces.*]
WAITER: Wait a minute, wait a minute. Did you ever do this before?
BOB: Yeah, in *Rio Rita* we did—
WAITER: Oh, you did! [*Waiter starts smacking both of them; the boys smack back as the scene fades out.*]

Not only is the interplay lively and animated, but Bert and Bob's timing is impeccable, and Wheeler's pantomime is incredibly clever, chock full of subtle expressions. Bert switches moods at the drop of a hat, conveying first suspicion, then fear, and finally sheer delight (once he's smacked Eddie Kane in the puss). The boys' playful give-and-take performances foreshadow their breezy roles in the top-notch *Peach O'Reno*, produced later in 1931.

Dorothy Lee appears in most circulating prints of the film for about five seconds. Those fortunate enough to catch the rarely shown original release print can see and hear her complete vignette, where she sings a few bars of "I Love You So Much" from *The Cuckoos*. Also clipped from latter-day prints was Maurice Chevalier belting "It's a Great Life, If You Don't Weaken" from his *Playboy of Paris* (1930) and Warner Baxter as the Cisco Kid crooning a Mexican-flavored ditty. Since each player warbled a single line from their specialty, the deletions seem gratuitous and silly. During the 1970s, Blackhawk Films, the finest of the now-defunct home-movie companies, edited out this footage through fear of legal reprisals from copyright gadflies at the American Society of Composers, Authors and Publishers (ASCAP). A word to the wise: Whistle a happy tune in public—but first be certain that the song is in the public domain.

The National Variety Artists later became better known to the general

Bob seems apprehensive, but Bert is delighted after slapping Eddie Kane's face in *The Stolen Jools*.

public as the Will Rogers Institute for Respiratory Diseases, located at Saranac Lake in upstate New York. (To most kids of the fifties and sixties, the name Will Rogers signified not the beloved humorist but "donation time" at the movie house.) Ironically, Bert, who was a two-pack-a-day smoker, contracted emphysema in the 1950s and spent his last years trekking from show dates to Saranac with distressing regularity. Yet Wheeler never wore out his welcome at the actor's sanitarium. Reinvigorated from the mountain air, Wheeler would stage performances to cheer up the other patients. After Bert's death, a new hospital wing was dedicated to his memory—a rare gesture toward a penniless comedian who could not bequeath any money yet was never miserly with his talent.

11
Caught Plastered (1931)

Directed by William Seiter. Produced by William LeBaron. Associate producer, Douglas MacLean. Original story, "Full of Notions," by Douglas MacLean. Adaptation and dialogue by Ralph Spence and (uncredited) Jane Murfin. Additional dialogue by Eddie Welch. Scenery and costumes by Max Ree. Photographed by Jack MacKenzie. Sound recording by J. Faulkner, Jr. Film editing by Jack Kitchin. Music by Victor Schertzinger. Dates of production: May 18 to June 9, 1931. Released by RKO on August 9, 1931. 68 minutes.

Cast: Bert Wheeler (Tommy Tanner), Robert Woolsey (Egbert G. Higginbotham), Dorothy Lee (Peggy Morton), Lucy Beaumont (Mrs. Talley), Jason Robards, Sr. (Harry Waters), DeWitt Jennings (Chief H. A. Morton), Charles B. Middleton (Flint), Josephine Whittell (Miss Newton), Bill Scott (Mr. Clarke), James Farley (Trolley Conductor), Grace Hayle (Corpulent Customer), Arthur Housman (Drunk Counter Patron), Nora Cecil (Patron).

Synopsis: Pauperized vaudevillians Tommy Tanner and Egbert G. Higginbotham (Bert Wheeler and Robert Woolsey) alight from a freight train after fleeing from their last play date. Stranded in the town of Lockville and starving, the boys board a trolley in search of theatrical work. They quickly make friends with a little old lady, Mrs. Talley (Lucy Beaumont), whose drugstore verges on bankruptcy. Harry Waters (Jason Robards, Sr.), a medicinal wholesaler, has extended the widow extensive credit, using her property as collateral. Waters offers Mrs. Talley three hundred dollars for the assignment of her business. Fortunately, Tommy and Egbert know a rat when they see one: the boys convince the widow not to sell the drugstore to Waters. Infuriated by their interference, Waters gives the widow thirty days' clemency before his bank forecloses.

Sure enough, Waters has been moonlighting as a bootlegger by selling his firm's booze to racketeers. He also has insider information that a ten-story office building is to be erected across the street from Mrs. Talley's prime location. Waters connives to grab the drugstore before Tommy and Egbert transform it into a success. Meanwhile, Waters's girlfriend, Peggy Morton (Dorothy Lee), seems to be falling hard for Tommy. Since Peggy's father is the chief of police (DeWitt Jennings), Waters decides to tag the boys as "two suspicious-looking characters from the East [with] all the earmarks of racketeers."

Overnight, Mrs. Talley's little enterprise becomes a booming success. Tommy and Egbert modernize the drugstore by equipping it with everything but drugs. With the widow's two hundred dollar savings, the boys stock the shop and establish a radio station within the store. Waters schemes with Clarke (Bill Scott), another crook, to sell the boys some phony "pepo-lemon syrup" (actually alcohol); when Peggy and the other customers have become roaring drunk on the premises, Chief Morton padlocks the drugstore and arrests the proprietor, old Mrs. Talley.

Fortunately for all concerned, Peggy recalls Clarke's hiding place, a nondescript tenement building. Tommy, Egbert, Peggy, and the Chief discover Clarke packaging moonshine in the cellar. Coincidentally, they also nab Waters, who blithely walks into the trap. All ends happily as Mrs. Talley is reunited with Peggy and the boys, just in time for their next radio broadcast.

★ ★ ★

RKO executives blundered in a big way when they split up the studio's favorite sons, but the home lot learned its lesson. On May 27, the same day *Variety* reviewed *Everything's Rosie*, RKO took out an explosive ad campaign in that trade paper, reassuring exhibitors of the studio's commitment to reuniting Wheeler with Woolsey. "THREE BIG WHEELER AND WOOLSEY SHOWS," the herald began. "These boys are the established favorites of millions of kids. THE YOUTH OF AMERICA AWAITS YOUR CALL—TITAN SHOWS GEARED FOR JUVENILE TRADE." Wheeler and Woolsey's original public was the urbane 1920s theatergoer, but in the early 1930s, Depression-era kids propelled Bert and Bob into Saturday-matinee superstardom. Alex Watz, the greatest dad in the world, turned seven in 1931 and started attending movies that year with his pals. To Dad and his friends, Wheeler and Woolsey were the reason you went to the movies.

> Laurel and Hardy and Wheeler and Woolsey were all that the kids ever talked about. But Laurel and Hardy mainly made short comedies, which were tossed into the bill. Wheeler and Woolsey made full-length pictures, so everybody knew a week in advance when they were coming to town. On the day a Wheeler and Woolsey film opened, the first show was packed. Many times we were forced to play hookey just to get into the theater. Then we'd stay there all day, or until our parents dragged us home.

While *Everything's Rosie* was being filmed, RKO purchased Douglas MacLean's original story "Full of Notions" on April 2 for Bert and Bob's return to the screen. MacLean pocketed $2,500 for the rights to his yarn, but the ring of familiarity should have made studio wags wary. The basic idea of "Full of Notions" was the formula used in *Hook Line and Sinker.* Worse, the "novel" ingredients interwoven into the plot (the boys befriend an elderly woman and revitalize her drugstore) were lifted verbatim from, of all things, a Hal Roach *Our Gang* comedy, *Helping Grandma.* That two-reeler was released to theaters January 3, 1931; before the year was out, the Roach studios produced two additional shorts with "little old lady" themes, Laurel and Hardy's *One Good Turn* and another *Our Gang* starrer, *Fly My Kite.* The three Roach shorts reinforced another point ignored by RKO: Wheeler and Woolsey's new plot might prove suitable for a twenty-minute comedy, but would audiences remain pleased for sixty-eight minutes?

If such questions were raised at RKO, they fell on deaf ears, because "Full of Notions" (retitled *Caught Plastered*) was filmed exactly as written during the late spring of 1931. Bert and Bob voiced no complaints about the carbon-copy plotting; possibly the boys were simply happy to be teamed again and chose to overlook the threadbare screenplay. The studio, anxious to make amends to its reigning box-office champs, indulged the boys' every whim. When Bert started riding his bicycle from stage to stage on the RKO lot, Bob complained to the studio brass that he wanted some vehicular contrivance for himself—and received a free motorcycle. Wheeler's desires were a tad less capricious. Paul Sloane, the team's director on *The Cuckoos* and *Half Shot at Sunrise,* was initially earmarked to make *Caught Plastered.* Bert respected the director's capabilities but knew that Sloane wasn't cut out for comedy: "That fella had no sense of humor." Although *Too Many Cooks* was a failure, Wheeler became friendly with director Bill Seiter and was impressed by the man's smooth, relaxed style. Based upon Bert's enthusiastic recommendation, Seiter was recruited to helm *Caught Plastered,* his first Wheeler and Woolsey film.

William Seiter's assured guidance gives *Caught Plastered* a genuine vestige of charm and wit. Seiter was able to imbue the scenes between the boys and old Mrs. Talley (Lucy Beaumont) with a benevolence that never becomes mawkish—high praise for a couple of smark-alecky comedians who used to laugh at each other's asinine jokes. Bert and Bob's characterizations are better delineated here and more fully integrated into the story line than ever before, and the picture even boasts two sprightly first-rate scenes.

The first highlight centers around Bert and Bob's attempts to lift Mrs. Talley's spirits when her situation looks bleakest. Bert, finding the widow crying, gently consoles her: "Oh, honey—I'm *sure* everything's gonna be all right." He hugs her reassuringly. "Things are never as bad as they seem. You know what they say about those clouds with the silver lining? Well, it's

"CAUGHT PLASTERED" *A Radio Picture*

Wheeler and Woolsey portray song-and-dance men bringing sunshine into Lucy Beaumont's life in *Caught Plastered*.

true!" The sequence is played honestly, affording viewers a glimpse of the real Bert Wheeler as friends like Dottie remember him.

Woolsey reprimands Mrs. Talley for feeling blue: "Didn't I say that from now on that we were going to do all the worrying around here?" "Yeah," adds Bert, "we've had a lot of practice lately." The boys decide to put on an act that they "did at the Elks." Bert and Bob proceed to tell a series of corny gags that fly over the old lady's head:

> BOB: Once upon a time a tramp went to a back door, and he said to the housewife, he says, "Lady, will you lend me a cake of soap?" And the housewife says, "What in the world do you want with a cake of soap?" And the tramp replied, "Me partner's got hiccups, and I wanna scare him!"
> MRS. TALLEY: Oh, why did they want to scare the poor fellow?
> BERT: [*to Bob*] We'd better tell her some of the new jokes.
> BOB: I think you're right.

Eventually Mrs. Talley understands the boys' tomfoolery ("We're gettin' her!") and laughs over the dopiest jokes imaginable, but this only adds to the charm of the scene. Bert and Bob next follow with a rendition of "While Strolling Through the Park One Day" and finish to an Irish clog dance, singing "She's the Daughter of Rosie O'Grady." Such innocent fun perfectly typifies the team's song-and-dance talents and provides a magical moment in a generally low-key comedy.

The other classic scene is Bert and Dorothy's duet, "I'm That Way About You, After All." Performed in front of a radio microphone, with Bob "accompanying" them on the piano, Bert and Dottie undulate to the peppy tune while a counter of drunk patrons (spearheaded by movies' number-one souse, Arthur Housman) jiggles in their seats. The "turn" is as delightful as any of Bert and Dottie's more elaborate musical numbers, but the scene does magnify the movie's primary problem: nearly everything occurs in that darned claustrophobic drugstore setting. RKO was tightening its purse strings when it doled out the budget for this production, and the story line seems as shaky as old Mrs. Talley's finances. To be sure, there is a surfeit of funny lines, but the film lacks punch and, unlike the classic W & W adventures, quickly wears thin with most viewers.

The best laughs occur in the drugstore setting, which could have easily fashioned a neat two-reeler distilling all the funny gags. Attempting to decipher a doctor's prescription, Bert comments, "Ya can't read it—it's written in pig latin!" "Pig latin?" Bob responds, "This one's written in wild boar!" A man comes in to buy a toothbrush. "How many in your family?" queries Bob. "Four," the man answers. "Then you want the large size," replies Woolsey. The customer then inquires about the price of the toothbrushes:

> CUSTOMER: How much are they?
> BOB: Fifty cents and one dollar.
> CUSTOMER: What's the difference?
> BOB: The fifty cent ones are all sold!

When a flirty dowager informs Woolsey that she wants to purchase a book that will make her feel "sentimental," Bob reads to her from *The Book on Love*:

> BOB: Here we are, the first page. It says, "When you meet a little girl that you like, when you take her little hand in yours—and then you sigh—and then you put your arm around her waist—and then you place her head upon your shoulder—and then you go for a stroll, 'way out into the lonely woods—"
> LADY: [*excitedly*] And after that, what does the book say?
> BOB: Well, after that, you don't need a book!

The low-voltage supporting cast lacks the force to buttress the conflict between the little drugstore owner and the devouring conglomerate. Jason

Robards, Sr., is too namby-pamby to be a threat, while Charles "Ming the Merciless" Middleton is tremendous in the bit role of a skinflint railroad inspector. Lucy Beaumont is more than adequate in the grandma part, although she can't make up her mind whether Robards's character should be called Mr. Walters or Mr. Waters (but then, does anybody care?). DeWitt Jennings could essay his stock-in-trade police chief role blindfolded (he doesn't); the following year, Beaumont and Jennings would portray Harold Lloyd's parents in *Movie Crazy*. Dorothy Lee is adorable in the sequence where she gets drunk on spiked soda, but has little else to do besides look cute.

The critics generally recognized *Caught Plastered* as inferior-grade Wheeler and Woolsey; *Variety* grumbled, "Will fit the combo programs on the picture's few laugh moments. Mostly chatter of a wisecracking nature, some of it new and much of it old." As to the performances, the reviewer felt that "only the Wheeler-Woolsey experience in handling gags saves the film from utter mediocrity." With a broadside directed at Dottie, *Variety* sniffed, "Miss Lee cannot handle dramatics, with her voice against her before she starts." Leonard Maltin later quipped, "Dorothy Lee came to the movies right out of high school, which stands as a strong argument for higher education. Still, she had great charm." In *Caught Plastered* the criticisms ring true. Dorothy admits, "I *couldn't* act when I was twenty. Bert wanted a musical comedy gal, and some of the pictures weren't written with that in mind." Great looks and allure were the only requisites for a W & W heroine. Dottie adds, "If Bert wanted an actress, there were a helluva lot of unemployed Katharine Cornells around in 1931."

Nevertheless, *Caught Plastered* cleaned up its initial playdates, grossing $20,458 in a fifteen-day run at the prestigious Chicago State-Lake Theater, proving that the team retained its powerhouse attraction for audiences. *Caught Plastered* dispelled any bad taste remaining from *Too Many Cooks* and *Everything's Rosie*, proving that Bert and Bob's popularity could withstand RKO's bungled team fission. Best of all, Wheeler and Woolsey were about to reward their patient fans with a true comedy classic.

12
Oh! Oh! Cleopatra (1931)

Directed by Joseph Santley. Story by Joseph Santley. Additional dialogue by Lew Lipton and Eddie Welch. Edited by John Link. A Masquers Comedy released by RKO-Pathé on August 17, 1931. 16 minutes.

Cast: Bert Wheeler (Marc Antony), Robert Woolsey (Julius Caesar), Dorothy Burgess (Cleopatra), Robert Frazer, Tyler Brooke, Tom McGuire, Claude Gillingwater, Mitchell Lewis, Montagu Love, Alec B. Francis, Crauford Kent, Kenneth Thomson, William Farnum, Walter Hiers, Hale Hamilton, Edmund Breese, Paul Nicholson, William Arnold, Richard Carlyle, George Harris, Tom Wilson, Eddie Sturgis, James Finlayson, Max Davidson, Maurice Black, William C. Camp.

Synopsis: A group of eminent professors hypothesizes on whether reincarnation is an actual possibility. Wheeler and Woolsey proceed to rediscover their past lives as Antony and Caesar in ancient Egypt.

★   ★   ★

While an anonymous collector somewhere in New England possibly owns a print of *Oh! Oh! Cleopatra,* no one has come forth to substantiate this claim. My observations are based solely upon scattered reviews at the time of its release. *Variety* was highly selective when reviewing short subjects (Warner Bros.' Vitaphone product had the inside track there) but the showbiz tabloid nevertheless did critique *Cleo*:

> Bert Wheeler and Robert Woolsey star in this production of the Masquers, Hollywood actor's organization similar to the Lambs, New York. Certain good comedy touches plus the cast names make the piece undoubted subject matter for any program and should get billing. One objection is that it's too long. Some of the chariot racing sequence which is strong-armed into the picture could be cut to advantage.
>
> One of the few shorts that attempts some kind of story continuity. Here it's a meeting of professional minds to listen to a Professor Waldo J. Sweinstein lecture about previous incarnations. He has pills that if swallowed will reveal to the swallower his retrospective life. Thus Wheeler

& Woolsey go back as Anthony and Julius Caesar with Dorothy Burgess as Cleopatra. Ends when the two come out of their trance.

The several Masquers comedies to resurface invariably reveal twenty to thirty performers enacting two-reel spoofs of movie genres—crime melodramas, Civil War stories, et cetera—somewhat like twenty-minute editions of *It's a Mad, Mad, Mad, Mad World* (1963). The available films are merely an actor's "in" joke; it is a wonder that the shorts were ever released to theaters at all (through RKO's short-subject unit, Pathé Pictures). The performers romp with all the professionalism of third graders in a Christmas pageant, most of them barely distinguishable beneath layers of makeup. Perhaps *Oh! Oh! Cleopatra* is different from other entries in the series (writers Lew Lipton and Eddie Welch were W & W regulars, while director Joseph Santley helmed the Marxes' *Cocoanuts*), but until this antiquity is properly excavated, we can only speculate on whether it is a museum piece.

Around the time this film was made, RKO hired another comedy team from the New York stage, Bobby Clark and Paul McCullough. Until the advent of VCRs and bootlegged videotapes, some reviewers spoke of Clark and McCullough in the same glowing tones reserved for Buster Keaton or Charlie Chaplin. Esteemed critics like Andrew Sarris heaped praise upon the team's "inspired" RKO two-reelers. Once the Clark and McCullough shorts reemerged on video and the real world could see how awful they actually were, the fuss died down. Bert and Bob had starred in an adaptation of C & McC's play *The Ramblers* in 1930, which became a different show with our boys in the leads. At that time Clark and McCullough had just finished a series of shorts for Fox. *Picture Play* magazine (June 1931) recounted the team's initial Hollywood fling:

> A ghastly contract—from the studio's viewpoint—was the signing of Clark and McCullough by Fox. These two men are as funny as they come on the stage, but in pictures it was a "verra, verra" different story. They had a year's contract at something like $8,000 a week. The studio put them in a series of two-reelers hopefully designed as "The Clark & McCullough Comedies" but they quickly became known around the lot as "The Clark & McCullough Tragedies." The end of that year couldn't come too soon for the studio.

Some comedy buffs will remark on the "similarities" between the two teams. Bert Wheeler and Bob Woolsey were both expert comedians whose personalities complemented each other. Bobby Clark's characterization was that of a revolting loudmouth, whereas Paul McCullough was merely a transparent straight man. In their films, Clark hastily loses his partner, spending his screen time with other members of the cast. (After McCullough's death in 1936, Bobby Clark appeared exclusively as a single with no change in his working methods—he was used to talking to himself.)

Clark and McCullough starred in twenty-two two-reel comedies for RKO through 1935, yet they never clicked with moviegoers. Sam White, who directed three Clark and McCullough shorts, reminisced about why they failed on film:

> Bobby Clark was a funny guy on the stage. In person, when we were filming, he was hyperactive. You'd think you just had witnessed a wonderful comedy performance, yet when we screened the footage, Bobby came across annoying. Clark was one of those comedians who had to be seen live. In pictures, he was flat.

Clark and McCullough's comedies are available today, but they rank among the worst short subjects ever made by any studio. RKO tried hard to bolster the films—capable directors helmed the series (White, Mark Sandrich, Ben Holmes) and production values were enhanced by the usual big-studio gloss. Reviews were almost never encouraging (the *Exhibitor* invariably found the shorts to be either "sporadically funny" or "dull and unfunny"). Whatever humor does emerge from the films comes from the terrific supporting casts—*The Iceman's Ball* (1932) features Vernon Dent, James Finlayson, and Walter Brennan effortlessly yanking the real laughs away from a frenzied Bobby Clark. Few comedians strained so hard to be so unfunny. Clark's babbling idiot strives miserably to amuse (his monotone delivery dutifully kills every line) while straight-man McCullough has even less of a screen presence than Zeppo Marx. Other Broadway comics invading Hollywood had a tough time trying to "tone it down" for the movies (witness the early Bert Lahr, Jimmy Durante, and Ed Wynn talkies). Bobby Clark eventually returned to his first love, the theater, but the miserable films he made with his partner occasionally crop up to baffle, irritate, or just plain disgust comedy fans today.

13
Peach O'Reno (1931)

Directed by William A. Seiter. Produced by William LeBaron. Supervised by John E. Burch. Original story by Tim Whelan, (uncredited) Louis A. Sarecky, and Bert Wheeler. Adaptation and dialogue by Ralph Spence, Tim Whelan, and Eddie Welch. Scenery and costumes by Max Ree. Photographed by Jack Mackenzie. Musical direction by Max Steiner. Sound recording by George D. Ellis. Film editing by Jack Kitchin. Dates of production: September 28 to October 14, 1931. Officially released by RKO on January 1, 1932. New York release date: December 23, 1931. 61 minutes.

Cast: Bert Wheeler (Wattles), Robert Woolsey (Swift), Dorothy Lee (Prudence Bruno), Zelma O'Neal (Pansy Bruno), Joseph Cawthorn (Joe Bruno), Cora Witherspoon (Aggie Bruno), Sam Hardy (Judge Jackson), Mitchell Harris (Ace Crosby), Arthur Hoyt (Secretary), Josephine Whittell (Mrs. Doubleday-Doubleday), Monty Collins (Vendor), Eddie Kane (Radio Announcer), Harry Holman (Counselor Jackson), Frank Darien (Another Counselor Jackson), Olaf Hytten (Croupier), Gordon (Bill) Elliott (Juror), Lita Chevret (cut from release print).

Synopsis: Aggie and Joe Bruno quarrel on their silver wedding anniversary and race each other to Reno for a quickie divorce. Their daughters Prudence and Pansy start for Reno, too, determined to reconcile their parents. Both divorce seekers fall into the hands of Reno's most successful lawyers, Wattles and Swift (Bert Wheeler and Bob Woolsey). Although they are partners in a firm, Wattles agrees to represent Joe's case while Swift unwittingly accepts Aggie's side of the affair.

Just when the boys are congratulating themselves on the Bruno case, Prudence and Pansy arrive, begging that the divorce be halted. Wattles falls in love with Prudence, ditto Swift with Pansy. To complicate matters, Ace Crosby, an ornery desperado from Arizona, arrives on the scene. Crosby is itching to shoot the man who got his wife a divorce, and his quarry is none other than Wattles, who hides while Swift staves the avenger off until nightfall.

Each night the huge law office is converted into a luxurious gambling casino. Desks flop over, revealing roulette wheels and gaming tables.

Stenographers strip down to skimpy chorus costumes; lawyers don tuxedos and become croupiers. A hot dance band emerges from a revolving wall while a hydraulic barroom rises from out of the floor.

Wattles masquerades as a woman in order to dodge Crosby; in the role of a professional corespondent, he pretends to be Joe Bruno's girlfriend. Swift plays gigolo with Aggie Bruno, but is sidetracked when Crosby's luck at the poker table threatens to bankrupt the casino. Meanwhile, Aggie falls prey to a rival law firm, Jackson, Jackson, Jackson, and Jackson. One of the Jacksons (Sam Hardy) has just been appointed district judge and will preside over the Bruno divorce trial. He vows that Wattles and Swift will never win a case presented before him.

Swift persuades Wattles (still dressed as an attractive widow) to flirt with Crosby in order to distract the gambler from cashing in his winnings. Wattles surreptitiously stuffs Crosby's poker chips down his bosom; as the pair shimmies across the crowded dance floor, Swift follows on all fours with a brush and dustpan to collect the cascading shower of chips. Bruno and Crosby both vie for the widow's affections until Wattles's wig inevitably comes off. Crosby shoots up the casino, pursuing Wattles, until the police arrive (they arrest Crosby for having parked next to a fire hydrant). The boys promise Prudence and Pansy to reunite their parents at the divorce trial.

The trial itself degenerates into burlesque proceedings. Inside the courtroom, a popcorn vendor hawks his wares while a glib radio commentator supplies a blow-by-blow description for the listening audience. Swift delivers an impassioned speech to the jury while Wattles takes out a violin and plays a soulful rendition of "Hearts and Flowers." With the entire courthouse weeping, Aggie and Joe break down and realize that they love each other after all. Wattles and Swift propose marriage to Prudence and Pansy while the jury suddenly produces musical instruments to play "The Wedding March" in a lively jazz combo.

★ ★ ★

Until *Peach O'Reno*, Wheeler and Woolsey comedies tended to look alike. From picture to picture the costumes changed, the locales shifted, and the casts were reshuffled, yet each film was marred by a humdrum sense of déjà vu. Audiences flocking to a Wheeler and Woolsey movie could expect an unsavory dose of palaver and a succession of scenes showing two funny guys saying unfunny things to each other. The duo—and numerous viewers—were at wits' end. Throughout 1930 and 1931, the Wheeler and Woolsey comedies accentuated "visual radio" (rambling dialogue routines that do not come full circle when they conclude, but stop—dead). A few of these films attempt stronger characterizations but end up creating a fuss over wafer-thin story lines. Although Bert and Bob were likable performers, their first five starring vehicles were disappointing, and seldom justified a seventy-minute running time.

In June 1931, *Variety* reported that "too much comedy sameness soured RKO on Wheeler & Woolsey pictures. No more home-gagged comedies for the lot." The article hinted that Bert might return to the stage when his contract expired on January 1, 1932. RKO recognized the poor quality of the team's releases, yet the studio was turning a handsome profit over some cheaply made merchandise, albeit at the expense of Bert and Bob's hard-earned reputations as versatile comedians. RKO's apparent apathy toward their biggest moneymaking attraction was typical of Hollywood's "good business" acumen: studios often feigned disinterest to keep contract renewal demands on the paltry side. (RKO had recently cultivated that ploy on Richard Dix, even though his *Cimarron* [1930] had won the studio not only some prestigious critical acclaim but its first [and subsequently, only] best picture Oscar.)

According to Dorothy Lee, Bert and Bob were upset over the quality of their recent films. "We were grinding out pictures so fast that they *had* to come out bad, so the boys complained a lot. Finally the studio gave us better stories just to shut them up."

After a season of strikeouts, Wheeler and Woolsey threw a curve ball that really connected: *Peach O'Reno* was a gem, the finest film Bert and Bob had made to date and one of the very best comedies of the period. Much of what was wrong with the earlier films was replaced by material that seemed unerringly right. The early Wheeler and Woolsey pictures often harken back to wheezy vaudeville routines; no matter how amusing individual sequences might be, viewers subconsciously anticipate the curtain to fall in lieu of a fadeout. From *Peach O'Reno* onward, Bert and Bob began to make bona fide movies, with comedy that really moved. After two years and nine pictures, the boys finally had hit their stride.

Peach O'Reno had its genesis in two eye-catching media events during the spring of 1931. In March, the Nevada State Legislature legalized gambling in the city of Reno; and on May 1, Reno passed a six weeks' residence law that granted disgruntled spouses a divorce in record time, forty-two days. With plenty of comedy angles to exploit, screenwriters began brainstorming ideas. *Variety* reported on May 20 that "Reno has knocked story departments for a cycle," [and] "almost every lot has a divorce and gambling idea slated." MGM was scouting Reno locations for a topical burlesque with Metro comedy queens Marie Dressler and Polly Moran, and RKO wasted little time in devising a similar opus for their own resident team. Staff writers Tim Whelan and Louis Sarecky concocted a "Reno story (outline) for Wheeler & Woolsey" by May 28; a first draft was then embellished by Whelan solo, who finished on June 18.

Whelan suggested several working titles for the picture, including *Six Weeks in Reno*, *Renovated in Reno*, and *Wedding Rings of Reno*. His rough draft contained quite a bit of the sharp satire, which ended up in the finished product, along with some interesting casting notes. Dorothy Lee's presence by now was a foregone conclusion, but ZaSu Pitts was suggested to portray Dottie's sister. Whelan wanted Edna May Oliver and Charles Winninger to play the quarrelsome Brunos, which would have furnished a *Rio Rita Meets Show Boat* flavor to the proceedings (Oliver and Winninger were the original Parthy Ann Hawks and Cap'n Andy in the latter production). An unfortunate loss was Stanley Fields, the gravel-voiced heavy of *Hook Line and Sinker* and *Cracked Nuts*, who was Whelan's choice for the role of the gun-toting badman.

The Reno story took on deeper relevance for Bert Wheeler. Life imitated art when a major argument erupted at the Wheeler household, culminating in Bert and Bernice's separation on June 8. Although the press announced the couple's reconciliation soon afterward, Bernice and daughter Patty remained at the Wheelers' Malibu Beach house while RKO sent the team on a personal appearance tour — of Europe. Considering how hastily the studio had announced its intentions to ditch Bert and Bob, it seemed darned nice of RKO to furnish them with such a swell "sendoff." Actually, the studio had little desire to lose such a successful attraction (unlike most RKO product that Depression year, Wheeler and Woolsey movies returned a profit), but if it were possible to retain the team's services for less money, a Hollywood charade was prime to be played.

"The studios were always ready to play cat-and-mouse games with the actors," Bert once told a friend. "After all, a lot of those joints were run by a rat."

On June 12, Bert, Bob, and RKO staff writer Eddie Welsh trekked east, with a two-week stopover in New York City. The trio went to the prizefights, attended a Lambs' Club gambol, and caught a performance of *Girl Crazy*, George Gershwin's hit Broadway musical, which RKO had purchased as a Wheeler and Woolsey vehicle. As a solo artist, Wheeler guested at a Friars' Club roast for George M. Cohan, and when buttonholed by a *Variety* reporter, Bert griped that Hollywood had caused him to become ten pounds underweight: "Getting up at six out there every morning to do pictures is all wrong." Finally, Bert and Bob sailed for Europe early in July, intending to return to New York by September 1 for a two-week appearance at the Palace Theatre.

The team was hoping for an enthusiastic reception on the Continent, but they did not anticipate the public outpouring of affection that greeted them throughout the British Isles. Woolsey considered English audiences to be "pushovers" for cornball humor, and was particularly intrigued by the Anglo-Saxon fascination for bad puns and ancient jokes. New gags were OK, but the British went into absolute hysterics over moth-eaten wheezes that could not even make it into a Wheeler and Woolsey film. Irish audiences were even better; fans greeted the bewildered comics like long-lost relatives and refused to accept payment for any of their purchases. Appearing in person in a Dublin theater, the duo was mobbed by fans who rushed onstage to congratulate them. Bert and Bob were so moved that they gave free shows throughout Ireland. They drove around for four days, doing an act on the main street of every town they passed through. Everywhere they went, the public was crazy about Wheeler and Woolsey—until Berlin. Berlin in the early 1930s was the hub of all European decadence, momentarily the city of such divergent celebrities as Kurt Weill and Albert Einstein, Max Reinhardt and Marlene Dietrich. The Great Depression only seemed to intensify the city's steamily erotic attributes. With the world going to pieces around them, Berliners exploited nearly every aesthetic interest to the hilt—theater, philosophy, literature, and (especially) sex. RKO's Berlin representative was a dyed-in-the-wool hedonist who was delighted to guide Bert and Bob through the city's wilder nightspots. As Tom Dillon relates,

> Bert and Bob were taken to a very special nightclub, the Eldorado. What made the place special was its clientele, which was comprised mainly of giant-sized transvestites. Apparently, Bob Woolsey was always trying to get Bert into a hassle in betting on things, and Bert never won once. So this time, Woolsey said to Bert, "Hey, I bet you won't dance with one of these things." Bert said, "You know I wouldn't!" Woolsey asked, "Why not? I'll give you fifty bucks if you dance with one of those gorillas." Bert told him to forget it. These guys were extremely tall and built like truck drivers.
>
> Woolsey finally said he'd give Bert $100 to dance with a male Amazon. So Bert figured, "Nobody is going to see me. I'm thousands of miles away from home. For once I can beat Woolsey on a bet."
>
> So Wheeler says, "OK, you're on." Bert gets up and goes over to this guy in a dress who's six feet tall, and motions that he'd like to dance. Little Bert is dancing up a storm with this giant across the floor. All of a sudden someone over on the other side says, "Hey, Bertie, what the heck are you doing here in Germany?" It was Jimmy Walker, mayor of New York, accompanied by his staff—all of them knew Bert!

Upon their return to the States on August 19, Bert and Bob raved to *Variety* about the hospitality they had encountered, but nary a word was spoken about the Berlin incident. Wrote *Variety*, "The boys said they had a good time abroad, but nothing especial excepting their stay in Ireland."

Plans for a personal appearance at New York's Palace Theatre were canceled while the team hustled back to the West Coast. *Peach O'Reno*, as the production was finally rechristened, was scheduled for shooting in the near future. Story conferences with the team dominated the next four weeks, with Bert particularly busy incorporating a number of bright ideas into the screenplay.

With ZaSu Pitts unavailable to portray Dottie's sister, producer William LeBaron had the good sense to cast Zelma O'Neal in the role. O'Neal had a prior career in musical comedy similar to Dottie's; Zelma's claim to a hazy immortality today rests with her 1928 Broadway showstopper, "The Varsity Drag" from *Good News*. "Poor Zelma—she was one of the greatest gals on Broadway," Dorothy Lee remembers. "She had a million dollar personality but photographed like twenty-five cents. In movies, Zelma just didn't photograph well."

Shooting commenced on September 28, 1931, with William Seiter directing his second film for the team. Principal photography was completed on October 14—the shortest schedule for a Wheeler and Woolsey picture thus far. The only incident during filming happened to Woolsey, who demonstrated that despite his looks, he was no prude between the bedsheets. Dorothy Lee remembers:

> While we were making *Peach O'Reno* a fire broke out in Woolsey's dressing room. There was a big hulabaloo—people screaming, running, not knowing what the hell they were doing.
>
> And in the middle of all this was Bob Woolsey standing in his undershorts, along with one of the chorus girls wearing his bathrobe! Woolsey had persuaded her to come to his room and "play house" with him — must've promised to make her a star or something. While they were together in bed, Woolsey was too lazy to get up and turn out the light, so he just threw a towel over the lamp. Then the towel caught on fire.
>
> The dumbest part is that Woolsey later bragged to everyone within earshot about what a dude he was, while Bert and I agreed about what a dope he was.

A handful of the best thirties comedies—the Marx Brothers' *Horse Feathers* (1932), W. C. Fields's *It's a Gift* (1934), and Laurel and Hardy's *Way Out West* (1937), among them—transcend the genre of funny pictures peopled by clowns. Add to this select list Wheeler and Woolsey's *Peach O'Reno*. Bert and Bob subsequently made several films that are funnier than *Peach*, but never before or again would they star in a movie so densely packed with gags that are meaningful to their comic screen relationship. *Peach O'Reno* demonstrates that Wheeler and Woolsey comedies could reap huge laugh dividends. *Peach* is a breezy, high-spirited comedy that borders on amiable lunacy—for a more rabid testimonial, turn to the team's severest critic, Dorothy Lee: "Lord knows, both Bert and I could tell you from experience that divorce is no picnic, but anyhow, divorcing is funny in *Peach O'Reno*."

Peach O'Reno (1931)   149

Bert and Bob's opening scene sets the stage for the double entendres that would typecast the team as purveyors of 1930s "adult" humor. But what passed for coolly sophisticated wit in 1931 emerges today as endearingly coy—as in the exchange between Bob Woolsey and a prospective divorcee:

> MRS. DOUBLEDAY: You remember me?
> BOB: Can't say that I do, no, can't say that I do...
> [*Mrs. Doubleday crosses her legs and raises her skirt slightly above the knee.*]
> BOB: [*recognizing her legs*] Oh—yeah, yeah!
> MRS. DOUBLEDAY: [*pointing down at her legs*] Are you looking at these?
> BOB: I beg your pardon, ma'am, I'm above that, I'm above that!

Joseph Cawthorn and Cora Witherspoon emerged as memorable foils, portraying the combative Joe and Aggie Bruno. Cawthorn marked his return engagement with the team (his trademark Yiddish accent was pretty much a dead herring in the magnolia fields of *Dixiana*). Here he acquits himself splendidly in a dialogue contretemps with Bert Wheeler:

> BERT: Where is this ball and chain of yours now?
> JOE: She's right here in Reno. She's getting a divorce, too.
> BERT: Well, that's fine! Tonight I'll arrange to have her see you with a beautiful woman.
> JOE: Couldn't you arrange for her *not* to see me?
> BERT: Aw, no, no. Your wife has got to see you with a beautiful woman.
> JOE: Well, it sounds dangerous—heh, heh! I place myself entirely in your disposition. But remember—none of these "breaches of promises" things!
> BERT: Aw, you're safe! Very few women would marry you.
> JOE: Very few would be enough!

Cora Witherspoon is best remembered today as the hatchet-faced spouse of Egbert Sousé in W. C. Fields's *Bank Dick* (1940). Her buzzardlike appearance in *Peach* brands her as fair game for Woolsey:

> BOB: What's the matter? Is your husband a sheik, or would that be insulting the Arabs?
> CORA: Oh, I've had so much trouble. Why, I've aged six months in the past year! All night long I've been doubled up with such a terrible pain—
> BOB: Ah, then, you're still living with your husband! Have you any children?
> CORA: Two lovely daughters—they look just like me!
> BOB: Well—what do you care, so long as they have their health! Do you contemplate getting married again?
> CORA: Listen, if I ever get married again, I want a man who's easily pleased—

> BOB: That's the kind you'll get.
> CORA: One thing you can bet: I'll never marry another man who snores.
> BOB: That's a good idea, and I'll bet you'll have a lot of fun finding out!

Things really start jumping when the Arizona badman Ace Crosby (Mitchell Harris) arrives on the scene, a-gunnin' for Bert. Crosby vows to kill Bert that very night in the team's casino parlors. While Bert hides, Bob strikes a fast-talk deal with Crosby for himself. Bert and Bob then indulge in the following consultation:

> BOB: I saved our lives, didn't I?
> BERT: You saved your own, but you certainly sprinkled lilies on *my* chest!
> BOB: Well, you don't want to separate the firm by having us both shot, do you? I've got a great idea: I'm going to be with Mrs. Bruno tonight, so you doll up and be Mr. Bruno's lady friend!
> BERT: Oh, no, no. I could never pass for a woman. I don't look masculine enough.
> BOB: Don't be a sap! If you're a woman, you'll escape this man-eater, Crosby.
> BERT: Gee, that's right!

The casino sequence occupies approximately half of the film's scant sixty-one-minute running time. It is one of the finest episodes in the entire Wheeler and Woolsey canon, with a standout performance by Bert in drag as the Widow Hanover. The character was apparently invented by Wheeler himself, as Tom Dillon relates:

> Bert told me that he got the idea for the female impersonation from when he and Woolsey appeared in the English music halls. Comedy female impersonators like Arthur Lucan (who was beloved by fans as Old Mother Riley) were a staple in the theater. Bert figured it was a comedy idea that maybe he could draw upon.

As the slightly tipsy and flirtatious widow, sporting a blond wig, silky evening gown, and mink wrap, Bert contributes an incredibly effective portrayal, rivaling the better-known impersonations of both Jack Lemmon in *Some Like It Hot* (1959) and Dustin Hoffman in *Tootsie* (1982). The characterization is flawless, proving beyond a shadow of a doubt that Bert Wheeler was a vastly underrated comedy performer. At one point Bert (as the widow) and Bob perform a dancing duet for the patrons; in a hilarious bit of sexual cross-purposes, each alternates trying to lead the other around the dance floor. When the puny Woolsey repeatedly fails to hoist his partner into the air, Bert grabs Bob by the neck in unladylike fashion and plants Woolsey on *his* shoulder.

Some of Wheeler's dialogue in the casino sequence was especially racy

Bob and Bert trip the light fantastic in *Peach O'Reno*.

and sent the editors of family magazines like *Parents* on the warpath. Adults enjoyed Bert and Bob's antics, but kids loved them, too. Their tender ears were polluted by the following vintage spice:

> ZELMA: Have you got a good lawyer, Pa?
> BERT: [*as the widow*] I should say he has! Charming fellow, too.
> DOTTIE: Oh, then you know him?
> BERT: [*forgetting himself*] Know him? I sleep with him!

Bert's encounter with Ace Crosby is another highlight. Speaking in a coquettish falsetto, the widow works "her" seductive charms on Crosby until he's lured onto the dance floor. Having stuffed Crosby's substantial poker-chip winnings down his dress, Bert proceeds to shimmy about with Crosby as Bob crawls along with whisk broom and dustpan to collect the falling chips. Nestled between the legs of the dancers, Bob takes the time to fastidiously brush one patron's trousers, and dallies long enough to admire a short-skirted flapper's legs.

Bert and Dorothy perform a delightful number called "From Niagara Falls to Reno," in which Bert tap-dances atop a huge kettle drum while Dorothy performs a ministriptease (she's wearing the 1930s equivalent of hot pants underneath a floor-length skirt). "It's a wonder I didn't take my blouse off!" Dottie remarks today.

The trial scene which concludes *Peach O'Reno* is somewhat of a disappointment, particularly after the great comedy stuff that preceded it. There is still some fun to be had, especially from the team's encounter with Judge Jackson, played with an erudite dishonesty by Sam Hardy (he's the urbane theatrical agent in *King Kong* [1933]).

For someone with an extensive background in comedy and music, Zelma O'Neal is assigned little of the former and none of the latter. A *National Exhibitor's Association* review (November 1931) of the film's preview sheds light on one of Zelma's deleted scenes:

> One particularly funny sequence is the farce love making of Woolsey and Miss O'Neal. It's a riot, with Miss O'Neal copping a slight edge for laughs. We never have been able to understand why this young comedienne, who was a tremendous hit on the Broadway stage, hasn't been in more demand in pictures. It's a safe bet that she will be after this picture.

A continuity summary of the film exists with a complete description of the expurgated scene. The sequence is outrageously funny in print, but the roughhouse romance between Zelma and Bob would have been the rawest kind of burlesque horseplay. The unlikely lovebirds affectionately wrestle about the room, culminating with Zelma wrapping her legs around Woolsey's waist while her head drags along the floor, surpassing even W. C. Fields's raunchy tooth-extraction routine from *The Dentist* (1932). *Peach O'Reno*'s episode was peppered further by this dialogue:

> ZELMA: Are girls the only thing you think about?
> BOB: Yes, but I'm very broadminded. You see, I'm a man about town and a fool about women.
> ZELMA: Well, start fooling around, will you? Don't tell me that you give up?

Woolsey and Zelma O'Neal's wrestling match–courtship was deleted from *Peach O'Reno*.

>BOB: I'm all in.
>ZELMA: That's all right, I'll wait.

Peach O'Reno was bestowed a favorable nod by the critics upon its release in late 1931. The *New York Daily News* called it "a very good wisecracking comedy," while the trade paper *Exhibitor's Herald* found *Peach* to be "another swell low comedy (we confess to liking [this type] when it's well done)." *Variety*, which understandably found much to gripe about in the team's recent releases, was not entirely bowled over by this movie's superiority: "Director and players seemed to feel that they were working with thin stuff and went to extremes to bolster it all up with rowdy byplay."

Producer William LeBaron was destined to be ousted from RKO within a matter of months; his replacement at the studio would someday be acclaimed as Hollywood's greatest producer and the creative force behind the decade's most prestigious film, *Gone with the Wind* (1939). By 1931, David O. Selznick aspired to make films of literary importance; yet somehow he had to digest the fact that RKO's chief moneymakers were a streetwise urchin, his cigar-chomping partner, and their flapper girlfriend. Selznick accepted the news but didn't enjoy the notion one bit. Things were about to change at RKO—and those plans did not include Bert, Bob, or Dottie.

14
Girl Crazy (1932)

Directed by William A. Seiter. Executive producer, David O. Selznick. Produced by William LeBaron. From the musical comedy *Girl Crazy*. Book by John McGowan and Guy Bolton. Lyrics by Ira Gershwin. Music by George Gershwin. Adaptation by Herman L. Mankiewicz. Screenplay by Tim Whelan. Dialogue by Eddie Welch and Walter DeLeon. Scenery and costumes by Max Ree. Photographed by J. Roy Hunt. Musical direction by Max Steiner. Sound recording by Hugh McDowell, Jr. Film editing by Arthur Roberts. Dates of production: December 15, 1931, to January 12, 1932. Retakes (directed by Norman Taurog) filmed mid–February to February 28, 1932. Released by RKO on March 27, 1932. 75 minutes.

Cast: Bert Wheeler (Jimmy Deegan), Robert Woolsey (Slick Foster), Dorothy Lee (Patsy), Eddie Quillan (Danny Churchill), Mitzi Green (Tessie Deegan), Brooks Benedict (George Mason), Kitty Kelly (Kate Foster), Arline Judge (Molly Gray), Stanley Fields (Lank Sanders), Lita Chevret (Mary), Crispin Martin (Pete), Nat Pendleton (Motorcycle Cop), Monty Collins, Alfred Cooke (Bartenders), Josephine Ramos, Esther Garcia (Señoritas), High Eagle (Eagle Rock), Max Steiner (Orchestra Leader).

Synopsis: Manhattan playboy Danny Churchill (Eddie Quillan) is sent to Custerville, Arizona, by his father, where he will be far removed from the allure of predatory females. Danny discovers that Custerville is a siesta village, populated by deadbeat cowpokes, in dire need of urbanization and fast women. He sets about converting a dude ranch into a stylish casino and imports a busload of cosmopolitan showgirls. Danny summons Slick Foster (Robert Woolsey), a crooked crapshooter from Chicago, and his wife, Kate (Kitty Kelly), to operate his gambling hall. Flat broke, the couple hails a taxi manned by Jimmy Deegan (Bert Wheeler) and make the two-thousand-mile trek in Deegan's dilapidated auto.

Custerville is no sleepy hitching-post town after all; each newly elected sheriff is routinely shot by the local outlaws, burly Lank Sanders (Stanley Fields) and his grinning sidekick, Pete (Crispin Martin). Arriving in Custerville, Slick ponders lynching and its ramifications when Lank Sanders selects Jimmy as "fall guy" for the latest dead sheriff. If Jimmy is lynched, Sanders can state that Deegan was responsible for killing the last sheriff, and Slick won't have to pay off his staggering cab fare. Fortunately for Deegan, local cowgirl Patsy (Dorothy Lee) halts the proceedings in the nick of time, while the arrival of Danny's New York showgirls permanently distracts the murderous cowpokes from their mission. Romance quickly blossoms between Patsy and Jimmy.

Danny falls in love with Molly Gray (Arline Judge), Custerville's petite postmaster. Molly becomes jealous when the Manhattan chorines flirt with Danny; to spite him, she socializes with George Mason (Brooks Benedict), a slick character from back East who hitched a bus ride with the girls. Also aboard as a stowaway was Jimmy's kid sister, Tessie (Mitzi Green), who is determined to collect the $465.30 taxi fare Slick owes her brother.

Opening night at Danny's casino is a smashing success. Meanwhile, business over at Lank Sanders's gambling hall suffers from the feminine competition. Scheming Lank announces his candidacy for sheriff, intending to close Danny's business once elected. Slick and Danny ponder whom they could nominate to run against Lank, knowing full well that running for sheriff in Custerville is akin to committing suicide. Naturally, naive Jimmy is selected to run for office. Jimmy wins the election when Tessie hides the ballot box, stealing Lank's votes.

Lank goes gunning for the new sheriff; Jimmy and Slick disguise themselves as Indians and escape detection. Molly catches Danny reminiscing about old times with his chorine friends; angered and hurt, she hastily decides to travel to San Luz, Mexico, with lecherous George Mason. Danny, Jimmy, Patsy, Slick, Kate, and Tessie follow in close pursuit, hoping to dissuade Molly from making any foolish mistakes.

Lank and Pete likewise follow the gang to San Luz, planning to kill Jimmy that very night. Slick tries to hypnotize Lank but is repeatedly thwarted in his attempts. Jimmy and Lank resort to a raucous exhibition of fisticuffs while Molly and Danny reconcile their differences. Jimmy and Slick overpower the heavies (with the aid of some giant vases), leading to a kissing fadeout for the three happy couples.

★ ★ ★

RKO was in a bottomless financial pit when David Sarnoff assigned dynamic movie maven David O. Selznick the herculean task of revitalizing his stricken studio. Although the young mogul had performed minor miracles at the beleaguered Paramount lot, Selznick was chafing under the restrictive control of B. P. Schulberg, Paramount's West Coast production chief. Assured by Sarnoff that he would enjoy near-total creative autonomy, Selznick arrived at RKO's Hollywood studio in October 1931.

Girl Crazy (1932)

Sizing up the pictures in progress, Selznick did not like what he saw. Dorothy Lee remembers the rest:

> During the Depression it was the Wheeler and Woolsey movies that got RKO on its feet, but Selznick wanted to produce "important" pictures. When he met the boys he said to them, "Which one is Wheeler and which is Woolsey?" Oh, he hated them! See, Selznick couldn't be bothered with people whom he didn't find interesting. It didn't matter whether or not your films made big money for the studio. "Cleaning house" gave Selznick the chance to change the company's image. We were on our way out, and he let us know it.

RKO employees were given a sixty-day probation period, after which Selznick would determine their further value to the company. Wheeler and Woolsey saw the handwriting on the wall, although their own arrangements would be slightly extended. Under the team's January 1931 contracts, they were signed for fifty-two weeks or until five feature-length pictures were completed. Bert and Bob had completed three films under this pact. The long-running Broadway hit musical *Girl Crazy* had recently been purchased for the duo at $33,000, quite a bargain during those rocky Depression days. *Girl Crazy* became the last RKO production to be personally supervised by William LeBaron. Supplemented by an outstanding score from George and Ira Gershwin, *Girl Crazy* would be RKO's first major musical since Hollywood's so-called moratorium on the genre in mid-1930.

Eddie Quillan was an appealing young comedian who had been appearing in energetic little comedies for Pathé like *The Tip Off* in 1931, when RKO acquired the Pathé Studio. Eddie recalled how he eventually landed a part in *Girl Crazy*.

> I was working at the RKO-Pathé Studio and had one more picture to make under my contract. I was there for five years. They told me that they didn't have a story for me, but that there was some interest over at RKO, the parent studio.
>
> So I went over there and met David O. Selznick. He talked about *Girl Crazy*—informed me about it being a big hit on Broadway (which I had known), and that Wheeler and Woolsey, Dorothy Lee, and Arline Judge would be in it. So I said, "Fine, because I haven't got a story over at my own studio, so I might as well go to work here." Later I received the script. When I read it, I went back to see David. I don't know exactly what I saw in the script, but I didn't particularly care for it.
>
> I told him, "The way this is written, I think you're going to have to go back and shoot a few weeks more of retakes." He said, "No, I think everything will be fine." So I said, "OK."

Girl Crazy was adapted for the movies by Herman J. Mankiewicz, the hellion screenwriter whose talent dazzled the brightest in collaboration with Orson Welles on *Citizen Kane* (1941). A great deal of rewriting was required to make the material palatable for movie audiences. Lower East Side favorite Willie Howard essayed the comedy lead on Broadway, portraying Gieber Goldfarb, a schmoozy Manhattan cab driver who brings his fare west to Arizona. According to RKO's synopsis of the play, Gieber hopes to seduce a pretty cowgirl named Patsy (Peggy O'Connor), "knowing his religion will protect him from marriage with an Irisher." Later, Gieber struggles with Lank (Carleton Macy), the villain of the piece, over a loaded shotgun. "Gieber gets possession and is about to shoot him. Lank offers $50 for the return of his gun. This is too much for Gieber's Hebrew blood, and he promptly sits down to make a bargain."

The offensive Jewish stereotypes were laundered out of the story line, while repugnant Gieber Goldfarb was anglicized into Jimmy Deegan, alias Bert Wheeler, a taxi driver transplanted to Chicago. Mankiewicz completed a revised draft on December 1, 1931, and submitted his final script on December 12. Shortly before filming began, Bert and his wife, Bernice, came to a parting of the ways. The split was amicable enough: "We just have different interests," Bernice confided to the press, "but we'll remain good friends." Bert's two-year-old daughter, Patricia, remained in her mother's custody. "Bert didn't seem to be distressed about his failed second marriage," Dottie remarks, "maybe because our careers were in bigger trouble, I don't know."

Filming began on December 15 under William Seiter's lively direction. Eddie Quillan remembers his first day of shooting:

> I made myself up for the part and came to the set. The scenes I had to do were with Woolsey. But the camera filmed me only from the back of my neck. So we got through that day. The next day when I came on the set, the camera positions were reversed from the day before. Bill Seiter said to me, "Eddie, you haven't got your makeup on." I asked, "Oh, you mean my face?" He said, "Yeah!" I said, "I worked with these guys all day yesterday, and you never saw my face, so I thought I'd just make up my neck." Bert got hysterical at that.
>
> Anyway, there were no major problems encountered, and I thought we had some marvelous numbers in this first cut. I'm so sorry now that I didn't get a chance to see the rough cut the first time we completed the picture.

Girl Crazy wrapped production on January 12, 1932. Dorothy Lee recalls that "we had finished the film and I had all these great Gershwin songs; I sang 'They're Writing Songs of Love but Not for Me.' I was looking forward to seeing this film when it was assembled." "But," Eddie

Quillan adds, "we were all called back to shoot for two more weeks' worth of rewrites." Norman Taurog, whom RKO had borrowed from Paramount to direct W & W's forthcoming *Hold 'Em Jail*, was paid a bonus salary to shoot new scenes for *Girl Crazy*.

"Selznick butchered all my scenes," Dottie, even today, recalls:

> Out of the clear blue sky, Arline Judge (she was under the right guy, Selznick) was given everything I had to do, and Kitty Kelly, who couldn't sing, was given "I've Got Rhythm." Kitty Kelly was going with William LeBaron, our producer, you see.
>
> I didn't want to do the thing anymore, but Bert said, "Well, we're getting a few thousand bucks for this. We're all out after *Girl Crazy*. Selznick hates us, so what do you care? Do it!" He was right.
>
> You know, I was pretty hurt because RKO starred the three of us in it and I ended up playing a bit part in *Girl Crazy*. That was Selznick's doing. He didn't care, didn't pay any attention to any of us. He stayed at RKO a year or so before going on to bigger and better things at MGM.

"None of us really cared about *Girl Crazy* anymore when we saw David [Selznick] reshooting perfectly good scenes with pointless ones," Eddie Quillan remembers.

> Instead of correcting the film's faults, David seemed to be intensifying the problems. So we all started to really loosen up. I would do double takes in rehearsals. They weren't really placed in the retakes that we were shooting—they would've been overdone. But it got to a point where Bert would call me "swivel neck" and he was trying to do these "takes" right back to me!

Quillan was disenchanted with the finished film. "I didn't want to see it then," Eddie recalls, "and I didn't ever see it until 1985. It's really chopped up from what we had done. The numbers I worked on were lost." Dot Lee didn't see the film at the time, and said, "I *never* want to see the damn thing!" The musical numbers in the Selznick version of *Girl Crazy* are bastardizations of the Gershwin originals. "I've Got Rhythm" is mutilated by a raspy-voiced Kitty Kelly, swamped by a ridiculously overblown presentation set in a dance hall, replete with mounted bison heads swaying to the music and crazy cacti performing stop-motion gyrations à la *King Kong*. "But Not for Me" is *recited* between Arline Judge and Eddie Quillan in record-breaking time, while "Bidin' My Time" is heard as background accompaniment in the film's opening scene. "Embraceable You" and "Sam and Delilah" were jettisoned from the film's score.

On November 27, 1931, RKO paid the Gershwins two thousand dollars for a "new" composition, "You've Got What Gets Me," to be sung in *Girl Crazy* by Bert Wheeler and Dorothy Lee. Actually, only Ira Gershwin's lyrics were new—George had composed the song for a 1927 musical, *Funny Face*, starring Fred and Adele Astaire. But Fred frowned upon the number as unsuitable to his style. Back in the trunk it went, only to be recycled as a delightful song-and-dance specialty for Bert and Dorothy.

David O. Selznick had a Hollywood reputation as a hedonistic hellcat (among producers, he wasn't alone) with an insatiable appetite for food, gambling, movies, and women. Actresses from Fay Wray to an underage Shirley Temple were reportedly propositioned or stalked around the office desk by the voracious producer; Dottie, too, recalled having to dodge out of his groping range, rebuffing Selznick's invitation to dally on the casting couch. She later suspected that he retaliated by undercutting her one number with Bert, employing numerous cutaways as she sang and selecting an unflattering camera angle (Dottie is hidden from view by a pillar) during their dance routine.

Variety claimed that Selznick's retakes exceeded $200,000, bringing the total negative cost of *Girl Crazy* up to $532,000, making it the most expensive of all of Bert and Bob's starring vehicles. The lavish, star-laden, and Technicolored *Rio Rita*, by contrast, cost only $33,000 more in the boom days before the stock market crashed. *Girl Crazy* would have to gross at least $750,000 before it could turn a profit, a virtual impossibility during those lean Depression years. For a man supposedly committed to economic efficiency, David O. Selznick was spending depleted company funds with a reckless abandon on a project he had not initiated and a comedy team he did not care for. To quote Eddie Quillan, "Don't even try to figure it out."

Despite numerous production difficulties and the botched musical numbers, *Girl Crazy* actually presents Wheeler and Woolsey at their comedic best. Their routines in this picture betray none of the strain that went into crafting the film, and it is a polished, stylish production. Today the 1932 *Girl Crazy* emerges as an abomination only in terms of its Gershwin score, but the 1943 MGM remake, with its overblown musical interludes, was no more faithful to the original intent. Only Ethel Merman and Ginger Rogers, from the original cast, could have recaptured the 1930 Broadway edition's spirit. RKO never had any intention of utilizing either actresses' services, however.

Bert and Bob's comedy turns in *Girl Crazy* are a sheer delight, beginning with their first encounter on a busy Chicago street corner. Woolsey and his wife (Kitty Kelly) have been hired to manage an Arizona gambling casino when Bob spots Bert's idle taxicab.

> BOB: C'mon, we'll take this cab to Arizona—
> KITTY: Are you crazy?
> BOB: Listen, I know what I'm doing! Has it ever struck you that railroads want money in advance for tickets?

KITTY: [*glumly*] It struck me.
BOB: Get the grip, Mama. [*to Bert*] Son! Custerville, Arizona.
BERT: Yes, sir—Where did you say?
BOB: [*regally*] Custerville, Arizona.
BERT: Arizona—is that east or west?
BOB: Go west, young man, go west!

While stopping for directions at an Arizona gas station, Bert's towline accidentally catches onto a life-sized mobile cutout of a motorcycle cop. Riding along the open highway, Bert eyes the "policeman" in his rearview mirror with mounting apprehension. Pulling to the side of the road, Bert and Bob share a laugh over Wheeler's discovery that the stern-looking officer is only a cardboard cutout. "Mama," Woolsey chortles to his wife, "it's a dummy!" "He was in good company," Kitty replies disgustedly.

Discarding the troublesome advertisement, Bert's jalopy continues, only to be tailed by a genuine highway patrolman (Nat Pendleton) who bears a striking resemblance to the fake "cop." Bob spots Pendleton first. "Hey," he calls to Wheeler, "I thought you said you got rid of that dummy!" "I did," Bert responds, staring in disbelief. "It must've got caught again. I'll shake it off." Wheeler weaves his cab across the road, nearly causing Pendleton to ram head-on into an oncoming sedan. Unable to ditch the cop, Bob begins tossing assorted junk at the hapless patrolman in an effort to "unhinge" him from their cab. Nat Pendleton's indignant reactions to this lawless affront are priceless (at one point he reflexively reaches for his holster). Having had his fill, Pendleton revs up his siren. "What are you blowing your horn for?" Bob asks Bert. "I didn't!" Wheeler replies. Bert tries his taxi horn for comparison—a wheezy honk—whereupon the boys realize that something is amiss. Pulling over to the side. Wheeler's good intentions at rectifying their mistake go awry (Bert explains to Pendleton, "We thought you was a dummy!"). Nat decides to acquaint the city slickers with a local jail for about ten days.

Finally on the open road again, Bert loses his brakes while careening down a steep, winding road. "Don't worry," a petrified Wheeler reassures his passengers. "I've never had a wreck and I've been driving this car for nine years." Panic-stricken, Woolsey retorts, "You mean you've never had a car but you've been driving this *wreck* for nine years!"

Some of the intended satire is still pretty sharp. Inducing Bert to run for sheriff, Bob inquires, "What do you know about politics?" "Nothing," Wheeler replies. "I came from an honest family." Bert wonders, "What does the job pay? Any graft? You know—not that I'd take any!" While Bert delivers a campaign speech, rival candidate Lank Sanders (Stanley Fields) arrives at Wheeler's election headquarters with murder in his eye. With Lank's six-shooter pointed at their backs, Bert and Bob attempt to convince the townspeople to cast their votes for the brusque badman:

High Eagle (left) and Stanley Fields seem doubtful of Bert and Bob's pedigree in *Girl Crazy*.

>   BOB: Folks, this is our last chance. They say that Lank ain't fit to sleep with a pig! Well, that's wrong—I say he is!
>   LANK: That's telling 'em!
>   BOB: Now you take his good points, one by one—
>   BERT: That makes two.
>   BOB: He can also give all his time to office, 'cause he's a bachelor. All his ancestors were bachelors.
>   BERT: Now, then, folks, I ask you—what does that make Lank?
>   [*The townspeople laugh uproariously*]
>   LANK: Go on—tell 'em, tell 'em!
>   BERT AND BOB: They know it, they know it!

The comedy only falters in one of the later Taurog-directed sequences. Bert and Bob have disguised themselves as Indians to hide from Lank; Lank happens to arrive on the scene with a genuine Indian, Eagle Rock (played by High Eagle). The boys are stymied until they begin conversing in pig latin with the streetwise brave. "And we thought you were a real Indian!" Woolsey tells the Native American between chuckles. Bert, Bob, and Eagle Rock perform a fast dance shuffle offstage. This silly and gratuitous sequence could have been performed wittily in the musical theater, but on film it is an irritating episode that disrupts the narrative flow.

A later encounter with some Mexican señoritas is likewise extraneous but still funny:

> SEÑORITA: [*grabs Bert's lapels*] I warn you, señor! When I love a man, I love him all over!
> BERT: [*nervously*] All over what?
> SEÑORITA: All over the house, the bathroom, the garden, the street!
> BERT: [*quavering*] Well, maybe I can last a coupla blocks, anyhow.

Bumping into Lank Sanders, Bob nicknames the burly menace "Frankenstein"—it is the movies' first, but by no means last, reference to Boris Karloff's monster-protagonist, who debuted on November 21, 1931.

After being forced to pull his punches in *Hook Line and Sinker* and *Cracked Nuts*, Stanley Fields tears loose with Bert in an uproarious last-reel donnybrook. Frenzied punches, open-handed slaps, furious yells, outrageous strangleholds, and spectacular tackles highlight the mismatch of the century. Bob tries to hypnotize Lank Sanders into unconsciousness, but ends up putting himself into a trance when a mirrored door is opened just as Woolsey says "Sleep." Wheeler can break the spell by snapping his fingers—only he is too nervous to produce the snapping sound. Poor Bert is chased all over the room, screaming "Snap-snap!" to no effect in a hilarious, breathtaking finale.

Girl Crazy received mixed notices from critics upon its release. *Time* merely synopsized the plot without indicating whether the movie was funny. As an afterthought, the reviewer stated that "Wheeler giggles constantly and Woolsey chews cigars"—thanks for the news. Mordaunt Hall of the *New York Times* raved about the film, declaring that "the melodious side of this adventure is unimportant, but with Bert Wheeler and Robert Woolsey at their best, it offers a brand of humor that few could resist."

Bert and Bob were about to write finis to RKO and Selznick with one last film, but Dorothy Lee was given the old heave-ho even sooner. On April 11, 1932, RKO formally divulged that Dottie was off the contract list—the same day that the studio announced a "strengthening" of Selznick's position among the RKO hierarchy.

15
Hold 'Em Jail (1932)

Directed by Norman Taurog. Executive producer, David O. Selznick. Associate producer, Harry Joe Brown. Unit manager, Charles Richards. Assistant directors, Mark Sandrich and Bert Gilroy. Screenplay by Walter DeLeon, S. J. Perelman, Eddie Welch, and (uncredited) Mark Sandrich. Story by Tim Whelan and Lew Lipton. Radio dialogue by John P. Medbury. Continuity by Al Ray. Art direction by Carroll Clark. Photographed by Leonard Smith. Musical direction by Max Steiner. Film editing by Arthur Roberts. Dates of production: April 4 to May 13, 1932. Additional footage filmed circa June 20–22. Released by RKO on September 16, 1932. 65 minutes.

Cast: Bert Wheeler (Curley Harris), Robert Woolsey (Spider Robbins), Edna May Oliver (Violet Jones), Robert Armstrong (Radio Announcer), Roscoe Ates (Slippery Sam Brown, Captain of the Bidemore Team), Edgar Kennedy (Warden Elmer Jones), Betty Grable (Barbara Jones), Warren Hymer (Steele), Paul Hurst (Butch), G. Pat Collins (Mr. C. White, aka Whitey), Stanley Blystone (Kravette), Jed Prouty (Warden Charles Clark), Spencer Charters (The Governor), John Sheehan (Mike Maloney), Monty Collins (Referee), Leo Willis (Riggs), Eddie Sturgis (Riggs's Pal), Mike Donlin (Coach), Harry Watson (Sam's Son), Ben Taggart (Doorman), Marshall Ruth (Nance Prisoner), Ernie Adams, Billy Engle, George Ovey, Charlie Hall (Assistant Referees), Al Alt (Doctor), Alfred Cooke (Timekeeper), Bobby Barber, Pat Harmon (Unnamed Jailbirds), Clem Beauchamp (Trusty), Lee Phelps (Spike), Frank Mills (Hood), George Magrill (Policeman), Charles Sullivan, Jim Thorpe, Dutch Hendrian, John Kelly (Football Players, Lynwood Team), Ward Bond, Ernie Pinckert, Marshall Duffield, Norm Dunca, Jim Kusick, Ray Baker, Dink Templeton, Harold Schlickemeyer, Nate Barrager (Football Players at Practice).

Synopsis: Elmer Jones (Edgar Kennedy), warden of Bidemore Prison, is an avid football enthusiast caught in a dilemma. His gridiron team of convicts is so awful that rival prison Lynwood would rather play against a boys' reform school. Butch (Paul Hurst), Bidemore's coach, places a distress call to mobster Mike Maloney (John Sheehan), president of Bidemore's alumni association. Maloney agrees to recruit players for the upcoming season, enlisting the aid of henchman Whitey (G. Pat Collins) to shanghai some fresh talent.

Curley Harris (Bert Wheeler) and Spider Robbins (Robert Woolsey) are high-pressure novelty salesmen determined to sell their trinkets to Maloney's nightclub. Spider brags about Curley's alleged prowess as a football hero, leading Whitey to frame them for a jail term. Whitey persuades the duo to pretend to hold up the club with toy water pistols and then substitutes real guns. The scheme succeeds, and the boys face a stretch in the hoosegow.

Romance develops as soon as the boys are escorted into the warden's office. Curley falls for Barbara Jones (Betty Grable), Elmer's nubile daughter, while Spider becomes enamored with crusty Aunt Violet (Edna May Oliver), the warden's flighty sister. Although Curley and Spider irritate Elmer to the brink of murderous intent, Aunt Violet's affection for Spider ensures that the boys are appointed as trusties.

The team foils a daring prison break by hosing down the escapees, but Curley also accidentally douses the hapless warden. As punishment, Curley is consigned to breaking boulders in a cliffside quarry. When Bidemore's greatest football star, Slippery Sam Brown (Roscoe Ates), is paroled, Spider fabricates a tale about Curley being "the greatest quarterback in the world." The boys immediately become the warden's pets and go into training on the team.

On the day of the big game between Bidemore and Lynwood prisons, Curley and Spider spot Whitey, now a convict himself, on the players' bench. Spider obtains a bottle of chloroform from the first-aid kit, and Curley surreptitiously knocks out members of both teams. As they keel over, replacements are brought on the field—including the reluctant Whitey. The boys simultaneously extract a signed confession out of the hood and win the game for dear old Bidemore.

★　★　★

Prison pictures were all the rage in the early 1930s, even before the first flourishings of the gangster-movie cycle. John Ford's *Up the River* (1930), Howard Hawks's *Criminal Code* (1931), and especially MGM's landmark *The Big House* (1930) set the trend for grim, uncompromising macho entertainment. The casts were predominantly male and the films were generally geared toward the masculine contingent in the audience. For once Hollywood brushed aside that all-important arbiter of a film's success—the woman's angle—and fashioned a series of films so ruthless and hard-hitting that male viewers alone could guarantee the films' box office-earnings.

Close on the heels of the new movie formula came the subgenre:

parodies, send-ups, and spoofs. Laurel and Hardy wasted little time poking fun at *The Big House* with their *Pardon Us* (1931), while Wheeler and Woolsey tapped all the major prison dramas for *Hold 'Em Jail*, an achingly funny distillation as hilarious today as it must have been over sixty years ago. With a retinue of six top writers (including the dean of the whimsical non sequitur, S. J. Perelman), *Hold 'Em Jail* is chock full of comic exuberance and gusto; you would hardly suspect it to be the team's swan song under Selznick's hostile sponsorship.

Director Norman Taurog became acquainted with Bert and Bob's style while shooting retakes on *Girl Crazy* several months earlier. Taurog was schooled in two-reel comedies under Jack White's Educational Pictures back in the 1920s; his work with the great neglected silent comedian Lloyd Hamilton ranks among the finest visual humor ever put on celluloid. Stringing his comedy scenes together like sausage links, Taurog concentrated his energies on individual gag sequences. Although a formal plot line is tossed to the wind, *Hold 'Em Jail* doesn't meander from the basic premise: Bert and Bob are framed and sent to prison; somehow they will prove their innocence, but in the meantime they try to survive behind bars. The subplot, featuring a football-fanatic warden (Edgar Kennedy) whose life revolves around his jailbird team, neatly anticipates *The Longest Yard* (1974), starring another Burt (Reynolds), with Eddie Albert essaying the Edgar Kennedy role.

Hold 'Em Jail was the first Wheeler and Woolsey picture filmed entirely away from RKO's Hollywood studio. Headquarters were established at the recently acquired Pathé lot in Culver City. From Pathé, the Wheeler and Woolsey unit would make the haul all the way across the street to Metro-Goldwyn-Mayer. MGM's high-walled prison facade, built for *The Big House*, was leased by RKO for Bert and Bob's epic about life in the calaboose. Securing use of the set could not have been too difficult, since Selznick was Louis B. Mayer's son-in-law.

Hold 'Em Jail went before the cameras on April 4, 1932, and was scheduled for a cozy three-week shoot. Perfectionist that Selznick was, he characteristically picked nits over every facet of the production, keeping the unit active past the allotted time frame, through May 13. Loath to let Wheeler and Woolsey go before every shot in the can met his exacting standards (their contracts would terminate upon completion of their roles), Selznick once again pushed the budget (ceilinged at $275,000) past the profit margin and into the red at $408,000. Once the dust cleared, *Jail* was destined to ultimately lose $55,000, despite good reviews and respectable business.

Even though the slammer setting would seem to be Bert and Bob's most restricting locale, a new spirit of anarchic humor permeates the halls of Bidemore Prison with the boys' arrival. Unlike poor Laurel and Hardy, whose good intentions continually landed them in solitary confinement, Wheeler and Woolsey's boisterous bravura earns them the run of the joint before long. Bob arouses the ire of their jailer (Stanley Blystone) by calling him "busboy" and instructing Blystone to "take this pillow out and have every feather in it washed and ironed before morning." *Hold 'Em Jail*'s most wildly comical scene follows, with the boys assigned to the forge in the blacksmith shop. Neatly anticipating the Three Stooges' classic Columbia shorts, Wheeler and Woolsey agree to aid a fellow felon (the genial but dumb Warren Hymer, repeating his role from *Up the River*) in removing his shackled ball and chain. Bob places a chisel on Hymer's ankle brace while Bert takes aim with a colossal sledgehammer. Bert swings mightily, but Hymer removes his leg just as Wheeler's mallet comes crashing down through the table. "That's too bad," Woolsey snorts. "If you hadn't moved your leg—we'd have had it off by now!" (Bert mutters to himself, "Stupid man!")

The boys give Hymer an anesthetic—a hammer applied to the noggin—which fails to work: "Don't do that," Warren laughs good-naturedly, "you might give me a headache!" Bert tries clamping Hymer's foot in a vise but manages only to worsen the problem. Finally the team decides to melt off the unwanted appendages in an open fire. As raging flames engulf the foot, Woolsey assures Hymer, "It may get a little warm, but don't mind it." The three men stare vacantly at the smoldering foot as though it were a yule log. "Say," Warren volunteers, "on second thought, I think my foot's burning." "Yeah," Bert nonchalantly agrees, "it looks like it's burning." Three-second pause. "Hey," Hymer suddenly realizes, "it *is* burning!" Dunking the scalding foot in a pail of water brings the desired results: the vise and the ball and chain drop off with the greatest of ease. "It's all very simple," Woolsey comments scientifically, "You see, when iron in the white heat hits the water"—Bob snaps his fingers. "Every time," Wheeler nods in agreement.

The captain of the guards (Blystone) sees that Warren is no longer enchained to his weighty accessories. As Hymer is taken away to solitary, Bert reminds him not to forget his ball and chain. "No thanks," the poor lug dejectedly replies, "I'll get another one."

"Helping a prisoner to escape?" Blystone sneers at the boys. "I'll put you on the rock pile for this!" "If you do," Bob retaliates, "we'll throw rocks at you!" Brought to warden Edgar Kennedy's office, the team is rescued by Kennedy's spinster sister (Edna May Oliver), who secures positions for the duo as houseboy trusties. "Don't be late for dinner," Bert instructs the harried Kennedy, "or we'll have to throw your soup in the sink."

Romance develops between Bert and the warden's nubile daughter, Barbara (played with a benign innocence by an eighteen-year-old Betty Grable). The warden's sister and the trusty concept were elements borrowed

Edna May Oliver is not impressed by the boys' imitations of her in *Hold 'Em Jail* (1932).

out of *The Criminal Code*, with Bert more or less parodying the Phillips Holmes role. Bert and Betty plan to rendezvous in the courtyard at nine o'clock that night. Unbeknownst to either of them, Riggs (Leo Willis) has planned a prison break at the same time. Woolsey inadvertently tips Kennedy off to the plot, allowing Edgar to reinforce the tower turrets with additional guards.

At nine sharp, Bert jauntily saunters into the darkened prison courtyard, incongruously holding a floral bouquet for his beloved. From the opposite direction comes Riggs with his gang. The guards turn a searchlight on Bert. "Heeeey!" whispers Riggs, "get outta here!" "You get out," Bert responds indignantly. "I was here first!" The searchlight tracks Wheeler as he ambles toward the would-be escapees. Bert has a grand old time playing hide-and-seek with the searchlight. An astonishing gag follows: while Wheeler uses the light beam to make shadow puppets, a machine gunner traces Bert's outline with bullets that ricochet off the wall. The racket disturbs Woolsey, who comes outside just in time to have his lantern shot out of his hand. Bert and Bob, with the angry gang in hot pursuit, take cover in the firehouse. Wheeler and Woolsey manage to keep the roughnecks

Edgar Kennedy and Paul Hurst regard the boys dubiously in the gridiron-prison spoof, *Hold 'Em Jail*.

at bay with a hose until the guards arrive. As Kennedy congratulates the boys, Bert shakes hands and forgets to crimp the hose, drenching poor Edgar.

Bob shares a delightful tête-à-tête with Edna May Oliver at the keyboard; she performs a classical duet with Woolsey that segues into "Chopsticks." Vocalizing horribly for the too-polite Woolsey, Oliver comments on her screechy delivery:

Hold 'Em Jail (1932)   171

EDNA MAY: That's funny—I can't seem to hit that top note.
BOB: Perhaps it's just as well. Where did you learn to sing, anyway?
EDNA MAY: I spent four years in Paris. Of course, I'm not a virtuoso.
BOB: Not after four years in Paris, no.
EDNA MAY: I trust we're both talking about the same thing?
[*Woolsey laughs and blushes as he hides his face behind a feather duster. He sneezes.*]
BOB: [*annoyed*] Somebody's been putting dust in this thing!

The football game that climaxes *Hold 'Em Jail* has many hilarious sight gags, but the loosely organized, overdrawn episode lacks the punch of the excellence that has gone before it. Compared by some to the football finale of the Marxes' *Horse Feathers* (made shortly after *Jail* and also cowritten by Perelman), it is more akin to the Three Stooges' early two-reeler *Three Little Pigskins* (1934), featuring a procession of crazy jokes that do not necessarily build to a powerhouse conclusion. Suffice to say that Bert manages to kick the ball backward, scoring for the opposing team; Bob intercepts the ball, only to be picked up and carried across the other team's goal line; Wheeler tackles teammate Woolsey; running with the ball, Bob pauses for a photo and is tackled; and the football gets wedged in Bert's voluminous trousers. Five weeks after Wheeler and Woolsey completed their scenes in the picture, Selznick hired radio humorist John P. Medbury to write a running commentary of the football match and filmed Medbury as the convict-announcer. Satisfied with Medbury's dialogue but not with Medbury himself, Selznick reshot the scenes using RKO contract player Robert Armstrong in what amounted to be a thankless bit part.

Young Betty Grable was no novice to films by this time (she already had been a Goldwyn Girl, featured in a showy bit for *Whoopee*), but she is used as a pretty prop for Bert to pine over. At $100 a week, Grable became bargain-priced following Dorothy Lee's $500-a-week terms. Edna May Oliver lets her hair down and indulges in some undignified horseplay, which proves what a superb low-comedy actress she could have been. At $15,125, she was the most expensive W & W costar, and worth every nickel. Master of the delayed take and the slow burn reaction, bald Edgar Kennedy blusters his way through *Hold 'Em Jail* and chews the scenery beyond the frameline.

Kennedy, who admitted to overacting but was quick to add, "at least I try to *act*," was a comedian's comedian and is fondly remembered by buffs who revere his "average man" short subjects series through the present day.

Hold 'Em Jail was held back from release until the early fall of 1932. Reviews were generally favorable, although most critics agreed with Mordaunt Hall of the *New York Times* when he wrote, "Messrs. Wheeler &

Woolsey are not nearly as funny as they have been in one or two of their other comedies." Perhaps not, but for a brief spell that year the team had bigger problems to worry about: headlines announced that Bert and Bob would not be making comedies for anyone anymore.

16
So This Is Africa (1933)

Directed by Edward Cline. Produced by Harry Cohn. Screenplay by Norman Krasna. Story by Norman Krasna, Lew Lipton, and Eddie Cline. Assistant director, C. C. Coleman. Photographed by Leonard Smith. Words and music by Bert Kalmar and Harry Ruby. Sound recording by Edward Bernds. Sound assistant, Irving (Buster) Libott. Dates of production: October 17 to November 23, 1932. Released by Columbia Pictures on April 22, 1933. 60 minutes.

Cast: Bert Wheeler (Wilbur), Robert Woolsey (Alexander), Raquel Torres (Tarzana), Esther Muir (Mrs. Johnson Martini), Berton Churchill (Studio Chief, Ultimate Pictures), Henry Armetta (Street Cleaner), Spencer Charters (Doctor), Jerome Storm (Production Manager), Spec O'Donnell (Johnnie, an office boy), Eddie Clayton (Elevator Operator), Clarence Morehouse (Josephine, an ape).

Synopsis: Wilbur (Bert Wheeler) and Alexander (Robert Woolsey) have five mangy lions (which they won in a raffle) featured in their vaudeville act. The act is so bad that it lasts for only one miserable performance. In the meantime, a Hollywood movie company faces the dilemma of either producing a stupendous animal picture or going broke. They have secured the services of beautiful Mrs. Johnson Martini (Esther Muir), the greatest expert on Africa in the world, to direct the picture. Since Mrs. Martini is actually afraid of wild animals, Wilbur, Alexander, and their toothless menagerie are hired to lend authenticity to the production.

Mrs. Martini and her expedition arrive in Africa. Decked out in a clinging evening gown, she takes Alexander into the jungle for a moonlit walk. She immediately starts making violent, passionate love to him. Wilbur, attired in pith helmet, sleeping gown, and combat boots (he anticipates walking in his sleep), wanders through the jungle in the opposite direction. He walks right into the arms of a native beauty, Tarzana (Raquel Torres), a petite member of the Amazon tribe—the most passionate women in the world. She brings the snoozing Wilbur up to her tree hut.

The next morning Mrs. Martini, still in pursuit of Alexander (who has stolen away from her), finds him with Tarzana and Wilbur. Suddenly the beating of native tom-toms is heard by the terrified group. It's mating season for the Amazon women, who are hot in pursuit of Wilbur and

Alexander. The Amazons carry them away to their camp. Mrs. Martini explains that only at night are they passionate; during daylight, the Amazons are merely ferocious. The boys nervously await their nocturnal fate—to be loved to death!

Suddenly an eclipse occurs, and the Amazons, thinking it is night, make a mad rush for our heroes. The pair escape and disguise themselves as native women, but Alexander's "Me no speak-um English" remark and omnipresent cigar give them away.

They are about to be ravished by the slavering women when a platoon of Tarzan men stalk the encampment and carry off the Amazons. Wilbur and Alexander, still attired in Amazonian regalia, are also carried off by the men. The last time we see the boys, they are in front of two washtubs, scrubbing laundry. Strapped to their backs are papooses. Just then Mrs. Martini and Tarzana step out of the hut to greet their loving husbands.

★ ★ ★

Dubbed by Hollywood wags as "His Royal Crudeness," street-smart Harry Cohn dominated Columbia Pictures' product for over thirty years, a longer tenure in command than the entire existence of RKO as an active studio. In 1932, Columbia was still regarded as a lucky indie, teetering on the brink of respectability with occasional A pictures from the Frank Capra unit. Cohn, who ran his fragile studio on gambles and hunches, hoped to lure Wheeler and Woolsey over to his fold with an offer too tempting to resist.

RKO had not kicked the boys out the back door the way Bert Wheeler later led colleagues to believe. On February 9, 1932, the team had asked for $125,000 per picture for a two-film deal; David O. Selznick proposed a counteroffer of $30,000 a picture for four films, later raising the ante to $40,000 a film. Bob was amenable toward a package deal, but Bert rejected the studio's cut-rate terms outright. The time was ripe for Harry Cohn to make his pitch.

Cohn personally intervened when a Columbia contract was proposed to Wheeler and Woolsey; according to Eddie Quillan, who socialized with Bert at the Hollywood Masquers Club, "Harry Cohn seemed to know exactly what to say to intrigue the boys, especially Bert." Informing the comedians that RKO's production chief David O. Selznick was a "dumb bastard" who "wanted to keep the profits to himself," Cohn explained how Columbia would gladly give the team a percentage of the film's profits. Bert later recounted to Eddie Quillan that Cohn pounded his fist on the table in indignation: "You guys know how much money you made for that studio," Cohn barked, "and see how they treat you. Come to Columbia and you'll share in the take." Under Cohn's sweet terms, Bert and Bob signed with Columbia for a single-picture deal. On April 4, *Time* magazine described the proposal as "an experiment to find a new way of paying actors. Last week Harry Cohn announced that he had hired Wheeler and Woolsey to make a picture for a royalty on its profits, an arrangement never before tried by a major producing company." Bert and Bob set about finishing *Hold 'Em Jail*, their last RKO picture, while Columbia went fishing for a suitable W & W comedy angle.

Bert and Bob completed their scenes in *Hold 'Em Jail* on May 13, 1932. The next day the team suddenly quarreled; on May 17, under the headline "Wheeler-Woolsey Split, with Bert East for Show," *Variety* mourned that the "team of Wheeler & Woolsey for pictures is no more. The two men have split with Bert Wheeler giving up further screen activity. Latter is now driving East and will probably go into the new Larry Schwab musical. The pair's deal with Columbia is cold." The following week *Variety* reported that "Harry Cohn says Columbia will hold Wheeler & Woolsey to their contracts, and if necessary will go to court and restrain them from other engagements until they meet their obligation." Meanwhile, Bert motored from Hollywood to New York in five days and five hours, a record at the time for amateur transcontinental driving. While Bert was not pinched for speeding, he got into trouble at a roadside stop in New Jersey for impressing local urchins with his target practice. The local cops who arrived at the scene were impressed, too; Bert was carrying a gun without a Jersey license.

No sooner did Bert return to Broadway than his deal with Larry Schwab fell through; he immediately returned to personal appearances on the Paramount Publix circuit, where he commanded a lofty $4,250 weekly and rave reviews at the New York Paramount Theater. As per *Variety*, Bert and his current gal Friday, Polly Walters, "go into the old Wheeler standby, of which there was no better among mixed dialogues in the old days, and everything lands, including the glycerine tears."

Meanwhile, Bob Woolsey explained his side of the breakup to Jack Grant of *Movie Classic* magazine:

> It seems I was the last man in town to know about Bert's heading East. You can't guess who told me. The headwaiter at the Roosevelt Hotel. He heard the deal arranged between Bert, his agent [Leo Fitzgerald], and an Eastern theatrical producer [Schwab]. The producer said that he had a part for Bert in a new musical show—a great part, one that would make him the most famous comic on Broadway. Imagine his giving up pictures to be famous on Broadway!
>
> But that's the way Bert is. A great little guy, but a lousy businessman. He's impetuous and can be easily sold. Bert has made over $400,000 in pictures and hasn't a thing to show for it.
>
> Bert was a little hot-headed. He burned plenty when he was told that

Selznick, the new boss at RKO, asked when he first came on the lot which was Wheeler and which was Woolsey. They told him that Woolsey was the guy with the cigar, and Selznick is quoted as saying it really didn't make any difference, as he didn't think either of us was funny. There are a lot of people who don't think us funny. But our pictures made money. After hearing that remark attributed to Selznick, Bert refused to sign the new contract RKO offered us. It wasn't for us [as] much money as we had been getting—but it wasn't anything to sneeze at.

However, he was all for arranging a deal with Columbia on a profit-sharing basis. The papers were drawn. Then a fellow who had acted as agent for Bert back East [Fitzgerald] popped up. After talking to him, Bert accused me of being hasty about the Columbia deal. And it was his idea in the first place!

Later I found out that Bert had signed several stage contracts, so perhaps he picked the fight just to break the partnership.

I'm sorry the curtain had to be rung down on our act. The team of Wheeler and Woolsey was lucky and enjoyed a great run. I wish Bert all the luck in the world, wherever he is.

Woolsey announced that he was teaming up with former silent comedian Harry Langdon, whose babylike mannerisms provided the contrast to Bob's "brazen braggart" characterization. According to Harry Langdon's widow, Mabel, "I was going steady with Harry at the time, and if Woolsey ever approached him about teaming up, that's news to me! Harry was too busy working on *Hallelujah, I'm a Bum*, a big Jolson picture for Joe Schenck." But before either Wheeler or Woolsey proceeded further with their plans, the team was reconciled. Bert apparently woke up to the fact that with the Depression worsening, nobody had the resources to back him in a lavish Broadway production. Big-time vaudeville—the only other avenue that appealed to him—was dying, and Wheeler had to hustle changing trains from New York to Chicago to St. Louis just to play the few remaining theaters left that could accommodate his hefty salary.

Variety reported on July 26 that "Bert Wheeler is due in Hollywood for his first Columbia talker with Bob Woolsey." Comedy maestro Leo McCarey, the man who developed Laurel and Hardy as a team during silent days, was slated to direct the picture, which had an August 20 starting date.

August 20 came and went with Columbia still working on a script idea for the boys. McCarey finally had to bow out of the picture due to other commitments. Meanwhile, RKO's newly appointed corporate president, Merlin Aylesworth, was carefully studying gross profit figures on the studio's Wheeler and Woolsey comedies. All of the films had posted huge gains except for the two on which Selznick had served as executive producer. Aylesworth was shocked at the exorbitant costs of *Girl Crazy* ($532,000) and *Hold 'Em Jail* ($408,000), convinced that both films would have racked up sizable profits had Selznick been judicious in the preproduction stages. Aylesworth strongly recommended that Selznick send studio representatives to negotiate with the two comedians for their safe return to the RKO fold; the studio had not nurtured the profitable perennials for disreputable Columbia to reap the harvest. For David O. Selznick, producer extraordinaire, it was a humbling lesson.

On August 30, *Variety* reported that RKO officials had been talking with Bert for two weeks but were at an impasse because Wheeler wanted double the figure that RKO had proposed. Bert "contended that the Wheeler-Woolsey combination stood above the RKO star group in draw value at the box office and figured their pay should be in proportion." Bert called off the negotiations when the studio continued to hem and haw the money issue. (Years later Wheeler remarked, "I was a tough little monkey in those days.") Selznick pursued the matter no further—for the time being.

Slowly but surely a story was shaping up for Wheeler and Woolsey's initial Columbia venture. Norman Krasna, a twenty-three-year-old former secretary to Broadway columnist Walter Winchell, had impressed Harry Cohn as a bright, witty kid with a knack for original and lively ideas. Krasna pressed the Columbia chief for a chance as a screenwriter; gambler Cohn acted on his instinct and assigned him to the Wheeler and Woolsey project. At Bert and Bob's behest, freelancer Eddie Cline was signed to direct and Lew Lipton was secured to assist Norman Krasna in bolstering the gag sequences.

RKO still had a hankering to re-recruit their exiled sons, but now the competition was just around the corner—literally. On October 11, RKO's neighbor, Paramount Pictures, was reportedly negotiating with the team to make a series of four pictures on the 1933 program. The proposition called for a flat $75,000 for each picture plus 25 percent of the net profits. Paramount would likely have been the ideal showcase for Bert and Bob's talents, since they were the one lot specializing in comedy, with the Marx Brothers, W. C. Fields, Mae West, Maurice Chevalier, Burns and Allen, Jack Oakie, Charlie Ruggles, and Mary Boland parading before the cameras at that time.

On October 12, the Motion Picture Producers and Distributors Association (the MPPDA), the industry's self-regulating board, returned the script of Norman Krasna's Wheeler and Woolsey effort *Bottoms Up* to Harry Cohn with a few recommendations. This standard procedure had been instituted in 1930 and was adhered to by all the major studios and most of the smaller independents. The Production Code—a list of screen taboos and their variants, was applied as a yardstick by the MPPDA to keep all films from going beyond a reasonable checkpoint. The association brought up several polite observations: the story's comic sex scenes "might go a little over the borderline, but we are sure your good taste will handle them"; the risqué dances of the native girls should be handled in long (faraway) shots; Woolsey should not strike a match on a girl's posterior; and a burning theater should not be presented onscreen, for fear that the movie patrons might believe that the real theater was ablaze and start stampeding. The MPPDA's greatest concern was over the depiction of an Italian sanitation worker:

> The Italians are getting a little sore about having their nation perpetually represented as a race of excitable, arm-waving comics, and they have already registered an official complaint on this score. May we suggest, therefore, that your character in this scene be not obviously an Italian.

Longtime Columbia filmmaker Edward Bernds later became the finest director of that studio's two-reel comedy unit (he holds the enviable distinction of having helmed the four funniest Three Stooges shorts: *Micro-Phonies* [1945], *Brideless Groom* [1947], *Who Done It?* [1949], and *Dopey Dicks* [1950]). Before his directorial debut, Ed Bernds was Columbia's top sound technician from 1929 through 1944. Director Frank Capra regarded Bernds's expertise so highly that he became an invaluable member of the elite Capra unit. Among Ed's many other assignments at Columbia, this Wheeler and Woolsey epic remains an especially memorable occasion. "I worked on that picture, and recall a lot of sexy stuff in the script. Right before shooting began, Harry Cohn summoned Eddie Cline and Norman Krasna to his office. Cohn said there might be a censorship problem. Both men assured him that everything would be handled 'in good taste,' so we made the picture without another thought about it."

Bottoms Up was retitled *That's Africa* when it went into production on October 17. Ed Bernds recalls that the opening segment in a vaudeville theater was shot at the "ancient Vitagraph Studio, which is still there at the eastern edge of Hollywood, only half a dozen stones' throw—if you could throw stones well—from the site of D. W. Griffith's enormous *Intolerance* set." An African village set was erected in nearby Sherwood Forest, which got its name from the first major production filmed there, Douglas Fairbanks's *Robin Hood*. "We spent a lot of time in Sherwood Forest doing nothing, waiting for sunlight," Ed recalls. "That was kind of unheard of at Columbia, where you were either told to go ahead and shoot it anyway or they sent out generator lights. But we had a lot of long-shot stuff—people swinging on vines between trees—and I guess the production office agreed we couldn't shoot into a lit gray sky for that stuff. So we laid out a softball diamond in the rough dirt and played ball until the sun came out, and we went back to work."

So This Is Africa (1933)

Whatever animosity Wheeler and Woolsey may have felt toward each other vanished by the time cameras started rolling for the boys' African junket. Buster Libott, Bernds's technical assistant, recalled Bert and Bob as being "totally different guys. Wheeler was a happy-go-lucky, feisty little guy. And Woolsey was always so businesslike. I remember there was always music coming from out of Wheeler's dressing room. The other guy would come out of his room when they'd call him, and his face would be scarlet." Ed Bernds remembers an especially telling moment while the film was in production:

> During shooting of the picture, I went to a movie one night. There was a newsreel segment that got one of the most explosive laughs I ever heard in the theater. It was an Australian newsreel covering a race in some obscure little town. The interviewer, a guy with a prissy British accent, was trying to make a big deal out of this small-time race. Finally, he interviewed the winner, a skinny, knock-kneed character with a funny-looking goatee. "And how, sir," said the pompous character, "do you account for the fact that you defeated so many men younger than you are?" The skinny old guy glared at the camera. You could see right away that he was a Donald Duck character, mad at everything and everybody. He snarled at the camera and said, "I don't drink, I don't smoke, and no monkey business!" The laugh in that theater was absolutely explosive. Why?
>
> The suggestion of sex spices the whole thing. Not the mention of sex or the presence of it but merely the thought that the old goat was, in effect, inveighing angrily against it. That was irresistibly funny.
>
> How does this discourse relate to Wheeler & Woolsey?
>
> Well, the following day in the studio Woolsey was telling a group of us that he had gone to a movie in Hollywood the night before and had seen that newsreel. He described the reaction in the audience. It was terrific, the same reaction as my audience. Bob Woolsey said, "If I ever got a laugh like that, I'd die happy!"

Although production continued for a lengthy five weeks, enthusiasm ran high throughout the making of the film, finally rechristened *So This Is Africa* before it was wrapped on November 23. Esther Muir, who played the world's foremost authority on Africa in the world, Mrs. Johnson Martini (a twist on the real-life jungle adventuress, Mrs. Martin Johnson), felt that "we made a hilarious takeoff on *Trader Horn*, Tarzan pictures, Frank Buck adventures, and those impressive documentaries that were all the rage." Bus Libott recalls the cast and crew as being "a happy set. We had a chorus of forty-two girls, so it *had* to be a happy set!"

Back at RKO, Merlin Aylesworth made a last-ditch effort to secure Bert and Bob's services. Without Selznick's influence at the bargaining table, RKO presented an extraordinary deal: $10,000 a week for the team with a seven-week guarantee, plus 20 percent of all profits over a $500,000

Esther Muir puts the make on Woolsey in the Tarzan-inspired epic *So This Is Africa*.

gross. As a bonus, RKO would send the team on a world tour upon completion of the picture, picking up the entire tab. Best of all, the pact was a one-picture deal, allowing Wheeler and Woolsey to negotiate an even better contract if their picture clicked big. Bert and Bob put their signatures to the RKO contract on November 16; that studio would remain home base for the rest of their days as a team.

The completed *So This Is Africa* was shipped to MPPDA officer James Wingate for official film-industry sanction. On December 29, 1932, Wingate wrote Harry Cohn that the film "seems to us to be satisfactory under the Production Code and free from elements to which official censorship could take serious action." The following day a similar summary was sent to Governor Carl E. Milliken, categorizing the film as "an amusing and rather boisterous comedy which should prove to be very popular." Only one aspect irritated Wingate:

> Henry Armetta does a very small bit in the first part of the picture as a discouraged street cleaner. He does it in his usual Italian hand-waving manner and although no mention is made of his nationality, he is easily recognizable as an Italian.

So This Is Africa (1933)

So far, so good. A ninety-minute version of *So This Is Africa* was previewed in San Bernardino on January 12, 1933. *Variety* called *Africa* "the best Wheeler & Woolsey offering to date although it is highly censorable, being overboard on blue gags which presages trouble in bluenose states, unless cleaned up. Lines, however, are smart and at the preview polled plenty of heavy laughs."

On February 16, 1933, the National Board of Review screened *So This Is Africa* and rejected the entire film, hurling broadsides at the picture: "Nothing as salacious has ever come before the National Board in eight years of reviewing.... It outrages every common standard of decency... has absolutely nothing to recommend it.... The Board would harm itself if it were to pass such a picture."

Frantic, Harry Cohn called the MPPDA's James Wingate, who had approved the original script. Wingate agreed to assist Columbia in "minimizing outstanding vulgarities" and making all prints conform to an acceptable version. In the meantime, word leaked out to the press that nearly half the picture had to be cut before it could be released. "I remember that Columbia had to go back and put in all these out-takes of the unfunny opening scene in the vaudeville house," Ed Bernds recalls. "The studio couldn't get Wheeler and Woolsey for retakes because they were no longer contractually bound to us. I believe that by this time, they were back filming at RKO." Even censor kingpin Will Hays was caught in a tight spot, having been told that if *Africa* were released intact, "nothing can stop the censorship bill pending before the Nebraska Legislation from passing.... It is the rawest picture ever seen."

What, you may ask, was eliminated that was so offensive? Modern readers may judge for themselves in considering these censoring instructions:

Eliminate following dialogue:

> BOB: Now you take the hot water bottle. Has that done away with marriage?
> BERT: What's the hot water bottle got to do with marriage?
> BOB: What's the hot water bottle got to do with marriage? Listen, you're lying in bed at night. You're cold. What's it you long for? What is it you cry for? What is it that you need more than anything in the world?
> BERT: Not a hot water bottle.

Eliminate views of group of native girls removing their outer garments and wiggling their hips.

Eliminate scene of camera on tripod with cloth over it. A man goes under the cloth and looks through the camera and comes out. A woman with a dark skirt goes under to look through it. Woolsey follows and instead of lifting the camera cloth lifts her skirt and puts his head under.

Wheeler remarking on the number of trees in the jungle:

> MRS. MARTINI: There are millions of them and they are all virgin trees.
> BERT: They look wild to me.
> BOB: That's why they're wild, that's why they're wild!

Eliminate dialogue as follows and accompanying action with wild native girl:

> BERT: No more kissing, not on an empty stomach! Look, boy hungry. I've got to have food. Look, something like this—see? Look, see? Nuts.
> TARZANA: Nuts.
> BERT: Yeah, nuts, right.
> TARZANA: [*grabs Bert to wrestle*] More!
> BERT: Hey!
> ECHO: Hey!
> BERT: Stop!
> ECHO: Stop!
> BERT: I'm hungry!
> ECHO: I'm hungry!
> [*Tarzana pulls Bert toward a cave*]
> BERT: I don't want to go in there with you!
> ECHO: Don't be a chump.

Eliminate views of Tarzana and Wheeler coming out of tree hut; Woolsey sees them:

> BOB: [*to Bert*]: Where were you last night? What happened? Whose fault was it? Answer me yes or no!
> BERT: Yes.
> BOB: Just as I expected. You ought to be ashamed of yourself.
> BERT: I was up a tree.
> BOB: Yeah? What were you doing?
> BERT: I was doing all right.

Eliminate scenes of Tarzana in heat, jumping up and down when she is trying to make Wheeler go back up into tree, and eliminate accompanying dialogue:

> TARZANA: More.
> BERT: [*to Bob*] Excuse me for a few minutes—perhaps you'd better make it a half hour.

Eliminate scene where monkey is trying to get Woolsey to go up into tree:

So This Is Africa (1933)

BOB: No, not tonight, Josephine. Not tonight. Oh, no. Wait a minute, wait a minute. I'll buy you a bottle of beer but I'm not going upstairs! Oh, all right, all right.

Eliminate scenes of Woolsey and monkey coming out of tree, monkey jumping up and down and Woolsey brushing himself off and speech by Woolsey, "Africa's killing me, boy. It's killing me. I can't stand it."

Eliminate Woolsey's retort to Wheeler: "Me? Oh, I was just monkeying around a little."

Where Wheeler says, "Sounds as if they've all been running uphill," eliminate close-up of girls panting.

Eliminate the following in scene where Woolsey, Wheeler and Martini watch gyrating native girls:

> MARTINI: Don't touch her. It may cost you your life! This is the most savage tribe in Africa. These women may seem peaceful now, but that's only one side of them. In the daytime they're just like ordinary women, but at nightfall, when it gets dark, they become wild and their worst side comes out in them!
> BOB: Who says it's their worst side?
> MARTINI: They don't love like ordinary women. Why, they will kill you with love!
> BOB: Yeah, well I want to be killed by the little one on the end down there.
> MARTINI: She's the most dangerous one of all. They tell me she has killed three husbands already.
> BERT: Yeah, I can understand that, all right.
> MARTINI: They don't love like ordinary women. They will love you to death!
> BOB: Oh death, where is thy sting?
> [*He takes out his watch and waits eagerly for night to fall; the Amazons stage a muscle dance, which is offensive in the extreme*]
> MARTINI: They become animals as night falls.
> [*Woolsey sees a monkey calling to him*]
> BOB: [*to monkey*] What, you too?

Eliminate rear view of girls stooping and moving their bodies and breasts in vulgar manner, and Wheeler's remark, "Oh, look at those Afri-*cans*!"

★ ★ ★

"You can imagine what a disaster this was for Harry Cohn," Ed Bernds comments. "The MPPDA cut such chunks of what they considered offending material and sent Columbia the mangled remains, which turned out to be too short to be released." The outtakes of weak footage reinserted into the film merely watered down whatever kick remained. To be sure, there are still several bright bits left: on safari, Bert and Bob watch tribal

Esther Muir, Bert, Bob, Clarence Morehouse (as gorilla), and Raquel Torres get ready to swing in *So This Is Africa*.

natives furiously running and leaping backward (courtesy of stock footage run in reverse, from the documentary *Africa Speaks*). "That's the famous Backward Tribe of Africa," Woolsey informs his partner. "They always run backward." "Yeah?" Bert inquires. "Why do they do that for?" Bob responds, "They don't care where they're goin', they just want to see where they've been." Rendezvousing with Mrs. Martini in the jungle, Woolsey wears a tuxedo while Martini is garbed in a clinging evening gown:

> BOB: What a lovely gown! That certainly is pretty.
> [*One of the straps falls off Martini's shoulder*]
> MARTINI: You think it becoming?
> BOB: It'll be coming off any minute now!

Although *Africa* was tame once the censors hacked it to bits, its notorious past spread by word of mouth, ensuring a box-office smash. *So This Is Africa* earned $20,000 in its first week at the Rialto in New York, "tremendous business," *Variety* declared, "for a house this size." By contrast, the previous W & W release, *Hold 'Em Jail*, had earned a respectable $11,000 in its week at the New York Mayfair. With only this one film,

Wheeler and Woolsey shot straight up to the number-two slot, behind square-jawed Jack Holt, among Columbia's profitable players for 1933—and Holt had no fewer than nine films in release that year. Polled for *Motion Picture Herald*'s survey of the "Biggest Money-Making Stars of 1932-33," Wheeler and Woolsey ranked number fifteen. Among comedians, only Joe E. Brown was in the top ten, while the Marx Brothers were slightly ahead of Bert and Bob, in thirteenth place. Laurel and Hardy, Buster Keaton, W. C. Fields, Harold Lloyd, and all the other major comics ranked behind W & W when final results were tabulated. RKO was bluntly informed that Wheeler and Woolsey vehicles could mean huge profit margins. For the rest of their partnership, Bert and Bob would find new and remunerative ways to remind the studio of their value.

Even though the expurgated edition of *Africa* ran a scant sixty minutes, *Variety* did an about-face, panning the new version as "giving the general effect of a two-reeler stretched out endlessly." *Variety* found the film to be a ragged production given over to crude jokes for rowdy blue-collar guffaws. Perhaps Marguerite Tazelarr in the *New York Herald Tribune* summed *Africa* up best when she wrote,

> While [Wheeler and Woolsey] lack anything approaching genius as comics, or even definitive style, they invariably contribute such gusto and breezy naivete to their performance that it has the semblance of refreshing and adroit comedy. This piece, fast moving, ribald, in sum total a nondescript accumulation of gags often bewhiskered, has still an amazing vitality which commands interest, though it lacks satire, subtlety, wit and real humor.

Bert and Bob did not see one penny of their anticipated profits materialize from *So This Is Africa*. At the close of 1933 the team griped to *Variety* that "Harry Cohn gave them a fast talk to close the proposition. Cost ran over $200,000, with $17,000 charged as incidentals. The two comics got nothing."

Ed Bernds has the final word:

> About Wheeler and Woolsey's "profit participation"—I didn't hear a word while making the film. Believe me, a sound man hears many things other crew people don't, and he hears a lot of things he isn't supposed to hear. But for several years after *So This Is Africa*, whenever there was a strange unidentified noise during filming, some wise guy would say, "That's Wheeler and Woolsey looking for their share of the profits!"

17
Diplomaniacs (1933)

Directed by William A. Seiter. Executive producer, Merian C. Cooper. Associate producer, Sam Jaffe. Screenplay by Joseph L. Mankiewicz and Henry Myers, from an original story by Joseph L. Mankiewicz. Settings by Van Nest Polglase and Al Herman. Photographed by Edward Cronjager. Musical direction by Max Steiner. Music and lyrics by Harry Akst and Edward Eliscu. Dance numbers staged by Larry Ceballos. Sound recording by John E. Tribby. Film editing by William Hamilton. Dates of production: February 15 to March 18, 1933. Released by RKO on May 12, 1933. 61 minutes.

Cast: Bert Wheeler (Willy Nilly), Robert Woolsey (Hercules Glub), Marjorie White (Dolores), Louis Calhern (Winkelreid, General Manager of the High Explosive Bullet Company), Phyllis Barry (Fifi), Hugh Herbert (Chow Chow), Edgar Kennedy (Chairman of Peace Conference), Richard Carle (Captain of the S.S. *Periwinkle*), Edward G. Cooper (Adoop Indian Chief), Dewey Robinson (Luke the Hermit), William Irving (Puppenschmerzen), Neely Edwards (Schmerzenpuppen), Billy Bletcher (Schmerzenschmerzen), Teddy Hart (Puppenpuppen), John Kelly (Army Sergeant), Eddie Hart (Pilot), William "Heinie" Conklin, Miki "Mike" Morita, Harry Schultz, Neal Burns, Michael Visaroff (Delegates to Geneva Peace Conference), Richard Alexander (Sergeant at Arms), Alfred P. James (Attendant), Charles Coleman (Marie, effeminate butler), Constantine Romanoff (Toughest Man in the World), Yola D'Avril (French Vamp), Shirley Chambers, D'Arcy Corrigan (Ship Passengers), Grace Hayle (Countess), Carrie Daumery (Deaf Dowager), Florence Hoo (Mrs. Chow Chow), Charlie Hall (Schaffner, Winkelreid's valet), Lon Poff (Bald Adoop Indian), Artie Ortega (Indian), Blackie Whiteford (French Apache), Jack Leonard (Gorilla).

Synopsis: A series of titles superimposed on the visage of an Indian introduces the picture: "There are three important things we should know about the noble red man. An Indian never shaves—because he has no beard—He has no left whisker—And he has no right whisker." With that tidbit, the film introduces Willy Nilly (Bert Wheeler) and Hercules Glub (Robert Woolsey), tonsorial wizards who have opened a barbershop on an Indian reservation. The boys haven't had a customer since opening day;

suddenly, the region's only other white man, Luke the Hermit (Dewey Robinson) arrives for a shave and a manicure. Business begins to boom. A dozen members of the Adoop Indian tribe crowd the shop. A knobby, bald-headed Indian (Lon Poff) has a dandruff-ridden scalp he wants cured. Willy promises to "clean-um up good."

Hercules engages Luke in the usual barbershop banter: "Now you take these international debts. Suppose you owed me a quarter." "Which is right," Luke responds, "after you get finished shaving me." "Then the whole world will call you a crook and a defaulter," Willy chimes in. "That's OK," Luke responds, "if I get my shave for nothing!" "Boy, do you learn fast," Hercules observes. "You're practically a diplomat right now. You could have a foreign affair." At the mention of the words "foreign affair," the Indians become incensed and escort Willy and Hercules to the Chief of the Adoop tribe (Edward G. Cooper). The Chief explains that the Indian nation is the only one not invited to the Peace Conference in Geneva. He commissions the boys to represent the Adoops and persuade the world's nations to sign the peace treaty. Willy and Hercules are each given one million dollars in expense money, with the promise of another million upon the successful completion of their mission. The Chief explains away his profligacy by pointing to the tribe's gushing oil wells. Willy and Hercules agree to accept the challenge.

Unbeknownst to our heroes, diabolical munitions manufacturers Puppenschmerzen (William Irving), Schmerzenpuppen (Neely Edwards), Schmerzenschmerzen (Billy Bletcher), and Puppenpuppen (Teddy Hart) realize that the success of the boys' mission would spell disaster for their industry. They hire a dirtier scoundrel than themselves, Winkelreid (Louis Calhern), to thwart the boys' bid for world peace. Aided by Dolores (Marjorie White), a love-starved vamp, and a smart-aleck Chinaman named Chow Chow (Hugh Herbert), whose dialect is strangely tinged with Yiddish, Winkelreid plots to prevent the signing of a peace pact.

At their Paris stopover Winkelreid enlists the services of the exotic Fifi, whose kisses make men swoon and smoke under the collar. Fifi and Dolores entice the boys to follow them into the Dead Rat saloon, where a gang of French Apaches descends upon them. Awakening in the gutter of a Paris street, the boys realize that their portfolio of secret documents has been stolen. Armed only with their wits, Willy and Hercules proceed to Geneva. Ready to quit and double-cross the Adoops, they receive a deadly warning. An arrow falls at their feet with instructions to achieve peace or die. The boys continue on to the conference hall.

The would-be diplomats arrive at the conclave just in time to find the chairman (Edgar Kennedy) aiming a machine gun for persuasion. Tossed out of the fray, Willy and Hercules hit upon the idea of entertaining the delegates. They go into a song, dance, and acrobatic act, scoring a hit and causing the conferees to consider the ramifications of a peace treaty. Fearful that the team will convince the representatives to ratify an agreement, Winkelreid forges a document supposedly signed by all the nations of the world and presents it to the boys, who then jaunt merrily homeward to enjoy the plaudits of a grateful world.

Alas, the fraud is exposed, and the misguided pacifists arrive at the Adoop reservation in time to be conscripted into service. The Second World War begins. Willy, Hercules, and the Adoops march off to battle as Fifi and Dolores, in Adoop costumes, cheer from the sidelines.

★ ★ ★

In Hollywood, happy endings usually happen only in the movies, but there are exceptions to every rule. Only a year after they had been drummed out of RKO by David O. Selznick, Wheeler and Woolsey were returning to the studio, feted as conquering heroes about to star in an important production. Selznick meanwhile was experiencing an attack of persona non grata at his own studio; RKO corporate president Merlin Aylesworth questioned the creative blunders Selznick had perpetrated during his one-year reign. Aylesworth undermined Selznick's authority by dictating contrary policies that challenged the mogul's judgment. As Merlin Aylesworth brought Bert and Bob back into the fold, Selznick gave RKO official notice of his resignation on January 2, 1933. Almost immediately, Selznick was hired by father-in-law, Louis B. Mayer, whose MGM studios were across town, in Culver City. With access to MGM's assets, bankable stars, and valuable properties, Selznick proved himself an outstanding producer of high-quality entertainment, but a studio in such frail health as RKO just was not able to withstand the rigors of so much "artistic" experimentation.

With the removal of the team's wunderkind nemesis, RKO wanted to let bygones be bygones and accommodate Bert and Bob as much as possible. RKO producer Merian C. Cooper (the man responsible for envisioning *King Kong*) was placed in charge of studio production. From all accounts, Cooper's easygoing and agreeable nature seemed a throwback to the happier days of Bill LeBaron. Remembering the boys' overtures from Paramount, RKO borrowed Joseph L. Mankiewicz from that studio to write a sophisticated satire along the lines of his *Million Dollar Legs*, a 1932 Paramount spoof of foreign intrigue and the Olympics. RKO paid Mank two thousand dollars for his original story *In the Red*, while his writing partner on *Legs*, Henry Myers, was brought onboard to assist. Throughout December 1932 Mankiewicz and Myers toiled at RKO, around the corner from their home lot, Paramount. Before long, studio spies were keeping an eye on Mankiewicz's activities. At one point Paramount producer Emanuel Cohen accused Mank of lifting material from the tentative Marx Brothers story in preparation, *Cracked Ice* (eventually to become *Duck Soup*). Mank was eventually cleared of all charges of plagiarism but did not appreciate the accusations. With six months of his four-year contract remaining, Mank resigned from Paramount at the end of the meeting.

RKO wasted no time in churning out publicity gimmicks, keeping Bert and Bob's faces in the newspapers. In January 1933, starlet Betty Furness was dispatched on a typically offbeat assignment with the boys:

> Bert, Bob, and myself appeared at Grauman's Theater wearing skirt suits—why, I don't quite understand or recall. Anyway, we met Tom Mix and Wallace Beery, who were pretty good sports. The four of them strolled down Hollywood Boulevard nonchalantly, Woolsey puffing away on his cigar—Lord, it was funny.

Short-subject specialist Mark Sandrich was slated to direct Wheeler and Woolsey's *In the Red*, soon to be retitled *A Five-Cent War*. Perhaps someone had cold feet over Sandrich's appointment, because William A. Seiter wound up helming the picture when it went before the cameras on February 15, 1933. General production manager Sam Jaffe (not to be confused with the Gunga Din actor of the same name) was assigned to supervise the production. In later years Jaffe grumbled that Bert and Bob were "mediocre talents"—but the likely cause for his grousing was the $70,000 that Wheeler and Woolsey split for this film, compared to the $1,000 Jaffe was paid for his services.

Diplomaniacs, as the film was finally christened, is a lighthearted, crazy confection that is still topical and delightfully fresh in the 1990s. Not everyone's cup of tea, the film nevertheless has an immense charm about it. Although *Diplomaniacs* turned a profit during that darkest of all Depression years, audiences were more likely intrigued with the music and sexy "cheesecake" angles than with the stinging satire (which is still potent). The best supporting cast Bert and Bob had ever assembled—Louis Calhern, Hugh Herbert, Marjorie White, Edgar Kennedy, Phyllis Barry, and Richard Carle—lent energy and vigor to the foray. Calhern and Herbert even occasionally outshadow the stars with their scene-stealing bon mots. "There wasn't a comedian in Hollywood who didn't want to work in our pictures because we would let them run wild," Bert recalled in 1966. "By them getting laughs, it was feathering our nests. We never said, 'Don't do this' or 'Don't do that.'" Hugh Herbert, as the maxim-spouting Chinaman Chow Chow, is wildly hilarious and gives the comedy performance of his life. At one point Louis Calhern informs Herbert that his stock has tumbled to a dollar a share. "If it falls any lower," Calhern notifies his esteemed colleague, "I shan't be able to sell short." Herbert

Bob, Wallace Beery, Tom Mix, Bert, and Beery's daughter, Caroline, promenade along Hollywood Boulevard, forty years before men in dresses became the fashion there.

solemnly replies. "In the book of the Bull and the Bear it is written, 'Stock that is down to one is no longer stock—it's *stuck*.'"

The suave Calhern, dressed in white tie and tails, makes an impeccably smooth villain, continually looking down upon his height-impaired colleagues. "How do I look, Schaffner?" he inquires of valet Charlie Hall. "Sir," Hall replies, "in that suit you can conspire freely." Although they are crossing the Atlantic in an ocean liner, Charlie nonchalantly dives out of the porthole when Calhern orders him to leave the room. Calhern asks Hugh Herbert whether his valet drowned; Herbert answers with a question: "It says in the book of the Rabbit, 'How much ocean can one man drink?'" "Oh, well," mutters Calhern, "he couldn't press a pair of pants anyway."

The witty subplot makes the weak W & W early sequences doubly distressing. Their tonsorial jokes were played to death in vaudeville and silent comedies, and backwoods dialogue—discussing a character known as Luke the Hermit, Bert asks Bob, "Why do they call him Luke?" "Because he's not so hot," Woolsey retorts—makes the opening segment appear to be almost a spoof of every bad W & W situation from their earliest, crudest movies.

Bert and Bob are virtual straight men for everyone else's punch lines in the opening segments of the film. Attempting to converse with an Indian chief, Bob asks in pidgin English, "You speak-um English?" "Not terribly fluently," the chief replies in an upper-crust British accent. "I was at Oxford for four years, and while I'm fairly conversant with the classics, my ear has not yet become attuned to your Americanisms." Dumbstruck, Bert finally asks his partner, "What language was he talkin'?" "Pig latin," Bob replies with certitude. "He was only foolin'." Fortunately, the boys gain control over the picture near the halfway mark and proceed to dazzle viewers with a passel of stylish highlights.

Despite a slim sixty-one minute running time, *Diplomaniacs* is crammed with nearly twenty minutes' worth of sprightly song-and-dance specialties. Max Steiner's rich orchestrations are certainly the finest arrangements of any Wheeler and Woolsey film. "Ood-gay Eye-bay" is an Indian motif production number pitting the boys against shapely squaws wearing skimpy halters and loincloths. Louis Calhern sings "Annie Laurie" at Bert's request in a devastating number that becomes uproarious once Bert chimes in. Wheeler resurrects his old crying bit from vaudeville days, chewing on a slice of bread and catching the spitball projectiles that spew forth from his quavering lips. "Sing to Me" is a wrestling-match love song/duet between Bert and Marjorie White, a spunky musical-comedy actress whose outrageous mugging must be seen to be believed. At four feet, ten inches in height, Marjorie was the shortest W & W heroine but also the most bombastic. The raucous White implores Bert to serenade her:

> MARJORIE: Sing to me!
> BERT: How about "One Hour with You"?
> MARJORIE: Sure! But first—sing to me!

The frothy "On the Boulevard" number is a neat spoof of Maurice Chevalier, with the boys waited upon hand and foot by a contingent of French maids in low-cut blouses. "No More War" is a spiritual performed in blackface by the delegates to the Geneva Peace Conference, led by Bert and Bob at the rostrum.

Sometimes Mankiewicz's script seems too clever for itself. There are more in jokes in *Diplomaniacs* than in all the other Wheeler and Woolsey films combined. Subjects touched on the surface include the Bronx, Bing Crosby, *Fu Manchu* movies, Greek diners, Mamoulian's *Love Me Tonight*, Jeanette MacDonald, homophones ("sheik," "chic," and "cheek"), Columbia University (Mank's alma mater), Al Jolson, the stock-market crash, and numerous oblique references that possibly baffled infrequent moviegoers in 1933. That these jokes go over at all today is a tribute to screen serendipity—the asides are basically aimed at films, actors, and genres that have become high camp with movie buffs.

Predictably, the censors found plenty to quibble about when the film was screened for industry approval. James Wingate of the Motion Picture Producers and Distributors Association wrote Merian C. Cooper on April 20, "It would be well to recall to your mind the serious censorship difficulties encountered by the previous Wheeler & Woolsey picture, *So This Is Africa*, because there is no doubt that *Diplomaniacs* will have to overcome some of the unfavorable reactions caused by this previous release." RKO actually hoped to capitalize on *Africa*'s notoriety; in a campaign similar to Columbia's, RKO promoted *Diplomaniacs* as "a sexpedition of international importance!" Wingate apparently failed to catch on to Bert Wheeler's spoof of Jeanette MacDonald's "lingerie" scenes, either. In the actress's early Paramount films, quite a few musical numbers were set in a boudoir, where, adorned in her negligee, she would serenade the audience. Bert's falsetto mimicry is superb, and Wingate's puzzled reaction is amusing:

> The scene where Wheeler & Woolsey get out of bed, Wheeler wearing a woman's bedcap and putting on a woman's feathered dressing gown. Inasmuch as there has been some complaint that the screen is attempting to portray sexual perversion, we believe this scene will be criticized in that light.

The sequence was left intact, but only after haggling among Cooper, Sam Jaffee, Wingate, and the morals czar himself, Will Hays. Not all criticisms were of a sexual bent. RKO agreed to delay the release of the film in Washington, D.C., due to a summit being held there by foreign diplomats. "If thrown in the face of foreign representatives now gathered in Washington," the MPPDA warned, "they would consider it an unfriendly gesture." Supposedly, foreign reaction to *Diplomaniacs* would be more favorable once the envoys were back on their *own* soil.

If *Diplomaniacs* has a serious flaw, it is the brevity of the film's "sketchbook" comedy turns. The gagging cannot stand still long enough to pursue any idea for more than three minutes. Bert and Bob are likable in these "blackout" excursions, but the choppiness eliminates the depth needed for their personalities to sparkle. Nevertheless, any film with the classic scene where Wheeler and Woolsey perform "Sing to Me" while a gang of thugs encircles them cannot be all bad. Again, it is the supporting cast that puts the jokes over with a vengeance. Plug-ugly Constantine Romanoff portrays the Toughest Man in the World so flat-footedly that it is funnier than a legitimate comedy role. Following Romanoff into a dive named the Dead Rat, Hugh Herbert laments, "I wish I were back in China with my wife—who I hate!"

A classic moment in *Diplomaniacs*: Constantine Romanoff (left of Woolsey) and friends get ready to annihilate our heroes.

Critics did not know what to make of this raggle-taggle assortment of gags, burlesques, spoofs, and songs. *Variety* labeled the film "a baddie," adding that Wheeler and Woolsey "are practically tossed into a tank and told to give themselves their own swimming lessons. It doesn't pan out." The *Hollywood Reporter* grumbled that the film "suffers terribly from bad writing and abounds in beautiful sets, excellent tunes and a rather competent cast, struggling vainly." Even today audiences run hot or cold on this film, with little rhyme or reason. Bert and Bob immediately went on a world tour following the completion of *Diplomaniacs,* and the film was generally forgotten (even in its own time) until Leonard Maltin's rediscovery for the Museum of Modern Art's Bicentennial Salute to American Screen Comedy. *Diplomaniacs* travels a rocky road, but the route is not without considerable pleasures. In many regions the film premiered just days after the highly popular *So This Is Africa*. Despite the direct competition and downbeat reviews, *Diplomaniacs* was a reasonable success (it cost $242,000 and earned RKO a $65,000 profit). Nevertheless, the studio had no intention of repeating such an oddball formula. Bert and Bob's next project, *Hips, Hips, Hooray!* emerged as a mainstream

Woolsey encountered the Sphinx (and camel) in Egypt during the team's second international tour, in 1933.

production—although the "girlie" slant was sensibly retained for box-office insurance. As Wheeler and Woolsey movies go, their next two films were ideal vehicles and, incidentally, among the finest comedies of the 1930s.

Before continuing with their screen careers, Bert and Bob embarked on their world tour. On April 7, 1933, the boys, together with Woolsey's wife, Minnie, and Bert's gal Friday, Pat Parker, cruised from Los Angeles to Honolulu on the liner *Mariposa*. Among the other passengers were Al Jolson, his wife, Ruby Keeler, director Frank Borzage and his wife, and the Pat O'Briens. On May 1 the boys continued toward Yokohama, Japan, where fans hounded the two comics day and night. "This 'round-the-world business is plain torture," Woolsey reported to Hilary Lynn in a *Photoplay* interview. "Believe me, the Orient's no place for a comic! Showing a funny man to an Asiatic is like showing a chunky side of beef to a jolly old lion—they just gobble you up. Maybe it's because they haven't any screaming comedies of their own there."

RKO handed Bert and Bob an all-expenses-paid vacation, but it turned into a whirlwind publicity stunt that never gave them a chance to breathe. "Imagine if you can," Woolsey continued, "being chased up and down Asia for three solid months—from Batavia to Singapore, from Mandalay to Calcutta, from Calcutta to Cairo, from Cairo to Bagdad. Chased by mobs of frenzied followers who grabbed for my cigar or my specs..." Bert and Bob were relieved to end their tour with a return to the British Isles. On the last leg of the journey, the boys were feted in Dublin by Ireland's president Eamon DeValera. Emerging from the presidential limousine, the weary Woolsey acknowledged the crowd's cheering with a brief speech, then stumbled and fell off the curb. Bob was exhausted, but his faithful subjects roared with laughter over the wilted comic's "impromptu" clowning. The comedians returned to Hollywood in the late summer of 1933, although within weeks they were contemplating another marathon tour, this time of the United States. An actor's need for applause is a strange thing indeed.

18
Signing 'Em Up (1933)

Directed by Leign Jason. NRA (National Recovery Administration) official featurette contributed by the Motion Picture industry. Filmed October 31, 1933. Released by RKO during December, 1933. 4 minutes.

Cast: Bert Wheeler, Robert Woolsey, Bruce Cabot, Roscoe Ates, Pert Kelton, Dorothy Lee (themselves), Sydney Jarvis (the director).

Synopsis: While shooting their latest picture, Wheeler and Woolsey are recruited by the studio boss to obtain NRA consumer pledges from stars on the lot. Their mission accomplished, Bert and Bob return to their next scene. Dorothy Lee is to rescue the boys, who are tied up next to a shack full of explosives. The scene begins, but the four o'clock whistle trills the end of the workday—causing everyone to instantly abandon the set. "Hey, what's the idea?" asks Bert. "NRA," Bob states didactically. "Everybody quits at four o'clock." "Yeah," Wheeler notices, "but what about that big black bomb?" "Aw," responds Woolsey, "who's afraid of the big black bomb?" The shack explodes, leaving the boys (in blackface) signing each other's pledge card.

★ ★ ★

By 1933 the worldwide Depression had penetrated every facet of the American lifestyle—including the public's moviegoing habits. Fewer dimes were earmarked for Bijou pleasures, particularly when radio offered free entertainment at home. The once-insulated film industry was bitten where it really hurt—in the pocketbook. Paramount, Warner Brothers, Fox, Universal, and Columbia were on the ropes and battling receivership or bankruptcy. Of all the major studios that year, only MGM managed to turn a profit; RKO especially felt the pinch, to the tune of a $4.4 million loss. In typically gung-ho, patriotic fashion, Hollywood rallied around the country's new president, hoping for a real-life movie miracle. One of Franklin D. Roosevelt's first presidential acts was to create the National Recovery Administration (NRA), a bureau established to regulate industry for economic reform and recovery. Hollywood responded with a

We Do Our Share: Bert and Bob badger Bruce Cabot for his autograph in *Signing 'Em Up*.

series of short subjects extolling the benefits of the NRA and distributed the films to theaters free of charge. Big-name talent was employed on some well-crafted little pictures: Charlie Ruggles teamed with Mary Boland in a Paramount short, enacting a domestic routine; Dick Powell sang for Warner Brothers and dreamed he met both Washington and Lincoln; and Jimmy Durante joked for Metro and met Moe Howard—portraying not a Stooge but a sober-minded businessman.

RKO entered the foray with this thoroughly enjoyable vignette. Wheeler and Woolsey filmed the impromptu, four-minute, fifteen-second short at the beginning of a shooting day for *Hips, Hips, Hooray!* their feature in production. The haste with which it was assembled is evident in the harsh sunlight and heavy shadows that alternate from shot to shot, but the home-movie atmosphere makes the short delightful to watch: Bruce Cabot comes into the scene, riding a camera dolly camouflaged as a go-cart. As Cabot signs a pledge card, he recites a complicated speech citing the virtues of the NRA; and he's obviously reading this little homily off the card. Bert and Bob's lines are effortlessly delivered, showing the pair in peak form. Inquiring where Pert Kelton can be found, the boys are told that she is sunbathing on the roof. "Sonny," Bob advises Bert, "suppose you get Richard Dix. I'll take care of Miss Kelton!" "Look," says Bert, "you know, I don't think you should climb away up on that roof. Didn't you just tell me that your feet hurt?" "I know, boy," Bob responds with mock heroism, "but this is for the NRA!" Racing up the stairs in a we'll-see-who-gets-her-first attitude, the duo encounters Pert at the top of the stairs. She gives the boys (and the motion picture audience) as sincere a testimony as can be expected, given the scatterbrained circumstances:

> BOB: We want you to sign this NRA card. Will you sign it?
> PERT: Will I sign it, I should say I will, I just love the NRA, I don't know what it means but I'm for it, I think they're the grandest people, bless their hearts, they're always doing something for somebody that can't help themselves, they're a swell bunch of kids, well, boys, go along now, I'll be seein' ya.

Like kids selling chances, Bert and Bob rush over to their director (Sydney Jarvis) and flaunt the signatures they have obtained: "William Gargan, Ann Harding, Richard Dix, Dorothy Jordan..." Hey, did we miss something?—these people aren't even in the film. Jarvis is puzzled by a scrawl on one of the cards. "That's Baby LeRoy," Bert explains—evidently the boys played truant and ran around the corner to Paramount.

Unseen and unknown for nearly half a century (a single 35 mm work print was unearthed by archivist Marty Kearns in 1982), *Signing 'Em Up* is as fresh today as it was during the Depression's darkest days.

19
Hips, Hips, Hooray! (1934)

Directed by Mark Sandrich. Executive producer, Merian C. Cooper. Associate producer, H. N. Swanson. Screenplay by Bert Kalmar, Harry Ruby, and Edward Kaufman. Story, music, and lyrics by Bert Kalmar and Harry Ruby. Art direction by Van Nest Polglase and Carroll Clark. Costumes by Walter Plunkett. Photographed by David Abel. Photographic effects by Vernon Walker. Musical direction by Roy Webb. Sound recording by Phillip J. Faulkner, Jr. Dances directed by Dave Gould. Sound cutter, George Marsh. Film editing by Basil Wrangell. Dates of production: October 17 to November 6, 1933. Released by RKO on February 2, 1934. 67 minutes.

Cast: Bert Wheeler (Andy Williams), Robert Woolsey (Dr. Bob Dudley), Ruth Etting (Herself), Thelma Todd (Amelia Frisby), Dorothy Lee (Daisy Maxwell), George Meeker (Armand Beauchamp), James Burtis (Detective Sweeney), Matt Briggs (Detective Epstein), Spencer Charters (Mr. Clark), Phyllis Barry (Madame Irene), Carlyle Moore, Jr. (Clark's Assistant), Marion "Peanuts" Byron, Jean Carmen, Patricia Parker (Lipstick Girls), Dorothy Granger (Miss Cole, a stenographer), Bobby Watson (Choreographer), Elise Cavanna (Miss Pilot, a radio announcer), Otto Fries, Walter James (Mountaineers), True Boardman (Himself, a sports radio announcer), Alfred P. James (Mule Driver), Stanley Blystone (Racing Car Driver), Nat Carr (Gas Station Proprietor), Joe Marba (Poolroom Proprietor), Lee Shumway (Policeman), Doris McMahon (Maid), June Brewster (Bit).

Synopsis: Despite a beautiful display of scantily clad models, Amelia Frisby (Thelma Todd) cannot entice any customers to her Maiden America Beauty Products store because Andy Williams (Bert Wheeler) and Bob Dudley (Robert Woolsey) are attracting the crowd with their flavored lipsticks and sidewalk comedy routines. Enamored of Frisby model Daisy Maxwell (Dorothy Lee) and troubled by her plight, Andy persuades Bob to turn their talent to the successful sale of her products. The police arrive on the scene and are about to arrest the boys for peddling without a license when Bob declares that they are not selling anything— they are giving the products away. From across the street, Daisy sees the crowd grabbing at the cosmetics and assumes that the boys are born salesmen. Forced to cough up the cost of the goods—$24.50—Andy and Bob have Daisy believing that their "modern salesmanship" methods will salvage Miss Frisby's company. Daisy arranges an appointment for the boys to meet her boss at their place of business.

Now Andy and Bob must acquire an office, which they do by ingeniously ejecting Mr. Clark (Spencer Charters), president of the Clark Investment Company, telling him that his house is on fire. Miss Frisby and Daisy arrive at "Doctor" Dudley's posh suite; so impressed is Miss Frisby with the boys that she hires them to manage her organization. This arranged, the boys hurry from the office just in time to escape the furious Mr. Clark on his return. By mistake they take his black bag containing valuable securities and leave Clark their satchel of lipsticks. Clark sets private investigators Epstein (Matt Briggs) and Sweeney (James Burtis) on their trail.

The engagement of Andy and Bob complicates life for Armand Beauchamp (George Meeker), Miss Frisby's crooked sales manager. Beauchamp has designs on Daisy, but she and Andy have fallen in love while Bob is making rapid amatory progress with Miss Frisby. Beauchamp vengefully snatches the securities and informs the boys that detectives are looking for two fellows of their description who stole a bag from Mr. Clark. Andy and Bob belatedly realize that they unwittingly took Clark's bag by mistake.

Beauchamp schemes to bankrupt Maiden America, Inc., by selling company secrets to a competitor, Madame Irene (Phyllis Barry). Deciding to eliminate Andy and Bob once and for all, Beauchamp summons Epstein and Sweeney, having planted the empty black bag in the boys' desk. Andy and Bob evade capture, but are exposed as thieves to the women they love. Miss Frisby and Daisy prove their loyalty by refusing to believe Beauchamp's revelation.

Andy and Bob find themselves in a small midwestern town at the time the Cross-Continental Motor Classic is racing through. Maiden America, Inc., has entered a car into the race, but Beauchamp has arranged to have the drivers abandon the vehicle at that very point. When the boys spot Epstein and Sweeney fast in pursuit, they leap into the Maiden America car, continue in the frenetic race across country, and eventually find themselves winners of the event. At the California finish line Clark's detectives rush to arrest them, but Daisy and Miss Frisby intervene, disclosing that Beauchamp confessed to the robbery in New York. Andy and Bob win the prize money, Andy has Daisy, and Bob has Miss Frisby.

★   ★   ★

Hips, Hips, Hooray! is one of Wheeler and Woolsey's most enjoyable movies and ranks as a personal favorite for many staunch comedy buffs.

Hips, Hips, Hooray! (1934)

Even William K. Everson, guru of film historians and a certified nonfan, ranks *Hips* "one of their best and glossiest films," while Leonard Maltin, a loyal W & W partisan, calls the film "an excellent example of comedy in the 1930s." Not everyone's favorite vehicle (I share Maltin's preference for *Cockeyed Cavaliers*), *Hips, Hips, Hooray!* is still the perfect introduction for anyone unfamiliar with the boys' sizable body of work.

Bert and Bob's first production under their new three-picture deal was assigned to a bold, brash, brand-new RKO producer, Harold Swanson. Billed on screen credits as H. N. Swanson and known affectionately as just plain Swanie, the neophyte movie executive had a seasoned background in comedy: Swanie was the former editor of *College Humor* magazine, the 1920s equivalent of today's *National Lampoon*. Outspoken and impetuous, it was Swanie who changed the title of an F. Scott Fitzgerald work to *The Great Gatsby* and who later walked out of a lucrative RKO production job because he was "too damn bored with making movies." Still opinionated and active into his late eighties, Swanie reminisced in 1987 about his producing days:

> In 1933 I came to RKO, where I was hailed as some great literate giant, so I was promptly assigned to a B picture unit. This was OK by me since I didn't want to make those candy-assed "woman's pictures" with Katharine Hepburn that guys like Pan Berman were falling over each other to do.
>
> Some people looked down on the Wheeler and Woolsey movies but I think at the time they made more money for that studio than any other star RKO had. I worked on one, *Hips, Hips, Hooray!*, and had a ball, because we had all these girls wearing lingerie throughout the picture. Girls were cuter then, or maybe I was just younger! Anyway, it's Hollywood tradition that when you have a birthday the whole set throws a party. I think the *Hips, Hips, Hooray!* company had a "birthday party" every other day.
>
> What's more, every joker on the lot would come at lunchtime to look our babes over. I was just about to chase one of these clowns away when he turned around and I saw it was Mr. [Merian C.] Cooper, my boss.
>
> Bert Wheeler and Bob Woolsey were funny guys. I thought [Dorothy] Lee was a game kid, too. Nobody's around today who wants to work their tail off to make people laugh the way those three did.

The comedy talents of Bert Kalmar and Harry Ruby, fresh from the Marx Brothers' *Duck Soup*, concocted a script full of racy gags in the risqué tradition of *So This Is Africa* and *Diplomaniacs*. Dorothy Lee made a welcome return to the fold at $500 per week, in addition to the stunningly beautiful comedienne Thelma Todd, borrowed from Hal Roach at $2,500 for eleven days' work. Years afterward, Bert Wheeler reminisced fondly about his work with Todd:

> I tell you, this was a running gag with us. At the same time the Marx Brothers and Laurel and Hardy were making comedies, and we'd all be fighting to get Thelma Todd. She used to laugh about it—she'd say, "I go from Laurel and Hardy to Marx Brothers to Wheeler and Woolsey." We'd fight to get her, because she was such a beautiful girl and such a sweet girl, and she would do anything. She just loved to be with us. See, that was her life, doing comedy. She was such a wonderful person to get along with. We loved her.

Torch singer Ruth Etting, immortalized by Doris Day in the biopic *Love Me or Leave Me*, was to suffer stoically in a subplot with suave villain George Meeker. Shortly before production began, Etting's scenes were whittled away until she was down to a single number, "Keep Romance Alive." Ruth Etting was considered a potent enough draw to receive billing over her female costars, plus a commanding $10,000 for her guest-star appearance. "I got ten thousand dollars," Etting recalled happily in a 1974 *Film Fan Monthly* interview. "Now remember, it was 1933 and that was big money in those days. I bought a house, furnished it, and a fur coat. Oh, it wasn't mink but it wasn't rabbit, either. I felt I was on top of the world."

Bert and Bob found an eager ally in their new director, Mark Sandrich. A two-reel comedy graduate brimming with ideas, Sandrich understood the dictates of musical-comedy plots better than any of the team's other directors. "A wonderful thing about Mark Sandrich," Dorothy Lee remembers, "was that he'd ask us for our own ideas. Bert, Bob and I had more of a creative hand with Sandrich than with our other directors. Believe me, you care more when the head guy solicits your input."

Filming proceeded without incident except when an artificial snowstorm engulfed Bert and smothered him under several hundred pounds of bleached cornflakes. "Well," he cracked to reporters a day after resting at home, "after all that snow it's pretty sure I'll never be a 'coke' addict!"

Bert and Dorothy's simple introductory scene bristles with the spontaneity and charm which teems throughout the little picture. As Bert commiserates with Dot (who is liable to lose her job), he nonchalantly peels a banana and breaks off half for her. She takes the piece and casually eats it while continuing to relate her tale of woe. There is nothing especially funny about the action—and yet, it is funny, watching these real-life friends behave like real people caught in a candid moment.

The film's centerpiece is an elaborate mock-ballet executed by Bert, Bob, Dottie, and Thelma in a vacated business office. Pretending to be an affluent entrepreneur, Bob visits Mr. Clark (Spencer Charters), president of the Clark Investment Company while Bert telephones the office, informing

Hips, Hips, Hooray! (1934)

Clark's receptionist that her boss's home is on fire. As the distraught executive scurries out the door, Woolsey inquires solicitously, "What kind of a house is it? Stucco, frame, or brick?" "Brick!" Clark replies while pacing for the elevator. "Oh well, then, you have nothing to worry about," Bob assures him. "Brick takes longer to burn." As a pledge of support, Bob hands Clark the bulky hallway fire extinguisher before the elevator starts its descent.

Once Bob meets Thelma Todd, nothing stands in the way of a felicitous corporate merger. Bert and Dorothy sit atop a penthouse ledge, trading small talk. "Isn't the view beautiful from up here?" he asks. "Yeah," Dot replies, "but it makes me dizzy." "I like 'em dizzy!" Bert retorts. The happy twosome engages in one of Kalmar and Ruby's smoothest ditties, "Just Keep on Doin' What You're Doin'." The "doin'" portion of the number is kissing, which Bert and Dottie pursue between verses and while exchanging goo-goo eyes.

Soon Thelma and Bob join the happy couple in an outrageous takeoff on ballet, making a mess of poor Mr. Clark's once-tidy office. Creative impulse compels the quartet to shatter every vase, jar, and assorted bric-a-brac as punctuation for the song, "Keep on Doin' What You're Doin'." The exhibition is a riot, with Bert and Bob attempting punk acrobatics on Dorothy (leaping into Bert and Bob's arms from a desktop, the trio collapses on the floor). Tossing Dottie into the air, where she grabs ahold of a ceiling fixture, Bert, Bob, and Thelma catch her in a Persian rug. (When Dottie fell on the rug, someone let go; she landed partly on the floor, injuring her spine.) Suddenly Clark returns (still clutching the fire extinguisher), only to be waltzed by Woolsey into a nearby closet. This exhilarating showpiece is *the* highlight in a film of many highlights.

Later on, Bert and Bob perform a lively tap dance as instruction for a gay choreographer (Bobby Watson, who enjoyed negative fame in the 1940s as the movies' number-one Hitler impersonator). When Bert concludes the number with a somersault that lands him on his posterior, Watson flamboyantly sniffs, "Oh, my girls could never do that—they'd bruise!"

Although *Hips, Hips, Hooray!* is not that heavily seasoned with sexual innuendos, it does contain one episode that raised the ire of censors and the eyebrows of everyone else—the notorious lipstick kissing scene. Bob invents a kissing game to guess the flavor of lipstick worn by his all-girl retinue. Each shapely young miss wears next to nothing and leaves nothing to the imagination. It's a sexy scene and a funny one (when Wheeler becomes preoccupied in an extended kiss, Woolsey implores him to "Say something!" "Hullo," Bert feebly replies, before returning to the business at hand). Petite Marion "Peanuts" Byron, so appealing as Buster Keaton's leading lady in *Steamboat Bill, Junior* (1928) but reduced to bit roles in

In *Hips, Hips, Hooray!* Bert and Bob sample flavored lipstick kisses on the RKO lot. Marion Byron is kissing Bert, while Bert's real-life girlfriend, Pat Parker, is to the right of Woolsey.

talkies, packs such a wallop in her smooching that Woolsey's legs levitate. Falling back to earth, Bob dubs the tiny dynamo "public enemy number one." For the record, Bert's current girlfriend, Patricia Parker, appears as one of the kissable kissers. She's the knockout blond who backs off, causing Bert and Bob to accidentally kiss each other.

Hips, Hips, Hooray!'s auto-race finale is one of the fastest and funniest of its kind, certainly the inspiration for a great many of the endings that climaxed the next decade's Abbott and Costello epics. The impressive sight gags are worked out perfectly. Whether tobogganing through the Rockies (the boys have put skis on the car's wheels) or sailing gracefully over the competition (Bert pumped helium into the tires), it's all plausible and all funny. The best moment comes when the midget racing car teeters precariously on a rocky peak; a yawning chasm awaits the boys. "Whooah!" shouts Woolsey, "Oh, boy, don't make a move. If you do, we're sunk!" "Wh-wh-wh-what am I gonna do?" asks Bert, "I've gotta hiccup! You'd better scare me!" Bob laughs nervously as he looks over the side at the terrifying drop; if the predicament they're in doesn't frighten

Patricia Dolores Wheeler and Bob do imitations of her dad outside the soundstages for *Hips, Hips, Hooray!*

Bert, what on earth will? Woolsey hesitates a moment before "shocking" his partner with a tiny "boo!" It's a superb comedy moment made even funnier by the boys' sincere straight acting.

Hips made a fortune for RKO and Wheeler and Woolsey, who collected 20 percent of the picture's gross receipts against a $75,000 guarantee of the profits. Andre Sennwald in the *New York Times* hypothesized, "There are three reasonably hilarious gags and perhaps fifty more that depend on whether you are for or against the ex-vaudeville clowns to begin with." *Time* magazine believed that "admirers of the agonized smile of small Wheeler and the brisk dignity of cigar-chewing Woolsey will relish" the comedy, while Marguerite Tazelaar in the *New York Herald Tribune* felt that the witticisms were "timed with the pride of all comics scattering pearls. ... Then there is Mr. Woolsey's weird war cry, which for some reason always draws astonished laughs from admirers."

Hips, Hips, Hooray! is vintage Wheeler and Woolsey, although by no means the team's masterpiece. Their next film would be both.

20
Cockeyed Cavaliers (1934)

Directed by Mark Sandrich. Executive producer, Pandro S. Berman. Associate producer, Lou Brock. Screenplay by Edward Kaufman and Ben Holmes. Additional dialogue by Grant Garrett and Ralph Spence. Art direction by Van Nest Polglase and Carroll Clark. Costumes by Walter Plunkett. Photographed by David Abel. Photographic effects by Vernon Walker. Musical direction by Roy Webb. Music and lyrics by Will Jason and Val Burton. Sound recording by Phillip J. Faulkner, Jr. Sound cutter, George Marsh. Edited by Jack Kitchin. Dates of production: March 29 to April 24, 1934. Released by RKO on June 29, 1934. 72 minutes.

Cast: Bert Wheeler (Bert), Robert Woolsey (Bob), Thelma Todd (Lady Genevieve), Dorothy Lee (Mary Ann Dale), Noah Beery (the Baron), Robert Greig (the Duke of Weskit), Henry Sedley (the Baron's Friend), Franklin Pangborn (Town Crier), Alfred P. James (Squire Dale, Mary Ann's father), Jack Norton (the King's Physician), Snub Pollard (the Physician's Assistant), Kate Price (Maid), Frank Mills (Brawler), Kewpie Morgan (Andrew), Billy Gilbert (Landlord), Charlie Hall (Coachman), Kit Guard (Peasant).

Synopsis: Bert Wheeler and Bob Woolsey are impoverished varlets wandering the countryside in seventeenth-century England. They are "riding the rods" beneath regal coaches of state when they meet the Duke of Weskit's intended wife, Mary Ann (Dorothy Lee) of Cranberry Cross, who is being forced to marry the Duke (Robert Greig) to repay a debt contracted by her father (Alfred James). Mary Ann masquerades as a boy to escape the Duke's advances and to make her fortune in the world. Bert and Bob are arrested when Bert's kleptomania compels him to steal the Duke's coach. Mary Ann, still disguised as a male, rescues the boys from pillory by starting a brawl. The trio escapes on horseback, resting at an inn after Bert has stolen everything from a nobleman's watch to the town curfew bell. Andrew (Kewpie Morgan), an official of Cranberry Cross, catches up with the trio, forcing them to make a quick exit for their lives; they annex the royal physician's coach and continue.

By coincidence they stop at the Duke's house, where the real physicians are expected to cure the latter's bellyache. Mary Ann must continue her masquerade; after Bert discovers that his traveling companion is a beautiful girl, he falls in love with her. Bob, meanwhile, cures the Duke with his unorthodox methods and falls for his niece, Lady Genevieve (Thelma Todd), the wife of a ferocious baron.

Returning from a hunting trip, the Baron (Noah Beery) discovers his wife's duplicity, but believing Bert and Bob to actually be the king's physicians, he is afraid to harm them. Meanwhile, the Duke threatens to punish Mary Ann's father unless his daughter arrives for the wedding. Mary Ann tearfully overhears the Duke's threat and hurriedly dresses for the nuptials. At this moment, it is announced that a wild boar that the Baron has attempted to capture is in close proximity. The Baron offers a reward for its capture, an amount that will cover the debt and liberate Mary Ann. In a wild chase sequence, the boys capture the boar, save the day, and straighten out their romances.

★ ★ ★

Cockeyed Cavaliers, Bert and Bob's greatest comedy, was envisioned almost as an afterthought. In December 1933, it was decided that the next Wheeler and Woolsey vehicle (entitled *Frat Heads*) would use a college campus as its backdrop for humor. Publicity photos were taken of the boys suffering through their dreary technocracy lessons, after which they embarked on an abbreviated personal appearance tour with Dorothy Lee. Meanwhile, writers Ben Holmes and Ed Kaufman met with producer Lou Brock to brainstorm gags and situations for the scholarly setting.

Apparently Bert, Bob, and Dottie did everything but assassinate the audience during the run of their tremendously successful tour. *Variety* caught up with the team January 26, 1934, in Baltimore at the Century Theater. "There's a solid-scoring fifty minutes of stage entertainment on tap here this week that's evoking grade A comment from the old-line vaudeville followers," the reviewer noted, "who in turn are giving the show such word o' mouth plugging, audiences are building into what will eventuate as a sweet box office session for all concerned." *Variety* continued,

> The marquee illuminators, Wheeler & Woolsey, undoubtedly drawing largely by virtue of their picture rep, but the hardy vets of the stage are also delivering in vaudeville fashion and swatting over their turn to sockerino proportions. Woolsey rassles with that giant perfecto and Wheeler pleased the old-timers by resurrecting the apple-gnawing foolery.
>
> Miss Dorothy Lee, brought on after an initial ten minutes, strong receptioned. Trio sits on apron, feet hanging down over pit, a new and epic audience proximity to this town, but lends effective intimacy with the mob in the pews. A song by Miss Lee supplied the boys with an

December 1933 publicity photo for an unmade film, *Frat Heads*. Bert's Eaton schoolboy outfit is the same one worn in his vaudeville days with Betty Wheeler.

opportunity for some pantomimic mugging and the trio then offed with hoke song and dance. The getaway afforded Miss Lee a chance to introduce some of her highly developed hip-grinding. Mob wouldn't be sated until the threesome stepped through four bends and a pair of curtain spiels by Woolsey.

"The boys were a smash wherever we played," Dottie recalls. "We were traveling all over the East in a tiny plane, going from city to city. Somewhere along the line we had a four-hour layover, so Bert and I figured we'd check out the town. Bob decided to hang around the airfield." The inevitable corps of reporters caught up with Woolsey at the airport, assailing him with the usual barrage of questions regarding himself, Hollywood, and his teammates. When queried whether or not Dottie was engaged to Marshall Duffield, Bob decided to have a little fun. "Naw," he drawled, "*I'm* the love of her life. We're gonna be married." Dot Lee recalls the rest:

> The next day, wherever we landed, the headlines in the paper read, "DOROTHY LEE TO WED ROBERT WOOLSEY." Oh God, I said to myself, am I dreaming?
> When I found out what Bob did, I gave him Hell and wouldn't let up until he explained to the press that he was just being funny. Some joke!

Back in Hollywood, the writers were experiencing serious snags nurturing *Frat Heads*. To begin with, the Marx Brothers had thoroughly covered the collegiate market with *Horse Feathers* in 1932. All story ideas pointed to the inclusion of a football finale for *Frat Heads*, but that would have infringed once again on the Marxian epic, not to mention the gridiron climax in *Hold 'Em Jail*. Someone—either Ed Kaufman or Ben Holmes—suggested placing the boys in a costume spoof of *The Three Musketeers*. Ideas thrashed around began evolving into a costume period piece somewhat akin to Will Rogers's *Connecticut Yankee in King Arthur's Court*, or Eddie Cantor's current gem, *Roman Scandals*. Inspired by the recent spate of historical pageants—*The Private Life of Henry VIII*, *Queen Christina*, *Catherine the Great*—not to mention Laurel and Hardy's megahit operetta *Fra Diavolo*—RKO dropped *Frat Heads* and ran with the new ball.

On its own merits, the completed script for *Cockeyed Cavaliers* is quite extraordinary, and not just because two comparatively unknown writers authored a sharper screenplay than those darlings of light musical comedy, Kalmar and Ruby. *Cockeyed Cavaliers* contains some of Wheeler and Woolsey's funniest comedy routines but, more importantly, has the firmest structure of any of their features. Despite its razor-sharp parody of costume epics, *Cavaliers* is essentially a latter-day adaptation of the English Restoration farce, which flourished in the late 1600s under King Charles II. The king, England's original good-time Charlie, was less concerned with the affairs of state than he was with the affairs of his boudoir. This dissolute monarch's lifestyle was reflected in the bawdy lampoons of the age, the best known of which is Henry Fielding's vintage spicy novel, *Tom Jones*.

Cockeyed Cavaliers (1934)

The raucous immorality of Restoration comedy was right up Hollywood's alley in the early thirties. No one would accuse Wheeler and Woolsey of going highbrow with an erudite, literate adaptation of a stolid, dead style. Best of all, Bert and Bob had been cited for peddling "dirt" to their audiences before, but who could denounce the boys for being raw when their humorous inspiration derived from the classics?

Other refreshing ideas abound in *Cavaliers.* Anachronisms are always funny when comedians find themselves transplanted in time, either backward (Eddie Cantor in *Roman Scandals*) or forward (Woody Allen in *Sleeper*); in another era, their twentieth-century savvy seems hilariously inappropriate (witness Eddie Cantor's attempts to explain Mickey and Minnie Mouse to an incredulous Nero, or Knight Will Rogers's winning a joust by lassoing his medieval opponent). Since the comic is displaced from his own age, there is a logical basis for the continual culture shock experienced by the funnyman throughout the entire picture. Not so in *Cockeyed Cavaliers*—Bert and Bob portray authentic vagabonds of the late 1600s yet spout modern vernacular, much to the confusion of everyone they encounter. Since all the other players speak in the stilted rhetoric style of the period (most of them affecting or possessing British accents), Bert's flat Brooklyn twang and Bob's midwestern drawl seem almost surreal and all the funnier. This hilarious wordplay erupts in the boys' very first scene, when the audience discovers them hitching a ride underneath a royal coach:

> BOB: Egad and gadzooks, to say nothing of a couple of bod hodkins—this Pullman service is awful!
> BERT: I wonder who this carriage belongs to?
> BOB: Oh, some great duchess, I suppose. I hope she doesn't find us under here—she's liable to have us beheaded.
> BERT: Behead us? Can she do that?
> BOB: Sure, she can be hed.

A running gag throughout the film is Bert's periodic spells of kleptomania; he goes into a trancelike state just before he pilfers whatever is in sight. Catching Bert going into a stupor, Bob soundly smacks his buddy's face:

> BOB: Get that silly look off of your face! Every time you do that I know you're ready to lift something—and you promised me you weren't gonna steal another thing!
> BERT: You know I can't help lifting things. It's a disease! Y'know, the doctor says that I'm a kleptomaniac.
> BOB: Yeah, well why don't you take something for it?
> BERT: I've taken everything. But you know, I don't really steal.
> BOB: Aw, no, you don't steal—you just find a lot of things that haven't been lost, that's all!

Baroness Thelma Todd is aware of two freeloading varlets in the team's best picture, *Cockeyed Cavaliers.*

Inevitably, Bert's kleptomania gets the duo in big trouble—first he steals the horses off the coach, and while Bob is returning the animals to the driver, Bert creeps away with the coach itself. Placed on public display in pillory, the boys are pelted with rotten fruit when Dorothy Lee arrives upon the scene. Dottie has disguised herself as a boy to evade the clutches of an amorous old Duke (Robert Greig) who desires her hand in marriage.

Cockeyed Cavaliers (1934)

She attacks the mob for their cruel actions, and while a free-for-all escalates, Bert and Bob make their move. Running down the street with their heads still trapped in the stock, the boys chance upon two oxen wearing a yoke. "I wonder what they're in stocks for?" Bob asks Bert. "They must be kleptomaniacs, too!" Bert replies matter-of-factly.

Breaking off the wooden beam, Wheeler and Woolsey rescue the "boy" Dottie and make their escape on her horse. Arriving that night at the Golden Boar Inn, Dottie appears on horseback while Bert and Bob are afoot, wearing straw pillows draped across their behinds. Without a sovereign to their names, Woolsey devises a scheme to obtain free meals for the three of them: after finishing their food, Bob will blow his nose, giving Bert the signal to throw a tankard of ale into Woolsey's face. Bob will then challenge Bert to a fight in the courtyard, where they'll make their getaway.

Naturally, everything that can go wrong, does; Bert continually mistakes other people's sneezes for Bob's cue, causing Woolsey to be unceremoniously doused several times. Seething, Bob wonders why Wheeler has splattered him:

> BERT: You blew your nose!
> BOB: I did not blow my nose—it was your imagination!
> BERT: Oh, no—my imagination doesn't make a noise like *that*.

Bert, Bob, and Dorothy encounter the lecherous Baron (Noah Beery, Sr.) who has come to the tavern for food, drink, and wenching. Introducing themselves, Wheeler and Woolsey perform a rousing song and dance specialty, "And the Big Bad Wolf Is Dead." Spirited lyrics, the team's enthusiasm, and expert hoofing atop a wooden table make for a glorious production number. Everyone joins in for another chorus and an encore—including the basso-voiced Noah Beery, whose throaty croak was an amusing revelation to 1934 audiences.

The arrival of the law causes the trio to escape, stealing the clothes and coach of the King's physician and his assistant (played respectively by a drunken Jack Norton and the equally soused Snub Pollard; incidentally, they—not Bert and Bob—are the "cockeyed cavaliers"). All duded up in royal finery, Wheeler, Woolsey, and Dottie (who they still believe is a boy) are trundled off to a country estate. Searching for clues regarding their newfound occupations, Bob locates a book left in the carriage and reads its title: "*Materia Medica*—ah, pig latin!" Arriving at the estate of the same duke to whom Dottie was betrothed, Bert and Bob are informed by the beautiful Baroness (Thelma Todd) that her uncle, the Duke, is suffering from insomnia. "You know, toots," Bob informs Thelma as he takes her arm, "you and I are going to be great pals. By the way—what does 'insomnia' mean?"

A magical music moment from *Cockeyed Cavaliers*: the boys perform "And the Big Bad Wolf Is Dead."

The boys attempt to cure the Duke by using a veterinarian's manual, treating the obese Greig as though he were a horse ("it says here if he kicks, trip him up, throw him on his back, and sit on his belly"). The unorthodox methods unexpectedly invigorate the Duke, who grows fond of his new royal acquaintances. Greig suggests that Wheeler and Woolsey secure the king's permission to stay on indefinitely as houseguests. "Aw, the king'll never miss us," Bob reassures his host.

A hot-blooded flirtation develops between coquettish Thelma Todd and ladies' man Woolsey. Dorothy confesses to Bert that she's really a girl, and romance quickly blooms for both happy couples. The foursome performs another exceptional song and dance, "Dilly Dally," with the boys executing jackhammer high jumps in slow motion.

When Baron Beery returns home, he finds Woolsey flirting outrageously with his wife. Preparing to skewer Bob with his rapier, Beery is reminded that the "physician" represents the king—thus compelling the murderous Baron to hold his anger in check. But when Beery eventually discovers the masquerade, he pursues Bob, ready for the kill. "Remember the king!" Woolsey remonstrates—to no effect—as Beery lunges at him.

Thelma Todd hides from Woolsey but Noah Beery seeks him out in the Restoration farce *Cockeyed Cavaliers*.

Bob adds, "Well, the queen, then—the jack—the ace—deuces wild!" Thelma informs Bob that her low-cut dress is "the coming fashion." "It must be coming," Woolsey observes, "because it all hasn't arrived." As Thelma stuffs her powder puff between her ample cleavage, Bob inquires if she'd like a little assistance. Bert's kleptomania overpowers him, and he steals the powder puff (off camera, of course) from Thelma's bosom;

Beery arrives on the scene to see Woolsey returning the item to its owner, while Todd remarks, "Oh, Doctor—how *ever* did you get it?"

The climax features a wild boar chase that is up to the thrills-and-laugh standards set in *Hips, Hips, Hooray!* The boar lands on top of Bert and Bob's coach, falling through the roof and frightening the boys. When they spot the boar chasing Noah Beery across a field, Bob instructs his partner not to shoot. "Why not?" Wheeler asks. Woolsey responds, "You might hit the boar."

Cockeyed Cavaliers is a nigh-perfect comedy, certainly the finest film Wheeler and Woolsey ever appeared in. *Cavaliers* was expertly directed by the versatile Mark Sandrich, who was about to be promoted by RKO to helm the big-budgeted Astaire and Rogers musical *The Gay Divorcee*. While she hardly recalls the making of this film, Dorothy Lee believes this to be one of the top W & W comedies, although she regrets that it was not filmed in color. "Those costumes were really lovely, and Thelma Todd was such a pretty girl." The trade press raved over the team's latest release, although cosmopolitan reviewers only grudgingly admitted their appreciation. "Despite all of its unhappy gags," Richard Watts wrote in the *New York Herald Tribune*, "there is an air of amiable lunacy about it that deserves to be encouraged. Andre Sennwald in the *New York Times* rationalized his amusement, noting that

> Mr. Woolsey tosses off his low vaudeville retorts so expectantly, that the defiant spectator, almost unwillingly, finds himself joining in the resultant laughter. Thus when Mr. Woolsey gazes thoughtfully down a patient's throat, shakes his head sagely, and says, "Just as I thought: flat feet," the jest is so unreasonably bad that it becomes perversely amusing.

Cavaliers did not live up to the box-office achievements of its predecessors. RKO distribution president Ned E. Depinet wrote studio chief B. B. Kahane on July 19 that *"Cockeyed Cavaliers* is not drawing as many theater patrons out in the sticks as *Hips, Hips, Hooray!* I think the results with *Cockeyed Cavaliers* should teach us not to put Wheeler & Woolsey in a period costume picture like this story." The effect was duly noted: if anything, the team's next vehicle was designed specifically for that audience "out in the sticks." As a result, Wheeler and Woolsey's next film would be the biggest box-office hit of their careers.

21
Kentucky Kernels (1934)

Directed by George Stevens. Produced by Lee Marcus. Associate producer, H. N. Swanson. Unit manager, Charles Stallings. Assistant directors, Jean Yarbrough and Bill Cody. Screenplay by Bert Kalmar, Harry Ruby, and Fred Guiol. Story, music, and lyrics by Bert Kalmar and Harry Ruby. Script girl, Ann Coleman. Art direction by Van Nest Polglase and Perry Ferguson. Costumes by Walter Plunkett. Photographed by Edward Cronjager. Second cameraman, Al Wetzel. Assistant cameraman, Henry Cronjager. Musical direction by Roy Webb. Sound recording by Phillip J. Faulkner, Jr. Sound assistant, Frank Ray. Film editing by James Morley. Property man, Syd Fogel. Second property man, Larry Haddock. Grip, Ralph Wildman. Gaffer, Bristow. Best boy, Armstrong. Wardrobe man, Tommie Clark. Wardrobe woman, Frances Winters. Makeup by Fred T. Walker. Hairdresser, Lillian Lashin. Dates of production: August 6 to September 4, 1934. British release title, *Triple Trouble*. Released by RKO on November 2, 1934. 77 minutes.

Cast: Bert Wheeler (Willie Dugan), Robert Woolsey (Elmer Doyle, aka the Great Elmer), Mary Carlisle (Gloria Wakefield), George "Spanky" McFarland (Spanky Milford), Noah Beery, Sr. (Colonel Wakefield), Lucille LaVerne (Hannah Milford), Willie "Sleep 'n' Eat" Best (Buckshot), Margaret Dumont (Mrs. Baxter), Louis Mason (Judge Ezra Milford), Paul Page (Jerry Bronson), Frank McGlynn, Jr. (Jess Wakefield), Richard Alexander (Hank Wakefield), William Pawley (John Wakefield), Marian Sheldon, Ruth Leslie, Frances Grant, Marge Dowell, Ruth Riley, Harriet Haddon, Valerie Traxler, Elizabeth Cook (Kentucky Belles), Dorothy Granger (Ethel, a secretary), Edgar Dearing (Policeman), Harrison Greene (Lawyer Aloysious T. Guilfoyle), Clarence Wilson (Lawyer Peck), Frank O'Connor (Officer), Charlie Hall (Cigar Stand Proprietor), Otto Hoffman (Station Agent), William Gould (a Milford), Roger Gray (Moonshiner), Harry Bernard (Destitute Man), Hank Potts, Jackie Goodrich (Doubles).

Synopsis: Out-of-work magician Elmer Doyle (Robert Woolsey) and his assistant, Willie Dugan (Bert Wheeler), live in a waterfront shanty, dreaming of the day that vaudeville comes back. Hearing the bell ring on their fishnet, their "catch" turns out to be Jerry Bronson (Paul Page), a wealthy suitor attempting suicide. Convincing Bronson that no woman is worth dying over, the boys persuade him to adopt an orphan baby as a heartache palliative. They urge him to choose Spanky Milford (George "Spanky" McFarland), without realizing that the adorable tyke has a habit of smashing windows. When Bronson's fiancée has a change of heart and elopes with Jerry, Elmer and Willie are assigned the task of watching Spanky until the couple's return.

Thanks to Spanky's unerring accuracy with a rock, Elmer and Willie sit shivering in their now-windowless shack. They are interrupted by two lawyers (Harrison Greene, Clarence Wilson) who inform them that Spanky has inherited the huge Milford homestead in Banesville, Kentucky. The boys deliver Spanky to his family and witness a feud raging between the Milford and Wakefield clans. The dynasties have been at war for over a century, destroying the romance between Colonel Wakefield (Noah Beery) and Aunt Hannah Milford (Lucille LaVerne). Elmer is determined to end the feud as romance develops between Willie and beautiful Gloria Wakefield (Mary Carlisle).

The Wakefields are invited to a Milford garden party, orchestrated by the too-amiable Elmer. The guests indulge themselves happily until Spanky opens a champagne bottle and the cork pop is interpreted as a pistol shot. The feud is on again! Milford and Wakefields open battle while the boys' peacemaking efforts fail dismally. Just as Elmer and Willie are about to be shot by Wakefields, a telegram arrives announcing that Spanky is not a true Milford after all. Realizing the foolishness of his pointless grudge, Colonel Wakefield buries the hatchet, paving the way to Willie and Gloria's inevitable marriage.

★   ★   ★

With Wheeler and Woolsey's popularity solidly rooted in the cotton belt and rural communities, it seemed only logical that the peregrinating duo would eventually wander into the bluegrass comedy *Kentucky Kernels*, the greatest financial success of all their starring films. Highly regarded in its day, *Kentucky Kernels* is a genial "family" picture whose mild humor and protracted slapstick lacks the bite and wit of their best vehicles.

Bert Kalmar and Harry Ruby fashioned an unusual narrative for the team, inspired by the legendary feud between the southern families the Hatfields and the McCoys, clans that were on opposing sides during the Civil War. The war ended but the feud raged on between the families for years afterward. Buster Keaton had already poked fun at honor and death on the old plantation in his classic *Our Hospitality* (1923), but nobody else tackled a noteworthy hillbilly spoof until *Kentucky Kernels*. Afterward, the mountain-man motif proved fertile ground for other teams, including the Ritz Brothers, Abbott and Costello and the Bowery Boys, not to mention the Ma and Pa Kettle series. Television found grass-roots humor alive and well in the 1960s with *The Beverly Hillbillies, Petticoat Junction,* and *Green Acres.* The rustic revue *Hee Haw* continued well into the 1980s; all of these shows can be found running in syndication today.

Kalmar and Ruby had written memorably for the team before (witness *Hips, Hips, Hooray!*) but now they were curbed by the suddenly omnipotent Legion of Decency, which was founded by the Catholic Church on April 11, 1934. Catholics were required to take a pledge at mass that bound them for one year to avoid all movies that the church labeled "indecent and immoral and unfit for public entertainment." The Legion's clout spread like wildfire—not only Catholics but citizens of all denominations refused to attend films that the church condemned as either "indecent and immoral" or those "that glorify crime." Fearful of ever-dwindling returns at the box office, the Motion Picture Producers and Distributors Association immediately created the Production Code Administration, headed by Will Hays's appointee, Joseph I. Breen. Under the declarations established, no scripts could go into production without Code approval.

One of Breen's earliest acts was an attack on films already in release. Breen categorized eighteen major studio releases as "Class I—the release of the picture be halted now and no additional contracts be taken on." Among the titles (*Affairs of a Gentleman, Baby Face, Melody Cruise, The Ex-Lady, Blondie Johnson*) was a Wheeler and Woolsey, the "notorious" *So This Is Africa.* Breen further specified twelve other titles as "Class II—the films be permitted to finish out their present contracts, but no new contracts be taken." On this list (*Fog Over Frisco, He Was Her Man, I'm No Angel, Manhattan Melodrama, Sadie McKee*) were two Wheeler and Woolseys, *Diplomaniacs* and *Hips, Hips, Hooray!* No other star attraction, not even the double entendre-spouting Mae West, was represented by more than one film on both lists combined. As Hollywood's leading offenders, Wheeler and Woolsey scripts would have to be scrubbed squeaky clean in order to appease vanguards of the team's kiddie audiences. Bert and Bob had to completely overhaul their approach to comedy—and they did not like the new setup one bit. Bob Woolsey griped to the press, "The censors are tougher on us than they are on the Fascist newspapers in Spain."

Help in cushioning the blow was the arrival of a new director—the affable young genius-to-be, George Stevens, a former Hal Roach cameraman who worked his way up from directing shorts to RKO B features. *Kentucky Kernels* was a feather in the cap of this twenty-nine-year-old aspiring maverick. In his autobiography, *The Salad Days,* Douglas Fairbanks, Jr., recalled that Stevens appeared "vague, dreamy, and inefficient, but this was a mask behind which his creative brain ticked at the speed of light." Bert and Bob took to their new maestro immediately. "I loved him," Bert Wheeler reminisced in 1958. "He's still the biggest director there is. He looked like a real college boy type. Never raises his voice. You wouldn't think he knew anything."

In keeping with the team's newly expurgated image, Bert and Bob's costar would be six-year-old George McFarland, better known to *Our Gang* enthusiasts as Spanky. Spanky was borrowed from the Hal Roach studios at a salary of $200 a week with a seven-week guarantee, $25 a week more than Bert's new leading lady, Mary Carlisle, would be receiving. Gruff Noah Beery again returned to the fold, playing the irascible Colonel Wakefield for a commanding $1,000 a week, while D. W. Griffith veteran Lucille LaVerne signed on at the same salary. The studio "desperately" sought to borrow Stepin Fetchit from Fox, but they were not desperate enough to pay Fox the $1,250 a week requested to secure his services. RKO settled on Willie Best, a lanky young black actor whose claim to fame was his ability to imitate Stepin Fetchit—a dubious honor, to say the least. Poor Willie Best was featured prominently throughout *Kentucky Kernels*, yet he received a meager $125 for his work on the entire picture. Best became somewhat of a talisman to Wheeler and Woolsey directors George Stevens and the later Fred Guiol, representing good luck for Stevens (*Kentucky Kernels*, *The Nitwits*) and bad luck for Guiol (*Silly Billies*, *Mummy's Boys*).

Filming commenced August 6 with a week spent shooting at the old Shelby Mansion on the Universal lot. Other exteriors were obtained at the RKO ranch in Encino. Allotted a generous budget of $287,150, *Kentucky Kernels* is a handsomely mounted production boasting the glistening camerawork you would expect from a George Stevens film. That it fails to elicit much genuine humor is the fault of neither the director nor his two stars; their divergent schools of comedy simply refused to mix. In fashioning a "wholesome" comedy, the script eschews the usual W & W repartee, which might be slightly censorable, and substitutes simon-pure slapstick, guaranteed to please the children. However, Bert and Bob are musical comedy stars, not slapstick comedians. They could execute individual sight gags extremely well, but they could not handle the mindless runaway buggy sequence in *Kentucky Kernels* any better than the nameless silent-comedy goons who stumbled through hundreds of mediocre two-reelers.

An equally vexing problem is Spanky McFarland. The cute-looking Spanky gives a lackluster performance, quite possibly the worst of his career. True, he was only six years old, but Spanky had been contributing expert portrayals to *Our Gang* since 1932. The poor kid, surrounded by strange actors, a new studio, and a different director, had been thrown for a loop. In his review of the film for the *New York Times*, Frank Nugent remarked, "There is little danger of any one mistaking Master McFarland for a male Shirley Temple."

Equally irksome is Spanky's role—not a lovable mischief maker, but a prepubescent pain in the ass. Tearing up Bert and Bob's $1,000 check, shattering every window in their freezing shanty, nearly getting Willie Best's head blown off by a shotgun, and instigating a second, deadlier feud, the kid has no redeeming qualities to make the audience want to "pull" for him. Bert does get to stick him in the behind with a sewing needle, but a dart gun might have been a more suitable implement.

Coy humor was not an attribute of the W & W pictures, and its appearance in *Kentucky Kernels* is out of sync with the team's established personas. The opening scene finds Bert washing dishes while Bob enjoys a smoke and the newspaper (*Variety*, of course). Bert is uncharacteristically whining to Bob as the scene begins:

> BERT: All you do is sit around the house all day and read the paper while I work my fingers to the bone!
> BOB: Didn't I take you to the movies tonight?
> BERT: Aw, what good is going to the movies when you have to come home and wash the dishes? And another thing—you know, it's very embarrassing for me to always have the neighbors see me in front of this sink washing dishes!
> BOB: You're right, and I'm gonna do something about it. I'll buy a shade for the window! Now will you stop complaining?
> BERT: Listen, you'd complain too if you had to stand in front of a hot stove all day long! Look at my hands! This dishwater has ruined them. If I'd only listened to my mother—
> BOB: Listen, I'm gettin' sick and tired of this continual nagging! If I hear one more word about your mother—
> BERT: You leave my mother out of this!
> BOB: That suits me, and it'll probably suit your old man, too. The poor devil never gets a chance to say a word. He opened his mouth once and three moths flew out!

Although some might consider the sequence cute, it certainly isn't funny. Granted, it is entirely different from anything the team had done previously, but change does not always do a comedy team any good. More in line with the boys' characters is the exchange following their rescue of Jerry Bronson (Paul Page) from committing suicide:

> BRONSON: It's awfully nice of you boys, but you really shouldn't have stopped me.
> BOB: Aw, you're crazy! No woman is worth dying for!
> BRONSON: You don't know my Joan. She's so beautiful. She's Juno, Venus, and Aphrodite all rolled into one!

BOB: Yeah? Well, I'll take Mae West.
BRONSON: Her father wouldn't let us get married, and I couldn't possibly live without her. Her eyes are sunbeams! Her hair is just like burnished gold! Her kiss is the gossamer touch of a zephyr breeze—
BERT: He's still crazy, let's put him back in the river—
BOB: Wait a minute, wait a minute. I know what he needs. You need something to get interested in. Now let's see—what would take a man's mind off a woman?
BERT: Another woman.

Once Spanky is introduced, the film steers a treacly course between false sentimentality and labored slapstick. Having destroyed Bert and Bob's shack, Spanky is told that he would be better off at the orphanage. "I like to play with you kids," Spanky informs the boys in a genuinely touching line, adding, "I've never had so much fun before." He happily glances at the windows and assorted bric-a-brac he's shattered. "Yeah," Bert says, "we get it." The audience gets it, too. Spanky is meant to be adorable but emerges instead as a cold-blooded gremlin intent on destruction of the world around him. At no time in *Kentucky Kernels* does Spanky receive a much-warranted thrashing. (Even W. C. Fields in the concurrently released *It's a Gift* manages to spit a grape into Baby LeRoy's eye—with Production Code approval.) Bert and Bob are unfailingly polite to the lad at all times, almost as a penitential rejoinder for their "filthy" pre–Code movies.

A halfhearted attempt is made to bring a touch of bawdy humor into the film when Bert and Bob accidentally find themselves trapped in the Wakefield homestead. Old Colonel Wakefield (Noah Beery, Sr.) pledges to "shoot those two scoundrels from up North!" The boys hide in the bedroom belonging to the Colonel's daughter, Gloria (Mary Carlisle). Bert hides under the bed, while Bob foolishly hides *in* the bed. Colonel Wakefield enters the room, sees the ruffled bedsheets, and yanks back the covers. Bob is unveiled, fully dressed and smoking a cigar. The camera stays on his motionless form for quite a spell, while the Colonel reacts outrageously and immediately arranges for a shotgun wedding. There's not a single innuendo spoken by Woolsey to add some spice to the scene; perhaps his silent image lying on the bed was supposed to garner laughs.

Mary Carlisle was one of the prettiest leading ladies who appeared with the team, but apart from her expert southern drawl *Kentucky Kernels* required little emoting from her. Noah Beery, Sr., so colorful in *Cockeyed Cavaliers*, is heavily subdued here; he is hardly a comic menace, and it appears that director Stevens has deliberately downplayed the actor's scene-stealing tendencies. It is a shame, too, because a tongue-in-cheek parody might have brightened the comedy considerably. Willie Best is reduced to enacting a shivering lackey who bears the brunt of Spanky's

Bob and Bert take orders from Spanky McFarland and seemed pleased at the prospect in *Kentucky Kernels*.

malevolence. Some television stations have clipped every shot of Best's scared reaction comedy out of the film, rendering entire portions incomprehensible.

The material is watered down Kalmar and Ruby at best, although a song, "One Little Kiss," is enjoyable if reminiscent of "I Love You So Much" from *The Cuckoos*. Even better than the legitimate verses are parody

Bert (right) disguises himself as a preacher man to keep Bob (center) from actually marrying Mary Carlisle. Noah Beery, Sr., Dick Alexander, and William Pawley are nearby. *Kentucky Kernels.*

lyrics sung by Woolsey to a jackass, of all things ("One little kiss / that's what I beg for / I'd break a leg for / one teeny little weeny little kiss"). While serenading the animal, Bob informs the audience, "I'm the one with the glasses on!"

Dull and predictable though it is, *Kentucky Kernels* reinstated Wheeler and Woolsey in the good graces of the Legion of Decency; the film received accolades for its "good taste" and "clean comedy." The moviegoing public reacted in the same way. Typical of the film's preview postcard comments is the following: "I liked the picture as it was clean entertainment—a picture that will not injure the minds of children such as a Mae West picture will do. Continue making clean entertainment for the minds of our coming generation." Apparently *Kentucky Kernels* struck the right chord at the right time; according to *Film Daily*, it became one of the fifteen top-grossing films of 1934–35. Parents dutifully brought their children to see the first Wheeler and Woolsey film specifically geared for the kiddie market, the same way a later generation trudged the family off to such dreary Disney corn as *The Shaggy Dog* simply because it was "wholesome."

Many reviewers saw beneath the sugary facade and realized what was being lost. The perceptive Frank Nugent (*New York Times*) noted that Bert and Bob "emerge from their white-washing as a pair of pallid funny men in a picture that may be approved, on moral grounds, by clean film advocates, but otherwise seems destined to be applauded most heartily by the 10-year-olds in the audience." The *Hollywood Reporter* indicated that "for a while the feud stuff is very funny. Then, as it gets more and more slapstick, it becomes boring." The *New York Sun* wrote, "*Kentucky Kernels* is their latest and, to a moviegoer who has managed to enjoy two or three of their frolics, their weakest comedy. This new feature can be designated to please only the tiny tots. Spanky McFarland is one of Hollywood's least spontaneous child actors." In England, where the film was released as *Triple Trouble*, the *London Chronicle* observed, "Though Wheeler and Woolsey are absurdly comic in their familiar way when opportunities permit, a plodding story gives them few such chances." Bad reviews were de rigueur for Wheeler and Woolsey, but such panning coming on the heels of their highly touted *Cockeyed Cavaliers* was a grim development.

Curiously, despite its excellent box-office performance, *Kentucky Kernels* was either forgotten or ignored by its participants. "Unfortunately," Spanky McFarland has told me, "I have no recall at all of *Kentucky Kernels*. Good luck with your book!" Mary Carlisle today is a wealthy California socialite who "was too busy making wedding plans at the time of *Kentucky Kernels* to care very much about the film." When the British National Film Theater planned a retrospective of George Stevens's work in 1970, he advised them that "there is no need for the program department to knock themselves out searching for prints [of *Kentucky Kernels*]."

Bert Wheeler hated sending telegrams, but he was in New York on October 8, 1934, when *Kernels* was successfully previewed in California. Wheeler sent the following message to George Stevens:

> CONGRATULATIONS TO MY FAVORITE DIRECTOR. HEARD THE GOOD NEWS. THANKS, BERT WHEELER.

At least Bert remembered.

22
The Nitwits (1935)

Directed by George Stevens. Associate producer, Lee Marcus. Unit manager, Charles Stallings. Screenplay by Fred Guiol, Al Boasberg, and (uncredited) George Stevens. Story by Stuart Palmer. Assistant directors, Jean Yarbrough and Doran Cox. Script girls, Ann Coleman and Gloria Gottschalk. Art direction by Van Nest Polglase. Associate art director, Perry Ferguson. Photographed by Edward Cronjager. Second cameraman, Al Wetzel. Assistant cameraman, Kay Norton. Musical direction by Roy Webb. Music and lyrics by Dorothy Fields and Jimmy McHugh, L. Wolfe Gilbert and Felix Bernard. Sound recording by Phillip J. Faulkner, Jr. Stage sound man, Frank Ray. Assistant sound man, Fred Stall. Film editing by John Lockert. First property man, Eddie Trickle. Second property man, Joe Behm. Rain machine effects, Harry Redman. Grips, Ralph Wildman and E. T. Harris. Gaffer, Cleo Crabtree. Best boy, Sgt. Caldwell. Wardrobe man, Clem Harrington. Wardrobe woman, Edith Clark. Dates of production: February 28 to April 2, 1935. Released by RKO on June 7, 1935. 81 minutes.

Cast: Bert Wheeler (Johnny), Robert Woolsey ("Newt" Newton), Fred Keating (William Darrell, alias the Black Widow), Betty Grable (Mary Roberts), Evelyn Brent (Alice Lake), Erik Rhodes (George Clark), Hale Hamilton (Winfield Lake), Charles C. Wilson (Captain Jennings), Arthur Aylesworth (Lurch), Willie Best (Sleepy), Lew Kelly (J. Gabriel Hazel "Nut"), Edgar Dearing (Riley the Cop), William Gould (Police Sergeant), Arthur Treacher (Englishman), Donald Haines (Office Boy), Joey Ray (Himself, a crooner), Joan Andrews (Singer), Frances Grant, Jack Ellis (Hoofers), Constantine Romanoff, Pat Harmon (Singing Prisoners), Gil Perkins (Double for Keating and Man in Skeleton Suit), Dick Gilbert, Pat West, Ham Kinsey, Fred Shackleford (Henchmen), Donald Kerr (Martin), Ed Peil (Detective Eddie), Dick Curtis, Bob Reeves (Cops on Stakeout), Jack Grant, Martin Cichy (Bits), John Kelley, Slim Talbot, Teddy Mengeans, Vera Eugene (Doubles), Dorothy Granger (Phyllis the Manicurist [part cut from film]).

Synopsis: A mysterious blackmailer known only as "the Black Widow" is terrorizing the wealthy denizens of a major American city. Among his latest victims is Winfield Lake (Hale Hamilton), head of a song publishing company, who engages William Darrell (Fred Keating), a noted private detective, to act as his personal bodyguard. Within Lake's building is a cigar counter operated by two would-be songwriters, Johnny (Bert Wheeler) and Newt (Robert Woolsey). Newt has invented an electrical apparatus intended to shock the truth out of any liar. Johnny is smitten with Mary Roberts (Betty Grable), Lake's secretary. Mary and Johnny play a punchboard to win a wedding ring prize, but to Mary's disappointment, she wins a revolver.

When Mary learns that Lake needs a murder theme song, she passes the tip on to Johnny. When Johnny goes upstairs to Lake's office, he finds the publisher trying to compromise Mary. Johnny belts Lake on the jaw and tells Mary to quit her job. Minutes later, Lake is found murdered.

A squadron of police arrive on the scene. Suspicion points to Mary because her punchboard gun is found on Lake's desk, where Johnny inadvertently left it. Johnny "confesses" to save Mary; Newt "confesses" because he thinks that Johnny actually did kill Lake; but the police arrest Mary, refusing even to book the boys on suspicion. The police, headed by blustery Captain Jennings (Charles C. Wilson), are nevertheless baffled. Any one of the dead man's enemies might have committed the crime — Lake's wife, Alice (Evelyn Brent), who was jealous of Mary; Lurch (Arthur Aylesworth), Lake's head auditor, who was falsifying accounts; George Clark (Erik Rhodes), a disgruntled songwriter who had quarreled with Lake over meager royalties.

Potential victims who receive threatening notes from the Black Widow are instructed to leave extortion money in the ventilator shaft of the Lake Building. On the appointed night, Johnny and Newton, turning amateur sleuths, install the truth detector on the chair Lake was sitting on when he was shot, expecting the murderer's return to the scene of the crime. When detective Darrell falls into the trap, he shouts, "I'm the Black Widow!" Puzzled as to why the renowned investigator would make such a statement, the boys conclude that the invention is just another one of Newt's failures.

Darrell now marks Newt and Johnny for death in the same manner Lake was killed, but Lurch accidentally receives the fatal bullet fired from Darrell's gun (poised through a hidden aperture in the ceiling). After a wild chase through a costume company, during which Darrell dons a skeleton getup to terrify the duo, Captain Jennings arrives, arresting Darrell as the Black Widow. He reveals that the supersleuth, while delivering Mary to the police as the killer, switched his murder weapon with her punchboard gun, which had never contained any bullets. Further, Darrell "advised" the victims of the Black Widow to deliver the money to the extortioner — himself.

All ends happily, as Newt, having won the punchboard ring (he punched out every number to get it), presents the gift to lovebirds Johnny and Mary.

★   ★   ★

Only in Hollywood could a success story travel from the sublime to the ridiculous and back again. In 1930, Bert and Bob were hailed as RKO's conquering heroes whose on-screen antics kept the studio solvent. Just two years later, RKO production chief Selznick accused the team of being unfunny, indistinguishable, and uncommercial. As 1934 drew to a close, Wheeler and Woolsey were back on top of the heap — or rather as darn near the peak as they would ever reach. *Variety*'s poll of the studios' biggest moneymaking attractions placed them second among RKO stars, ranking only behind 1934's Academy Award recipient Katharine Hepburn. Bert and Bob's position is remarkable in light of the fact that *Cockeyed Cavaliers* performed beneath box-office expectations, while final returns were not in yet for *Kentucky Kernels*. (*Kernels* did not premiere in New York until January 1935.) *Variety* reported that this lowbrow twosome "far outshadowed" such stellar performers as Fred Astaire and Ginger Rogers (as a team), Ginger Rogers (as a solo), Irene Dunne, Ann Harding, Richard Dix, Diana Wynward, and Clive Brook — and this in the year of Astaire and Rogers's milestone musical success, *The Gay Divorcee*.

The boys trekked east for personal appearances with *Kentucky Kernels*, stopping off at Rockefeller Center to revise a point on their new three-picture contract. Terms were similar to their last pact: the team would receive $7,500 weekly for ten weeks per film, plus 15 percent of all gross receipts. Fearing a W & W glut on the market, Woolsey's only stipulation was that their exposure be limited to two features per year. RKO's home office readily agreed. With "prestige" pictures like *Of Human Bondage*, starring Bette Davis, and John Ford's *Lost Patrol* barely clearing the ledger, the New York office could rest peacefully, knowing that their dynamic duo would continue to profitably prowl RKO theaters, at least for another eighteen months.

On November 9, 1934, the *Hollywood Reporter* announced that *Murder in Tin Pan Alley* would be the next Wheeler and Woolsey vehicle. With a title that told it all and no other instructions to follow, mystery novelist Stuart Palmer concocted a murder story set in a music publishing house. Al Boasberg, who had not worked with the team since *Cracked Nuts*, was hired December 9 to fashion the screenplay. Boasberg dictated an "outline treatment" December 22 for *Mellodicks*, as the picture was achingly rechristened. On February 5, 1935, George Stevens was again slated to direct the boys, but he was not pleased with the script; accompanied by his faithful writing associate Fred Guiol, Stevens went to work February 7 revising the screenplay. The final script owes as much to Stevens as it does to the credited authors.

Stevens and Guiol had their hands full trying to mesh elements from two disparate drafts, but they tackled the task in record time. Filming was originally scheduled to commence February 18; rewrites delayed shooting by another ten days. The roles had already been cast, but the rescheduling forced two performers to bow out due to other commitments. The absence of pip-squeak comedian Etienne Giradot was a blessing to the production (see how Giradot's performance as a mousy religious fanatic ruptures the otherwise taut screwball farce *Twentieth Century*). However, another defector was irreplaceable: the superbly slimy screen villain Lionel Atwill. Atwill's gallery of debonair dastards, urbane fiends, and cultivated mad scientists had already made their mark in lurid thrillers like *Mystery of the Wax Museum* and *The Vampire Bat*. Renowned for his scene-stealing proclivities and tendency to slice the ham rather thick, it would have been fun to see Atwill spar with the team.

Unhappy with the title *Mellodicks*, producer Lee Marcus offered a fifty-dollar prize to any RKO employee who could come up with a less noxious appellation. Here are a few of the gems that were submitted: *Murder Out of Tune*, *Death Strikes a Chord*, *Quick Watson, the Needle*, *Homicide Blues*, *The Dead Soprano*, *Slay It with Music*, *Murder in 3/4 Time*, *Little Men, What Next?* and *Little Men, So What?* Marcus eventually settled on a generic title that had been bouncing around the lot since 1930—*The Nitwits*.

Filming began February 28 on Stage 12 at the Pathé Studios in Culver City. There is not a single genuine exterior shot in the entire film; production-wise, *The Nitwits* looks like a B picture laced with A picture attributes. George Stevens's surefooted direction, coupled with Edward Cronjager's low-angled photography and the eerie atmospheric effects, reveals the painstaking care which gave the picture an elegant gloss. Total budget for *The Nitwits* was $252,292—some $35,000 less than *Kentucky Kernels*—but Stevens was still afforded an expansive twenty-eight day shoot and the luxury of shooting the film in sequence. Stuntman Gil Perkins recalls how cast and crew benefited from this technique:

> When you're shooting a picture in sequence, you can always build upon what you've already done. On *The Nitwits*, Wheeler and Woolsey quite often ad-libbed. They'd shoot a scene and say, "Wait a minute, George! Wouldn't it be funnier if we did this?" And he'd say, "What? Let's hear it. OK, let's try it." They'd shoot it—and if they thought it was funny, they'd use it. Incidentally, I always thought Bert Wheeler was the more creative one when it came to thinking up routines, but that's just an opinion.

The Nitwits (1935)

Lionel Atwill was replaced in the pivotal role of the Black Widow with Fred Keating, a former stage magician turned dramatic actor. Keating's low-key delivery and quiet underplaying was much admired at the time; today his performances in films like this and the all-star *Captain Hates the Sea* resemble narcolepsy attacks or, at the very least, a world-weary boredom. Keating's greasy looks were adequate for "bad guy" roles but he was about as colorless a villain as can be imagined. His lackluster contributions to *The Nitwits* supplies this musical murder mystery with its one jarring note.

If Keating acts as though he is slumming, perhaps it is because he was reluctant to appear in the film at all. Originally signed for the RKO musical *Hooray for Love*, his part was subsequently written out. Reassigned to *The Nitwits*, Keating refused the task, claiming that he was not under contract to RKO to act in that film. Keating and RKO management came to an unusual arrangement: regardless of his feelings, he would report to work in *The Nitwits*. Following his first day's services, he had the right to withdraw from the cast without further obligation. Keating chose to stay put; with a four-week guarantee at $1,000 a week, he would have been foolhardy to walk out. Fred Keating was not worth the aggravation, however: several days into filming his scenes, he was stricken with appendicitis. Gil Perkins remembers the rest:

> I worked as a stuntman in Laurel and Hardy and Charley Chase two-reelers for Hal Roach when George Stevens was a cameraman there. George was familiar with my work, so he hired me to perform all the acrobatic stuff for *The Nitwits*. When Fred Keating got appendicitis, he was laid up for three weeks. They didn't want to hold the picture up, so they called me in. I put on Keating's suit and they filmed me in long shots, over the shoulder, from the back—I was in the whole picture. When Fred Keating recovered, they brought him in for the last week of shooting and shot all the close-ups of him.

Keating notwithstanding, *The Nitwits* is a top-notch comedy, extremely well crafted, and featuring several outstanding sequences that rank among the team's funniest. Bert and Bob's opening scenes deliberately soft-pedal the jokes, introducing the boys' characters instead and establishing audience support for the team. Even at this early stage in his directorial career, George Stevens sacrifices the team's outrageous throwaway gags that might interrupt well-delineated characterizations.

Interestingly, George Stevens's inventiveness becomes a double-edged sword—yes, we do care about Bert and Bob in *The Nitwits* when they're warm and funny, but did we care for them any less in *Peach O'Reno*, *Diplomaniacs*, or *Cockeyed Cavaliers*, when they were merely whimsical and hilarious? In order to transform Wheeler and Woolsey into two "real" people whom he can believe in, Stevens must yank them out of the musical-comedy tableau that has been their specialty. Gone not only are the breezy plots but also the parade of outrageous supporting players: Stanley Fields, Edna May Oliver, Hugh Herbert, Jobyna Howland, Joe Cawthorn, Zelma O'Neal, Edgar Kennedy, Noah Beery—all of whom were replaced with fairly "normal" actors in colorless straight roles. *Colorless* and *straight* also describe the parts written for Bert Wheeler in these dramatic comedies. Beginning with *The Nitwits*, the fairly normal-looking Bert starts losing his unique comic persona—much the same way that Harpo Marx was relegated to the backseat in the Marxes' later MGM movies. Apart from an avuncular concern for his partner, wisecracking Bob Woolsey hardly changes at all: with his naturally goofy looks and the need for some silly banter, he is the last joker left in the deck. But Woolsey popping off one-liners to dead air eventually became too much of a strain, both on Bob and the audience.

Happily, George Stevens was a brilliant craftsman able to camouflage these radical changes within W & W's formula; it was only when his no-talent assistant, Fred Guiol, inherited the director's reins that these same techniques sabotaged the series. Guiol imitated Stevens's pattern passably enough; what Guiol could not duplicate were the wonderful gags that sprang from George Stevens's fertile comedy mind.

Director Stevens skillfully mixes plot, characterization, and hilarious gags in the film's first major comedy sequence. Bob uncovers circumstantial evidence convincing him that Bert has murdered Winfield Lake (Hale Hamilton). Naturally he is mistaken, but Woolsey goes to great lengths to protect his little buddy—Bob shoves Bert in an elevator when the cops arrive. In an effort to discourage the police from finding his partner, Bob tells Captain Jennings (Charles C. Wilson) that the elevator is out of order. At that moment the elevator returns to the lobby, with an indignant Bert asking Woolsey what is the big idea. Understandably suspicious, Captain Jennings assigns Officer Riley (Edgar Dearing) to keep an eye on Bob.

Woolsey slowly begins to walk toward the doorway. "Where do you think *you're* going?" Riley asks. "I thought I was goin' out," Bob replies, "but I guess I'm not." Woolsey schemes to distract the cop so that Bert can escape undetected. Bert, being innocent, has not the foggiest notion about his partner's motives. Bob produces his pocketwatch and demonstrates how its alarm works; Riley is intrigued and becomes absorbed in fiddling with the little bell. As Woolsey tiptoes down the hall, he glances back at Riley and Bert—they're both playing with the watch. Bob stalks back just in time for Riley to return the timepiece to its frustrated owner.

So it goes: Bob diverts the cop by pretending to faint; Bert runs away, only to return with a pitcher of water to throw in Woolsey's face. The cop

Gil Perkins, Bob, and Bert give director George Stevens their undivided attention on the set of *The Nitwits*.

implores Wheeler to leave. "No," Bert responds adamantly, "I'm not going to leave my pal!" When Bob manages to toss Riley's cap through the door, Wheeler runs out of the building. Woolsey is delighted, figuring that Bert has escaped. Instead, Bert returns with the officer's hat. Bob's diversionary tactics are so aggravating that Riley decides to handcuff Woolsey to the staircase.

A detective arrives to bring Bert upstairs for questioning. "I'll be right back," Wheeler assures his partner. "Yeah," Woolsey comments, "in about twenty years!" Bob proceeds to effortlessly slide the handcuffs off his wrists. Riley is dumbfounded by Woolsey's smooth technique, but Bob dismisses his skill, informing Riley that "even you could do it." Naturally the cop has to learn the trick and permits Bob to handcuff him to the railing. However, Riley has a bit of a problem. "You can't get 'em off?" Woolsey inquires politely. Negative. "That's all I want to know!" Bob responds before racing up the stairs.

The terrific interplay between the three characters makes the scene remarkable. Dialogue is limited throughout the sketch, so the flawless body language carries the comedy. Bert Wheeler is excellent, but based upon his acting in earlier films, you would hardly expect otherwise. Bob Woolsey is the surprise standout; for a guy who is consistently deadpan, limited to communicating only through his mouth, Woolsey contributes a sly performance rivaling the subtlety of the great silent comedians.

The second great scene comes when the boys play amateur detectives on an eerie, rainy night. Anticipating the murderer's return to the scene of the crime, Bert and Bob enter Lake's offices and eventually encounter Mr. Darrell, who is also wandering through the building. Although the boys do not realize that Darrell is the Black Widow, he decides to eliminate them anyway. Pretending to enlist their aid in reenacting the murder, Darrell summons Bob to play Mr. Lake while Bert is stationed in Mary's office. As Bob makes himself at home sitting behind Lake's desk, Darrell pretends to wait in the head auditor's office. Actually he runs upstairs and places his gun through the aperture in Lake's ceiling, directly above the victim's chair. Darrell adopts the Black Widow's trademark—a fake spider on a string—in order to position his victim for the slaying. When the spider is lowered on to the desktop, Bob will become a suitable target as he reaches for the bug. In an encounter that is both nerve-wracking and hilarious, Woolsey thwarts the Black Widow's plans as he casually flicks away spider after spider. "The place is full of cockaroaches!" Bob notes as he swats the last one.

Lurch, the crooked auditor who conspired with his boss to falsify composers' royalties, enters the scene armed with a gun. Bert and Bob start running toward the door. Lurch stops them, saying, "Just a moment—please." "It's a good thing he said 'please,'" Bob nervously quips. The boys are forced to stick 'em up and face the wall while Lurch rifles Lake's desk. The unfortunate auditor becomes another victim when he stands point-blank beneath the Black Widow's gun. A single gunshot rings out, killing Lurch; Bert and Bob are still facing the wall. "I'm shot," Bert informs his partner, "but it don't hurt!" "He must've hit you in the head," Bob responds. The terrified team races through the building, finally encountering Darrell, who knocks them out cold with an oversized sledgehammer.

The third and final classic sequence immediately follows. The Black Widow's intended victims have been instructed to leave extortion money in the building's ventilator shaft; the money then travels through a wind tunnel to the air vent at the upstairs costume company. Unfortunately for Darrell, a group of men running a crap game discovers the whirlpool of dollars and begins pocketing them. Darrell dons a skeleton outfit and, screeching in a scary falsetto, chases the men off. Bert and Bob enter the room, which is littered with money. "Call an ambulance," Bob advises his friend, "I think I'm crazy!" (His scripted remark was better; "If you wake up and find out this is a dream, walk quietly.") The Skeleton Man returns to collect his cash. Bob spots him first; letting out a traditional cry of "Whooah!" Woolsey's eyeglasses literally pop off his face and back on again. "Look," Bob advises Bert, "Mr. Lake is back!" Wheeler glances at the gruesome specter. "He's certainly lost a lot of weight," Bert observes. Petrified, the boys run away, but Wheeler wises up quickly. "Say, do you know who that is?" he asks Woolsey. "Sure," Bob answers, "it's Death taking a holiday." Bert tells him it is none other than the Black Widow collecting payoff money. A wild chase ensues throughout the costume company, involving Bert, Bob, the terrified gamblers, gangsters, and the Black Widow disguised as a skeleton.

Seven days were spent making this exciting, hilarious scene, which is described ever so simply in Stevens's straightforward script: "A chase follows with gags, including the [card] players, Bob and Bert, Darrell in the skeleton costume and possibly Hazel (Lew Kelly), for about eight or ten scenes." Inspired by a similar sequence in *High Gear* (1931), a Hal Roach "Boy Friends" comedy also directed by Stevens, this exhilarating escapade is perhaps the funniest of its kind. The combination of breathtaking stunt action (prolific Gil Perkins leaps about as a skeleton) and sight gags (Woolsey calmly flings bottles at thugs with unerring accuracy) mixes wonderfully for a climax that anticipates Stevens's comedy fight scenes in *Gunga Din* (1939).

Captain Jennings arrives to arrest the man in the skeleton suit (apparently for parading around in a Halloween costume out of season). Unmasked as the Black Widow, Darrell sneers, "Great police work! But it took those two nitwits to catch me!" "Yeah," Woolsey answers in rebuttal. "Well, we had the finger on you right from the beginning!" Bert and Mary (Betty Grable) are now free to start making plans for their wedding — and for their "own little children." Inadvertently she sits down in Woolsey's truth-detecting chair. "Well," Bob inquires, "how many of these little blessed events do you expect to have?" "One or two," she replies as she sits back into the chair, "but no more than three — four — five — six — seven — eight — nine — ten..." "Here, here, now," Bert instructs Bob, "shut that thing off."

The Nitwits earned some of the team's best reviews. "Wheeler & Woolsey have their funniest," the *Hollywood Reporter* noted. "Anyone who imagines that knockabout comedy and slapstick has lost its power to roll 'em down the aisles should have heard the preview audience yell their heads off. It's rowdy comedy with no brakes and the muffler cut out, and there's just as much money in it as there was fifteen years ago." The film went on to rack up a fortune for RKO, with a handsome percentage going to the boys.

While *The Nitwits* was Betty Grable's second appearance with the team, she's hardly featured in the film at all; her major scene, singing and

"It's two against one—but oh, that one!" Bob and Bert with stuntman Gil Perkins in *The Nitwits*.

dancing "Music in My Heart" with Bert, was heavily trimmed when preview audiences felt that it disrupted the flow of the narrative. A later reprise of the number, where Betty, Bert, and Bob are accompanied by a chorus of singing felons (Constantine Romanoff leads the jailbirds in song), is much cuter and funnier. Dorothy Fields and Jimmy McHugh wrote some of the most enduring song standards ("I Feel a Song Comin'

The Nitwits (1935)

On," "I'm In the Mood for Love," "Exactly Like You") but "Music in My Heart" certainly was not one of them. The film's other tune, "You Light Up My Eyes," heard in snippets and as background music for the team's comedy routines, is a catchier number, although its composers (L. Wolfe Gilbert and Felix Bernard), like the song itself, are forgotten today.

RKO executives were pleased as punch with George Stevens's directorial ingenuity. Like Mark Sandrich before him, Stevens was elevated to "important" productions, the first of which was a Katharine Hepburn starrer, *Alice Adams* (1935). Stevens recommended that his friend and collaborator, Fred Guiol, be promoted to helm the Wheeler and Woolsey series. No one at the studio had any objections—certainly not Bert and Bob—and no one could have predicted the disastrous ramifications this move would have on Wheeler and Woolsey's screen careers. Like most of the disasters that befell the team, it seemed like a good idea at the time.

23
The Rainmakers (1935)

Directed by Fred Guiol. Produced by Lee Marcus. Screenplay by Grant Garrett and Leslie Goodwins. Story by Albert Traynor and Fred Guiol. Additional material (uncredited) by Stanley Rauh. Art direction by Van Nest Polglase and Feild Gray. Costumes by Walter Plunkett. Photographed by Ted McCord. Photographic effects by Vernon Walker. Musical direction by Roy Webb. Music and lyrics by Louis Alter and Jack Scholl. Sound recording by George D. Ellis. Sound effects by Walter Elliot. Film editing by John Lockert. Rehearsals: July 8 to July 16, 1935. Dates of production: July 17 to August 16, 1935. Released by RKO on October 25, 1935. 80 minutes.

Cast: Bert Wheeler (Billy), Robert Woolsey (Roscoe), Dorothy Lee (Margie Spencer), Berton Churchill (Simon Parker), George Meeker (Orville Parker), Frederic Roland (Henry Spencer), Edgar Dearing (Kelly), Clarence Wilson (Dennis P. Hogan), Jack Richardson, Ed LeSaint (Engineers), Harry Bernard, Leo Sulky (Firemen), Billy Dooley, Harry Bowen (Switchmen), Eddie Dunn (Dispatcher), Peggy Waters (Secretary), Edwin Brady, Edwin Sturgis, Frank Moran (Farmers), George Magrill, Eddie Borden (Hoboes), Lon Poff, Bill Wolfe, Edward Hearne, Pat Harmon, Nelson McDowell, Bob Milash, Robert McKenzie, Donald Kerr, Bob Graves, Warren Jackson, Don Brodie, Billy Bletcher, Billy Engle, Frank Hammond, John Ince (Townspeople), Joe Marba, Jack Curtis, Sam Lufkin, Olin Francis (Bits).

Synopsis: The ranch community of Lima Junction, California, is plagued by a drought. Simon Parker (Berton Churchill), a wealthy but crooked rancher, has a relief plan to construct an aqueduct to bring water to the farmers. Parker has tricked his neighbors into mortgaging their homesteads to him, and intends to eventually foreclose on their properties. Henry Spencer (Frederic Roland), president of the local bank, takes an entirely different approach toward solving the drought crisis. He sends for Roscoe (Robert Woolsey), the scientific rainmaker, to induce some well-aimed cloudbursts over the stricken region. Roscoe has just escaped from angry midwestern farmers and also from the dust storm they blame on him. One hapless farmer, Billy (Bert Wheeler), loses his house to the windstorm and decides to try his luck working for Roscoe.

Roscoe and Billy arrive at Lima Junction just as Parker threatens to audit poor old Spencer's penniless institution. Roscoe's boasts about producing rain delight the decrepit banker, while Billy wastes little time in romancing Margie (Dorothy Lee), Spencer's pretty daughter. Roscoe explains that a vast crowd is required for the rainmaking properties to take effect. A public demonstration is arranged, but Parker uses his influence to bar Spencer's radio advertisements from the airwaves.

Puzzled by the lack of a turnout, Roscoe decides that the only way to elicit crowds would be to stage a stupendous spectacle: the collision of two ancient train locomotives. Roscoe pretends to be president of a railroad line, artfully purloins two engines, and prominently advertises the event.

The following day as crowds gather for the show, the train engineers refuse to cooperate when dynamite is discovered in the tenders. Unbeknownst to Roscoe and Billy, the engines were peppered with explosives to ensure a resounding smashup. Realizing that the crowds will disperse if the show does not commence, the boys hop into the cabs to start the locomotives. Billy accidentally pulls and breaks the reverse lever; Roscoe throws his throttle open and gives chase. After a wild and prolonged excursion over the countryside, Roscoe rescues Billy while switchmen frantically route the runaway engines back to Lima Junction.

Roscoe and Billy escape from the cabs just moments before the two engines connect head-on. The explosion stimulates the rainmaking machine, drenching the crowd while Parker disgustedly tears up his liens against the other farmers. The midsummer rain suddenly turns into an unseasonal snowfall because, Roscoe explains, "the engine is cold!" Billy and Margie huddle arm in arm while the populace revels in the chilly relief from the skies.

★ ★ ★

Having enjoyed one success after another during a four-year reign, Wheeler and Woolsey's comedy oasis finally dehydrated with *The Rainmakers*. Like *Diplomaniacs*, *The Rainmakers* is topically rooted in the newspaper headlines of the 1930s, in this case the infamous dust bowl that plagued the central United States throughout the decade. The subject matter is documented impeccably—watching *The Rainmakers*, you experience the same irritation, sweat, and parched throat (not to mention headache) felt by the original dirt-poor sharecroppers. The trouble is, this is no *Grapes of Wrath* but an agonizingly dull comedy whose aged and arid jokes are caked underneath piles of dust. More gagging seems to waft among the viewers than up on the screen.

This snail's-paced tale of cracker-barrel intrigue is more akin to the folksy Will Rogers and Chic Sale films of the era than to Bert and Bob's customarily breezy format. Both Rogers's and Sale's vehicles were lovingly built around minutely etched portraits of smalltown Americana. Action was subordinate to monologues, as the homespun philosophers literally stopped the film dead in its tracks to muse upon a rustic truism. Since Rogers and Sale were the darlings of the *Farmer's Almanac* set, their leisurely plotted films were quite popular (the United States was still primarily an agrarian nation), with Rogers's movies consistently leading at the box office. Putting Wheeler and Woolsey within a rural milieu was simply not good comedy planning; throughout *The Rainmakers* they seem dazed and behave as though they have wandered onto the wrong set. From a comedy fan's perspective, the boys obviously were on the wrong set.

Foremost among the team's problems was their new director, Fred Guiol, a man whose association with comedy stems back to the Hal Roach studios and 1918. Guiol began as a prop man for Roach, working predominantly on Harold Lloyd's pictures, from the early one-reelers through such classic features like *Grandma's Boy* and *Safety Last*. At Roach's, he eventually became a cameraman and finally graduated to director status, helming much of the studio's second-string product. Ever so rarely the Comedy Muse smiled upon Freddy: *Don't Park There* (1924), with Will Rogers, was a deft satire on traffic congestion that grows timelier by the minute, while *The Second Hundred Years* (1927) is the first great Laurel and Hardy short, with the boys escaping from prison by disguising as painters and whitewashing their way to freedom. But the bulk of Guiol's silent shorts were adequate though seldom clever. Hollywood's conversion to sound in 1929 accentuated his shortcomings; Guiol's talkies proved to be among the Roach studio's worst.

With the Depression's onslaught in 1930, Guiol was laid off, thereafter freelancing as a gag writer. It was in the latter capacity that George Stevens selected Guiol to assist on the screenplays of *Kentucky Kernels* and *The Nitwits*. When RKO promoted Stevens to more ambitious projects, he recommended Guiol as his replacement. The choice seemed logical, since Guiol, along with Stevens, Mark Sandrich, and Eddie Cline, had a long apprenticeship in the two-reel comedy leagues. What RKO could not foresee was Guiol's incompetence with feature-length productions.

Stuntman Gil Perkins worked on Wheeler and Woolsey pictures for both Stevens and Guiol; observing the two men firsthand, he recollected that

> George Stevens was a bright guy who was always thinking, "What can I change in the script to make this scene a little better," while Freddy Guiol honestly believed his own stuff to be perfect. But really, Stevens's scripts were good to begin with, while Guiol's material was usually junk.

Fred Guiol littered his scripts with hoary silent comedy jokes, much like a burnt-out Borscht Belt comic who uses an unfunny routine simply because it has been committed to memory. Throughout the films he scripted or directed, Guiol indiscriminately lifted gags from the dinosaurian likes of silent funsters such as Snub Pollard and Clyde Cook; he made little attempt to tailor these crude antiquities to Bert's and Bob's unique personalities.

The Rainmakers even followed the pattern of old-time silent comedy "construction": the last scene, a chase between two locomotives that ultimately crash, was written first. The rest of the picture was ponderously contrived to arrive at this finish. Guiol and Albert Treynor then proceeded to write a "legitimate" story about rainmakers in southern California, which would be beefed up with slapstick gags. Guiol probably remembered how well this recipe worked for Harold Lloyd in pictures like *Doctor Jack* and *Safety Last*, but Lloyd himself outgrew and abandoned this method by the mid–1920s. Unfortunately for the Wheeler and Woolsey series, poor Freddy Guiol never noticed the unsuitability of silent-movie technique for a couple of song-and-dance men.

Wheeler and Woolsey were musical comedy stars, not slapstick comedians; yet *The Rainmakers* resembles an early Harold Lloyd or Buster Keaton silent with the visual wit drained out of it. The antediluvian gags assigned to Bert and Bob harken back to the Ben Turpin school of humor, but at least Turpin's moronic pastiches were short, and they moved. One look at Guiol's directorial approach convinces the viewer that he should never have left the prop room; his amateurish meandering causes every scene to drag without a hint of comic tempo. *The Rainmakers* has the pace of a taffy pull and the thrills of a quilting bee; although it concludes with a locomotive crack-up, *The Rainmakers* chugs along like the Little Train That Couldn't, stalling long before the finish line.

The staged train wreck which concludes *The Rainmakers* is the sole novel incident in the entire movie. Steam railroad buffs might cringe at the filmed destruction of priceless locomotives today, but nearly a century ago these spectacles were enjoyed by thousands of ticket-buying patrons. It was William G. Crush, vice-president of the Katy railroad that ran between Kansas and Texas, who conceived the idea in 1896 of staging a train wreck in order to stimulate free publicity for his line. But an Iowan farmer nicknamed "Head-On Joe" Connolly concocted the most ingenious locomotive collisions, seizing the public's imagination for nearly forty years and pocketing over a million dollars' profit in the process. Connolly's most successful show was presented in 1911 at the Brighton Beach racetrack in Brooklyn, New York, when a crowd of over 100,000 assembled for the occasion. After Connolly retired in 1932, interest in staged train wrecks waned and died altogether with the scrap-metal drives of World War II.

The Rainmakers went into rehearsals on July 8, 1935, with actual filming commencing on July 17. The production was so uneventful that when Bob's brother Charles made a rare foray into Los Angeles and visited the set, RKO issued a press release noting the remarkable resemblance between the two brothers—a dubious distinction, to be sure! Dorothy Lee rejoined the team under her old salary of $500 per week, but with only a two-week guarantee in place of her former three-week contract on *Hips, Hips, Hooray!* and *Cockeyed Cavaliers*. Filming was completed on August 16, with an extra day spent taking studio portraits of Bert, Bob, and Dottie sporting yellow slickers and sprouting giant umbrellas.

The Rainmakers begins with a promising comedy sequence. Bob seeks refuge from a dust storm at a country farmhouse belonging to Bert (it is never explained how Wheeler's weed-chewing rube happened to acquire a Brooklyn accent, but this picture needs every comic absurdity it can grasp at). Woolsey enters Bert's storm cellar just as the farmhouse is lifted into the air, à la Keaton's *Steamboat Bill, Junior*. "Too bad about your house," Bob commiserates. "Aw, that's all right," Bert replies. "The roof leaked anyway." Woolsey decides to commit suicide to spite the townspeople who rebuffed him ("Here I am a great genius and nobody knows it but me. I'll get even with 'em!"). There's a sublime lunacy to the rest of this scene that nothing else in the film comes close to achieving. Bob dramatically asks Bert if he has a piece of rope. "Um-hmmm," Bert matter-of-factly responds, handing the rope over to Woolsey. Bob quickly reconsiders killing himself in such a manner ("You don't want me hanging around here anyway"). Bob next asks Bert if he has any poison. "Um-hmmm," Bert replies as he lackadaisically hands Bob a jar of rat poison. This method is likewise rejected by Woolsey ("If I can't die like a man, I'm not gonna die like a rat!"). Bob next asks if Bert has a gun. "Um-hmmm," Bert says for the third time as Bob mutters, "I was afraid of that!" Woolsey aims the revolver away from his head. "You've got that pointed the wrong way," Bert observes. "How do you know which way I want to die?" Woolsey rejoins. Bob shoots the gun upward; the discharge is so loud that he decides it's "too much noise. Why, a thing like that's liable to scare you to death!"

Bert persuades Bob to abandon his self-destructive notions and instead proceed to California, where people are expecting him to produce a rainfall. "What's going to happen to you?" Woolsey asks Wheeler. "Oh, there's nothing much for me to do around here," Bert replies. "I guess I'll go out and look for my house." Bob asks Bert to team up with him:

> BOB: I could use a bright boy like you! You could be my assistant. Do you know anything about machinery?
> BERT: I know all about plows and tractors and things—
> BOB: Good! Then I'll be your assistant.

The Rainmakers (1935)

After this solid start the movie virtually stops in its tracks, becoming a sober and sedate film. Comedic ingenuity bites the dust, as in the sequence where the boys decide to stage a train wreck. Just how do they obtain two locomotives from the division manager of the Trans-Pacific Railroad? Very simply—Woolsey happens to have a pocketful of business cards. One of the cards reads, "Trans-Pacific Railroad, Cornwall Flint, President." Mr. Hogan (Clarence Wilson), the division manager, believes Woolsey to be his own employer, in the flesh. This desperate ploy is a cheap enough trick to pull on the audience, but the assault doesn't end there. The portrait of Cornwall Flint hanging in Hogan's office just happens to be a photograph of Woolsey sporting a beard. Bob dismisses the differences in appearance with the bum quip, "That was taken when I was much older." Woolsey's retort comes across as even more painfully unfunny when he utters those wit-defying words on film.

With the censors declaring a moratorium on risqué jokes and double entendres, kiddie humor abounds everywhere. Infantile gags infest the film: a water pump spouts dust, Bob kicks an adversary in the shins, Bert topples over a table of sandwiches. Guiol stages his dumb comedy with the solemnity of *War and Peace*, which for the viewer equates to boredom and hell.

Occasionally a funny joke does assert itself. Bert and Bob stage a rainmaking demonstration for the town's hostile chamber of commerce members. Before activating the "hydro-electric diversifier," Bob addresses the townspeople:

> BOB: Are there any questions?
> FARMER: [*angrily*] Aw, we can see through you!
> BOB: [*to Bert*] When you get the machine started, drown him first, will you?

Bert and Dorothy do get to perform a nostalgic duet entitled "Isn't Love the Grandest Thing?" The number is stodgily photographed and there is no dancing involved, but it has more than a glimmer of the old charm. Bert and Dottie sing to each other underneath a "magic tree," or as Dottie describes it, "If you're under that tree, and you tell even a teeny weeny little lie, an orange falls off." "Is zat so?" Bert asks. "How'd you find out?"

Bert and Dottie end up singing and spooning beneath the magic tree, and of course the oranges keep dropping on their heads, punctuating each little lie in their love song. "We'll never fight like other folks do, will we?" Dottie asks. "Never!" Bert replies, precipitating an avalanche of cascading oranges (most of which appear to be of grapefruit dimensions). "Isn't Love the Grandest Thing?" was the last hit song to come out of a Wheeler and

Woolsey movie and the final classic set piece featuring this endearing couple. Although Dorothy Lee is usually ultracritical about her film work, she recently considered this number to be "one of the cutest things we ever did."

The rest of the movie is an aching time-killer sweated out by the subdued cast. The pace is so slow and episodes so interminable that viewers are subjected to such dubious treats as watching Woolsey and Frederic Roland play an extended round of Parcheesi. The camera seems to plunk down contentedly as the actors gingerly move their pieces around the board ("I rolled a five and a six. Let's see—one, two, three, four..."). There's not much more to the scene than the above, yet the routine drags on for a minute and a half of screen time.

The supporting cast acts as though performing underwater, including blustery Berton Churchill, who usually appears on the verge of a coronary but who is quietly muted here. Frederic Roland as Dottie's dad is such a mouse that he provides an unwelcome *Little Women* atmosphere to this out-of-kilter comedy. Apart from his first excellent scene, Bert continues playing the no-nonsense straight man, as he did in *The Nitwits*. Dottie does little more than traipse, starry-eyed, after Bert.

All of which leaves the comedy element upon Robert Woolsey's knobby shoulders. Bob works hard with the punkish gags he's been assigned, but the other players' low-key performances only cause Woolsey's bombastic acting style to resemble comedic overkill. Out of step, out of touch, and out of date, Bob becomes a meddlesome busybody perpetually poised to interject his two cents' worth into the proceedings: barging into conferences, badgering Dottie's dad, or unwisely challenging one of the townspeople to a fight (the challenger turns out to be a giant), Bob's abrasive demeanor runs amok to no appreciable effect.

The locomotive chase that climaxes the picture is just about the dreariest of its kind in motion picture history. Rear-screen projection is always easy to detect and lessens the credibility in action scenes, but swift pacing and editing (not to mention genuine humor) can overcome all these obstacles—witness Bert and Bob's climaxes for *Hips, Hips, Hooray!* and *Cockeyed Cavaliers*. W. C. Fields furnished marvelous stunt chases to conclude *The Bank Dick* and *Never Give a Sucker an Even Break*, while fourteen Abbott and Costello films were graced with the widest variety of vehicular conveyances for slapstick wrap-ups of varying quality. The Marx Brothers' *Go West* had the best of these climaxes, peppered with beautifully executed railroad sight gags devised by Buster Keaton (oddly enough, none of the existing Keaton or Marx books notes Buster's extensive contributions to this justly famous ending). In comparison, *The Rainmakers* features one of the lengthiest chases, bogged down with unfunny, drawn-out bits: Bert hangs from a plank wedged between the two locomotives for what seems an eternity; the boys knock themselves out repeatedly in their efforts to save each other; Woolsey continually has his hat blown off by steam escaping from the safety valve. Worse, the rear-screen projection is entirely out of proportion with the action, rendering the sequence so patently phony that boredom is instantaneous. The actual crack-up is an impressive moment, but ten seconds of action do not warrant a seventy-nine minute wait.

The critics were understandably hostile when *The Rainmakers* crawled into town during October of 1935. The *Hollywood Reporter* echoed the complaints of many reviewers:

> There isn't even any attempt made to lift this above the intelligence of a five year old. Strictly for the kiddie matinees. Most of the comedy is pretty grim ... however, there's a runaway train sequence that the children will laugh at, if they don't get too tired. The cutting does keep the train going around the same darned curve for hours. Wheeler and Woolsey deliver as much as possible in their particular style, but they aren't given much to start with, and very little action to cover up the lack. Guiol's direction can only suffer from Guiol's original story. He gave himself nothing to do in the first place.

In 1945, veteran gag writer Monty Brice was rummaging through old RKO scripts in pursuit of a vehicle for Wally Brown and Alan Carney, RKO's cut-rate version of Abbott and Costello. Brice proposed a remake of *The Rainmakers*, and while producer Sid Rogell was interested, wiser heads prevailed: *The Nitwits* was remade instead. It is a shame that those same sage executives were not consulted when *The Rainmakers* got the OK the first time around.

24
Silly Billies (1936)

Directed by Fred Guiol. Produced by Lee Marcus. Screenplay by Al Boasberg and Jack Townley. Story by Thomas Lennon and Fred Guiol. Assistant director, Jean Yarbrough. Art direction by Van Nest Polglase and Feild Gray. Photographed by Nick Musuraca and J. Roy Hunt. Photographic effects by Vernon Walker. Musical direction by Roy Webb. Music and lyrics by Dave Dreyer and Jack Scholl. Sound recording by John E. Tribby. Film editing by John Lockert. Dates of production: December 5, 1935, to January 3, 1936. Released by RKO on March 20, 1936. 64 minutes.

Cast: Bert Wheeler (Roy Banks), Robert Woolsey (Dr. Philip "Painless" Pennington), Dorothy Lee (Mary Blake), Harry Woods (Hank Bewley), Ethan Laidlaw (Trigger), Delmar Watson (Martin), Dick Alexander (John Little), Chief Thunderbird (Chief Cyclone), Maurice Black (Bandit with Toothache), Leo Willis (Bandit), Ivan Christie (Bandit), Richard Powell (Stagecoach Driver), Nelson McDowell (Horse Trader), Dick Elliott (Mayor Culpepper), Anna Demetrio (Humming Bird), Stanley Blystone (Cavalry Captain), Frank Hammond (Barker), Phillip Armenta, Carl Mathews (Indians), Jim Thorpe (Medicine Man), Willie Best (Excitement, a hired hand), Edward Hearn (Mark, Martin's brother), Lafe McKee (Pioneer), Blackie Whiteford (Settler), Tommy Bond, Joan Breslau (Students), Georgia Odell, Allen Sears, Jack Rice, Harry Bernard, Mabel Forrest, Olin Francis, Blanche Rose, John Ince, Jane Keckley, Ivar McFadden, Jack Curtis, Joe Marba (Bits).

Synopsis: In the year 1850 Dr. "Painless" Pennington (Robert Woolsey), an itinerant dentist, and Roy Banks (Bert Wheeler), his assistant, are traveling by stagecoach to Little Town, where, unbeknownst to the boys, the citizens are preparing to leave en masse to join the gold rush.

As the townspeople prepare to evacuate, John Little (Dick Alexander), a crooked real-estate agent, sells the town's choice location to newcomers Doc and Roy before plying them with liquor. When the duo finally sobers up, they are startled to find they have situated themselves in a ghost town.

A covered wagon eerily clatters into town, carrying a dead man with a note in his hand indicating that the pioneers have been betrayed and that they will be slaughtered by the Indians. Mary Blake (Dorothy Lee), a schoolmarm whom Roy is smitten with, is also with the caravan. The boys speed off in the wagon, overtake the settlers, and warn all of their danger. They overhear Hank Bewley (Harry Woods) and Trigger (Ethan Laidlaw) scheming to deliver the pioneers to the Indians, but are themselves suspected of the betrayal. As the vigilantes prepare to lynch Doc and Roy, the boys sink out of sight in quicksand.

The following morning, Indians spot top hats on the ground and discover Doc and Roy's heads protruding beneath them. They bring the pair to Chief Cyclone (Chief Thunderbird) to be burned at the stake. However, Doc finds the Chief in pain and extracts a tooth for him. The Chief adopts them into his tribe.

Bewley tells Chief Cyclone of a change in his plans. He does not recognize Doc and Roy, who have changed into Indian garb. The duo escapes by arranging a foot race. They overtake Bewley, knocking him out and taking his clothes. They arrive at the wagon train and warn the people, but Trigger convinces the group that Doc and Roy are still in league with the Indians.

As the boys are about to be hanged for the second time, the bloodthirsty Indians come racing over a hill. Roy dips sponges into chloroform as Doc, with the aid of a slingshot, bowls Indians off their horses with the potent sponge missiles. The Indians are finally routed.

A pesky boy hits Doc with his own slingshot and an unusual-looking rock. Doc realizes that the "rock" is actually a gold nugget—which the boy found in Little Town. The wagon trains make a mad dash back to the ghost town as Doc, Roy, and Mary are happily reunited.

★   ★   ★

Bert and Bob moseyed with the Texas Rangers in *Rio Rita*, tangled with banditos in *The Cuckoos*, and hotfooted it away from the badmen of *Girl Crazy*, yet after seventeen features the team still had not made a bona fide Western comedy. *Silly Billies* was intended to fill that void. It contains the necessary ingredients to spoof the cowboy genre: a stagecoach holdup, the new schoolmarm, a gold rush, ornery cowpokes, unfriendly Indians, an attack on the wagon train and the last-minute rescue by the U.S. cavalry, all set against the backdrop of RKO's sprawling Western town, originally erected for *Cimarron*. But what should have been an on-target satire emerges instead as another tedious five-finger exercise. Fred Guiol, the man who wrote, directed, and effectively ruined *The Rainmakers*, was back in the saddle again.

Guiol's treatment (written with the unhelpful assistance of Thomas Lennon) involved murders, lynchings, scalpings, and assorted skullduggery, without a hint of comic possibilities. Guiol and Lennon's outline reads like a mournful parody of James Cruze's epic, *The Covered Wagon* (1923), which at least had the scene-stealing character actor Ernest Torrence to rustle up some laughs. RKO studio head B. B. Kahane did not like what he read, which prompted an anxious plea from producer Lee Marcus on October 4:

> Wheeler and Woolsey both being absent from Los Angeles, I cannot get their opinions about the story, however, Mr. Guiol and I both feel that we can make a good picture from this outline. Mr. [George] Stevens, incidentally, has read the outline and thinks it has excellent possibilities for a good vehicle.
> In developing the continuity, we will be able to strengthen up some of the obviously weak spots. As to the hokey element, I think this is pretty essential for the ultimate success of this type of picture.

Lee Marcus's unswerving faith in Fred Guiol's methods sealed the picture's fate even before the screenplay was written. The last thing Bert and Bob needed was an assortment of bewhiskered routines coming on the heels of *The Rainmakers*. Marcus, without any sense of comedy savvy, hired Jack Townley to work on the screenplay with Guiol. Townley's extensive background in scripting cheap two-reelers could be relied upon to fill out the picture with the huskered corn so "essential" to W & W's brand of humor. What Marcus, Guiol, and Townley all failed to realize was that even hokey comedy teams garner their biggest laughs when tired gags are emblazoned with fresh twists.

Bert and Bob returned to Los Angeles from New York on October 6, and immediately began haggling with Marcus over the quality of the story line in progress. The team induced RKO to secure the services of gagman Al Boasberg, who had buttressed the laugh quota on *The Nitwits* earlier that year. Boasberg had recently contributed some high-powered comedy scenes to the Marx Brothers' *Night at the Opera*, most notably the famous stateroom sequence, in which the Marxes and a host of other characters are crammed into Groucho's sleeping quarters. Boasberg went to work at RKO on October 14, with the script already taking shape as *The Wild West*.

The very next day RKO announced that it was considering removing Guiol from the director's chair and turning the reins over to Boasberg. Boasberg has previously directed some Leon Errol shorts for RKO, and the Universal feature *Myrt and Marge* (1933), starring Ted Healy and the Three Stooges. Boasberg's work on the Healy-Stooges picture proved that he knew how to pace a comedy, but Marcus's loyalty to Guiol eventually won out. Boasberg stuck to his typewriter while Guiol retained his megaphone.

Actually, there was little that Al Boasberg could do to bolster the screenplay. The project had been virtually completed by a trio of slapstick gagmen; unable to alter their deadly course, Boasberg's contributions amounted to doctoring the existing script and tinkering with the dialogue. Boasberg's best efforts could be likened to decorating the *Titanic* with Christmas ornaments after she hit the iceberg: It looks pretty, but you know the ultimate outcome.

Several good ideas were sabotaged before production began. The screenplay originally opened in Boston, with Woolsey cast as a crap-shooting plumber who, through a roll of the dice, wins the implements of a dentist's profession. Convinced that there's a demand for tooth-pullers in California, Bob heads west in a stagecoach—which is where the actual film begins.

Instead of portraying a boastful imposter, Woolsey is introduced in the completed film as a genuine dentist. By simplifying the screenplay, the filmmakers bypassed some surefire comedy situations. Any comic tension involved in watching Bob bungle his way through a tooth extraction has been thwarted. It is not nearly as funny when a tough hombre shoves a six-shooter between Bob's ribs and growls, "You're a painless dentist, eh? You'd *better* be painless!" The viewer now expects Woolsey to perform a competent job, and he does—without any laughs. Bob Hope's *Paleface* (1948), the plot of which is remarkably similar to *Silly Billies*, does not rob viewers of the enjoyment in watching a sweaty Hope bluff his way through one orthodontic anguish after another. *Silly Billies* tosses out several other promising ideas of Boasberg's; one wonders why the studio bothered to hire him in the first place.

The industry's censorship board (which could spot promiscuity in a Mickey Mouse cartoon) received an estimating script for the projected film on November 12; two days later censor Joe Breen sent RKO a list of objections, which included the following curios:

> The business and dialogue connected with peeking through the hole in the tooth, and the dialogue about looking through the little hole and seeing the dancing girl of Paris, should be deleted, as possibly having a vulgar meaning.
>
> We request the changing of Bewley's reply to the ugly woman when she asks, "You're sure there's no chance of being attacked by Indians?" and his reply, "I know *you* won't be, lady."

Another letter from the censorship board sniffed about "the problem" with Wheeler and Woolsey movies: "Wheeler and Woolsey have put out some terribly smutty things in the past and can benefit by something entirely clean for a change." Apparently this censor had not seen the team's last three antiseptic adventures. Perhaps the Legion of Decency was still reeling from the aftershock of *So This Is Africa*.

Dorothy Lee recalls how the team felt about the bowdlerized final script. "We were out on location, and Bert was sitting with his elbows on his knees and his hands on his chin," she remembers.

> He really looked down in the mouth. I asked him, "Why don't you fellows complain about the script? This stuff is really awful." He looked up at me with those big blue eyes and said, "Lee, this studio could care less about our pictures. We'll be kicked out of here before long. So we'll say our lines, take the money, and the hell with 'em."

Silly Billies is actually a better film than its predecessor, *The Rainmakers*, but it is leagues beneath the comedies the team had been making just a year earlier. The film's most repellent aspect is its title, which was heartily endorsed by studio head Benjamin B. Kahane in a memo to RKO vice-president Ned E. Depinet:

> Like suggested title *The Indian Sign* for Wheeler Woolsey picture but prefer another title which has just been suggested—*Silly Billies*. This is along lines of other Wheeler Woolsey titles—*Nitwits, Cuckoos, Cracked Nuts*, etcetera. If you like *Silly Billies*, please advise if clear legally and with Hays office.

The new Wheeler and Woolsey picture was officially baptized *Silly Billies* on January 5, 1936; two days later, B. B. Kahane was ousted from his position as production chief and replaced by former Columbia executive Samuel J. Briskin. It is doubtful whether Kahane's rechristening of the W & W epic influenced RKO's decision to demote him but in Hollywood you never can tell.

Silly Billies starts promisingly. Bert, Bob, Dorothy Lee, a horse trader, and an old maid share a lethargic stagecoach ride into Little Town. Woolsey attempts conversation with a fellow passenger:

> BOB: Nice day, isn't it?
> OLD LADY: [*nastily*] I answered that two days ago!
> BOB: That was a nice, friendly little visit. [*Bob observes Bert mooning at Dottie.*] Why don't you speak to her? You've been gawkin' at her for two days.
> BERT: I can't—I haven't got the nerve.
> DOTTIE: [*offering the boys an apple*] Will you have one?
> BERT: [*sweetly*] No thanks, we're not hungry.
> BOB: Listen pal, our hearts may beat as one, but we have separate stomachs. I'm hungry!
> BERT: Don't mind him, Miss—ah—

BOB: Blake—Mary Blake.
DOTTIE: How did you know my name?
BOB: Process of elimination—I saw your name on your suitcase.
BERT: Blake—that's an awful pretty name. Er—this is Doctor Pennington. [*pointing at Bob*]
DOTTIE: Oh, Doctor Pennington—and are you going to Little Town to practice?
BOB: I don't have to practice. I'm perfect.
BERT: Miss Blake, how long are you going to stay in Little Town?
DOTTIE: Well, I'm sure of at least one term.
BOB: A jailbird!
DOTTIE: No, I'm a schoolteacher.
BOB: Well, I'll say one thing, you've got some class! You know, I was stuck on a schoolteacher once. She had a lot of class but no principle.
BERT: Don't pay any attention to the doctor. He's always joshing. You know, you have the prettiest hair, the rosiest cheeks, and the most beautiful eyes—
BOB: Check her teeth.

Good as the opening sequence is, the picture rapidly disintegrates into a farrago of absurdities. Two lengthy comedy sequences are strung back to back in the first half of the film. The routines are crude and gritty but become tolerably amusing through sheer force of the boys' personalities. In the first episode, Bert and Bob get drunk with a crooked real-estate agent:

BOB: Now then, what'll we drink to?
AGENT: To success!
[*Bert and Bob swallow their drinks and immediately begin to choke.*]
BOB: [*to Bert*] What did we drink to?
BERT: Success.
BOB: I'd rather be a failure.
BERT: Doc, now we gotta drink to you. C'mon, we're gonna have a drink to the doctor.
AGENT AND BERT: To you, Doc!
BOB: I don't think I'm worth it, but—to me.
[*Bert and Bob gulp their drinks and react horribly.*]
BERT: Doc, I think you're right!
AGENT: Now then, let's drink to my wife and kids.
BOB: Ah now, that's a sweet thought.
BERT: Fill it up!
BOB: How many kiddies have you got?
AGENT: Fourteen.
BOB: Whooooah!

After the agent departs, the now-sodden duo mistakes a bearded billy goat for an elderly gentleman suffering from a toothache. It is the most

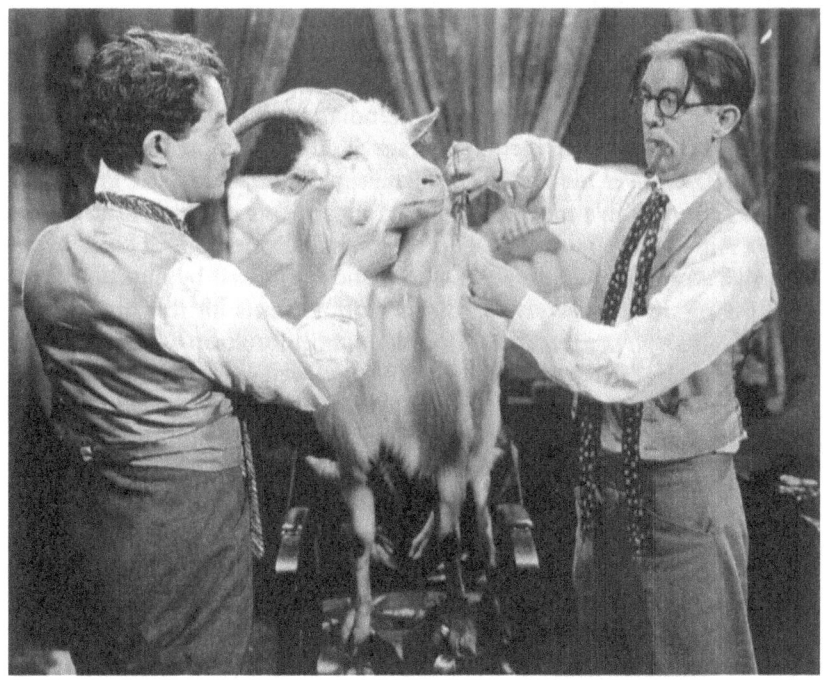

Cheap gags abound in *Silly Billies*. Preview audiences selected the goat's performance as the film's standout.

asinine situation ever concocted for the team, but via sheer audacity the boys play the scene for all it is worth. Bob orders Bert to "get him (the goat) off his hands and knees and put him in the chair." As Bert maneuvers the goat into the dental seat, his casual ad-lib provides the scene with its funniest line: "C'mon pop." Bert tearfully asks Bob not to hurt the "elderly gent" because "he reminds me of my old man." "He *reminds* you of your old man?" Woolsey sobs. "He *smells* like mine!"

As the boys sober up, so does the movie. Bert and Bob suddenly find themselves in a ghost town. A driverless wagon clatters eerily down the road, not unlike the phantom coach in *Dracula*. Stopping the wagon, Bob sees a dead man's hand protruding from the buckboard, clutching a scrap of paper. The blood-stained message warns of a pending Indian ambush; Wheeler and Woolsey ride off to warn the pioneers. This unsettling vignette is all that remains of Fred Guiol's "dramatic" subplot. The censors had objected to Guiol's graphic depiction of an Indian massacre in a family comedy but conceded on this grisly bit. Perhaps Guiol should have recast the picture as a straight Western with Hoot Gibson and Harry Carey. At least the audiences would not have been expecting genuine humor.

The second half of the film contains no mirth-making moments. Bert, Dottie, and Bob sing a so-so ensemble number, "Tumble On, Tumbleweeds, Tumble On," which is pleasing to the ear but a far cry from the Wheeler-Lee duets. The appearance of Indian actor Chief Thunderbird in *Silly Billies* elicited much media coverage. Today it is impossible to fathom the hullabaloo over his appearance; the superannuated duffer grunts his dull way through five minutes of screen time. More curious is the role of Native American athlete Jim Thorpe as a medicine man. Thorpe's appearance was unheralded by the studio and unnoticed by film historians until the recent rediscovery of RKO's casting sheets for this film.

The finale of the film, with Bob shooting chloroform-soaked sponges at the Indians, is strikingly photographed and well edited but it is just not funny at all. After the first Indian tumbles off his horse in a dead faint, the gag is repeated without a single variation. The scene continues endlessly before screeching to a halt without a satisfactory conclusion. Although *Silly Billies* is a scant sixty-four-minute misadventure, the film's second half seems much longer.

For Dorothy Lee, the making of *Silly Billies* was an unpleasant experience: "Every morning we had to get up before dawn and be driven out on location, to the studio's big ranch out in the San Fernando Valley, not far from the Malibu Mountains." The winter California mornings were "terribly cold," but Dottie felt especially sorry for the actors portraying Indians: "There must have been 150 Indians, and we had to be on the set at 6:30 in the morning, and these poor guys were coming in with just a cloth on, colder than a well digger's ass. It's a wonder they didn't freeze to death."

Like *The Rainmakers*, *Silly Billies* harvested some of Wheeler and Woolsey's worst reviews. Most of the damaging comments were reserved for the personnel behind the camera. The *Hollywood Reporter* noted that "the direction of Fred Guiol is pretty much routine and does little to save the situation." *Variety* grumbled, "two authors and two scripters get credit for this script, and there's not enough credit for one." The *New York Herald Tribune* astutely observed that "Fred Guiol seems to have a sense of comedy, but should restrict himself to one or two reels of film; at least *Silly Billies* could have packed all its humor into a short with nothing lost." *Motion Picture Herald* featured a weekly section entitled "What the Picture Did for Me," wherein exhibitors offered their own opinions on studio product. One perceptive theater manager wrote about *Silly Billies*:

> This is the poorest picture this pair has turned out, not due to their acting, but the story they had to work with. But they still brought in more than some of the so-called "specials."
>
> The silliest thing about this one is that RKO chooses to throw away a

Silly Billies (1936)

good comedy team in trash like this. No story value, few really funny incidents, no musical numbers, no production values. In short, everything's against the stars before they even started.

Upon completing *Silly Billies* Dorothy Lee decided that she had had enough, and retired from motion pictures. Bob quickly negotiated a three-picture deal with RKO, guaranteeing the team $75,000 per picture plus a percentage of the profits. Bert obtained a divorce from his wife, Bernice, on February 19, 1936, and promptly sailed for Honolulu with his girlfriend, Sally Haines. Producer Lee Marcus had to sweat it out alone when the new RKO brass finally previewed *Silly Billies*. On February 24, Sam Briskin sent the following memo to Marcus's attention:

> If you are writing a treatment on the next Wheeler and Woolsey, I would like to see the treatment or discuss the line-up whenever you are ready. If on the other hand you are going into continuity, please discuss with me first.
>
> After I saw *Love on a Bet* [a highly regarded RKO B], I can't believe the same producer could make *Silly Billies*.

Not only could Marcus make *Silly Billies*, but he was all set to give Fred Guiol one more try in the director's chair. Some people never learn.

25
Mummy's Boys (1936)

Directed by Fred Guiol. Produced by Lee Marcus. Screenplay by Jack Townley, Phillip G. Epstein, and Charles Roberts. Story by Jack Townley and Lew Lipton. Assistant director, James Anderson. Art direction by Van Nest Polglase and Feild Gray. Costumes by Edward M. Stevenson. Photographed by Jack Mackenzie. Musical direction by Roy Webb. Sound recording by James G. Stewart. Film editing by John Lockert. Dates of production: May 23 to June 23, 1936. Released by RKO on October 2, 1936. 68 minutes.

Cast: Bert Wheeler (Stanley Wright), Robert Woolsey (Aloysius C. Whittaker), Barbara Pepper (Mary Browning), Moroni Olsen (Dr. Edward Sterling), Frank M. Thomas (Dr. Phillip Browning), Willie Best (Catfish), Francis McDonald (Haschid Bey), Charles Coleman (Kendall, the butler), Frank Lackteen (Haschid Bey's assistant), Mitchell Lewis (Sheik Haroun Pasha), Tiny Sandford (Construction Foreman), Frederick Burton (Professor Edwards), Gerald Rogers (Cockney Sailor), Dewey Robinson (Hotel Manager), Frank Moran (Larson, a sailor), Ethan Laidlaw (Peters, a sailor), Edward Keane (Ship's Captain), Jack Rice (Second Officer), George Lollier (Third Officer), Rita Rozelle (Telephone Operator), Donald Kerr (Steward), Edith Craig (Sheik's Wife), Noble Johnson (Tattoo Artist), Pedro Rigas, Nick Shaid (Fakirs), John Davidson (Café Manager, Cairo), Pat Somerset (English Officer), Gil Perkins, Al Haskell (Native Cops).

Synopsis: Rain and wind pummel the Long Island home of archaeologist Phillip Browning, who paces nervously within. A year before, Browning headed an expedition in Egypt that uncovered and plundered the tomb of King Pharatime. Now, only a matter of months later, nine of the thirteen people who entered the tomb are dead, supposedly of natural causes. Browning has decided to return the ancient artifacts to the tomb, hoping to ward off the curse; visiting Professor Edwards scoffs at the idea. Suddenly Edwards slumps over dead. Now only Browning, his daughter, Mary, and his associate, Edward Sterling, remain.

Ditch diggers Stanley Wright and Aloysius C. Whittaker notice Browning's ad for excavators in a Long Island paper and walk off their job to apply for the position. Browning has already engaged the services of the mysterious Egyptian Haschid Bey, but agrees to bring the boys along on the expedition as well. Stanley is instantly smitten by Mary.

The sea voyage is a jinxed one, with mechanical defects plaguing the ship, an eerie fog impeding progress, and a near-shipwreck throwing passengers into a panic. Catfish, a black stowaway discovered in the hold, is about to be tossed into the brig when Stanley and Aloysius convince Browning to hire him on as well.

In Cairo's Hotel D'Orient, Stanley and Aloysius run afoul of Sheik Haroun Pasha, whose wives are in the habit of running away from his harem. Dr. Sterling vanishes from his hotel room, where a note hinting that he has been killed is found. Fearing that he will be the next to vanish, Browning entrusts Stanley and Aloysius with a sealed letter of instructions and a map to the Pharatime tomb. Annoyed that Stanley repeatedly loses the valuable map, Aloysius has a native artist tattoo the chart onto Stanley's back.

More mysterious goings-on occur as the expedition ventures into the Valley of the Kings. A falling boulder nearly crushes Browning. One morning Stanley, Aloysius, Mary, and Catfish awaken to find that they are the only ones left in camp; Browning and the camels have vanished. Determined to carry out the mission, Aloysius uses the map to determine the location of King Pharatime's tomb, and the men begin to dig. They unearth the ancient catacombs and enter with Mary, but a sudden cave-in seals the entrance. Sinister eyes watch the foursome from a hiding place.

The mystery figure is the mad Dr. Sterling, who has trussed up Browning in a secret chamber. Sterling explains to Browning that he had secretly managed to inject each of the ten dead expedition members with a slow-acting poison that leaves no trace. Toting his deadly hypodermic, Sterling joins Stanley, Aloysius, Catfish, and Mary, explaining that he has no idea how he ended up in the tomb. Sterling accidentally drops his diary, which is found and read by Stanley. In it, Sterling admits to being the killer.

A crazy chase ensues, with Sterling dressing himself up as a mummy at one point and menacing the boys with his hypodermic. Stanley and Aloysius are at last able to overpower Sterling and tie up the madman and seal him in a sarcophagus. Browning wriggles free of his bonds and rejoins the others. Haschid Bey, who is in actuality a member of the Secret Police, arrives on the scene with a troop of constables who dig their way into the tomb and free our heroes.

★ ★ ★

With the quality of the Wheeler and Woolsey vehicles slowly headed downhill, it seems only appropriate that the pair should find themselves literally underground in *Mummy's Boys*, weakest of the comedy duo's twenty-one feature films. One of the first spoofs headlining an established comedy team, *Mummy's Boys* is an embarrassment from shaky start to forced finish.

The original story for *Mummy's Boys*, written by Jack Townley and Lew Lipton, was submitted to RKO on Friday the 13th of March, 1936, as an "Untitled Mystery Comedy for Wheeler and Woolsey." The studio hoped to duplicate the comedy/whodunit success of *The Nitwits*, Bert and Bob's last certified hit. Clearly the inspiration of the tale was the 1922 discovery of King Tutankhamen's fourteenth century B.C. tomb by Lord Carnarvon and his American assistant, Howard Carter. "The greatest archaeological discovery of all time" made headlines all over the world, but the big news came later. Probably taking their cue from the untimely demise of Lord Carnarvon, who died from an insect bite as the tomb contents were being cataloged and shipped, the press manufactured the story of a "pharaoh's curse" striking a score of individuals who had desecrated the burial site. The stories were false but the public ate it up. The legend persists to this day.

Working from the Townley-Lipton story, Charles Roberts, Townley, and Phillip G. Epstein (whose later screenwriting credits included *Casablanca* and *Yankee Doodle Dandy*) fashioned a screenplay that gave Bert and Bob an eerie and highly unique backdrop: the ancient tombs of Egypt. The film opens with a favorite horror movie bromide, a howling storm pelting an isolated house; inside, Professor Edwards (Frederick Burton), one of the Browning expedition members, shrugs off the deaths of nine of his thirteen fellow explorers. ("It's horrible, isn't it? But death is notoriously unscientific," Edwards pooh-poohs, delivering the first of the film's many clunker lines.) Edwards expires moments later and Mary Browning screams as Jack Mackenzie's camera dollies to take in a sinister-looking Egyptian figure viewing the tragic scene from outside a rain-streaked window.

Even though the scene is a cliché, it catches our interest and mildly raises our expectations; mediocre as this opener is, however, nothing else in the picture comes up to its level—particularly not Bert and Bob, whose bag of tricks has begun to run perilously low. The boys are their dependable selves and they dish out their material with gusto, but in *Mummy's Boys* they have been scandalously let down by their writers; there is not a funny line or situation in the entire sixty-eight minutes.

Wheeler suffers especially, playing a character afflicted with what the pressbook laughingly calls "jumping amnesia." He is unable to remember events from one moment to the next, and the only thing that jogs his memory is a short nap. (Apparently the writers were hoping to nurture a running gag similar to Bert's kleptomaniac spells in *Cockeyed Cavaliers*.)

His jumping amnesia is established in his first scene (Woolsey tries to serenade him to sleep at the bottom of the ditch they have dug, hoping Bert will remember where he put their lunches), but there is nothing even remotely funny about it. Townley, Epstein, and Roberts keep flogging that dead horse, though: Bert dives on the floor or into the arms of other characters throughout the movie, catching forty winks and then leaping up to tell what he has remembered.

Woolsey, too, is victimized by the poor script, which presents him as a particularly obnoxious and belligerent simpleton. Purposely squirting ink into the face of a hapless sheik, pawing the poor man's wife in front of him, peeking under the sacred veils of women he sees on the street, and loudly inflicting himself on everyone within earshot, Woolsey's character greatly deserves a painful comeuppance that never materializes.

While Woolsey's take-charge character dominates every frame he's in, Wheeler is especially mild; without even a song to serenade the heroine, Bert emerges as little more than a mute Harry Langdon clone, obsequiously falling in line as Woolsey barks his commands.

Straight scenes are handled just as maladroitly; there is the seed of a good idea in *Mummy's Boys*, but so little imagination went into the production that its possibilities are squandered. The "surprise" ending (Sterling is the killer) is telegraphed long in advance when the man disappears rather than turning up dead. Even the cave-in scene in the tomb is robbed of suspense when the camera cuts to a pair of eyes watching Bert and Bob; obviously there is a second entrance to the ancient crypt. The scene where W & W are confronted by a walking mummy also had potential, but this too is spoiled when director Fred Guiol shows Moroni Olsen tediously wrapping himself up in bandages beforehand. Few films have gone this far out of their way to dilute suspense and prematurely tip their hands.

Mewling in the established Dorothy Lee tradition, Barbara Pepper turns in a thoroughly indifferent performance. She bulges her eyes and screeches mildly at one or two points, but throughout the rest of the film she moseys around with the same expression of ennui; her meager $100 a week salary on *Mummy's Boys* was more than she deserved. Once a Ziegfeld Girl and later a Goldwyn Girl, Pepper gained weight and drifted into bit parts. Her last role was on television's *Green Acres* playing the wife of Fred Ziffel (Hank Patterson), owner of Arnold the Pig; there is no resemblance between the flirtatious blond of *Our Daily Bread* (1934) and Barbara of *Green Acres*. She died in 1969.

Mummy's Boys might have benefited from the presence of a horror star who would have added to the atmosphere (the chronically unemployed Bela Lugosi must have been available), but the cast is filled instead with ho-hum actors like Frank Thomas, Sr., Moroni Olsen, and Francis McDonald. Thomas fills the bill in the role of expedition leader

Browning, although at one point the dignified actor debases himself by joining Bert and Bob in a painfully dumb and protracted routine that they had already performed, word for word, in *Cracked Nuts* (the three are too tongue-tied to speak the phrase "as the crow flies"). Playing the sort of unnecessary subordinate character who always turns out to be the killer, Moroni Olsen is also adequate as "Doc" Sterling, although he tends to ham it up in his "mad" scenes; chasing Bert and Bob around a crypt chamber, he huffs and puffs and slow-burns at every irritation, bungling a dozen opportunities to nab one or both of the boys. (Mitchell Lewis, as the much-put-upon pasha, falls into the same trap.) Noble Johnson and Frank Lackteen, veterans of Universal's *Mummy* pictures, lend a welcome presence in their microscopic parts. Playing the stereotypic frightened black, Willie Best adds nothing to the picture; he simply serves as a target for Woolsey's mildly racist jibes (chiding Best for being afraid of ghosts, Woolsey deadpans, "They couldn't see you in the dark").

The film's pressbook insults the intelligence of exhibitors and audiences the same way the film does. Exhibitors were encouraged to bury a homemade mummy on private property (with the permission of the owner), then send a brigade of patrons out with picks, shovels, crowbars, and a vague map. Another press blurb asserted that Woolsey smoked an average of 700 cigars per picture, 20,000 in his entire career; and that if the 20,000 six-inch cigars were laid end to end, they would reach from Hollywood to Chicago. (A few seconds of mental arithmetic are all that is needed to figure out that that string of cigars would give out within two miles; just how dumb did RKO perceive Wheeler and Woolsey fans to be?)

Not unexpectedly, *Mummy's Boys* proved to be Fred Guiol's swan song as the team's director. His lack of style and stone-age directorial technique is the only recognizable "Guiol touch" in the three W & W pictures he helmed. Guiol might have gone on to sabotage additional Wheeler and Woolsey comedies had he not committed the unpardonable sin and exceeded his budget and schedule. *Mummy's Boys* was slated for a comfortable twenty-one-day shoot; by June 10, with the picture in production nineteen days and no end in sight, studio chief Sam Briskin issued a stern warning to producer Lee Marcus: "Regarding *Mummy's Boys*, I see no reason for its being behind, and it is important that you try to get it up on schedule immediately." Gil Perkins, who doubled for several actors and played a bit part in the film, recalled that "poor Freddy Guiol wanted to duplicate the exciting climax we had in *The Nitwits*, but the camera setups needed were beyond his ability." The crew finally wrapped production on June 23, at thirty days a lengthy shoot for a comedy without musical numbers. "My God," Perkins recalls, "it seems like we were filming that finale forever. After that, Guiol was through as a director at the studio."

Guiol was soon rescued by his former protégé, George Stevens, who

Director Fred Guiol gives Bert some last-minute advice on how to play a scene in *Mummy's Boys* as Barbara Pepper eavesdrops. Bob seems dubious.

faithfully recruited the ex-director as a screenwriter on his major productions, including *Gunga Din*, *Vigil in the Night*, and *Giant*. When Guiol's writing services were not required, Stevens appointed him either as an associate producer or assistant director on his remaining pictures. Guiol's charmed movie career continued for as long as Stevens requested his services. He died a wealthy man in 1964 at the age of sixty-six.

Bert and Bob could not go to work for George Stevens, but they could start worrying about their future in the movies. The *New York Times* interviewed Woolsey during the summer of 1936; Bob was anxious that he and Bert complete a tour of the British Isles before their latest films were released there. "Otherwise," Woolsey mournfully confided to the *Times*' correspondent, "we're sunk."

Producer Lee Marcus put up a brave front, giving himself a self-congratulatory pat on the back when he wrote Sam Briskin that *Mummy's Boys* was "infinitely better than the last two we made." But preview postcard comments dispelled any smug notions. Typical of the reactions was the patron who remarked, "the picture was about eight reels too long" (*Mummy's Boys* was a seven-reeler).

Exhibitors writing to the industry trade journal *Motion Picture Herald* found plenty to moan about when *Mummy's* went into general release:

> The poorest picture this team has turned out. I can't understand why the producers don't give this famous team some story to work on. They are just as good as they ever were if given half a chance, but this last story couldn't get a laugh in a feeble-minded institution.

More insulting still was a lawsuit brought against the studio, the writers, and Bert and Bob themselves by a disgruntled would-be screenwriter named Earle Ross. Ross, who had submitted a story idea called *Fabricators* to RKO in 1933 as a possible Wheeler and Woolsey project, waited until August 1937 to press charges that *Mummy's Boys* had plagiarized his outline. He sued the defendants for $200,000 of the picture's profits to date (*Mummy's Boys* grossed approximately that sum in the domestic market). A comparison of the two plots indicates not a trace of similarity except for the notion that Bert and Bob portray archaeologists in both stories. Amateurish as Ross's screenplay is, it could not have made a worse comedy than the film created by the professional filmmakers. The case was dismissed in 1939, with RKO pocketing some twenty-odd dollars from Ross for secretarial expenses relative to the trial. If anyone at all had a legitimate gripe about scene-swiping, it would have been producer Sam Goldwyn, whose 1934 Eddie Cantor vehicle *Kid Millions* contained several sequences that were baldly copied in *Mummy's Boys*.

In the ensuing decades many comedy teams would endeavor to tackle horror spoofs, with greater or (usually) lesser degrees of success. The Three Stooges took on a phony mummy in *We Want Our Mummy* (1939), but probably the best-known encounter between pharaoh and funny men occurred in 1955 in *Abbott and Costello Meet the Mummy*. In a plot somewhat similar to that of *Mummy's Boys*, Bud and Lou wind up on an archaeological dig and find themselves in the sacred tomb of Klaris (played by stuntman Eddie Parker, who gulps and mugs like a bandaged Creature from the Black Lagoon). The film was A & C's last for Universal, and Bud and Lou go through their paces with little heart, even calling each other by their real names rather than the character names established in the story. The boys' tired delivery, the bright, antiseptic tomb sets, and Parker's gawky, goose-stepping Mummy gave the picture a hangdog air.

Variety's Hurl, writing on *Mummy's Boys*, was generous when he allowed that the "net result of the dialog is about four snickers." The lamest of the Wheeler and Woolsey comedies, *Mummy's Boys* is awash in groaner lines and asinine situations, and presents Bert and Bob at their boorish worst.

26
On Again—Off Again (1937)

Directed by Edward Cline. Produced by Lee Marcus. Screenplay by Nat Perrin and Benny Rubin. Based on the play *A Pair of Sixes* by Edward H. Peple. Assistant director, Edward Donahue. Art direction by Van Nest Polglase and Feild M. Gray. Set dressing by Darrell Silvera. Gowns by Renie. Photographed by Jack Mackenzie. Musical direction by Roy Webb. Songs by Dave Dreyer and Herman Ruby. Sound recording by John L. Cass. Film editing by John Lockert. Rehearsals: April 15–18, 1937. Dates of production: April 19 to May 8, 1937. Released by RKO on July 9, 1937. 68 minutes.

Cast: Bert Wheeler (William Hobbs), Robert Woolsey (Claude Horton), Marjorie Lord (Florence Cole), Patricia Wilder (Gertie Green), Esther Muir (Nettie Horton), Paul Harvey (Mr. Applegate), Russell Hicks (George Dilwig), George Meeker (Tony Toler), Hal K. Dawson (Sanford), Kitty McHugh (Miss Parker, a secretary), Pat Flaherty (Mr. Green), Alec Harford (Slip Grogan), Jack Carson, Edward Gargan (Policemen), Maxine Jennings (Miss Meeker), Alan Bruce, Frank O'Connor (Attendants), Frank Anthony (First Mug), Donald Kerr (Second Mug, a butler), Ann Hovey (Cheerleader), William Corson (Smith), Marie Marks (Secretary), Eunice Healey (Dancer), Mosette Du Crai (Maid), Dorothy Moore, Charlotte Dabney, Arleen Whelan (Bit Girls), Jane Walsh (Nurse), George Barton (Chauffeur), Lillian O'Malley (Cook), Phyllis Kennedy (Worker), Jerry Frank (Party Guest).

Synopsis: Claude Horton and William Hobbs (Robert Woolsey and Bert Wheeler), owners of a digestive pill company, cannot stomach each other and continually threaten to dissolve their lucrative partnership. Trouble is, Horton designed the vitamin-fortified tablet while Hobbs conceived its sugar-coated topping: success of the product is contingent upon Horton and Hobbs's continued association. The company's attorney, George Dilwig (Russell Hicks), sarcastically suggests that the feuding partners wrestle each other, with the loser becoming the victor's valet for one year. The loser must pay a hundred-dollar fine for every act of insubordination, and should either break the contract, he must forfeit his half of the business. Much to Dilwig's surprise, Horton and Hobbs readily consent to the ridiculous proposal and stage an immediate match.

Scrawny Horton accidentally wins during the first round; Hobbs, ashamed and humiliated, sends his fiancée, Florence (Marjorie Lord), to Florida without divulging his faux pas as he ponders his next move. Horton assigns Hobbs a host of demeaning tasks in the hope that his partner will resign. Instead, Hobbs plays a psychological game on his nemesis, pretending that he is having an affair with Horton's wife (Esther Muir). Horton retaliates by inviting Hobbs's fiancée to a party on his estate.

When Hobbs learns that Florence is coming, he gives the servants a vacation and hires gold digger Gertie Green (Patricia Wilder) and her gangster friends to masquerade as flunkies. The party deteriorates until Horton orders Hobbs to entertain his guests. Although Hobbs disguises himself with a beard, the getup falls from his face when he sings a song off-key. Florence recognizes her beau and believes Horton's insinuations that Hobbs has been two-timing her. Tearfully, she cancels their engagement.

Oily salesman Tony Toler (George Meeker) talks Horton into a worthless business merger without consulting Hobbs. That night, Hobbs conspires to steal the contract back from Horton's wall safe. Toler hires someone to beat him to it, purloining the document to double-cross Horton and Hobbs with his own corporate takeover. Fortunately, Gertie Green clobbers Toler before he has a chance to flee the estate. In a tell-all mood, attorney Dilwig casually informs the boys that their master/servant contract was invalid after all—neither one had signed it. Florence and Hobbs are reunited, and our final shot of the partners accelerates many years into the future, with the doddering duo squabbling happily ever after.

★ ★ ★

On Again—Off Again is tangible proof that miracles sometimes did occur in Depression-era Hollywood. It was not much of a miracle, but the film rates as a certified jewel alongside the five ponderously plotted pictures that preceded it. This pleasant programmer strikes pay dirt from a long-neglected source, the breezy Broadway musical comedies of the 1920s. Much maligned in recent years (Leonard Maltin commented that the film should have been cut up and used as protection leader), there is nothing in *On Again—Off Again* to embarrass any comedy devotee. It is the team's best film since *The Nitwits*; its laugh content outweighs not only the three Fred Guiol–squeezed lemons but also George Stevens's highly touted *Kentucky Kernels*. Wheeler and Woolsey's enthusiasm in *On Again—Off Again* is contagious, raising the viewer's expectation level considerably. Neither the boys nor the gags muff this chance for a memorable last hurrah.

During July 1936, Bob Woolsey griped to John McManus of the *New*

York Times that the team had exhausted story possibilities and "are desperately staving off the day that repetition must set in." McManus recorded his visit with the morose comedian:

> Mae West (whom Mr. Woolsey suggested we take, for instance) gets away with murder in the name of drama. Katharine Hepburn or (here Mr. Woolsey groped and groaned), well, Richard Dix, they can go to the Broadway stage and get material. "But us, we have a children audience. Nothing gets by the censors." The result is that Wheeler-Woolsey production depends largely on chaste inspiration on the lot. "Synthetic," he says, "like bathtub gin."

Apparently Woolsey's barbs struck the right target, because on August 12 the *Hollywood Reporter* announced that RKO acquired the play *A Pair of Sixes* from Paramount as the next Wheeler and Woolsey vehicle. While the 1914 farce was considered creaky by the midthirties, RKO was keenly interested in adapting *A Pair of Sixes*' popular musical remake, *Queen High*, produced by Paramount in 1930. This story was a pre–Production Code throwback, featuring risqué comedy situations, suspected marital infidelities, and implied sexual contretemps. RKO obtained the property handily enough (they traded Paramount the story rights on *The Other Passport* in an assignment deal). However, two snags had to be dealt with: the original source material was a 1914 antique in need of a 1936 facelift; and an update of the script would only stimulate the Legion of Decency's expurgating propensities. Although the shooting script eventually concocted would be more potent than synthetic gin, Joe Breen's censors could systematically distill hard cider into applesauce pablum "for the whole family."

Nat Perrin, the able-bodied comedy writer best remembered today for his contributions to several Marx Brothers pictures, sifted through *A Pair of Sixes* and *Queen High* to fashion a new script entitled *Easy Going*. While Perrin's story was completed by December 9, 1936, censorship interference and extended litigation with Paramount over remake rights delayed the picture's starting date until March 1937. By that time RKO had nine productions scheduled to get underway, forcing the studio to rent space off the lot and detaining *Easy Going* an additional six weeks.

Throughout the preproduction phase, RKO was bombarded with advice from the Motion Picture Producers Production Code Administration. Some of censor Joe Breen's objections were so puerile that one wonders if cloistered nuns were giving him counsel. To wit:

> All scenes showing Dilwig in the steam cabinet, or in the bath, will have to be handled with greatest possible care, if these scenes are to be acceptable. It is better that you merely suggest his presence in the steam cabinet,

> or bath, rather than to show it. In any event, his body should not be exposed at any time.
>
> The statue of Venus must be draped, so as not to be objectionable.
>
> The final fade-out is highly questionable, both from the standpoint of the Code and political censorship. We urge and recommend that you find some ending other than that of the business of Horton's sticking a pin into his own posterior.

To the last request Nat Perrin meekly responded, "I have not been able to think of a better finish yet. I will insert it as soon as I do." (He did.)

Breen's sanctimonious admonitions occasionally irked producer Lee Marcus. In response to Breen's request, "the character of Tony Toler must not be portrayed as a pansy," Marcus scribbled back, "Why—is he?"

RKO accommodated the team's demands within B picture constraints, signing one of their favorite directors, Eddie Cline, to a one-picture deal two weeks before filming began.

While Bob Woolsey continued to argue with Marcus over the quality of recent W & W epics, Bert was content to remain on the sidelines, remarking, "I let Woolsey do all the battling in studio business problems. He likes it, and I don't." Bert instead found new and expensive ways to deplete his own personal fortunes as an astoundingly inept businessman. Playing Broadway angel, Wheeler cofinanced, along with showbiz confreres George Burns, Georgie Jessel, Jack Benny, and Harry Ruby, Frank Craven's flop play *Glory for All*, to the tune of twenty thousand dollars. (You'd think that Bert would have known better, having starred in Craven's *Too Many Cooks*.) Wheeler built his own hotel, the Lone Palm, in Palm Springs, opening the establishment in October 1936. Almost immediately the hostelry became a money pit, causing Bert to bring in a partner, Ziegfeld alumnus Charlie Hill. Overrun by creditors seeking payment and old vaudeville friends seeking handouts, Wheeler quipped, "Instead of the Lone Palm, I should've called the place the *Loan* Palm. Everybody around here wants to slap me for a buck."

On February 26, 1937, Bert tied the knot for the third time, marrying Sally Haines at director A. Edward Sutherland's home. "I was so choked up I could hardly say the words," Bert told reporters. Friends believed that Wheeler had finally found the right mate, someone who truly cared for him as a human being and not just for his celebrity status.

Easy Going went into rehearsals on April 15. According to Nat Perrin, Bert was especially pleased with the script, plunging into his work with zest, delighting cast and crew with practical jokes and improvised displays of tap dancing. Esther Muir, Bert and Bob's costar from *So This Is Africa*, was recruited to portray Woolsey's nagging wife. Muir was re-creating the role she had essayed when *Queen High* opened as a Broadway play in 1926. She noticed a distinct change in Woolsey's appearance since last acting opposite him. "As always, Bert Wheeler was very good to work with, but Bob Woolsey was very ill at that time." Earlier that year Woolsey had learned that he was suffering from a kidney ailment that was beginning to sap his energy. "As a matter of fact, he didn't complain, but Eddie Cline, our director, let us know about Bob's problem. Bob was ill—and he looked ill."

Despite Woolsey's health problems, an air of camaraderie prevailed on the set. Eddie Cline encouraged Bert's hijinks, and writer/comedian Benny Rubin was on hand as a script doctor to supply bits of dialogue as needed. Rubin contributed little more than theatrical anecdotes to amuse the crew, but his name was plastered across the screenplay credits anyhow. Rubin gently chided Wheeler about Bert's superstitions back during the Bert-and-Betty vaudeville era. As Rubin related the story, Bert and his wife believed that it was bad luck to hear applause garnered by other acts on the bill. While an act onstage was taking its bows, the Wheelers would huddle together in their dressing room, running the water faucet at an open throttle and singing loudly over the audience's din. Asked by Eddie Cline if he still took such precautions, Bert replied, "Nah, I don't have to be superstitious anymore. Now I just stuff my ears with cotton!"

Marjorie Lord, best remembered for her appearances as Danny Thomas's wife in the 1950s sitcom *Make Room for Daddy*, was an RKO starlet cast opposite Bert as his petite vis-à-vis. Professing only "the sketchiest memory" of this early venture, Lord could recall only "my beautiful wardrobe designed by Renie and that I was nicknamed 'Peach Blossom' by the boys when I appeared in a peach negligee." Marjorie was a delightful enough presence in the film to warrant an encore appearance in *High Flyers*, the team's next and final picture. Her reminiscences of the latter film were far more memorable, due in no small part to the eyebrow-raising shenanigans of costar Lupe Velez.

Production went smoothly under Eddie Cline's spirited guidance; the picture wrapped up two days under schedule and just slightly under its $214,000 budget. As shooting completed on May 8, the pleased-as-punch RKO executives signed up Cline to direct the next Wheeler and Woolsey starrer, tentatively titled *The Fall Guys*. Meanwhile, to avoid confusion with Paramount's concurrently produced *Easy Living*, Bert and Bob's *Easy Going* was retitled, at the eleventh hour, to *On Again—Off Again*.

On Again—Off Again sets its tone with a briskly paced opening sequence, establishing Bert and Bob as disgruntled partners who can barely tolerate each other's presence. Striding neck and neck to the firm's pep rally, the boys' comic rivalry overflows into a snappy specialty number, "One Happy Family." The song's finish incorporates the patty-cake face-

Marjorie Lord's lovely presence brightened *On Again—Off Again*, the last enjoyable Wheeler and Woolsey film.

slapping routine used in *The Cuckoos* (Bert is stymied in his attempts to smack Bob, while Bob whacks Bert's face rhythmically, as if on cue). Although this material is recycled, the team's lively interplay makes the nonsense seem novel, a trait lacking in their overworked and undergagged recent pictures.

For the first time in their careers Bert and Bob portray friendly enemies instead of erstwhile buddies, giving a fresh slant to many of the gags. Thankfully, the question-and-answer format used by the team to telegraph a joke is absent; there would be no point in trotting out such inanities in Nat Perrin's taut screenplay. Instead Wheeler and Woolsey maintain a seething animosity toward each other, regulated just a degree or two below the boiling point. Sly insinuation and veiled sarcasm replace the sledgehammer wit that laced *The Rainmakers*, *Silly Billies*, and *Mummy's Boys*. The effect is off-beat and genuinely funny.

A number of amusing lines result when Bert is demoted to the position of Bob's lackey. Bob attempts to induce Bert to quit, while Bert tries to convince Bob to fire *him*, since whoever breaks the contract forfeits his half of the business:

> BERT: The servants have all quit.
> BOB: You're crazy!

Bob and Bert consult the script to *On Again—Off Again* with director Eddie Cline. Jack Carson (rear) is overawed by the presence of greatness.

> BERT: There they go, takin' the bus. . . . They said they wouldn't work for a stupid-lookin' egg like you.
> BOB: And you let 'em call me a stupid-looking egg?
> BERT: Well, there *is* a resemblance, sir.
> BOB: That'll cost you one hundred dollars.
> BERT: You better make it two hundred.
> BOB: Two hundred?
> BERT: I told them what I thought you looked like.
> BOB: You're fired.
> BERT: Gee, thanks!
> BOB: Wait a minute—you're hired again.
> BERT: Whew—what a layoff *that* was!

With the clever dialogue comes an extra dimension to Bert's characterization. Ever since *Kentucky Kernels*, Bert Wheeler's role in W & W comedies had been regressing into that of a subordinate dolt, blindly obeying an overbearing, garrulous Woolsey. The nadir of this pattern is the dreadful *Mummy's Boys*, which resembles nothing so much as one of MGM's Buster Keaton and Jimmy Durante atrocities, inflicted upon the public a few years earlier. Luckily, *On Again—Off Again* discards the slapstick formula of imbecile-rooked-by-smart-aleck, restoring Wheeler to equal partnership opposite Woolsey. The team's nuances, gestures, and wisecracks are delivered with such split-second precision that *Variety* perceptively noted, "both lads play with unusual effectiveness. . . . Proving they really have the stuff, they slap each laugh neatly in place."

The two comics have a field day playing off of each other, Bert especially scoring as he pretends to be the obediant servant, but actually kills his master with kindness. "C'mon, drink your milk," Bert chides Bob. "It'll make your hair curly." "I hate curly hair," Bob grumbles. "I don't even like rosy cheeks!" Bert forces a tumbler of milk down Bob's throat, spilling most of it over Woolsey's face. Traipsing out of the room, Bert announces that he's bringing Woolsey's wife her tea, punctuating the comment with an adagio kick and a parting "Woo-woo!" Bob mutters to himself, "I don't like that 'woo-woo'" before hightailing it after Bert.

Wheeler's gift for mimicry is displayed in a funny sequence where he intercepts Bob's call to an employment agency. Bert assumes an indecipherable British dialect, confusing Bob with esoteric superlatives while describing the quality of his agency's domestics. Later Bert reworks his famous crying routine into the song "Thanks to You." The business is still deliciously funny, but was showcased better in *Diplomaniacs*; here it is contrived to find Bert filching bread off of a harried waiter's tray so that his quavering tenor voice can also emit spitballs.

The movie concludes with Woolsey being pursued by a gun-toting, jealous husband, in and out of bedrooms à la Leon Errol's two-reeler imbroglios. Events accelerate toward the fadeout until a major scripting blunder stops the film dead in its tracks. Just as the boys are about to embark on a wild, no-holds-barred chase to the airport, the villain is apprehended—directly in front of the house. The film promises us an exciting conclusion in the tradition of *Hips, Hips, Hooray!* and *Cockeyed Cavaliers* but instead comes up empty-handed. An examination of Perrin's original draft indicates that a slam-bang finale was never intended, but denying such a wrap-up after promising so much simply reinforces the notion that we are watching a B picture. If *On Again—Off Again* had not been such a superior W & W vehicle up to this point, this cheater ending would not have been so insulting to audiences.

Despite the fizzle-out climax, *On Again—Off Again* has ample assets, not the least of all a sprightly background score and some impressive-looking sets representing Woolsey's stately mansion (a running gag has Bob literally tearing up and down his immense staircase while spying on Bert; at one point the exhausted Woolsey quips, "I gotta get a scooter!"). Esther Muir foils beautifully for Bob (she considered the finished picture "a real blues-chaser"), while George Meeker, in his third and final W & W film, continues to be the epitome of the sniveling cardboard cad. Jack Carson has a mere bit as a hassled cop, but Marjorie Lord, Patricia Wilder, and Russell Hicks buttress the comedy with stylish support.

The trade press genuinely liked *On Again—Off Again*, with *Motion Picture Daily* finding it "better in entertainment and production quality than other recent films featuring the pair." *Motion Picture Herald* lauded the newest release, commenting that

> Managers think well enough of the W-W drawing power to rate this pair as Blue Ribbon stars. Continued perusal of "What the Picture Did for Me" further denotes that exhibitors find the brand of entertainment of the comedians pleasing to their patrons. Wheeler & Woolsey attract a lot of customers.

The team's popularity was at its peak despite their recent spate of bad movies. Loyal—and very patient—Wheeler and Woolsey fans were rewarded with a treat that summer when *On Again—Off Again* was released on double bills. About that same time, the Marx Brothers' *Day at the Races* hit neighborhood screens. The Marx film, with its big-budgeted gloss and MGM hype, predictably emerged as the hit comedy of the season. Today *A Day at the Races* seems unfunny and pretentious, an overblown mélange of mediocre routines performed by the Marxes in calculated slow motion. But the modest *On Again—Off Again* has hardly dated after half a century; it is one of the most enjoyable W & W comedies to introduce to modern audiences. Bert and Bob's penultimate film was a worthy comeback, a refreshing change of pace, and the last delightful romp we would ever get from this unjustly neglected duo.

27
High Flyers (1937)

Directed by Edward Cline. Produced by Lee Marcus. Screenplay by Benny Rubin, Bert Granet, and Byron Morgan. Based on the play *The Kangaroos* by Victor Mapes. Art direction by Van Nest Polglase and Feild M. Gray. Gowns by Renie. Photographed by Jack Mackenzie. Special effects by Vernon L. Walker. Musical direction by Roy Webb. Songs by Dave Dreyer and Herman Ruby. Sound recording by John L. Cass. Film editing by John Lockert. Rehearsals: August 9 to 11, 1937. Dates of production: August 12 to September 4, 1937. Released by RKO on November 26, 1937. 70 minutes.

Cast: Bert Wheeler (Jeremiah "Jerry" Lane), Robert Woolsey (Pierre "Pretty Boy" Potkins), Lupe Velez (Maria Juanita Rosita Anita Morena del Vaya), Marjorie Lord (Arlene Arlington), Jack Carson (Dave Hanlon), Paul Harvey (Horace Arlington), Margaret Dumont (Martha Arlington), Herbert Evans (Hartley), Charles Judels (Fontaine), Lucien Prival (Panzer), Herbert Clifton (Stone, the butler), George Irving (Chief of Police), Frank M. Thomas (Parole Officer Collins), Soledad Jiminez (Auntie), Otto Fries (Fat Man on Kiddie Ride), Bruce Mitchell, Frank Fanning, Phillip Morris, Stanley Blystone, Jim Pierce (Policemen), Bud Geary (Bosun's Mate), Bruce Sidney (Ship's Officer), Mike Pat Donovan (Radio Cop), Monte Vandegrift (Cop Announcer), Don Brodie (Accomplice on Boat), Donald Kerr (Barker), Florence Promis (Bit).

Synopsis: Millionaire Horace Arlington (Paul Harvey) is upset over a rash of petty robberies at his estate, not realizing that the thefts are merely the work of his mischievous bull terrier, Squeezy. Arlington is expecting delivery of the valuable Markoff diamonds, due to arrive the following morning by steamship. Newspaperman Dave Hanlon (Jack Carson) lolls about the Arlington household, pretending to be interested in Arlington's daughter, Arlene (Marjorie Lord). Actually, Hanlon has his eyes set on the Markoff jewels, and schemes to steal them with the aid of his crooked associates, Hartley (Herbert Evans), Fontaine (Charles Judels), and Panzer (Lucien Prival).

Jerry Lane (Bert Wheeler) and Pierre Potkins (Robert Woolsey) run an airplane kiddie ride at a nearby amusement park. Hanlon induces them to fly out to sea and retrieve a life preserver that will be thrown overboard from an incoming ship. The life preserver allegedly contains exclusive "scoop" photos of the Royal Family for Hanlon's newspaper. Unbeknownst to the team, Hanlon "borrows" a Harbor Patrol seaplane for the mission. Pierre admonishes pilot Jerry for flying recklessly, admitting to Lane that this is only his second airplane trip. Jerry cheerfully confesses that he has never flown before, but not to worry, he has read every book on aviation ever written.

The duo locates the life preserver, which to their astonishment contains a collection of gems and some cocaine powder. The wind blows the powder into their faces, making them both temporarily and uproariously "high." Meanwhile, the Coast Guard opens fire on the seaplane with anti-aircraft guns. Jerry steers for an immense pool on the Arlington estate, but cracks up the plane in a tree. Arlington, mistaking them for detectives investigating the mysterious thefts, has the maid, Juanita (Lupe Velez), show them to a room. Pierre instantly becomes enamored of Juanita, but Jerry wants only to flee the house. The duo knows that they have Arlington's jewels but are afraid to turn them over to him, thinking they may be arrested.

Pierre begins imitating a tough-as-nails detective by interrogating members of the household. Jerry meets Arlene and they proceed to quarrel as he simultaneously falls for her. Dave Hanlon, hearing of their antics on the Arlington estate, assures Arlene by telephone that Jerry and Pierre are "mentally deranged—escaped lunatics—but if you humor them they're quite harmless." Hanlon arrives at the house accompanied by his trio of crooks, whom he introduces as psychiatrists. The thieves endeavor to find where the jewels are, and in the ensuing fracas the worried Arlingtons phone for the police. Jerry confesses that he hid the jewels in the fireplace, but Squeezy the dog has subsequently buried the parcel in the garden.

Jerry, Pierre, the crooks, and the police start digging up the garden, searching for the jewels. Mrs. Arlington (Margaret Dumont) finds the gems, which are stolen by Squeezy and finally recovered by Dave Hanlon. Hanlon shows his true colors when he shoves the Arlingtons into a ditch and makes a mad dash to escape with the diamonds. Jerry fires off a revolver, which brings the police back in time to arrest the crooks. Arlington finds a note in the jewel case indicating that he is holding only fake stones—the real gems are locked up in his office. Jerry gets Arlene, Pierre gets Juanita, and Squeezy the kleptomaniac gets Mr. Arlington's false teeth to wear in a fade-out close-up.

★   ★   ★

After Wheeler and Woolsey's comedy slump of 1935-36 and partial recovery with *On Again—Off Again* (1937), one harbored hopes that *High*

High Flyers (1937)

Flyers would conclude their years of teamwork on a final up beat. Alas, this final W & W outing is leagues beneath its predecessor, and while it is certainly not their worst film (*Mummy's Boys* reserves that distinction), *High Flyers* comes awfully close to the lower depths.

High Flyers was based upon *The Kangaroos*, a three-act farce written by Victor Mapes in 1926. Mapes's play remained unproduced (a blessing in disguise for the theater, no doubt) and was purchased by RKO on January 25, 1930. The studio paid $2,500 for assignment rights to the original story, in what seemed a bargain until someone sat down to read the actual manuscript. A June 8, 1931, reader's report dug out of the RKO story files is a tip-off to the quality of this vehicle: "A mechanically constructed comedy that lacks even comedy. Not suited to any one at this studio. NOT RECOMMENDED."

The Kangaroos (the title refers to the name of an airplane within the show) gathered dust on the shelf until 1937, when comedian/screenwriter Benny Rubin convinced RKO studio brass that he could squeeze a few shekels out of the worthless property. Rubin, one of the least appealing and most untalented of all 1930s movie buffoons, attempted to forge a new Hollywood career by doctoring unusable stories. Rubin argued that he could salvage *The Kangaroos*, transforming it into a Wheeler and Woolsey script at a fraction of the cost of an original story development. Producer Lee Marcus liked his rough draft of February 18 and gave Rubin the go-ahead to write a continuity script, with assistance from Byron Morgan. On February 26 it was announced that Betty Grable had been set for the female lead in *The Kangaroos*. Rubin and Morgan meanwhile went back to work, scribbling a completed script by April 3. Marcus was impressed with the writers' expedience, while the higher studio echelon echoed similar sensibilities. Whether *The Kangaroos* was actually funny seems to have been a minuscule point to RKO's bigwigs, certainly not an issue worth bandying.

Not too surprisingly, the studio hierarchy was more intent upon renaming *The Kangaroos* than in assessing the screenplay's merits. In an April 14 memo from studio head Sam Briskin to Lee Marcus, Briskin inquired, "What is your opinion of the titles *Fall Guys* and *The Sleep Walkers* to replace *The Kangaroos*?" Penciled in the corner was Marcus's reply: "Don't like either." Briskin immediately shot back:

> I don't agree with you on the title *The Sleep Walkers*. I think it is a very funny title for a Wheeler & Woolsey, and, anyway, some people might misinterpret it to mean *The Street Walkers*, thereby insuring the picture of doing a good business. Incidentally, a very prominent woman in this town told me that the other day she found a shoe store where she purchased shoes that made streetwalking a pleasure.

On May 10 the *Hollywood Reporter* noted that *The Fall Guys* (*The Kangaroos*' rechristened title) would be the next W & W picture, slated for a June 14 starting date. By June 7 Betty Grable was replaced as leading lady with Marjorie Lord, while the starting date was reset to June 15. However, June 15 came and went without a Wheeler and Woolsey film in the works. Finally, on June 26, the *Hollywood Reporter* revealed that "the Wheeler & Woolsey picture was postponed indefinitely at RKO because of Woolsey's illness." This first, tenuous allusion to Bob's kidney ailment barely ignited a reaction from the press. Probably the severity of Woolsey's affliction was downplayed by the studio, which rescheduled the picture's starting date to August 9 and rebaptized the movie for the last time, to *High Flyers*.

Marjorie Lord, so pert and attractive as the ingenue in *On Again—Off Again*, made a welcome return to the cast. Despite Woolsey's illness, she recalls the making of the picture as a continuous party for the entire crew:

> The director, Eddie Cline, had a great sense of comedy and there was always great humor bouncing between him, the cast, and the crew. The tone was especially frenetic when Lupe Velez was on the set. Her provocative antics opened my young eyes a good deal.

Mexican comedienne Lupe Velez was making her "comeback" to the screen after a season of personal appearances and one British "quota quickie," the stupendously dull *Mad About Money* (1937). Arriving on the set of the Wheeler and Woolsey picture, Lupe would call out, "Where is Lee Marcus, my seducer—I mean, producer!" She would continually grab the befuddled Marcus by the ears and plant smeary lipstick kisses atop his naked pate. At other times the "Mexican Spitfire" would dramatically swirl about her producer, wearing only a dressing gown, and "moon" him to the gasping laughter of the crew (like her Brazilian counterpart, Carmen Miranda, Velez apparently had an aversion to underwear).

"Naturally I was shocked," Marjorie Lord recalls, adding, "Keep in mind that I was only eighteen years old at the time, and at the very beginning of my film career. I never again encountered such an outrageous character like Lupe—never!"

Despite a generous twenty-one-day shooting schedule, *High Flyers* was not a trouble-free production. A three-day rehearsal period was interrupted on August 10 when Bert and Bob were subpoenaed to appear in Los Angeles Federal Court as codefendants in their *Mummy's Boys* plagiarism suit. Actual shooting of *High Flyers* was disrupted by the unprofessionalism of character actor Robert Emmett O'Connor. O'Connor was engaged for a week's salary at $500, worked two days, and refused to return for one final day of filming. A memorandum from Marcus to studio chief Sam Briskin ominously notes, "It might be advisable to keep this

No time for comedy: the team appeared in court between rehearsals for *High Flyers*.

attitude in mind when future work comes up for O'Connor." Shortsighted O'Connor's scenes were scrapped and refilmed with $250-a-week contractee Frank M. Thomas.

Bob Woolsey's worsening physical condition necessitated the attendance of a doctor and nurse on the set as *High Flyers* wobbled toward its completion. The studio hired a photographic double for Woolsey's climactic shots in the picture and enlisted Bert Granet to rewrite a number of scenes to reduce Bob's screen participation. "Bob Woolsey was not well, as I remember, and spoke of retiring," Marjorie Lord reminisced. "Bert Wheeler seemed a happier, freer man, perhaps due to better health." Bert himself recalled the anguish that his partner was suffering.

> Woolsey was very sick, and we knew he would never finish the picture. The director knew it. He got all these close-ups. Everything was done. And we used a double in all the long-shots. It was a patched-together picture, and it looked pretty bad. Woolsey wasn't in for the last ten days of shooting that picture. We put him in the car and we knew that was the finish.

Although press releases stated that Bob was experiencing a kidney ailment, Bert offered a different story:

> He had cirrhosis of the liver. He drank, but he didn't eat. When he was healthy he weighed 110 pounds. And how he drank! He couldn't sleep at night, so instead of taking sleeping pills (as a person would later, which was almost as bad, I guess), he would drink this whiskey to knock him out. Poor little fellow had a solid year in bed.

Woolsey completed his role on August 27 with a fever of 102 degrees and was immediately confined to his bed for rest.

Despite the production hurdles, *High Flyers* was completed on schedule and $3,000 under its $220,000 allotted budget. Accounting ledger sheets may have comforted the front office, though there's little actual entertainment value to be cited in *High Flyers'* grueling seventy-minutes. The only rewarding aspect about this talky, cream-puff farce is Robert Woolsey's performance itself. Physically, it is evident that something is very wrong with Bob: his speech is slightly slurred and his gaunt figure appears somewhat bloated. But his gestures are as lively as ever, full of the old verve and sparkle. Ill though he was, Woolsey literally gives the performance of his life in his final movie.

High Flyers actually contains two of Wheeler and Woolsey's best musical numbers amid the dreary trappings. As in *On Again—Off Again*, both highlights are nostalgically laden: Bob performs "I'm a Gaucho" with Lupe Velez, recalling both his "I Can Speak Español" from *Rio Rita* (1929) and "I'm a Gypsy" from *The Cuckoos* (1930). Bert's dance specialty reaches back into antiquity, and is an even bigger treat: an abbreviated version of his 1915 vaudeville act, imitating Charlie Chaplin.

Woolsey's number comes first, at approximately midway through the picture. After a dull tête-à-tête with Lupe Velez, Bob arbitrarily picks up a

High Flyers (1937)

"I'm a Gaucho," Woolsey's last-ever movie scene, with spicy Lupe Velez, from *High Flyers*.

gaucho's hat and places it on his head. This gesture prompts Lupe's perceptive comment, "Oh, señor, you look like a gaucho," which cues Woolsey to break into song. "I'm a Gaucho" (or, "The Gosh-Darndest Gaucho, You Bet") is neither novel nor witty (lyrics inform us that "Gaucho is Spanish for 'he-man,'" and, rhythmically for the next couplet, that Woolsey is "An A, B, C, D, E, F, G-man"). Bob's voice during the number is so weak that he appears to be whispering instead of singing, while Lupe's lung power is enough to revive audiences already dispatched to slumberland. But midway through the number the pair goes into a fiesta dance with tambourines; Woolsey's fiery fandango of nimble footwork with arms akimbo is vivid, lively, and wonderfully comic (Bob holds high a tambourine for Lupe to kick; when Lupe reciprocates the gesture, Woolsey hastily lowers the tambourine to a few inches off the floor). He and Lupe execute a complicated series of identical maneuvers with split-second precision, gracefully skipping off-camera in perfect unison. Ironically, the "Gaucho" dance, which took two days to film, marked Woolsey's final appearance before the cameras.

Bert's turn follows shortly afterward. Dipping into Marjorie Lord's makeup kit, Bert shapes a Chaplinesque mustache, purloins a nearby cane and bowler hat, musses his hair, and begins tap-dancing furiously. The mimicry is flawless, but Wheeler's dazzling skill as an eccentric dancer and human firecracker transforms the piece into magic. Whether jackknifing his derby from head to toe, catching a twirling cane between his legs, or recklessly running in place while his torso appears immobile, Bert's turbo-charged comedy streaks through the scene with a fury that would charm Fred Astaire. Yet instead of bolstering the movie, this galvanizing specialty number simply emphasizes the anemia of the rest of the picture.

The supposed "gags" that clutter up the film are so forgettable that they are hardly worth recounting. Stupidity reigns supreme in the following exchange between Bob and Mr. Arlington:

> BOB: Mr. Arlington, have you any bad habits that you're not aware of? Answer yes or no.
> ARLINGTON: No, uh...
> BOB: Ah! You mean that you don't know that you have any bad habits?
> ARLINGTON: Yes—why...
> BOB: Oh, you admit that you have bad habits?
> ARLINGTON: Say, you don't think that I'd rob my own house?
> BOB: Well, you may be a somnambulist. You do it while you're asleep.
> ARLINGTON: I certainly do not!
> BOB: How do you know that you don't?
> ARLINGTON: Well, I—I...
> BOB: Well, there you are, there you are. It's an open-and-shut case.

Comic "third-degree" scenes, where the comedian suspects the hapless victim, were so overworked by the late 1930s that Rubin's script merely substitutes a hollow joke for real wit. Groucho Marx fared just as badly when grilling a midget in *At the Circus* (1939). For the record, the best comedy interrogation sequence is probably in Buster Keaton's *Sherlock Junior* (1924)—and that classic movie is a silent picture.

As if to compensate for his asinine behavior in *Mummy's Boys*, Bert emerges as the smarter team member in *High Flyers*. But in making Bert intelligent, the screenwriters forgot to make him funny, although he is still several notches above Woolsey's character, whose brainless infatuation with Lupe Velez allows the duo to be entrapped by the villains. Bert and Bob struggle heroically with the ho-hum material, and turn in performances that rank among their best. But the closest *High Flyers* ever gets to a real laugh sequence was nearly botched by the censors, who sacrificed wit in the name of prudence at every turn of the script's pages.

The episode in question occurs near the beginning of the film, when Bert and Bob commandeer a stolen seaplane to pick up the "loaded" life preserver. Completing their mission, the boys continue in flight while Woolsey anxiously "opens" the catch, only to find a collection of jewels and some parcels marked "Parvadon." Bert examines the box's contents, a powdery white substance, and Wheeler reacts instantly. Taking his hands off the steering column and nonchalantly crossing his legs, Bert announces to Bob, "I think I'll turn this ship around and head for London!" Bert's giddy demeanor and ghost-white face causes Woolsey to grouse, "Laugh, clown, laugh!" Bob likewise opens a box and the stuff similarly coats him—only Woolsey decides that "we won't stop until we get to Moscow!" (Woolsey *would* want to go to Moscow.) The two squabble over a preferable destination until an antiaircraft attack from the Coast Guard quickly sobers them up. While the budgetary limitations hurt an otherwise clever piece of business (the tacky cockpit set resembles an empty broom closet), this episode affords *High Flyers* its only honest laughs, as well as the rationale for the film's title.

The Motion Picture Producers and Distributors Association failed to see the humor of the situation. Watchdog Joe Breen, the industry's censor, read the script and objected in a June 14 letter to Sam Briskin:

> The suggestion that Jerry and Pierre [Bert and Bob] have found some dope in the form of white powder in a box and the fact that they subsequently use it to strengthen their courage is unacceptable under the provisions of the Code. There must not be any suggestion of illegal drugs, or their traffic, and this business must be changed.

Briskin conferred with Breen on June 23, and reached a compromise whereby the studio agreed not to identify the white powder as cocaine, but instead to "use some ridiculous name ... to get away from any suggestion that the white powders were dope." This logic itself is ridiculous, since it is blatantly apparent in *High Flyers* that the boys' ebullience was induced by potent nose candy. Charlie Chaplin's *Modern Times* (1936) used a similar coke motif for comedy purposes, but "getting high" was virtually taboo in major studio releases of the era.

The most intriguing business in the script for *High Flyers* was never filmed, but this discarded last scene bears repeating:

> EXTERIOR: Marathon Street Gate—RKO Studio
> Wheeler & Woolsey are running down past Café and Little Theatre towards gate, being chased by a bald-headed man with two large Australian bull whips, one in each hand. Whips are being cracked in exaggerated sound effect. As figures approach CAMERA, we discover bald-headed man is [Lee] Marcus.
> MEDIUM SHOT: Wheeler and Woolsey passing through gate.
> MEDIUM SHOT: Gate—SAM BRISKIN standing on sidewalk.
> SAM BRISKIN [*disgustedly*] And stay out!

This coda reads like an in-joke not meant to be taken seriously by anybody, though another alternate ending neatly anticipates the Hope and Crosby *Road* pictures: the action accelerates one year into the future, where we find Bert and Bob have married their girlfriends and become fathers. Bert and Marjorie are the proud parents of quintuplets, all of whom resemble Bert. Bob and Lupe have one child—who also looks like Bert. Whether the censors axed the scene or the studio opted for a conventional tag is unknown, but it would have been a memorable finale for the last Wheeler and Woolsey comedy.

The supporting cast fared no better than the stars of *High Flyers*. The usually zesty Lupe Velez was given little to do, although at $1,500 a week with a three-week guarantee, she was the highest-paid W & W heroine since Thelma Todd. Paul Harvey played his typically harried business tycoon with cardboard dimension, while Margaret Dumont was her reliable matronly self in a thankless bit. Up-and-coming Jack Carson revealed his smooth comic touch, although the script afforded him few opportunities. He does supply an unintended laugh in the opening scene, when the camera spies Carson alongside a swimming pool, his potbellied physique outlined in what resembles a 1900 bathing suit. The gag may be accidental, but it is an honest laugh in this deceptively dull excuse for a comedy.

A finished print was shipped east for approval on October 15, five weeks after photography was completed. New York vice-president Ned Depinet flaunted his lack of movie business acumen when he wrote Sam Briskin a gushing testimonial:

> I consider [*High Flyers*] the best Wheeler & Woolsey that we have released in some time. It is fresh, funny, with good music and gags. It certainly should roll up a better gross than its recent predecessors. Congratulations.

Film critics, with nothing to lose by telling the truth, ravaged the movie. *Variety* went for the jugular: "Yarn is noisy, hectic, absurd, overlong

High Flyers (1937)

and witless." *Time* called it "a prettified thing of unfunny gags and attenuated plot," while the *New York Daily News* found *High Flyers* "a potpourri of misapplied and misdirected talent—and when we call it talent we give Wheeler and Woolsey the benefit of the doubt."

When RKO reissued a number of programmers in 1947, *High Flyers* was the sole Wheeler and Woolsey included in the package. Reactions could not have been encouraging; Bert Wheeler, who had not seen the picture initially, caught it at a revival house and promptly fell asleep—which is possibly the only smart way to deal with this misnamed mélange of sunken opportunities. *High Flyers* never leaves the ground.

Epilogue

Robert Woolsey died of his chronic kidney and liver ailments on October 31, 1938. He was just forty-nine years old. Bert Wheeler had recently returned to the United States after completing a music-hall tour of England; he had last seen Bob alive back in June. "I knew Woolsey was very, very ill, and when I saw him lying there suffering, and I knew what he was going through—you felt that soon God would take him and it would be a good thing. Because he didn't have a chance and he knew it, and he didn't try to fight it. He knew he was finished."

Woolsey's funeral attracted crowds that rivaled Jean Harlow's passing of the previous year. The press offered glowing, front-page eulogies for the late comedian, who was buried in Forest Lawn not far from the final resting places of John Gilbert and Marie Dressler. Robert Woolsey took his final bow while at the peak of his profession, with the applause still ringing in his ears; Bert Wheeler would outlive his partner by thirty years, carving a new niche for himself in show business yet never recapturing the popularity he had shared with Woolsey.

Around this same time, Henny Youngman appeared with Bert at both New York's Casa Mañana nightclub and Chicago's Palace Theater. Says Youngman today,

> Bert Wheeler was one of the funniest guys I'd ever worked with. I remember he had a great act that began, "Question: What do elephants have that no other animals have? Answer: baby elephants!" The guy was a genius because he could take silly, simple stuff and make you believe in it—and laugh. He worked intimately, quietly.
>
> Now, after Woolsey died, Hollywood could only see Wheeler as the straight man—but he wasn't just that. They didn't let him work in pictures as a single. Why not? If you can tell me the secret, then maybe the studios will knock on my door, kid.

Bert did return to pictures with *The Cowboy Quarterback* (1939), an ultracheap fifty-four minute quickie for Warner Brothers. In a partial remake of two Joe E. Brown comedies, *Elmer the Great* (1933) and *Bright Lights* (1935), Wheeler was stymied by a trashy script and forced to affect a midwestern twang reminiscent of Brown's natural cadences. The film was a disaster, causing such low-grade W & W fare like *Mummy's Boys* and *High Flyers* to look like classics in comparison. A momentary highlight is Bert's drunken rendition of "Mother Macree," reviving his crying routine with help from real-life crony Eddie Foy, Jr. Slightly better was *Las Vegas Nights* (1941), produced at Paramount under faithful William LeBaron's aegis and cowritten by longtime W & W author Eddie Welch. Bert sang "Dolores" delightfully with the Tommy Dorsey Orchestra (band vocalist Frank Sinatra sat on the sidelines), but despite some encouraging reviews, the film was a flop. "It was a real turkey," Bert recalled. Responding to the film's appearance on CBS-TV's "Early Show" in 1966, Wheeler quipped, "A picture like that can come back and haunt you."

Bert's money problems had forced him to star in these two pathetic potboilers. His Palm Springs hotel, the Lone Palm, folded when partner Charlie Hill died and creditors began hounding Bert. In 1939, wife Sally Haines divorced him, claiming that Bert was "anything but funny around the house." Wheeler found himself unemployed, unwanted for the first time in his career, and with plenty of time to kill. A proposal by Chuck Reisner to produce (for RKO) and direct feature comedies starring Bert and Dorothy Lee did not proceed past the planning stage. Although Dottie could not recall the movie offer, she remembered a more poignant incident from that same time. "When Bert's career was going badly, he asked me to join his stage act. My husband didn't want me returning to show business, but I told him, 'Too bad, Bert needs me!'" Dottie's presence bolstered Bert's enthusiasm and transformed their Chicago engagement into a success. "If I wasn't intent on becoming a mother, we probably would've teamed up like Bert and Betty did. But instead I retired from showbiz, while Bert's solo career finally caught on."

Bert appeared in a number of successful stage shows throughout the 1940s, including *Priorities of 1943* (1942) with Henny Youngman, *Laugh Time* (1943) with Frank Fay and Ethel Waters, *Harvey* (1946, earning rave reviews as Fay's summer replacement), and *All for Love* (1949), with Grace and Paul Hartman. For many in the audience, Wheeler had been away from Manhattan's footlights far too long. About *Priorities of 1943*, the *New York Post* mocked their own dim recollections: "Bert Wheeler is a pretty funny fellow. It was so long since we had seen Mr. Wheeler that we had all but forgotten his style. Several persons informed us before the show opened that he always eats an apple."

Not everyone appreciated the comedian. *Three Wishes for Jamie* (1952) was a "book" musical starring John Raitt, Anne Jeffreys, Jeff Morrow, and Ralph Morgan, with Bert, third billed, as comic relief in the guise of a defrocked village priest. Wheeler had replaced temperamental Cecil Kellaway when the actor began demanding outrageous script changes. Morrow felt that Bert was out of his element and out of touch with the times:

This was really a beautiful show about an ancient Irish legend; it could have been another *Brigadoon*. We had some wonderful actors in it, and John Raitt was in fine voice, but then we had this old-time, hokey buffoon, this vaudevillian, this *idiot*, this Bert Wheeler, whose idea of comedy was to hitch his trousers, cock his hat, and blurt his jokes out to the audience as though they were deaf—or stupid, maybe.

I'm not saying Wheeler wasn't funny—he got enough laughs legitimately—but he wasn't used to making his points in a character part. He was always playing Bert Wheeler, so he threw the whole show off kilter, and in my opinion, he ruined it.

In 1952, Wheeler married showgirl Patsy Orr, whom he had been dating on and off since the mid-1940s. Bert's fourth and last marriage lasted less than four years; he never referred to this failed union in subsequent interviews. In 1950 he made a pair of comedy short subjects for producer Jules White at Columbia Pictures. "Bert was a cute little man," Jules reminisced. "I believe he was bankrupt at the time and strapped for cash. Customarily, we paid our leading comedians $500 a picture, but I think I was able to wrangle $1,000 per short for Bert. He was a cooperative, friendly fellow in spite of his troubles." Unfortunately, the resulting two-reelers, *Innocently Guilty* (1950) and *The Awful Sleuth* (1951) were lackluster pastiches, filled with Three Stooges–style slapstick and lacking the qualities that were Wheeler's forte.

In 1954 Bert was hired to portray the Indian sidekick Smokey Joe on the television series *Brave Eagle*. Director Paul Landres recalled, "Bert Wheeler had an established name as a comic and he played his part well. I think his name enhanced the series. If the series would have gone into more episodes, I'm sure there would have been many stories about Smokey Joe." Bert's contributions to the one-season show were not especially notable, but they accomplished their task, providing him with steady work and paying his bills. *Brave Eagle* represented Wheeler's last regular employment in Hollywood. Shortly thereafter he abandoned the West Coast and returned to his beloved Broadway.

Bert wasn't the only great comedian relegated by Hollywood to has-been status—Stan Laurel was similarly neglected by the industry he had served for so many years. Bert had known Stan back in vaudeville when they were both Chaplin imitators. They later became close friends when Laurel was directing Clyde Cook for Hal Roach in the mid-1920s. During the 1930s, when Wheeler and Woolsey were the only comedy duo to rival Laurel and Hardy's popularity, it was Bert who encouraged Stan to hire their mutual friend, Bill Seiter, to direct L & H's *Sons of the Desert* (1933). In 1958 Wheeler reminisced about his final visit with Stan Laurel:

> A year and a half ago, I went out to say good-bye to Stan. He was the last person I saw before I left Hollywood. He's so cute, that Stan Laurel—and

a sense of humor! You know, I made that television thing—that *Brave Eagle*—I only did it because I needed a job. He told me that the first time he saw me playing that Indian, his wife had to grab him, saying, "We're going to be thrown out of the place!" I'm playing it on the level—it's not a comedy part—I'm a real Indian. But when he saw me playing this Indian, with this wig, it just hit him so that he got absolutely hysterical.

Bert journeyed east in a house trailer, settling along the Jersey Palisades while he "practically started all over again in show business." The challenge of again appearing before live audiences revitalized Wheeler's comic touch. He developed the hilarious "old biddy" nightclub routine (which partner Tom Dillon describes in this book's introduction). Bert was ecstatic about the act and its possibilities, while the club dates reminded Bert of "vaudeville with microphones." He later remarked, "I wouldn't care if I never saw anything else—all I want is to play these clubs. I get myself $600 or $700 for one show, and walk out—twenty minutes and I'm out of there. This thing is sensationally funny." Calling themselves Wheeler and Son, the act became a hot attraction, appearing at prestigious nightclubs in New York, Lake Tahoe, and Reno; as the shipboard entertainment on ocean cruises; and at private parties for major corporations. When the duo appeared at an affair for sports announcer Mel Allen and officials of the New York Yankees, Casey Stengel cornered Bert and admitted he was Wheeler's biggest fan. Stengel rattled off every theater Wheeler appeared in and recounted every gag from the Bert-and-Betty days. "If I ever saw a pro," Casey told the crowd as he pointed at Bert, "there's one!"

When Dillon and Wheeler appeared at Reno's Riverside Hotel in 1958, Bert visited someone he had not seen in thirty years—his first wife, Betty. "I didn't accompany him, because I knew how personal this was," Tom remembers, "but I know he gave her everything in his pockets—his salary for the engagement." Bert and Betty made their peace and parted as friends. Betty Wheeler died that same year, at the age of sixty-one.

Wheeler took time out from his newfound career for a final Broadway fling, *The Gang's All Here* (1959). For Bert it was a tour de force in dramatics, appearing as he did with Melvyn Douglas, E. G. Marshall, Jean Dixon, Arthur Hill, and Victor Kilian in a gripping account of President Harding's scandalous administration. Although the other performances were sober-minded and serious, Bert's role as a presidential sidekick required Wheeler to be himself. The script describes Bert's character as "a short, bubbly little man whose face has the mobility of a clown's, who darts about with good spirits." Screen sex kitten Yvette Vickers (*Attack of the 50 Foot Woman, Attack of the Giant Leeches*) abandoned sci-fi movies to expand her repertoire in the same play. Says Yvette today,

Epilogue

A candid moment on *The Ed Sullivan Show* (1960): Bert in costume as a little old lady interrupts "son" Tom Dillon's act. Ed Sullivan (right) watches approvingly.

Bert was always "on." Oh, he was a sweetheart! He was warm and charming and giving. He had a lot of energy. He was one of those dynamos: very, very energetic and alive. And I was very curious about show business when he was a young boy coming up: what was it like? So before we'd go onstage, waiting in the green room, Bert would tell me all his old stories. You can imagine—getting stranded at the railway station in the snow; the manager running away with all the salaries; barnstorming in a different town every night. It was colorful and fun to listen to.

In the show I played a party girl—what else?—hired by Bert to dance for the president, Melvyn Douglas. I remember distinctly that our director, George Roy Hill, was tough on the dramatic actors but Bert was pretty much left alone to do what he wanted to do. Bert was so friendly and down to earth. You could tell that just by looking at his old movies.

Wheeler sold his trailer and, to be closer to the theater district, took up residence in a tiny twenty-dollar-a-week room at the Lambs, the professional actor's club located on West Forty-fourth Street. After a near-fatal boating accident in 1960, where Wheeler clung to a buoy for forty-five

Alberta MacDonald, Yvette Vickers, and Bert Wheeler whoop it up in *The Gang's All Here* (1959).

minutes in the frigid night air of Long Island Sound, Bert was reconciled with the Catholic Church. "A priest visited me, and it dawned on me how lucky I was to be still active in this business," he mused. "Now I'm surrounded by happiness. I go to mass and take communion nearly every day." Wheeler was financially broke yet resilient in spirit: "I'm not getting rich, but I make all I need. I keep working all the time." E. G. Marshall, who appeared with Bert when the little comic guested on television's *Defenders* (1961), remarked, "Here was a wonderful man who was one of the major comedians of the 1930s, and had been extremely wealthy, but what pleased him most was his return to the church."

Wheeler's modesty and lack of pretense were so unlike the behavior of other veteran laughmakers that it continually caught observers off guard. Bert Lahr's son, John, recalled his own introduction to Bert:

> When I met Bert Wheeler, he was a genial old guy hanging around the Lambs Club. He was sprightly and warm-hearted, at least in the company of my father. I didn't really know who he was, or that he even had been a Broadway star. He didn't make a point of letting you know he'd once been big. But I remember at one Lambs' gambol that Dad took me

to, seeing him get up and improvise something and bring the house down. It startled me because in person he was so unprepossessing.

Musical comedy historian and author Miles Kreuger reminisced about his own touching encounter with Bert at this time:

> I was attending an event in the dining room of the Lambs and happened to be seated next to Bert Wheeler. When I told him how much I admired his work, he scoffed that I could not even know who he was, let alone ever have seen any of his work. I promptly raced through a long list of his film titles with the speed of a Gilbert and Sullivan patter song. He actually began to sob a little and spent the next ten minutes walking around the room remarking that "that young man actually knows my old movies."

Bert's emphysema attacks during the 1960s curtailed his acting appearances. On July 16, 1965, he made his final visit to California, when Warner Bros. tested him for the Indian role in *Petticoats 'n' Pistols*, a comedy Western series. Bert lost the part to Lon Chaney, Jr., but the plucky comic continued to work with Tom Dillon. Wheeler joked with a reporter, "How do I want to go? To drop dead on a stage, that's my ambition!" Instead Bert retired, making his final appearance at the Garden City Hotel, on Long Island, during Christmas 1966. This was the same resort where Charles Lindbergh rested forty years earlier, canceling plans to see Wheeler and Woolsey in *Rio Rita* the night before his historic flight.

On his seventy-first birthday in 1966, Bert Wheeler was elected President of the Catholic Actor's Guild, an appointment that tickled the elder statesman of comedy: "Imagine — an old reprobate like me — president!" But he took his job seriously, attending official functions and happily leading the members into Sunday mass at Saint Patrick's Cathedral, where the veteran mischief maker occupied the first pew.

Occasionally interviewers asked him for his views on comedy and comedians; his responses were always insightful and, at times, provocative:

On Buster Keaton: "I knew Buster very well. I don't know what finished his career; I think he was such a great pantomimist, but I don't think he was ever great with dialogue. I was at a lot of parties with him, and I was always crazy about him, but I didn't know his inside career. I didn't know what the dickens was happening to him [in the 1930s]. As far as anybody knew out there, to know him was to love him."

On Laurel and Hardy: "I was in the same golf club with Babe Hardy for twenty years, I guess. Babe loved to play golf and he loved to gamble: play bridge, play poker, play anything. Stan loved the gals — and liquor. Stan Laurel is as good a director as ever lived. You couldn't tell Stan how to fall down or do anything, could you? Stan and Babe never went around together, they had their different circles, but they got along well."

Supper dance at the Catholic Actor's Guild at the New York Hilton: Ed McMahon, Bert, Merv Griffin, Horace McMahon, and Iggie Wolfington, May 6, 1966.

On Jack Benny: "There's a smart operator. I know him very well. I've worked with him a whole lot—in vaudeville and in afterpieces. We're not friendly and we're not unfriendly. I figure I did a lot of things for Jack Benny, and he's never done anything for me. But I still admire him. He's a great performer, and as smart as he is great."

On George Burns: "I like him. He's a lucky guy. He has nothing. He's a good straight man, but I could run him out of a theater, right tonight. He makes his own TV show in Hollywood—he stands out there with a cigar and does a monologue—but he's the one that dubs in the laughs. I'd like to see him out in front of an audience getting those laughs. He's a funny guy offstage, and he's a nice guy. They tell me he takes himself very seriously now."

On Lucille Ball: "Lucy is a great talent. Desi [Arnaz] is nothing—but he's lucky."

On Fred Allen: "One of the most beloved men and one of the most humorous men who ever lived, but I never thought he was a great comedian. I thought he was even funnier with his pen and ink; some of the things he wrote were beautiful. He was a good comedian, but he wasn't great. He never moved funny or did anything real funny to me. But he's a great man, and a great, great, humorist."

On Comedy in the 1960s: "If comedy's dying now, it's not the fault of

Out of makeup, this unretouched photo shows Bert looking his seventy-one years yet obviously full of the old mischief (April 1966).

the comedians. It's because they haven't got time to practice. That television is a tough racket. You go out there and you've got to do it so fast and so furious! In vaudeville in the old days, we would walk out and start very, very slowly. Sometimes the audience would be heckling you in the beginning. You'd have a situation that you were slowly but surely getting to. You can't do that on television. You've got to walk out and kick their brains in."

Bert was Dottie Lee's houseguest while appearing in Chicago's *Show Boat* revival (July 1958). "I hadn't seen him for a few years," Dottie recalled, "and it surprised me that he had to nap every afternoon. I never thought about how old he was because he never acted like that before." Lambs Club member Frank Melfo remembered Bert's attempts to perform a time-step dance for an actors' affair in the 1960s. During rehearsals, Bert requested a recording of "Tea for Two." Melfo obliged by getting musician Eddie Webber to record the song on tape. Bert set the beat while "Tea for Two" was recorded, but after rehearsing Wheeler complained, "Frank, what are you doing to me? It's so fast, I can't keep up with it! I'm all out of breath!" Melfo responded that it was Wheeler who had set the timing, but that he would get Webber back to rerecord the tune. But no tempo was slow enough for Bert; he just was not up to performing any longer, even at private parties.

When Frank Melfo married shortly afterward, Bert presented the newlyweds with a bottle of champagne, remarking, "I know you kids are

going to make it. I've been a five-time loser [he included his relationship with Pat Parker], but I can tell you kids are gonna make it."

Bert Wheeler died of emphysema on January 18, 1968, at Saint Clare's Hospital in Manhattan. He was seventy-two. Ironically, his only child, Patricia Wheeler Walters, had died of cancer just weeks earlier (December 31) in California. She was survived by her son, Michael, and daughter, Bonita.

The comedian who earned and lost a fortune was buried in the field for impoverished actors at Calvary Cemetery, Queens. Megastar celebrities like Frank Sinatra and Bob Hope paid him verbal tribute, but fittingly, it was a member of the oldest surviving comedy team, Smith and Dale, who had the last word. Joe Smith remarked, "He was one of the funniest men I ever knew. He was the kindest man show business ever saw."

Appendix: Miscellaneous Film Appearances

The Voice of Hollywood **(1929, Tiffany Productions)**
Producer/director: Louis Lewyn.
Bert Wheeler hosted this down-home short, set at the fictional Hollywood radio station STAR and featuring guest appearances from Ken Maynard and his horse Tarzan, Marceline Day, Marjorie "Babe" Kane, and Wesley Barry. Bert munches on an apple between the acts and signs off with his vaudeville signature, "Love and no kisses." One reel.

The Voice of Hollywood **(1930, Tiffany Productions)**
Producer/director: Louis Lewyn.
Bob Woolsey hosts his own STAR entry, with Buster Keaton, Raquel Torres, Cliff Edwards, Lew Cody, Gwen Lee, Al St. John, Nancy Welford, Johnny Walker, Mary Carr, and the Meglin Kiddies. Woolsey steals a pie that Mary Carr has baked for Johnny Walker, who is leaving on an Alaskan vacation. Bob starts wolfing it down as the short fades out. One reel.

Screen Snapshots **(1930, Columbia Pictures)**
Producer: Harry Cohn.
Bert and Bob appear with Dorothy Lee, Sue Carol, Jack Mulhall, and songwriter Harry Tierney (the composer for *Rio Rita* and *Dixiana*). Tierney explains to the guest stars how a Hollywood theme song is written, demonstrating on the piano his new composition, "Let's Pretend We're Sweethearts." One reel.

The Voice of Hollywood **(1930, Tiffany Productions)**
Producer/director: Louis Lewyn.
Bert and Bob appear with two unidentified starlets on the dance floor of bandleader George Olsen's supper club; other celebrities dancing include Arthur Lake, June Clyde, and Rena Torres. Monte Blue and Buster Keaton are among the dinner guests, while Kenneth Harlan and the Sisters G (two German girls with the last name of Gutohrlein) emcee the short. One reel.

Grand Hotel Premiere **(1932, Metro-Goldwyn-Mayer)**
Short subject filmed at Grauman's Chinese Theater, featuring Conrad Nagel, Jean Harlow, Norma Shearer, Irving Thalberg, Wallace Beery, Joan Crawford, Johny Barrymore, Lionel Barrymore. Bert and Bob step up to the microphone and do a comedy bit before hustling into the theater. One reel.

Appendix

Hollywood Handicap (1932, Universal Pictures)
Director: Charles Lamont.
Bert is in this comedy sponsored by the Thalians, a Hollywood actors' club; other cameos include Vernon Dent, Anita Garvin, Monty Collins, Marion Byron, Ivan Lebedeff, Jack Duffy, James Burke, Dickie Moore. Two reels.

Hollywood on Parade (1932, Paramount Pictures)
Producer/director: Louis Lewyn.
Bert and Bob pull a gag on their old *Peach O'Reno* and *Stolen Jools* costar, emcee Eddie Kane. Other celebs: Tom Mix, Jimmy Durante, Douglas Fairbanks, Jr., Bebe Daniels, Ben Lyon, Anna May Wong, Billie Dove, Roscoe Ates, Jackie Cooper, Frankie Darro, Bob Bromley's Puppets. One reel.

Hollywood on Parade (1933, Paramount Pictures)
Producer/director: Louis Lewyn.
He-man Woolsey appears in shirt, tie, and sweater on his Malibu beach-front property along with Buster Collier and John Boles. Bob plays straight man for a bum joke by Collier; greeting former *Rio Rita* costar Woolsey, John Boles asks, "How's the ol' Kinkajou?" "OK, kid," Bob replies. Other movieland participants: emcee Johnny Mack Brown, Mary Pickford, Bebe Daniels, Ginger Rogers, Patricia Ellis, Gloria Stuart, Boots Mallory, Harry Green. One reel.

Hollywood on Parade (1934, Paramount Pictures)
Producer/director: Louis Lewyn.
Speeding to the premiere of their latest movie, the boys get a ticket from a cop without a sense of humor. Other stars: Mary Pickford, Tom Mix. One reel.

Hollywood on Parade (1934, Paramount Pictures)
Producer/director: Louis Lewyn.
Bert and Bob are seen watching the horse races at Agua Caliente racetrack in Mexico, along with Alice White, Constance Bennett, Joan Bennett, Carole Lombard, William Powell, Harry Langdon, Mabel Langdon, Claudia Dell, Raquel Torres, and Polly Moran. One reel.

A Night at the Biltmore Bowl (1935, RKO)
Producer: Lee Marcus. Director: Alf Goulding.
Bert appears at a popular Hollywood nitery with other film folk including Lucille Ball, Betty Grable, Edgar Kennedy, Grady Sutton, Anne Shirley, Dennis O'Keefe, Preston Foster, and Jimmy Grier's orchestra. Two reels.

Sunday Night at the Trocadero (1937, Metro-Goldwyn-Mayer)
Producer: Louis Lewyn. Director: George Sidney.
Bert turns up in familiar surroundings once again, only this time the short was filmed in gorgeous three-strip Technicolor. Among the other notables: Robert Benchley, Groucho Marx, Chester Morris, Connee Boswell, Reginald Denny, Peter Lind Hayes, Sally Blane, Glenda Farrell, Frank McHugh, Toby Wing, Stuart Erwin. Two reels.

Sources and Notes on the Chapters

Except where noted, the author interviewed the following individuals for information included within this book:

Joey Adams, May 20, 1988
Marilyn Cantor Baker and Mike Baker, June 7, 1988
Edward Bernds, November 19 and 25, 1987, August 12, 1988
George Burns (letter to author), January 27, 1986
Mary Carlisle, October 3, 1985
Alice Dillon, September 22, 1988
Tom Dillon, September 22, 1988, October 14, 21, 26, 1988, November 12, 1988, December 1, 1988, April 11, 1989
Betty Furness, June 9, 1989
Janet Cantor Gari, June 7, 1988
Joe Hardy, October 21, 1988
Pat Harrington, Jr., November 24, 1984
June Havoc, November 12, 1986
Florence Henderson, February 25, 1986
Buddy Howe, April 1, 1980
Madge Kennedy (letter to Cody Morgan), January 1985
John Lahr, July 9, 1986
Charles Lamont, August 13, 1988
Paul Landres, August 10, 1988
Mabel Langdon, July 17, 1979
Dorothy Lee, September 21, 1989, May 23, 1990, April 15, 1991, also interviewed by Joe Savage, December 20, 1976; interviewed by Savage and Maurice Terenzio, August 27, 1977; interviewed by Savage and Terenzio, December 1977; interviewed by Savage and Terenzio, May 8, 1978; interviewed by Cody Morgan, October 1989
Buster Libott, August 12, 1988
Marjorie Lord, February 24, 1986
George "Spanky" McFarland, January 28, 1986
Missy McMahon, September 22, 1988
E. G. Marshall, October 15, 1987
Frank Melfo, October 14, 1988
Jeff Morrow, interviewed by Tom Weaver, May 1987

Esther Muir, June 6 and 10, 1989, July 7, 1989, August 17, 1989
Gil Perkins, August 30, 1987
Nat Perrin, August 14, 1988; also interviewed by Cody Morgan, September 1987
Eddie Quillan, August 31, 1987, August 16, 1988
Buddy Rogers (letter to author), February 13, 1986
Raymond Rohauer, comments and information about Bert Wheeler obtained off-the-cuff while assisting Rohauer on his (abandoned) Buster Keaton and Harry Langdon book projects; over a four-year period, 1977–81
Joe Smith, July 1, 1979, August 15, 1979
Harold N. Swanson, January 22, 1987
Elwood Ullman, June 2, 1981
Rudy Vallee (letter to author), February 6, 1986
Yvette Vickers, August 11, 1988
Eli Wallach, June 7, 1988
Jules White, July 17, 1979, May 31, 1981
Sam White, March 9, 1990
Henny Youngman, May 20, 1988, June 7, 1988

Notes on the Chapters

Bert Wheeler

Information about Bert's boyhood came from sources in his hometown, at the Paterson Free Public Library in New Jersey. I am indebted to librarian Linda Brown for tracking down issues of the *Paterson Press* (1895–1968), the 1895 Paterson Census Report, street directories of that era, and, most gratefully, for providing a parking space in the library's guarded compound.

The brick tenement house where Bert was born still stands, serving the same purpose it did in his day, providing apartments for a new wave of immigrant families. On the day that Tom Weaver and I stopped outside 10 Ward Street to take a snapshot, we were mistaken for undercover cops. Paterson, alas, is not always the friendly city it had been when native sons Bert Wheeler and Lou Costello roamed its streets.

Sister Margaret Mary Lawler of the Paterson Diocesan Center located Bert's birth and baptismal records and refused to accept payment for her invaluable—and much appreciated—efforts.

Former New York City mayor Ed Koch was helpful in cutting through municipal red tape to locate Bert and Betty Wheeler's marriage license when NYC's bureaucratic superstructure threatened to crash upon my head; now there's a man who gets things done.

Articles and reviews from *Variety*, *Billboard*, the *New York Star*, and the *New York Dramatic Mirror*, for this chapter and all subsequent ones, come from the archives of the Lincoln Center Library for the Performing Arts. Knowledgeable assistance was dispensed by the library's ace reference staff.

Although Bert and Betty toured England in 1919, *Variety* was strangely silent on this point in their weekly overseas reports. Bert frequently made reference to this trip when interviewed—without ever relating any anecdotes about the tour.

Reviews from *The Ziegfeld Follies of 1923* were gleaned from the scrapbooks of Ned Wayburn, preserved at Lincoln Center.

Fannie Brice became a close pal of the Wheelers during the *Follies* fun. She backed Bert in a show that Wheeler wrote, *The Brown Derby* (1925). It never made Broadway, but in 1926 *Derby* was adapted as a movie vehicle for comic Johnny Hines, with Bert's involvement receiving heavy promotion in trade advertisements.

Salary lists of Ziegfeld performers were culled from the Billie Burke collection at Lincoln Center. The late actress (Mrs. Ziegfeld offstage) donated her husband's financial records for the period 1925 through 1929, which covers Bert and Bob's prime time with Ziegfeld.

Transcripts of Bert and Betty's divorce proceedings were obtained from the anonymous clerk at the circuit court of Cook County, Chicago.

The question remains: Did Bert Wheeler ever make a silent film? For years it was assumed that Bert appeared in the 1922 Robertson-Cole production *Captain Fly-by-Night*, but keen detective work by both Sam Rubin and Sam Gill, discovered the Bert Wheeler of that film to be an elderly, white-haired gent. (Vaudeville coincidentally had a "trick bicyclist" named Bert Wheeler; and misguided librarians across the country brought out files on the late senator from Montana, Burton K. Wheeler, time after time after time...)

Robert Woolsey

The most useful source for this chapter was a serialized article about Bob, written in 1934 and syndicated anonymously in many newspapers. It was possible to substantiate and elaborate upon this material when tracing Bob's career through the sketchy trade journals of the 1910s and 1920s.

Wheeler and Woolsey scholar Mike Hawks speculated on the path Woolsey's career might have taken if Bob had gone to work for Charlie Chaplin in 1915. Mike notes, "He could've become another Albert Austin," referring to Chaplin's gagman, stooge, and close associate of this era. Or perhaps Woolsey's performances would have been scissored and his ideas simply palmed by the ego-driven Chaplin, as later happened to Eddie Sutherland, Henri d'Arrast, Chuck Reisner, Robert Florey, Alfred Newman, Jack Oakie, Billy Gilbert, Henry Daniell, Buster Keaton, Orson Welles...

Early stage photographs of Robert Woolsey were especially difficult to track down. The Apeda Studios in New York photographed virtually every big-time stage star from the teens through the thirties. Apeda is still around snapping pictures, but they junked their negatives during World War II—for the silver content—about three cents apiece. The long-defunct White Studios photographed many of the shows that played Broadway in the 1920s. The annotated file cards in the Robert Woolsey holdings at Lincoln Center are not promising: *The Right Girl*: "negatives junked"; *The Blue Kitten*: "negatives emulsified—junked"; *The Lady in Ermine*: "negatives lost (?)" The *Poppy* negatives were in an advanced state of decomposition but were copied because of W. C. Fields's perceived value. The inevitable deterioration of these negatives is not Lincoln Center's fault—they work with limited funds granted to preserve a set number of stills per year. Photos from *The Right Girl* and *The Blue Kitten* survive only because they had been featured—and thus preserved—in theater magazines of the 1920s.

Rio Rita

Information about the stage version of *Rio Rita* derives from the Billie Burke files at Lincoln Center, and the Theater Arts Library of UCLA. Movie script and production information on *Rio Rita* and on all subsequent RKO titles likewise resides in the Theater Arts Library of UCLA.

In 1987, I was able to examine all of the RKO files on Wheeler and Woolsey at the RKO Research Center in Los Angeles. Through the courtesy of their able librarian, John Hall, I transcribed by pen and paper everything relevant to Wheeler and Woolsey for this book. Subsequently, in 1989, I photocopied those same files at their new repository under Ted Turner for my own permanent record. I am especially grateful to Dick May and Roger Mayer of Turner Entertainment for their kindness in allowing me a second look at this material.

Production information on Bert Wheeler's Vitaphone short *Small Timers* was obtained by W & W acolyte and expert Cody Morgan from Warner Brothers' Archives at USC.

The Cuckoos

The 1926 prompter's script for the play *The Ramblers* resides in UCLA's Theater Arts Library, along with various drafts and screenplay treatments of *The Cuckoos*. *The Ramblers* parodied California filmmaking, with Clark and McCullough combating an on-location film crew. Transplanted to film, *The Cuckoos* avoided spoofing Hollywood; instead, the movie seems to parody Broadway plays.

In 1955 the C & C Corporation licensed exclusive television rights to 740 RKO pictures (which included all the Wheeler and Woolsey titles except for *Rio Rita* and *Girl Crazy*, both of which MGM had acquired years earlier). Until the early 1980s these C & C prints were the only circulating versions on many RKO titles. The films were quickly exploited in penny-pinching ways; C & C sent original 35 mm fine grain material to a wholesale South American lab that sloppily ground out 16 mm negatives of varying quality. All the films had their original main title cards chopped off with a stock "C & C Movietime" herald inserted in its place. The end title was also redone, with the exit music clumsily cut in midtheme. *The Cuckoos* suffers more than most C & C prints. The original nitrate negative had already begun to diminish when it was copied. Careless lab work produced television prints that are slightly out of focus most of the time. Whether the original camera negative of *The Cuckoos* still exists today is open to question.

Budgetary figures for this film and other titles were provided by Raymond Rohauer, who had incomplete cost sheets of various RKO releases for 1930, 1936, and 1937. What his interest was in *The Cuckoos*, I'll never know.

Dixiana

Down and Out at RKO: A few words about director Luther Reed: he was responsible for RKO's first three major musicals (*Rio Rita, Hit the Deck*, and this film) and was slated to direct Everett Marshall in *Heart of the Rockies* before being given the boot (along with Marshall) following *Dixiana*'s poor performance. The following year found Reed unemployed, bankrupt, and severely beaten at his Malibu home by his estranged wife. At the ensuing assault trial, Bert and Bernice Wheeler testified as eyewitnesses on Reed's behalf. By the mid-1930s, the once-respected director was again employed—cranking out humble potboilers for a minor league studio, First Division.

Half Shot at Sunrise

Three Little Words—"Get 'Em Cheap": The Rhythm Boys (Bing Crosby, Harry Barris, and Al Rinker) performed Kalmar and Ruby's song "Three Little Words" on "The RKO Hour: *Half Shot at Sunrise*," a half-hour NBC radio program highlighting this film and starring Wheeler and Woolsey, Dorothy Lee, and Leni Stengel, aired live from Los Angeles on October 7, 1930. Two telegrams from Victor Baravalle, RKO music director, to New York administrator Lee Marcus are worth citing: September 9: "Whiteman Rhythm Boys will cost us $300 to broadcast. . . . Let me know if you think it's worthwhile spending this amount"—and September 11—"Can get Whiteman Rhythm Boys $50 cheaper if we announce them as Cocoanut Grove Rhythm Boys. Does this meet with your approval?" Unfortunately, we do not have Marcus's reply, but I'll bet that Cocoanut Grove title won out. Bing Crosby, of course, would be making $3,000 a week all by himself just two years later.

Hook Line and Sinker

Cline on the Spot: Eddie Cline's directorial career continued steadily (if unremarkably) throughout the 1930s until he became a fixture at Universal in

1939. Lauded for his W. C. Fields trilogy (*My Little Chickadee*, *The Bank Dick*, *Never Give a Sucker an Even Break*), Cline's other Universal product was assembly-line stuff, featuring people like Hugh Herbert, the Ritz Brothers, and Olsen and Johnson.

According to Eddie Quillan, Cline sealed his own fate: "We were shooting *Slightly Terrific* (1944) with Leon Errol, a fine comedian and a fabulous guy. I was doing a scene with Anne Rooney; when the action was over, there was a long pause before the assistant director finally yelled 'Cut!' Cline—our director—was nowhere to be seen. Then I spotted him, off in the corner, on the phone, holding a racing form and placing a bet!

"After he hung up, he turned to the script girl and asked, 'How'd that last scene look to you?' Eddie Cline hadn't even bothered to watch it! Well, you can imagine—you can't hide actions like that from the front office forever. He didn't last at Universal much longer."

Video: This title is available in the VHS format through Turner Entertainment. Picture and sound quality of the preprint material surpass all expectations.

Cracked Nuts

Some modern critics do find *Cracked Nuts* to be very entertaining—so please take a look at the film and decide for yourself. Regarding Bert and Bob's solo scenes, Maurice Terenzio offers his observation that not all comedy teams functioned as a unit: "Take the Marx Brothers. They are always portraying three (or four) guys who spend most of the time doing things separately: playing the piano, playing the harp, singing a solo—*avoiding* each other as much as possible! Where does real teamwork come in?"

On the other hand, other comedians could not exist without easy access to their partners—the worst scenes in any Abbott and Costello film are the ones where Lou performs without Bud. As Tom Weaver sees it, "Costello was such an undisciplined, sloppy performer that he needs Bud around to (a) interpret what he's doing, (b) give the act a vestige of quality and (c) *force* Lou's asinine behavior to seem funny. Take Bud away and what have you got? Lou Costello acting like a jerk."

Anyhow, it is to Bert and Bob's credit that their solo sequences in *Cracked Nuts* are characteristic, pointed—and funny.

Caught Plastered

The original credits for *Caught Plastered* featured a clever cartoon sequence involving a happy-go-lucky locomotive (not unlike the little train featured in *Shining Time Station*, Ringo Starr's kid-video series of the nineties). *Caught Plastered*'s cartoon train was scrapped when C & C Movietime remade the opening titles for television prints. Fortunately, Ted

Peach O'Reno

Peach O'Reno was the target of a plagiarism suit that RKO quickly settled out of court for $3,000. An interoffice memo dated May 9, 1932, from the RKO legal department states that "most of the ideas in the script of *Peach O'Reno* which were lifted ... were included therein upon the suggestion of Wheeler. If you will recall, Woolsey did practically the same in the case of *Everything's Rosie*." As discussed elsewhere in this book, *Rosie* was a blatant imitation of the 1923 play, *Poppy*. The RKO legal report concludes with a cryptic observation: "We, of course, have no action against Wheeler and, since we have had considerable trouble with him already, I do not believe it is worthwhile to bring the matter to his attention."

Girl Crazy

China Knew Best: In 1939 Metro-Goldwyn-Mayer bought the rights to *Girl Crazy*, intending to fashion a vehicle for Eddie Cantor. The project was temporarily shelved but RKO went about dutifully recalling all prints from circulation. A studio memo dated June 30, 1939, states that "the only territory where the picture is being currently exhibited and where any revenue at all is still being received from the picture, is the territory of China, where we distribute through our own exchange. Recently we received the munificent sum of $1.07 from the exhibition of this picture in China. We can stop the distribution of the picture in China and destroy all prints there at any time we are instructed so to do."

Very Good Eddie: Beloved Eddie Quillan could not say an unkind word about David O. Selznick, the man who effectively sabotaged *Girl Crazy*; when I spoke with Eddie about *Crazy*, he seemed puzzled rather than upset at Selznick's unnecessary extravagance and poor judgment calls. Eddie noted that "years later, when I ran into David at a party, he made it a point to introduce me to people who might offer me a part in a film. That's how a few roles came my way during the 1950s. I think that was David's manner of apologizing for what he did to *Girl Crazy*." Selznick also awarded Eddie the small but pivotal role of the heroic airplane pilot in *Made for Each Other* (1939, Selznick-International), which starred Carole Lombard and James Stewart.

The Mummy Dances: Horror aficionados have long maintained that young Creighton Chaney (later known as Lon Chaney, Jr.) appeared in his first RKO film, *Girl Crazy*, as a "chorus boy." A close viewing of the film, however, demonstrates otherwise. Possibly his footage was deleted by Selznick during retakes, because no chorus boys appear in the finished film at all.

Gershwin Recycled: For the record, the original title written for the melody "You've Got What Gets Me" was entitled "Your Eyes! Your Smile!" written by Ira Gershwin in 1927 for the musical *Funny Face*. I am indebted to Michael Feinstein for this nugget of Gershwiniana. For some peculiar reason, several recent books about George and Ira Gershwin mistakenly claim that Arline Judge and Eddie Quillan, not Bert and Dottie, sing "You've Got What Gets Me" in the 1932 *Girl Crazy*.

Hold 'Em Jail

Freelance actor Paul Hurst was engaged by RKO to play the role of Butch in *Hold 'Em Jail*, at a rate of $750 for ten consecutive days' work. After finishing his part and being closed out of the picture, Hurst was called back three weeks later for a day of close-ups. Hurst cashed a $166.66 check for this one day, but subsequently entered a claim against RKO for $2,666.66, claiming it was the salary owned him for the lay-off period. Eddie Quillan remembered Paul Hurst as "basically a nice guy, though capable of doing dopey things." The RKO legal department eventually settled Hurst's claim for $500. Instead of barring him from the studio, producer Selznick was amused by Hurst's nerve—or stupidity. Years later, Selznick assigned Hurst a memorable bit part as the renegade soldier Vivien Leigh shoots point-blank in *Gone with the Wind*.

So This Is Africa

Crass Krasna: Norman Krasna (1909–84), who received his first important screenplay assignment on this film, went on to great success with mainstream writing credits like Alfred Hitchcock's *Mr. and Mrs. Smith*; Rene Clair's *Flame of New Orleans*, with Marlene Dietrich; Bing Crosby's *White Christmas*; and *Indiscreet*, starring Ingrid Bergman and Cary Grant. Krasna also cowrote the play *Time for Elizabeth* with his mentor and friend Groucho Marx and produced or directed several feature films. Like the later W & W director George Stevens, Krasna recanted his earliest successes once he became a "prestigious" talent. He happily mocked his involvement with *Africa* when interviewed by Pat McGilligan: "It's only when we sit here in later years that we say, 'Oh, no, I wouldn't have done a cheap comedy.' Yet I did a Wheeler & Woolsey when I was a kid. [Harry] Cohn said, 'Can you do a Wheeler & Woolsey so we can start in six weeks?' I did it in *three weeks*. Wheeler & Woolsey! You can't tell me I had any aspirations towards great art there" (from *Backstory*, edited by Pat McGilligan [Berkeley and Los Angeles: University of California Press, 1986]).

Howard Prouty of the Academy Library in Beverly Hills took an active interest in the archival research for this book; he indulgently loaned me the Academy's Production Code files on the Wheeler and Woolsey comedies. These copious reports on censorship issues began with *So This Is Africa* and continued through *High Flyers*. The dossier on *Africa* alone was over thirty pages; Howard told me that this was the longest list of industry complaints he had ever seen, "even more objections than on Mae West's *She Done Him Wrong*."

For half a century *So This Is Africa* has been a "lost" film; it was never reissued, Columbia Pictures never included it in their Screen Gems television package, and home video has not yet discovered it. The only source for reappraisal was one 35mm fine grain print, leading a lonely existence at the Library of Congress Film Depository in Washington, D.C. Just recently, *Africa* resurfaced in 16 mm, which is how I finally caught up with it. With his usual insight, Len Maltin told me that "the most remarkable thing about *So This Is Africa* is not that it is such a good picture; what is surprising is how *similar* it is to all the comedies Bert and Bob were making over at RKO."

Diplomaniacs

Converging Opinions: Ned E. Depinet, RKO's vice-president in charge of sales, was bowled over by *Diplomaniacs* when he saw the film in a New York theater: "It is a fine audience show," he wrote his staff on April 26, 1933. "A well-filled house laughed its way through the full run of the picture; at places the laughs came so fast they were drowned out by the preceding ones. I had several people with me and two of them remarked that *Diplomaniacs* is a better show and more entertaining than *Forty-second Street*. Several numbers are very tuneful.... The picture is clean and wholesome fun. With the present conferences in Washington, the Geneva episodes are timely and the audience is quick to appreciate its humor. I, of course, am not foolish enough to even hope that it will do as much business as *Forty-second Street*, but I believe we have in *Diplomaniacs* a show that ... is certain to click and who knows but what it will click in a very big way."

On the flip side of the coin, Will Hays, the morals czar of the film industry, passed along to RKO this June 27 letter from one A. J. MacBeth of Toronto, Ontario: "Never have I seen a more debasing and vulgar picture [than *Diplomaniacs*]. At a time when the world looks to Geneva ... it holds up to ridicule in the most flagrant and objectionable manner the activities of the League [of Nations] and interpolates the grossest kind of slapstick comedy. It seems almost a vehicle of propaganda and, as the type of moronish pictures being produced in the States at present, is a national disgrace. I have taken the matter up with the local Board of Censorship, who tells me it has already been cut considerably! I appeal to you, as a patriotic citizen of the world, to stop producing and showing such a disintegrating spectacle." In spite of Mr. MacBeth's squeamishness, *Diplomaniacs* made a respectable profit in the worst year of the Depression.

Bert and Bob were referenced in RKO's *Morning Glory* that year. When a haughty actress barges into the office of showmen Douglas Fairbanks, Jr., and Adolphe Menjou, she exclaims, "Well, if it isn't Wheeler and Woolsey playing straight for each other!"

What Made Pistachio Nuts?: A book with this probing question as its title was published in 1992 by Columbia University Press. Subtitling this volume Early Sound Comedy and the Vaudeville Aesthetic, author Henry Jenkins takes a stimulating look at the 1929–34 era, freshly examining overworked icons (Mae West, the Marx Brothers, W. C. Fields) and delving into uncharted film careers (Joe E. Brown, Eddie Cantor, Wheeler and Woolsey). *Diplomaniacs* receives a fascinating chapter unto itself; author Jenkins is clearly familiar with W & W's entire body of work. I recommend this incisive study to all comedy buffs, particularly those fans who are interested in the early sound era.

Video: Diplomaniacs is available in the VHS format from Turner Entertainment. Once again, the transfer quality is what you'd expect from Turner—outstanding.

Hips, Hips, Hooray!

What Every Scholar Knows (Maybe): For the record, F. Scott Fitzgerald's original title for *The Great Gatsby* was *Trimalchio of West Egg*, which H. N. Swanson felt at the time (1925) was "the rottenest title imaginable for anything." (Since then, I believe that the movies *have* done worse.)

Word leaked to the press that *Hips*' publicity photos included shots of nude girls in glass bathtubs. The Production Code office put pressure on RKO to destroy the negatives, and that was that.

Producer Swanson had an interesting idea for the film's main title sequence, which he pitched to Douglas MacKinnon of the Producers Association on October 26, 1933: "After our trademark goes off the screen, fade in on three French maids dressed in musical comedy fluffy skirts, highly exaggerated. The girls' backs are to the camera. Then the first girl turns her head, winks and tosses her skirts up at the audience in a provocative manner. The letters of the words "HIPS" then appear over the figure (we do this by double printing). The next girl turns her head and repeats the movement, and the second "HIPS" comes on. The last girl does the same, and "HOORAY" pops out, to give us our main title. Okay by you? Sincerely, Swanie." On October 30, James Wingate of the censorship board curtly responded that "we have discussed this and believe it to be highly censorable. We suggest that you give the matter serious reconsideration." Result: French maids do not traipse across the main title of *Hips, Hips, Hooray!*

Cockeyed Cavaliers

The Hays Office was kind to the boys when *Cockeyed Cavaliers* was screened for industry sanction. Joseph I. Breen, one of Will Hays's most valued lieutenants on the Censorship Board, wrote RKO producer Pandro S. Berman on May 28, 1934, that "the manner in which [*Cockeyed Cavaliers*] has been handled reflects great credit on your organization." Privately Breen wrote

Hays on June 7, "*Cockeyed Cavaliers* represents, we believe, a tremendous improvement over [Wheeler and Woolsey's] recent releases."

Kentucky Kernels

George Stevens admitted in 1970 that his Wheeler and Woolsey movies were *not* the films he wanted to be remembered by. Fair enough, but at least he preserved his notes, scripts (leather bound!), revisions, clippings, and reviews on *Kentucky Kernels* and *The Nitwits*. This cache is part of the George Stevens Collection reposing at the Motion Picture Academy Library in Beverly Hills. I was able to draw extensively from this material, which included a daily shooting diary for both pictures.

Cranky Spanky: Did George "Spanky" McFarland really forget about working with Wheeler and Woolsey? Ron Hutchinson, a remarkable film enthusiast and great guy whom I did not get to know until after this manuscript was completed, told me about a personal appearance that Spanky made with *Kentucky Kernels*, circa 1990. Spanky spoke affectionately of director Stevens and costars Mary Carlisle and Noah Beery, and commented that Bert and Bob "were perfect gentlemen, treating me as though I were their favorite nephew." Based upon this account (and several public outbursts when Spanky threatened fans with lawsuits), it is with some regret that Ron, several other buffs, and I concur that Spanky cooperated only when silver graced his palm. Spanky died in 1993 at age sixty-four.

Video: *Kentucky Kernels* is available on VHS from Turner Entertainment, in another superlative film-to-tape transfer.

The Nitwits

As with *Kentucky Kernels*, I was able to examine George Stevens's personal files on *The Nitwits*, which were voluminous in comparison to the "official" files retained by RKO.

The Rainmakers

My source for information about staged train crack-ups is *Train Wrecks for Fun and Profit*, by F. A. Schmidt (Ontario: Boston Mills Press, 1982). It is a fact-filled book with many gripping photographs that graphically tell the story, and a must for all railroad buffs.

★   ★   ★

There was no additional information to cite on the remaining Wheeler and Woolsey features: *Silly Billies*, *Mummy's Boys*, *On Again—Off Again*, and *High Flyers*. Oh, well, you can't have everything!

Index

Numbers in **boldface** refer to pages with photographs.

Abbott, Bud 11, 70, 114, 125, 206, 221, 248, 249, 267, 310
Abbott and Costello Meet the Mummy 267
Actor's Fund of America 3
Adams, Joey v, 305
Albee, Edward F. 129, 130
Alexander, Dick **226**, 251
Alice Adams 239
All for Love 292
All Night Long 100
Allen, Fred 298
Alvarado, Don 55
The Americano 115
Amos 'n' Andy 123
Anderson, Gilbert M. "Broncho Billy" 44
Animal Crackers 52, 120
Anna Christie 105, 108-109
Arbuckle, Roscoe "Fatty" 77, 95-97
Arce, Hector 20
Archainbaud, George 77
Armetta, Henry 180
Armstrong, Robert 171
Arnaz, Desi 298
Arsenic and Old Lace 118
Astaire, Adele 160
Astaire, Fred 17, 125, 160, 231, 286
At the Circus 286
Ates, Roscoe 121, 166
Atwill, Lionel 232, 233
Avon Comedy Four 21
The Awful Sleuth 293
Aylesworth, Arthur 230
Aylesworth, Merlin 176, 177, 179, 189

Baker, Marilyn Cantor v, 305
Baker, Mike v, 305

Ball, Lucille 298
The Bank Dick 149, 248
Barry, Phyllis 190, 202
Barrymore, John 1, 15
Baxter, Warner 131
Beaton, Welford 116
Beaumont, Lucy 133, 135, **136**, 138
Beery, Caroline **191**
Beery, Noah, Sr. 210, 215, 216, **217**, 218, 220, 222, 224, **226**, 234
Beery, Wallace 190, **191**
Benedict, Brooks 156
Benny, Jack 272, 298
Berle, Milton 1, 3
Berman, Joe 8, 9
Berman, Pandro S. 70, 203, 314
Bernard, Felix 239
Bernds, Edward v, 42, 178, 179, 181, 183, 185, 305
Best, Willie 222, 224, 225, 265
The Big House 166, 167
Bletcher, Billy 188
The Blue Kitten **48**, 90
Blystone, Stanley 168
Boasberg, Al 114, 116, 117, 231, 253, 254
Boles, John 55, 63
Borge, Victor 3
Borzage, Frank 195
The Bowery Boys 221
Brady, William A. 124
Brave Eagle 293, 294
Breen, Joseph I. 221, 254, 271, 272, 287, 314
Brennan, Walter 141
Brent, Evelyn 230
Brice, Fannie 34, 35, 307
Brice, Monty 249
Brideless Groom 178
Briggs, Matt 202

317

Index

Bright Lights 291
Briskin, Sam 255, 259, 265, 266, 281, 282, 288
Brock, Lou 210
Brook, Clive 231
Broun, Heywood 34
Brown, Joe E. 1, 185, 291
Brown, Katharine 70
Brown, Wally 249
The Brown Derby 307
Bruckman, Clyde 125, 126
The Bubbles Revue 46
Burke, Billie 307
Burns, George v, 43, 272, 298, 305
Burroughs, Edgar Rice 64
Burtis, James 202
Burton, Frederick 263
Byron, Marion 205, **206**

Cabot, Bruce **198**
Calhern, Louis 188, 190, 191, 192
Calvert, Elisha H. 93
Cantor, Eddie 19, 32, 36, 211, 267, 311
Capone, Al 107
Capra, Frank 174, 178
Captain Fly-by-Night 307
Carey, Harry, Sr. 108, 257
Carle, Richard 190
Carlisle, Mary v, 220, 222, 224, **226**, 227, 305
Carney, Alan 249
Carol, Sue 123
Carson, Jack **275**, 277, 279, 288
Casablanca 263
Catlett, Walter 45, 46, 47, 51, 75
Caught Plastered 133-138, **136**, 310
Cawthorn, Joseph **48**, 85, 88, 90, 149, 234
Chandler, Edward 86
Chaney, Lon, Jr. 297, 311
Chaplin, Charlie 15, 21, 22, 23, 24, 25, 44, 77, 115, 140, 284, 286, 287
Charters, Spencer 202, 204
Chase, Charley 233
Check and Double Check 123
Chevalier, Maurice 131, 177, 192
Chief Thunderbird 252, 258

Chierichetti, David 91
Churchill, Berton 241, 248
Cimarron 95, 122, 145,
Citizen Kane 158
Clair, Al 61, 62
Clark, Bobby 12, 75-77, **76**, 95, 140, 141
Clark, Harvey 113
Cline, Eddie 105, **106**, 110, 112, 115, 116, 121, 122, 177, 178, 272, 273, **275**, 282, 309, 310
Clyde, June 73, 78
Coca, Imogene 3
Cocchi, John vi
Cockeyed Cavaliers 2, 209-218, **214**, **216**, **217**, 314, 315
The Cocoanuts 79, 114, 121, 140
Cohan, George M. 146
Cohen, Emanuel 190
Cohn, Harry 174, 175, 177, 178, 180, 181, 183, 185, 312
Collins, G. Pat 107, 166
Como, Perry 3
Compson, Betty 123
Conaty, Richard vi
Connery, Sean 3
Convict 13 122
Cook, Clyde 293
Cooper, Edward G. 188
Cooper, Merian C. 189, 193, 203
Corbett, James J. "Gentleman Jim" 34
Correll, Charles 123
Costello, Lou 11, 70, 114, 125, 206, 221, 248, 249, 267, 310
The Covered Wagon 253
The Cowboy Quarterback 291
Cracked Nuts 113-122, **119**, 265, 310
Craven, Frank 124, 125, 272
Creelman, James Ashmore 104
The Criminal Code 118, 166, 169
Cronjager, Edward 232
Crosby, Bing 40, 192, 288
Cruze, James 253
The Cuckoos 73-83, **79**, **82**, 97, 112, 308

Dale, Charlie 3, 4, 16, 21
Daniels, Bebe 55, 63, 85-87, 90, 123

Index

Davis, Bette 231
Dawn, Hazel 36
A Day at the Races 114, 277
Dearing, Edgar 235
Delmar, Harry 7
Dent, Vernon 141
The Dentist 152
Depinet, Ned E. 218, 255, 288, 313
DeRuiz, Nick 71
DeValera, Eamon 196
Dillon, Alice v, 4, 8, 9, 16, 305
Dillon, Tom v, 3, **4**, 5, **6**, 7, 8, 9, 16, 17, 19, 31, 41, 42, 61, 74, 147, 150, 294, **295**, 297, 305
Diplomaniacs 95, 109, 187-196, **191**, **194**, **195**, 221, 242, 276, 313
Dix, Richard 123, 145, 199, 231, 271
Dixiana 85-92, 95, 149, 309
Dixon, Jean 294
Don't Park There 243
Dopey Dicks 178
Dorsey, Tommy 292
Dotson (dancer) 32, 34
Douglas, Melvyn 294, 295
Down to Their Last Yacht 77
Dressler, Marie 104, 105, 145
Drew, William M. vi
Duck Soup 114, 115, 190, 203
Dumbrille, Erwin vi, vii
Dumont, Margaret 280, 288
Dunne, Irene 231
Durante, Jimmy 141, 198, 275

Edeson, Robert 104
Edwards, Gus 19
Edwards, Leo 20
Edwards, Neely 188
Elmer the Great 291
Epstein, Phillip G. 263, 264
Errol, Leon 36, 253, 276
Etting, Ruth 204
Evans, Herbert 279
Everson, William K. 203
Everything's Rosie 125-127, 134, 138, 311
Excess Baggage 53

Fairbanks, Douglas, Jr. 221, 222
Fairbanks, Douglas, Sr. 115, 178
Family Business 3
Fay, Frank 3, 4, 5, 7, 38, 292
Feet First 125
Feinstein, Michael 312
Fetchit, Stepin 222
Fields, Dorothy 238
Fields, Stanley 107, 109, 111, 112, 114, **119**, 122, 146, 155, 161, **162**, 163, 234
Fields, W. C. 15, 36, 37, 49, 50, 105, 114, 148, 149, 152, 177, 185, 224
Fine, Larry 19
Finian's Rainbow 16
Finlayson, James 141
The Firefly 20
Fishkin, Steve vi
Fitzgerald, F. Scott 203, 314
Fitzgerald, Leo 61, 175, 176
Ford, John 166, 231
Forty-Five Minutes from Broadway 19
Forty-second Street 90, 313
Foy, Eddie, Jr. 292
Fra Diavolo 211
Francis, Arlene 4
Francis, Noel **53**, 58
Frankenstein 114, 118, 119, 163
Franklin, Bob vi
Franklin, Joan vi
Frat Heads 210, 211, **212**
Free and Easy 121
The Freshman 105
Friars' Club 146
Funny Face 160
Furness, Betty v, 190, 305

The Gang's All Here 294, 295, **296**
Gari, Janet Cantor v, 305
The Gay Divorcee 218, 231
Gear, Luella 49
Gemora, Charles **184**
The General 125
Gershwin, George 76, 146, 157, 158, 159, 160, 312
Gershwin, Ira 157, 158, 159, 160, 312

Index

Gibson, Hoot 257
Gilbert, L. Wolfe 239
Gill, Sam vi, 307
The Gingerbread Man 20
Girardot, Etienne 232
Girl Crazy 42, 146, 155-163, **162**, 311
Go West 248
The Gold Rush 67
Goldstein, Nat 3
Goldwyn, Sam 74, 267
Gone with the Wind 154, 312
Gordon, Alex vi
The Gorilla 116
Gosden, Freeman 123
Grable, Betty 166, 168, 171, 230, 237, 238, 281, 282
Grae, Margaret Bruce Kudner *see* Wheeler, Betty
Grand Hotel Premiere 303, 304
Grandma's Boy 243
Granet, Bert 284
The Grapes of Wrath 242
The Great Dictator 115
Green, Mitzi 156
Greene, Harrison 220
Greig, Robert 209, 214, 216
Grele, Ronald vi
Gribbon, Harry 20
Griffin, Merv **298**
Griffith, D. W. 178, 222
Guiol, Fred 222, 232, 234, 235, 239, 243, 244, 249, 252, 253, 257, 258 259, 264, 265, **266**, 270

Haines, Sally 259, 292
Half Shot at Sunrise 93-101, **96, 98**, 309
Hall, Charlie 191
Hall, John vi, 91, 308
Hallelujah, I'm a Bum 176
Hamilton, Hale 229, 235
Hamilton, Lloyd 61
Harbaugh, Harriet **52**
Harding, Ann 231
Hardy, Joe v, 305
Hardy, Oliver 11, 114, 125, 148, 167, 185, 204, 211, 233, 293, 297
Hardy, Sam 144, 152

Harolde, Ralf 85, 90, 103, 109-111
Harrington, Pat, Jr. v, 305
Harrington, Pat, Sr. 5
Harris, Dennis 4
Harris, Mitchell 150
Hart, Teddy 188
Hartman, Grace 292
Hartman, Paul 292
Harvey 292
Harvey, Paul 279, 288
Havoc, June v, 30, 31, 305
Hawks, Howard 166
Hawks, Mike 307
Hays, Will 181, 193, 221, 313, 314, 315
Healy, Ted 253
Hello Yourself 1, 63
Hellzapoppin' 109
Henderson, Florence v, 16, 305
Hepburn, Katharine 231, 239, 271
Herbert, Hugh 103, **108**, 109, 111, 188, 190, 191, 193, 234
Hicks, Russell 269, 277
High Eagle **162**
High Flyers 279-289, **283, 285**
High Gear 237
Hildegarde 19
Hill, Arthur 294
Hill, Charlie 272, 292
Hill, George Roy 295
Hill, Gus 20
Hines, Johnny 307
Hips, Hips, Hooray! 2, 201-208, **206, 207**, 221, 314
His Majesty, the American 115
Hoffman, Alan vii
Hoffman, Dustin 3, 150
Hold 'Em Jail 165-172, **169, 170**, 211, 312
Hollywood Handicap 304
Hollywood on Parade 304
Holmes, Ben 141, 210, 211
Honest Liars 51, **52**, 99
Hook Line and Sinker 103-112, **106, 108, 110**, 309
Hope, Bob 1, 43, 254, 288, 301
Horse Feathers 148, 171, 211
Hot Water 105
Housman, Arthur 137
Howard, Curly 13
Howard, Moe 198

Howard, Shemp 11
Howard, Tom 75
Howard, Willie 158
Howe, Buddy v, 305
Howland, Jobyna 73, 80-81, 85, 90, 112, 234
Hurst, Paul 165, **170**, 312
Hutchinson, Ron 315
Hymer, Warren 168

I Live for Love 90
The Iceman's Ball 141
Innocently Guilty 293
Intolerance 178
Irving, William 188
It's a Gift 148, 224
It's a Mad, Mad, Mad, Mad World 140

Jaffe, Sam 190, 193
James, Alfred 209
The Jazz Singer 56
Jeffreys, Anne 292
Jenkins, Henry 314
Jennings, DeWitt 133, 138
Jessel, George 2, 19, 20, 272
Johnson, Chic 12, 95
Johnson, Noble 265
Jolson, Al 176, 192, 195
Judels, Charles 279
Judge, Arline 156, 157, 159

Kael, Pauline 122
Kahane, Benjamin B. 218, 253, 255
Kaiser, Helen 56, 69
Kalmar, Bert 76, 203, 205, 211, 220, 225
Kane, Eddie 129, 131, **132**
Karloff, Boris 11, 113, 114, 115, 117, 118, **119**, 163
Kaufman, Edward 210, 211
Kearns, Marty 91, 199
Keating, Fred 230, 233
Keaton, Buster 1, 61, 105, 121, 122, 125, 140, 185, 220, 244, 246, 248, 275, 286, 297

Keeler, Ruby 195
Kellaway, Cecil 292
Kelly, Kitty 155, 159, 160
Kelly, Lew 237
Kelton, Pert 198, 199
Kennedy, Edgar 165, 167, 168, 169, **170**, 171, 188, 190, 234
Kennedy, Joe 62
Kennedy, Madge v, 49, 305
Kentucky Kernels 219-227, **225**, **226**, 270, 315
Kerr, Donald 16
Kid Boots 36
Kid Kaberet 19
Kid Millions 267
Kilian, Victor 294
King, Charles 36
King, Dennis 90
King Kong 189
Koll, Don 94
Krasna, Norman 177, 178, 312
Kreuger, Miles vi, 297
Kueppers, Brigitte J. vi

Lackteen, Frank 265
The Lady in Ermine 48, 49
Lahr, Bert 3, 7, 141, 296
Lahr, John v, vi, 296, 297, 305
Laidlaw, Ethan 252
Lambs Club vi, 3, 4, 5, 6, 7, 139, 146, 295, 296, 297, 299
Lamont, Charles 304, 305
Lamparski, Richard vi, 83
Landres, Paul v, 293, 305
Langdon, Harry 100, 105, 176, 264
Langdon, Mabel 176, 305
Las Vegas Nights 292
Laugh Time 292
Laurel, Stan 11, 21, 41, 61, 114, 125, 148, 167, 185, 204, 211, 233, 293, 294, 297
LaVerne, Lucille 220, 222,
Leach, Marjorie 46
LeBaron, William 63, 64, 78, 124, 148, 157, 159, 189, 292
Lebedeff, Ivan 73
Leddy, Mark 4
Lee, Dorothy v, 1, 2, 16, **17**, 42, 43, 56, 63, 69, **71**, 73, 75, 77-79,

82, **83**, **89**, 93, 97-100, 103, 107, **108**, 112, 113, 121, 122, 123, 124, 125, 127, 131, 133, 136, 138, 145, 146, 148, 152, 154, 156, 157, 158, 159, 160, 163, 171, 201, 203, 204, 205, 209, 210, 211, 212, 214, 215, 216, 218, 242, 252, 255, 258, 259, 292, 299, 305
Lee, Gypsy Rose 31
Leich, Fred D. vi
Leigh, Vivien 312
Lemmon, Jack 150
Lennon, Thomas 252, 253
LeRoy, Baby 224
Lewis, Jerry 90
Lewis, Mitchell 73, 79, 265
Libott, Buster v, 42, 179, 305
Lindbergh, Charles 297
Lipton, Lew 140, 263
Little Giant 125
Lloyd, Harold 21, 30, 60, 61, 115, 117, 125, 138, 185, 243, 244
The Longest Yard 167
Lord, Marjorie v, 270, 273, **274**, 277, 279, 282, 284, 286, 288, 305
Lorraine, Lillian **48**
The Lost Patrol 231
The Lost Squadron 77
Love Me Tonight 192
The Love Parade 115
Lucan, Arthur 150
Lugosi, Bela 11, 118,

McAveny, Margaret Wheeler 18, 19
McCaffrey, Bill 38
McCarey, Leo 176
McCullough, Paul 12, 75-77, **76**, 95, 140, 141
MacDonald, Alberta **296**
McDonald, Francis 264
MacDonald, Jeanette 192, 193
McFarland, George "Spanky" v, 220, 222, 223, 224, **225**, 227, 305, 315
MacFarlane, George 93, 99
McGilligan, Pat 312
McGiveny, Owen 32, 33, 34
McHugh, Frank 106

McHugh, Jimmy 238
Mackenzie, Jack 263
MacKinnon, James 314
MacLean, Douglas 116, 124, 134, 135
McMahon, Ed **298**
McMahon, Horace **298**
McMahon, Missy v, 305
Mad About Money 282
Maid to Love 46
Maltin, Leonard v, 12, 94, 138, 194, 203, 270, 313
Mamoulian, Rouben 192
Mandel, Joe 34
Mandel, Willie 34
Mandel Brothers 32
Mankiewicz, Herman J. 158
Mankiewicz, Joseph L. 189, 192
Mapes, Victor 281
Marcus, Lee 232, 253, 259, 265, 266, 272, 281, 282, 288
Marion, George F., Sr. 103, 107-109, **108**
Marshall, E. G. v, 294, 296, 305
Marshall, Everett 85, 86, 90, 309
Martin, Crispin 155
Marx, Chico 11, 121
Marx, Groucho 19, 20, 41, 52, 120, 121, 286
Marx, Harpo 20, 234
Marx, Zeppo 141
The Marx Brothers 11, 76, 79, 111, 114, 120, 121, 125, 148, 171, 177, 185, 190, 204, 212, 234, 248, 271, 277, 310
Masquers Club 139, 140
Maurel, Raymond 85
May, Ada **53**
May, Richard 91, 308
Mayer, Louis B. 167, 189
Mayer, Roger v, 308
Mayflowers 50
Me and Mickey 25
Medbury, John P. 171
Meek, Donald 46, 52
Meeker, George 202, 204, 270, 276
Melfo, Frank v, 299, 300, 305
Micro-phonies 178
Middleton, Charles 138
Milliken, Carl E. 180
Million Dollar Legs 115, 122, 189

Index

Mix, Tom 116, 190, **191**
Modern Times 287
Monte Carlo 115
Moorhead, Natalie 107
Moran, Polly 145
Moran, Tom 25, 26, 27
Morgan, Byron 281
Morgan, Cody vi, 305, 306, 308
Morgan, Kewpie 209
Morgan, Ralph 292
Morley, Victor **48**
Morning Glory 313
Morrow, Jeff v, 292, 293, 305
Movie Crazy 138
Muir, Esther v, 30, 42, 173, 179, **180**, **184**, 270, 272, 273, 276, 306
Mulhall, Jack 123
Mummy's Boys 261-267, **266**
Mutt and Jeff 20
My Princess 51, 52
Myers, Henry 189
Myrt and Marge 253
Mystery of the Wax Museum 232

Nagel, Conrad 8
National Variety Artists 129, 130, 131
Never Give a Sucker an Even Break 248
The Newsboy's Sextette 20
A Night at the Opera 114, 253
The Nitwits 16, 229-239, **234**, **238**
Norton, Jack 215
Norton, Ruby 45

O'Brien, Pat 195
O'Connor, Robert Emmett 46, 282, 283
Of Human Bondage 231
Oh! Oh! Cleopatra 139-141
Oliver, Edna May 93, 99, 113, 116, 117, 121, 122, 146, 166, 168, **169**, 170, 171, 234
Oliver Twist 32
Olsen, Moroni 264, 265
Olsen, Ole 12, 95

On Again—Off Again 269-277, **274**, **275**
One Night in the Tropics 72
O'Neal, Zelma 148, 152, **153**, 234
Orr, Patsy 293
Our Hospitality 220

Page, Paul 220, 223
The Paleface 254
Palmer, Stuart 231
Pardon Us 167
Parker, Eddie 267
Parker, Pat 195, **206**, 300
Pasha, Kalla 81-82
Pawley, William **226**
Peach O'Reno 90, 105, 125, 143-154, **151**, **153**, 233, 311
Pendleton, Nat 161
Pennington, Ann 34
Pepper, Barbara 264, **266**
Pepper, Jack 5
Perelman, S. J. 167, 171
Perkins, Gil v, 232, 233, **234**, 237, **238**, 243, 265, 306
Perrin, Nat v, 271, 272, 274, 306
Petticoats 'n' Pistols 297
Pitts, Zasu 146, 148
Playboy of Paris 131
Poff, Lon 188
Pollard, Snub 215
Poppy 49, **50**, 126, 311
Postal Telegraph Boys 20
Powell, Eleanor 19
Priorities of 1943 292
Prival, Lucien 279
Proscia, Joe vi
Prouty, Howard vi, 312, 313

Quillan, Eddie v, 30, 42, 43, 61, 105, 155, 157, 158, 159, 160, 174, 306, 310, 311, 312
Quillan, Johnny 42

Radio Ramblers 77
Radio Revels 77
The Rainmakers 241-249, **245**, 315

Raitt, John 292
The Ramblers 75-77, **76**, 140, 308, 309
Rappe, Virginia 77
Raye, Martha 3
Reed, Luther 64, 106, 309
Reed, Mignone Park *see* Woolsey, Minnie
Reisner, Chuck 292
Renevant, Georges 55
Rhodes, Erik 230
The Right Girl 46, **47**
Rio Rita (1929) 1, 11, 12, 13, 17, 43, 55, 62-72, **68**, **71**, 74, 75, 83, 160, 308
Rio Rita (1942) 72
Rio Rita (play) 12, 51, **53**, 54, 56-61, **59**, 297, 308
Ritchie, Billie 21
The Ritz Brothers 1, 221
Roach, Hal 203, 243, 293
Robards, Jason, Sr. 133, 137, 138
Roberta 125
Roberts, Charles 263, 264
Robin Hood 178
Robinson, Bill "Bojangles" 90
Robinson, Dewey 188
Robinson, Edward G. 106
Robinson, Roberta 93, 99
Rogell, Sid 249
Rogers, Buddy v, 306
Rogers, Ginger 5, 17, 125, 231
Rogers, Will 32, 36, 211, 242, 243
Rohauer, Raymond v, 306
Roland, Frederic 241, 248
Romanoff, Constantine 193, **194**, 238
Room Service 125
Rosita, Eva 71
Ross, Earle 267
Rubin, Benny 273, 281, 286
Rubin, Sam vi, 307
Ruby, Harry 76, 203, 205, 211, 220, 225, 272

Safety Last 105, 243
Sale, Chic 242, 243
Sandford, Tiny 67
Sandrich, Mark 141, 190, 204, 218, 239

Santley, Joseph 140
Sarecky, Louis 145
Sarnoff, David 62, 63, 156
Sarris, Andrew 140
Savage, Joe vi, 305
Schenck, Joe 176
Schmidt, F. A. 315
Schnitzler, Joseph 61
School Days 19
Schulberg, B. P. 63, 156
Scott, Bill 134
Screen Snapshots 303
The Second Hundred Years 243
See America Thirst 107
Seeger, Alan vi
Seeley, Blossom 7
Seiter, William A. 125, 135, 158, 190, 293
Selznick, David O. 70, 154, 156, 157, 159, 160, 163, 167, 171, 174, 176, 177, 179, 189, 311
Sennett, Mack 61
The Shaggy Dog 226
She Done Him Wrong 313
Sheehan, John 165
Sherlock Junior 286
Sherman, Lowell 123
Show Boat 299
Signing 'Em Up 197-199
Silly Billies 251-259, **257**
Silverbush, Sam 62
Silverman, Sime 60, 83
Silvers, Phil 3
Sinatra, Frank 292, 301
Sloane, Paul 77, 106, 135
Small Timers 62, 308
Smith, Joe 3, 4, 16, 21, 27, 30, 40, 301, 306
Smith, Kate 3
Smith, Queenie 46
So This Is Africa 12, 42, 173-185, **180**, **184**, 193, 194, 221, 272, 312, 313
Some Like It Hot 150
Sons of the Desert 125, 293
Spence, Ralph 116
Steamboat Bill, Junior 246
Steiner, Max 192
Stengel, Casey 294
Stengel, Leni 93, 100, 113, 120, 122
Stevens, George 221, 222, 224, 227,

231, 232, 233, **234**, 235, 237, 239, 253, 265, 266, 270, 312, 315
Stevenson, Douglas 48
The Stolen Jools 129
The Story of Vernon and Irene Castle 95
Strike Up the Band 76
The Strong Man 105
Stroud, Clarence 39, 40
Stroud, Claude 39
Sullivan, Ed 4, **295**
Sunday Night at the Trocadero 304
Sunshine, Marion **48**
Sutherland, A. Edward 272
Swanson, H. N. v, 203, 306, 314
Syncopation 63

Taurog, Norman 159, 162, 167
Tell Me Again 53
Temple, Shirley 223
Terenzio, Maurice vi, 13, 17, 305, 310
Thomas, Frank 264, 283
Thornton, Frank **119**
Thorpe, Jim 258
Three Little Pigskins 171
The Three Stooges 11, 114, 168, 171, 178, 253, 267, 293
Three Wishes for Jamie 292
Tibbett, Lawrence 90
Tierney, Harry 57, 87, 88
Tillie's Punctured Romance 105
The Tip Off 157
Todd, Thelma 1, 201, 203, 204, 205, 210, **214**, 215, 216, **217**, 218, 288
Tombes, Andrew 45, 75
Too Many Cooks 124, 125, 135, 138, 272
Tootsie 150
Torrence, Ernest 253
Torres, Raquel 173, **184**
Townley, Jack 263, 264
Tramp, Tramp, Tramp 105
Trevor, Hugh 73, 78, 93, 99
Turner, Ted v, 70, 308
Turpin, Ben 114, 121, 122, 244
Twentieth Century 232

Ullman, Elwood v, 306
Up the River 166, 168

The Vagabond Lover 104
Vallee, Rudy v, 306
The Vampire Bat 232
Velez, Lupe 273, 280, 282, 284, **285**, 286, 288
Vickers, Yvette v, 294, **296**, 306
The Voice of Hollywood 303, 304
Von Stroheim, Erich 77

Walker, Jimmy 147
Wallach, Eli v, 306
Walters, Bonita 300
Walters, Michael 300
Waltzing Around 76
Waring, Fred 1, 63, 64, 75
Waters, Ethel 292
Watson, Bobby 205
Watz, Alex 134
Way Out West 148
Wayburn, Ned 32, 307
We Want Our Mummy 267
Weaver, Tom vi, 305, 306, 310, 311
Welch, Eddie 62, 140, 146, 292
Welcome Danger 125
Welles, Orson 158
West, Billy 21
West, Mae 177, 221, 226, 271
Wheeler, Bernice 60-62, 74, 146, 158, 259
Wheeler, Betty 2, 20-40, **22**, **29**, **33**, **39**, 294
Wheeler, Burton K. 307
Wheeler, James 18, 19
Wheeler, Katharine Foley 18
Wheeler, Patricia 62, 74, 126, 146, 158, **192**, 300
Whelan, Tim 105, 145, 146
When Dreams Come True 20
White, Jack 167
White, Jules v, 293, 306
White, Marjorie 188, 190, 192
White, Sam 141, 306
Whiting, Jack 5

Who Done It? 178
Whoopee 171
Why Worry? 105, 115
The Widow from Chicago 106
Wilder, Patricia 270, 277
Will Rogers Institute 8, 132
Willis, Leo 169
Wilson, Charles C. 230, 235
Wilson, Clarence 220, 247
Winchell, Walter 20
Wingate, James 180, 181, 193, 314
Winninger, Charles 146
Witherspoon, Cora 149
Wolfington, Iggie **298**
Woods, Harry 252
Woollcott, Alexander 34
Woolsey, Charles 43
Woolsey, Minnie 45, 195

Woolsey, Sarah 43
Woolsey, Thomas 43
Wynn, Ed 141
Wynward, Diana 231

Yankee Doodle Dandy 263
Young Donovan's Kid 122
Youngman, Henny v, 291, 292, 306

Ziegfeld, Florenz 32, 34, 35, 40, 51, 54, 56, 57, 60, 61, 74
Ziegfeld Follies 32, 33, 54, 56
Ziegfeld Follies of 1923 34, **35**, 36

www.ingramcontent.com/pod-product-compliance
Lightning Source LLC
Chambersburg PA
CBHW051208300426
44116CB00006B/471